7/11/12

W9-BEU-174

2012

Red-Blooded Risk

Red-Blooded Risk

THE SECRET HISTORY OF WALL STREET

Aaron Brown

WILEY

John Wiley & Sons, Inc.

Published by John Wiley & Sons, Inc., Hoboken, New Jersey.
Published simultaneously in Canada.

For general information on our other products and services or for technical support, please contact our Customer Care Department within the United States at (800) 762-2974, outside the United States at (317) 572-3993 or fax (317) 572-4002.

Wiley also publishes its books in a variety of electronic formats. Some content that appears in print may not be available in electronic books. For more information about Wiley products, visit our web site at www.wiley.com.

ISBN 978-1-118-04386-8 (cloth); 978-1-118-14015-4 (ebk); 978-1-118-14017-8 (ebk); 978-1-118-14016-1 (ebk)

Printed in the United States of America
10 9 8 7 6 5 4 3 2 1

Contents

Acknowledgments

The ideas presented in this book are the fruit of an informal collaboration of mathematically inclined researchers who became obsessed with the idea of betting—real bets for significant stakes versus all comers—on the results of their analyses. It is difficult to assign individual credit in a collaboration, and in any case there were too many participants to list here, even if I knew all of them. So I will take the easy way out and dedicate this book to anyone who ever made computations, bet on them, and learned enough from the experience to become successful.

More specifically, I acknowledge the tremendous benefit I have from arguing over these ideas in several places. I thank my colleagues at the various financial institutions I have worked for, and participants in risk conferences over the years, including those run by the Global Association of Risk Professionals, the Professional Risk Managers International Association, *Risk* magazine, and others. A special mention goes to the triennial conferences on gambling and risk taking produced by the University of Nevada at Reno, which attract a far broader variety of participants than the other conferences.

I also had the benefit of discussing these ideas at online sites, including Wilmott.com, NuclearPhynance.com, QuantNet.com, and TwoPlusTwo.com. And speaking of Internet sites, everyone connected with eRaider.com helped forge my ideas.

It is a little weird to dedicate a book to fictional characters, especially ones the author made up himself. But Red Blood, Blue Blood, Cold Blood, Thin Blood, Hot Blood, Unblooded, and Blood Sucker are composites of real people I have worked with over the years. So I acknowledge here my debt to the dozens of people who provided slices of various characters' history and attitudes.

Many people read part or all of the manuscript and sent useful comments. Brandon Adams, Gustavo Bamberger, Bill Benter, John Bogle, Rick Bookstaber, Reuven Brenner, Eugene Christiansen, Emanuel Derman,

Art Duquette, Dylan Evans, Doyne Farmer, Justin Fox, Kenneth French, Lisa Goldberg, James Grosjean, Ian Hacking, Michael Heneberry, Carey Hobbs, Craig Howe, James McManus, Michael Maubossin, Nick Maughan, Perry Mehrling, Robert Merton, Joe Nocera, John O'Brien, Deborah Pastor, Scott Patterson, William Poundstone, Kevin Rosema, Myron Scholes, James Stoner, Nassim Taleb, Edward Thorp, Whitney Tilson, James Ward, Paul Wilmott, and Bruce Zastera were particularly helpful. The title comes from my daughter, Aviva Pastor. Tiffany Charbonier, Bill Falloon, Stacey Fischkelta, Meg Freeborn, Sharon Polese, and other folks at John Wiley & Sons provided essential feedback and support.

Muhammad Cohen edited every word I wrote, and I rarely overrode his corrections. This book is far more readable for his efforts. Eric Kim provided the drawings. He is a true manga artist, not an illustrator for hire, and the give-and-take we went through added tremendously to the content.

My family, Deborah, Jacob, and Aviva, provided helpful advice and support throughout the process.

Red-Blooded Risk

1

What This Book Is and Why You Should Read It

Life is full of choices. At a job interview, you can give short, pleasant answers to questions. Or you can burst into an impassioned rant about how you will add value to the enterprise. You can dress sedately and behave discretely at a party, or go for maximum drama in your clothes and demeanor. In a basketball game you can throw up a quick shot, or pass the ball so the team can work into position for a higher-percentage shot. You can walk on by an interesting-looking stranger, or throw out a remark or a wink. These choices all concern risk.

In the basketball example, you have a coach. When the team is ahead late in the game, the coach will give one kind of advice. On offense, take plenty of time and get a high-percentage shot. On defense, deny the opponents easy shots and do not foul. Why? Because this style of play minimizes the variance of outcome, which is to the advantage of the team in the lead. The trailing team will try to shoot three-point shots quickly and will play aggressively for steals and blocks on defense. They don't mind fouls because those can change the score without running time off the clock. They are trying to maximize variance of outcome.

If you're not familiar with basketball, the same idea applies in virtually every competitive sport. The player or team that is ahead wants to minimize risk, whereas the opposing player or team wants to maximize it. In baseball, a pitcher with a lead throws strikes; when his team is trailing he will work the corners and throw off-speed pitches.

In soccer with a lead you try to control the ball and keep your defense back; when behind you attack aggressively. In hockey, the trailing team will sometimes even pull the goalkeeper. In American football, the team with the lead will run the ball up the middle and play prevent defenses, while the other team blitzes and throws long passes.

In the job interview, the short, safe answers are indicated if you think you're likely to get the job and just don't want to blow it. But if you're a long shot to be hired, maybe it's time to dust off that rant. Going to an obligatory party for your job, one you know will be boring? Navy suit, say as little as possible and only about the weather, don't drink, and leave early. But if you want to be the life of the party, have a great time, and maybe change your life? Think hot pink. And before you wink at the stranger, ask yourself if you're a bit bored and looking for new adventures—or is your life exciting and complicated enough already and you need peace and quiet more than a new friend?

Risk is something you dial up or down in order to accomplish a goal. It is neither good nor bad in itself. This is the sense in which I always use the word *risk* in this book. Compare this to the "risk" of a basketball player getting injured. I will use the word *danger* for this, not *risk*. Dangers should be minimized, subject to constraints. For example, we don't want to require so much protective padding that a game is not fun, or the cost is too great. So we don't try to set danger of injury to zero, but we also don't "manage" it; we never increase it for its own sake.

The counterpart to a danger on the good side is an "opportunity," such as the opportunity for a pitcher in baseball to get a no-hitter. This is considered so valuable that a manager will almost always leave a pitcher with a chance at a no-hitter in the game, even if he is tiring and a relief pitcher would increase the probability of winning the game.

Risk, Danger, and Opportunity

There are three tests to determine if something is a risk rather than a danger or an opportunity:

1. **Risks are two-sided; you can win or you can lose. Dangers and opportunities are one-sided. If you have a sudden change of**

health while playing football, it is highly unlikely to be an improvement.

2. Dangers and opportunities are often not measurable, and if they are, they are measured in different units than we use for everyday decisions. We can't say how many points a broken collarbone is worth, or whether two sprained ankles are better or worse than a broken finger. There is no dollar figure to put on the glory of setting a record or winning a championship. Risks, however, are measurable. In order to manage an uncertainty, we need some way of assigning relative values to gains and losses.

3. Dangers and opportunities often come from nature, and we usually have only limited ability to control them. Risks always refer to human interactions, and their level must be under our control—if not, they may be risks to somebody else but they are facts of life to us.

The distinction is not inherent in the uncertainties themselves; it is our choice how to treat them. For example, NASCAR has been accused of manipulating its rules to get an optimal number of fatal crashes per year: enough to keep a dangerous, outlaw edge but not so many as to kill all the popular drivers or provoke safety legislation. I have no opinion on whether this charge is true or false. If true, it means NASCAR is treating as a risk something that most people consider a danger. That might be immoral, but it is not illogical or irrational.

Some job applicants treat every question as a danger, carefully probing for traps and giving minimal answers to avoid the chance of mistake. They seldom get hired. Others treat every question as an opportunity to posture or boast. They never get hired. Some people go to parties that should be fun, and dress and act more appropriately for a funeral, letting the danger of embarrassing themselves over-whelm rational consideration of risk. Other people treat funerals as parties, grasping for opportunities that do not exist.

Another example of mixing up risk and danger is a famous memorandum by Ford Motor Company concluding that the cost to the company of settling lawsuits for Pinto owners burned to death in low-speed rear collisions was less than the $10 per car it would cost to shield the gas tank. This story, although widely believed, is a distortion of the facts, and Ford is innocent of any such decision. I mention it only to emphasize that the distinction between risks and dangers is in the eye of the beholder.

There are also things we can choose to treat as risks or opportuni-ties. In *On the Waterfront*, protagonist Terry Malloy makes the famous lament, "I coulda had class. I coulda been a contender. I coulda been somebody, instead of a bum, which is what I am," blaming his brother for persuading him to purposely lose a boxing match for the sure thing "short-end money." He is not complaining that there was not enough short-end money, but that he sold something that was literally price-less. His brother treated his opportunity like a risk, and managed it.

A coward treats risks as dangers, whereas a thrill seeker treats them as opportunities. We call them thin-blooded and hot-blooded, respectively. A cold-blooded person treats both dangers and oppor-tunities as risks. *Red-blooded* refers to people who are excited by challenges, but not to the point of being blinded to dangers and opportunities. To keep this straight, think of the classic movie plot in which the red-blooded hero and his hot-blooded sidekick push aside the thin-blooded person in charge, to fight the cold-blooded villain. We admire the first two people in different ways, feel sorry for the third, and hate the fourth.

Red-Blooded Risk Management

In emotional terms, thin-blooded people are motivated mainly by fear, hot-blooded people by anger and other passions—or even merely thrills—and cold-blooded people by greed. Red-blooded people feel anger and fear and greed like anyone else, but under-stand successful risk taking is a matter of calculation, not instinct.

This is not a self-help book. I do not have any advice for how to achieve this psychological state, if that is what you want to do. What I can tell you is how to compute the red-blooded action in risk situa-tions. It's mathematics, not psychology. Red-blooded risk management consists of three specific mathematical techniques, which have been thoroughly tested in real-world applications. Although quantitative skills are required to implement them, the ideas are simple and will be explained in this book without math. The techniques are used to:

- Turn any situation into a system with clearly delineated risks, dangers, and opportunities.
- Optimize the risks for the best possible outcome.
- Arrange things so both dangers and opportunities make the maximum positive contributions.

This field was invented by a cohort of quantitatively trained risk takers born in the 1950s. In the 1970s, we rebelled against conventional academic and institutional ideas of risk. We sought wisdom from actual risk-takers, which took us to some disreputable places. In the 1980s, we found ourselves taking risks on Wall Street, and developed the ideas described in this book between 1987 and 1992, although of course most of the ideas can be traced to much earlier work. University of Chicago economics professor Frank Knight, for example, made a distinction between risk, with known probabilities and outcomes, and uncertainty, which is something akin to our dangers and opportunities. But he did this to emphasize the limits of mathematics in decision making under uncertainty. He did not appreciate the power of quantitative methods for separating risk from uncertainty, nor the tremendous benefit from applying mathematics to optimize risk taking. Most important, he failed to see that mathematics can be brought to bear just as fruitfully on nonquantifiable uncertainty as on risk. Knight was a deeper thinker than any of the Wall Street risk takers, but we had far more experience in making successful quantitative risk choices.

This group of risk-taking rebels became known as "rocket scientists." That was partly because several of us actually worked on rockets (I myself spent a summer on satellite positioning, which technically uses rockets, but not the big ones that lift payloads into space; anyway, my contribution was entirely mathematical. I never saw an actual rocket firing except on film, so the experience certainly doesn't make me a real rocket scientist.), but mostly to capture the combination of intense and rigorous mathematical analysis tied firmly to physical reality, exploration, and adventure. Recall that one of our generation's defining moments was the Apollo moon landing. We weren't astrophysicists and we weren't engineers. We didn't know exactly what we were, but we knew it was something in between. A more general term for people who use quantitative methods in finance is "quant," but that term also describes less rebellious researchers with quantitative training who came to Wall Street later and called themselves "financial engineers."

I am aware that "rocket scientist" is a stupid name, both boastful and inaccurate. I didn't make it up, and don't use it much. I describe myself as a "quant" with a lowercase q, unpretentious as in, "just a simple quant." I'm not humble, as you'll figure out if you keep reading, but I'm not given to overstatement. What I do isn't rocket science, most of it is trivially simple and the rest is more meticulous care than brilliance. But to be historically accurate, we're stuck with the term, and it does convey some of the spirit of the group.

We contrasted ourselves to people we called "Einsteins," an even stupider name. We had nothing against Albert Einstein, but we disagreed with people who thought risk was deeply complex and could be figured out by pure brainpower, without actually taking any risk or observing any risk takers. "Einstein" was rarely used as a noun. It was more common as an adjective. "He had a good insight, but went Einstein with it," or "He used to be a rocket scientist but got offered a tenure track position and went Einstein." Don't blame me. I don't defend the usages, I just report them.

The rocket scientists rebuilt the financial system from the ground up. I compare these changes to the differences between a modern digital camera and a point-and-shoot film camera from 1980. They look similar. They both have lenses and flashes and shutter buttons. They both run on batteries, in some cases the same batteries. They are used to take pictures of vacations and parties and family members. They cost about the same. From the standpoint of sellers and users, the difference seems to be just an improvement in technology for the same basic device.

But for someone making cameras, there is no similarity at all. The modern technology is built on entirely different principles from the old one. From 1982 to 1992 rocket scientists hollowed out the inside of Wall Street and rebuilt it. We didn't set out to do that; it just happened. Most people, including most people working on Wall Street, didn't notice the fundamental change. They saw some of the minor external design changes, and noticed one day there was no more film to develop, but missed that something unprecedented in history had been created.

At the same time, with even less intention, we figured out the 350-year-old riddle at the heart of probability theory. As has always been the case with probability, practitioners ran ahead of theory. No doubt we will someday have a coherent theoretical explanation of how modern financial risk management works. Until then, all I can do is show you how and why it came into being, and what it is doing to the world.

Risk and Life

Risk taking is not just a quantitative discipline, it is a philosophy of life. There are basically two sensible attitudes about risk. The first is to avoid it whenever possible, unless there is some potential payoff worth the risk. The second is to embrace risk taking opportunities that appear to offer a positive edge. The advantage of the second course is that you take enough gambles that the outcome of any one, or any ten or hundred, doesn't matter. In the long run, you will end up near your expected outcome, like someone flipping a coin a million times.

In my experience, people incline to one of these two strategies early in life. Perhaps it's in our genes. In this context, I always think of a highway sign you can see if you drive from Nice to Monte Carlo. There is a fork, and the sign points right to "Nice Gene" and left to "Monte Carlo Gene." On that choice, I'm a leftist. That doesn't mean I take huge risks; it means I take lots of risks. I have learned from others and invented myself ways to balance these to ensure a good outcome, insomuch as mathematics and human efforts can ensure anything.

There are three iron rules for risk takers. Since your plan is to arrive at an outcome near expectation, you must be sure that expectation is positive. In other words, you must have an edge in all your bets. Expectation is only an abstraction for risk-avoiders. If you buy a single $1 lottery ticket, it makes no practical difference whether your expected payout is $0.90 or $1.10. You'll either hit a prize or you won't. But if you buy a million tickets, it makes all the difference in the world.

Second, you need to be sure you're not making the same bets over and over. Your bets must be as independent as possible. That means you cannot rely on systems or superstitions, not even on logic and rationality. These things will lead you to make correlated bets. You must search hard for new things to bet on, unrelated to prior bets, and you must avoid any habits. In many cases you find it advantageous to make random decisions, to flip coins. For risk avoiders taking only a few big chances, correlation is a secondary concern and flipping a coin for a decision makes no sense.

Finally, risk takers must size their bets properly. You can never lose so much that you're taken out of the game; but you have to be willing to bet very big when the right gambles come along. For a risk avoider, being taken out of the game is no tragedy, as risk taking was never a major part of the life plan anyway. And there's no need to bet larger than necessary, as you are pursuing plans that should work out if nothing bad happens, you're not counting on risky payoffs to succeed.

While moderation is often a good strategy, I don't think you can choose a middle way between risk avoiding and risk taking. Consider an investment portfolio. You can invest in high-quality bonds with payoffs selected near the times you expect to need the money, and possibly hedge your bets further by buying hard assets. Or you can buy stocks and hope for the best. If you choose the latter route, the risk-taking approach, you should seek out as many sources of investment risk as you think the market compensates— that is, all the securities for which there is a positive edge. Both strategies make sense, but it's crazy to split the difference by buying only one stock. You either avoid risk as much as practical, or you try to find as many risks as you can.

You could, of course, put half your portfolio in bonds and the other half in diversified risky assets, but this still makes you a risk taker, seeking out as many risks as possible. You just run a low risk version of the strategy. There's nothing that says a risk taker has to have a high-risk life. In practice, however, once investors take all the trouble to create a broadly diversified portfolio, or individuals learn to embrace risk, they tend to exploit the investment.

It's good that people make this choice young, because each route requires skills and life attitudes that would be fatal to acquire playing for adult stakes. Risk takers must enjoy the volatility of the ride, because that's all there is. There is no destination. You never stop gambling. Risk avoiders must learn to endure volatility in order to get to the planned destination. The world needs both kinds of people.

If you are a risk taker, you need the material in this book to survive, assuming you haven't already figured it out for yourself. We know a lot about the mathematics of risk taking that no one in the world knew a quarter century ago. If you are not a risk taker, you should still understand the mathematics of risk due to its effect on the world.

Quantitative risk models from Wall Street are in considerable disrepute at the moment. I hope to convince you that attitude is wrong. Whether or not I do, I can tell you that these models have changed the world completely, and the pace of that change will only accelerate. So even if you think they are worthless or harmful, it's worth understanding them.

Play and Money

I'm going to cover some topics you might not expect in a book on risk. First is play. One of the characteristics of play is that it takes place within a delineated area—physical or mental—which is not allowed to interact with the rest of the world. Basketball, for example, takes place on a court with clearly defined physical boundaries—and has people to blow whistles if the ball goes beyond those boundaries, stopping play until the situation is rectified. You are not allowed to buy a basket for money or any other consideration outside the perimeter of the game. Whether two players like or dislike each other is supposed to be irrelevant; their actions depend only on whether they're on the same team or on opposing teams. This is what allows us to treat the in-game events as risks. When the outside world intrudes, as with an injury or an equipment failure, those events cannot be managed as risks, because by rule they are incommensurate with baskets.

Although the world is not supposed to intrude on play, play can have enormous effect on the world. Elections, trials, and some wars are contests governed by rules that occur in designated times and places. Market competition can be considered a game, and game theory is a major part of the study of economics. Less serious games constitute a large portion of the economy: sports, gambling, video games, hobbies, and many other activities represent sizable aggregate demand for products and services. We will look deeply into these matters because risk management depends on the kind of delineation and isolation required by play. In a deep sense, risk is play and play is risk.

We're also going to discuss money. When economists consider risk, they usually assume that the types of stakes don't matter—gambling for money is no different from gambling for anything else of value. That turns out not to be true. Optimizing requires goals and constraints. Optimizing risk requires that the two be interchangeable. One way that can happen is if both are measured in money. It also turns out that any time you set up a risk-taking activity with the same units used for goals and constraints, you create a form of money.

One of the major schools of mathematical probability makes betting the fundamental definition of probability. It is called Bayesian theory. Bruno de Finetti's famous example concerns the probability that life existed on Mars one billion years ago. It seems difficult to put a number on that, or even to know what a number would mean. But suppose there is an expedition that will determine the answer tomorrow. There is a security that pays one dollar tomorrow if life existed on Mars one billion years ago, and nothing otherwise. There is some price at which you will buy or sell this security. According to de Finetti, that price *is* the probability that life existed on Mars a billion years ago. It's subjective to you; someone else could have a completely different price. But there is always a definable probability for any event, because you can always be forced to name a price at which you would buy or sell. Saying you don't know the probability of something is saying you don't know what you think.

Rocket scientists were the first group to see the implications of that formulation and ask some obvious questions. We noticed that the bet involved money and asked, "What currency are you betting with?" For example, suppose you would buy or sell the security that pays $10 for 10 cents, suggesting that the probability that life existed on Mars one billion years ago is 1 percent. But this expedition to Mars financed itself by selling bonds denominated in Mars Expeditionary Currency, or mecs. Mecs are the currency colonists will use. Each mec sells for $1 today. But if the expedition discovers there was life on Mars one billion years ago, the value of each mec will soar to $10 because of the potential value of artifacts and scientific discoveries, and because it makes it more likely that Mars can be made hospitable to life today. If you would pay 10 cents for a security that pays $10 if there was life on Mars, you would pay 10 centimecs for a security that pays one mec in the same circumstance. That has to be true, because the 10 centimecs you pay is worth 10 cents today, and the one mec you collect if you win will be worth $10 in that circumstance. So priced in mec, the probability is 10 percent that life existed on Mars one billion years ago. How can the probability depend on what you are betting?

It might seem you can get around this by using a currency that has the same value in all futures states of the world. But no such thing exists, any more than there is an absolute frame of reference in physics. Real risk can only be analyzed using real probabilities, which require some kind of real money in their definitions. Rocket scientists grew up in an era in which the value of money was highly uncertain. We were acutely aware that not everything can be bought or sold for dollars, and that the value of a dollar was highly dependent on future states of the world. We witnessed uncontrollable inflation and hyperinflation. Tax laws were complex and changed frequently, and the marginal rates were often very high. Governments were imposing wage and price controls and rationing many commodities—or forbidding buying or selling altogether. There were alternative currencies and abstract numeraires (a numeraire is a unit of account that assigns relative values to a set of items without necessarily being a medium of exchange or a store of value; an example is inflation-adjusted dollars), of course, but none were perfect. Therefore, we rejected the idea of a fully defined probability distribution that covered all possible future events. Our probability distributions might cover 95 percent or 99 percent of possible events, but would leave 5 percent or 1 percent as undefined outcomes, states of the world in which money was worthless, or in which outcomes were dominated by considerations that could not be priced.

Frequentism

Frequentism is the second major branch of probability theory. It uses long-term frequency as the fundamental definition of probability. This does not require money to define. Unfortunately, frequentism can't tell us the probabilities we want to know, like the probability that if I take a certain drug it will help me, or the probability that I will make money buying a certain stock. It can only tell us about probabilities created by the experimenter, and not even about specific probabilities, just average probabilities of groups of predictions. In a frequentist interpretation of a drug trial, there is no estimate of the probability that the drug works, only of the probability that the randomization scheme for assigning subjects to treatment or control groups—randomness the experimenter created—produced the observed result under the assumption the drug had no effect. Things are actually worse for observational studies where the researcher does not create randomness, such as an econometric study of the effect of monetary policy on inflation. For these, the researcher makes a statement about the probability of randomness she pretends she created.

A frequentist might test hypotheses at the 5 percent level. She can tell us that in the long run, fewer than 5 percent of the hypotheses she rejects will turn out to be true. That's mathematically true (at least if her other assumptions are correct) without reference to a numeraire. But why would we care? What if the 95 percent she's right about are trivial things we knew anyway and the 5 percent she's wrong about are crucial? Only if we can somehow add up right and wrong predictions to get a net gain or loss will her probability statement be useful for decision making. Moreover, the statements must have equal stakes or, as we'll see later, we must be in control of the stakes.

Both Bayesian and frequentist textbooks often obscure this issue by treating only problems in which only one kind of thing is at stake, or by assuming some perfect numeraire. But real problems almost always combine lots of different considerations, which means we need a numeraire to relate many different kinds of things, in other words, a form of money. Since no numeraire is perfect, we need to separate out the dangers and opportunities that cannot be measured in the money we are using for the probability calculation. To do otherwise is to be cold-blooded, to treat all dangers and opportunities as risks. This does not work in any human setting. It may be theoretically possible to imagine a perfect numeraire that puts a price on everything from God, honor, winning a game, and human life; to iPods, toilet paper, sex, and cocaine; to excitement, boredom, pain, and love; but if you make decisions based on probabilities stated in this numeraire, you will come to disaster. This is an empirical observation that I believe strongly. There is a better way to compute probabilities, a better way to manage risk.

If someone says, "Given my study of river height variation, there is a 1 percent chance this levee will be breached sometime in the next year," it sounds like a statement of physical reality, that might be right or wrong, but either way has objective meaning. That is not in fact true. The statement contains implicit assumptions about the value of human life versus property damage, since both are at stake. To a Bayesian, that assumption is implicit in the definition of the probability. Someone with different values would set the betting odds at a different number. To a frequentist, the statement doesn't make sense in the first place. The analyst should say, "I reject the hypothesis that the levee will be breached sometime next year at the 1 percent level." That statement is perfectly consistent with the knowledge that this levee is certain to be breached, but 99 other levees whose breach was also rejected at the 1 percent level are certain not to be breached. Only if I don't care about the difference between 100 levees each having a 1 percent probability of being breached versus 1 levee certain to be breached and 99 levees certain not to be breached, is the original statement a reasonable guide to action. That, in turn, requires that I regard each levee breach as having the same fixed cost that can be added up and that I care only about the expected number of breaks, not variation around that number. In a sense, it requires that I don't care about risk.

Looking at it another way, the original statement seems to imply that the researcher is indifferent between paying $1 for sure versus paying $100 if the levee is breached next year. But it also has to imply the researcher is indifferent between killing one person for sure versus having 100 people die if the levee is breached. There is no logical reason why a person has to accept the same stake ratio in both cases, and evidence from both behavioral and neuroscientific studies show that people do not, in fact, make the same answer. We call the person who pays a dollar for sure "a prudent insurance buyer" and the person who kills one person for sure "a murderer." We treat them very differently. We have not considered the more difficult case of how many dollars the statistician would pay for sure to save 100 lives if the levee is breached. And the probability could be different still if used for species extinction, votes, or excitement as numeraires.

Rationality

This is a deep insight into the nature of risk, money, and rationality. Suppose I observe that you will bet one apple against one orange on some event. I don't know what probability you assign to the event, because I can't divide apples by oranges. But then suppose I see you trade one apple for two oranges. Now I know you were giving two to one odds, meaning you think the event has at least two chances in three of occurring. I have separated your decisions into preferences—how much you like apples versus oranges—and beliefs—how likely you think the event is. This is the basic separation required for the modern idea of rationality, the assumption underlying most modern economic utility theory. It depends crucially on both gambling and exchange—on randomness and money.

A little reflection will show that this separation is entirely arbitrary. It's not how you think about risk. Suppose you're driving along an unfamiliar road and see that you're low on gas. You see a gas station charging 15 cents a gallon more than you usually pay. You have to decide whether to stop and pay the extra for at least a partial tank, or to drive on hoping to find a cheaper station before you run out of gas. In conventional theory, you estimate the probability and cost of running out of gas before finding another station, and also the probability distribution of gas prices at stations up the road. You have to also weigh the value of money versus the inconvenience of running out of gas. But no one does anything remotely like this, at least not consciously. You weigh probabilities and preferences simultaneously, without clearly separating between them. And people often act in ways inconsistent with any reasonable separation into beliefs and preferences.

Of course, the way you think about how you think can be misleading, whether compared to findings of neuroscientists and cognitive psychologists, or to actual behavior. Research does show that many risk decisions can be modeled as separation into beliefs and preferences, that is, to a probability distribution and a utility function. However, there are many different distributions and utility functions that are equally good at explaining brain activity and behavior for individual decisions, and no distribution and utility function that explains all decisions, even for one individual at one time. Intelligent risk management has to begin with a numeraire, plus the awareness that the numeraire does not cover all possible outcomes of the decision.

One of my favorite statistics stories illustrating the essential importance of getting the numeraire right occurred during World War II. The Allied Air Force was trying to decide the optimal amount of armor to add to bombers. This seems to be a problem in which the numeraire is obvious. Each pound of armor means one less pound of bombs, which means more bombing runs to deliver the same payload. Armor has to protect more airplanes than are lost on the additional runs. Wartime examples usually teach bad statistics, because war forces people to treat most dangers and opportunities as risks. Problems get brutally simple.

Anyway, the Air Force collected statistics on what parts of bombers suffered the most flak and shrapnel damage: leading edges took more than trailing edges, for example, and the underside took more hits than the rest of the plane. Obviously the places with the most frequent damage would benefit the most from armor. It sent the data to the great statistician Abraham Wald, asking him to indicate the areas where the armor would do the most good. Wald sent back a diagram that shocked the analysts. He put armor everywhere no damage had been recorded, and no armor on the places with most frequent damage. When Wald was asked why he put armor in places the bombers never took damage, he replied, "The bombers hit in those places never came back."

In this problem, using the obvious numeraire led to exactly the wrong conclusion. Putting armor where it seemed to do the most good meant protecting bombers against damage that was rarely fatal. You have to reverse the numeraire in this case, from protecting against recorded damage to protecting against everything but the recorded damage. After hearing the story, most people laugh at the foolish Air Force analysts. But the identical mistake is made frequently both by professional statisticians and nonstatistical professionals working probability judgments. It may be the single most common error in quantitative decision making.

Bets

Rocket scientists asked two more questions that occur immediately to anyone making an actual bet. Who are you betting with, and who is doing the betting? For the first question, are you going to name the same price for the Martian-life security when betting with a loudmouth idiot in a bar as with a scientific expert—or with a little green man from a flying saucer who lands in your back yard? If the other person knows less than you, you will set the price somewhere between what you think and what you think he thinks, in order to maximize your expected profit. If the other bettor knows more than you, you'll set the price at what you think he thinks, in order to minimize your expected loss. Traditional theorists usually have you betting with yourself, which is entirely pointless.

From a frequentist point of view, suppose someone tells you he rejects the hypothesis that it will snow in New York City tomorrow at the 5 percent level. He can say this every day with perfect accuracy, since it snows in New York City on fewer than 5 percent of days. But the statement is useless for practical decision making. Some days have essentially zero chance of snow; on other days snow is virtually certain. You could make money betting on this probability only if you are betting against an idiot, perhaps someone who thinks New York City is in Australia. If someone can make money predicting snowfall accepting odds set by the National Oceanic and Atmospheric Administration's National Weather Service, I'm willing to call that a useful probability. I'm even more impressed if the person can show a profit posting New York City snow odds on BetFair and taking all comers, or best of all, if the person can make money trading weather futures.

More generally, a frequentist probability claim says nothing about the strength of evidence backing up the computation. The person saying there is a 1 percent chance of the levee being breached might have simply looked at a list of historical levee breaches and noticed they happen on average once per hundred years. He might not know anything about this particular levee. He is violating no standard of statistical practice by making the statement without examining the levee, knowing which river it contains, searching out contrary opinions, or testing any assumptions. He could even put 99 true statements in a hat, along with a piece of paper reading, "The levee will not be breached this year," and pick one at random. If he picks the levee paper, he can say with complete accuracy that the chance of drawing an untrue statement out of a hat with at least 99 percent true statements is 1 percent or less, so he can reject the null hypothesis that the levee will be breached at the 1 percent level. It is not the significance level that tells you the reliability of a frequentist statistical claim; it is the vigor and sincerity of the falsification efforts undertaken in measuring the significance. But academic papers always report the former. In too many cases the latter is either omitted or amounts to the authors betting against themselves.

It's just as important to know who is doing the betting. There may be lots of people making profits betting on something, quoting different odds. This is easiest to explain in thinking about financial markets. Suppose I study all the people making markets (that is, setting prices at which they will buy from or sell to anyone) in, say, oil futures. They set different prices, implying different betting odds on oil prices in the future. I'm only interested in the market makers generating consistent profits. But even within this group there is a variety of prices and also differences in the positions they have built up.

You might argue that the differences in prices are going to be pretty small, and some kind of average or market-clearing price is the best estimate of probability. One issue with this is none of the prices directly measure probability; all of them blend in utility to some degree. A person who locks in a price for future oil may not believe the price of oil is going up. She may be unable to afford higher prices if that does happen, and is willing to take an expected loss in order to ensure survival of her business.

Two other issues have greater practical importance, at least in risk management. Some of these market makers may just be lucky, pursuing strategies that generate small profits most of the time but occasional disasters that more than offset any gains. Following their probabilities leads to disaster. Other market makers may actually lose money on their oil future bets, but make money overall because they use the oil bets to hedge other bets in an overall profitable strategy. Following their probabilities is also bad. The probability we care about is that of a hypothetical risk-neutral oil market maker who makes consistent money in stand-alone oil futures trading averaging over all future scenarios. That turns out to give significantly different probabilities than our subjective estimates, or long-term frequency, or market-clearing prices; even if we agree on numeraire and the identity of the bettors on the other side.

The result of all this is rocket scientists invented their own notion of probability. A probability distribution can only be defined with respect to a numeraire, and therefore cannot be defined for all possible outcomes. If you flip a coin, heads you win a dollar and tails you lose a dollar, the coin could stick to the ceiling or land on its edge, you could win the bet and not get paid, or you could get paid but dollars might be worthless at the time—or a 100 percent tax on gambling winnings could be passed while the coin is in the air, or you could die before the coin lands. You might try to list all possible events and assign probabilities to each, but it's a hopeless task for practical risk decisions. On the other hand, we made the empirical discovery that estimating the sum of the probabilities you could define reliably was highly illuminating, often a more valuable quantity to know than the statistic you were estimating in the first place. Meaningful probabilities also might not exist because no active betting market or reasonable hypothetical betting market existed to define whom to bet with, or because no one could be trusted to make a profit in that market.

That may seem to be a defective definition of probability, but consider the alternatives. Bayesians claim there is always a probability, but there must be one for every individual. In practice, Bayesians often find they have to resort to "improper priors" in which probabilities do not add up to one or choose probabilities for mathematical convenience rather than subjective belief. Bayesians who refuse to do this on principle must live in ivory towers, because they cannot tackle real decision problems. Frequentists often find no probability is defined, and the same hypothesis will have a different probability for every experiment. There is no rigorous way to combine probabilities from different experiments into a single number. Frequentist probabilities also do not add up to one. When a frequentist rejects a hypothesis at the 5 percent level, that does not mean the negation of the hypothesis has a 95 percent chance of being true. It's possible to have a set of mutually exclusive hypotheses, all of which can be individually rejected at the 5 percent level.

Rocket scientists also believed that probabilities could not be defined exactly, only up to a bid/ask spread. Unless someone can make a profit taking bets from everyone, there is no one competent to define the probability of an event.

Exponentials and Culture

But we're not going to talk only about play, probability, and money. There will be an entire chapter on exponentials. The mathematical definition of an exponential is something with a rate of growth proportional to its level. The bigger it gets, the faster it grows. These relate to risk for three reasons.

The first reason is that if you examine a sudden, dramatic change, it usually turns out to be an exponential. It was small and growing slowly for a long time, and was unnoticed as a result. Exponentials work both ways: The smaller it is, the more slowly it grows. Once it starts getting big, it grows so fast that it seems to come out of nowhere.

By that time it has lost its exponential character, as nothing physical can grow forever. It hits up against some limit. People describe it as a Black Swan, an unanticipated event—in fact, one that was impossible to anticipate—and focus on the sudden growth and spectacular collision with its limit. Anyone serious about risk has to concentrate on the exponential nature instead. Once the thing becomes obvious, it's usually too late either to avoid its danger or to exploit its opportunity. Nonexponentials are much easier to deal with. If they are big or fast growing, you notice them. If they are small or slow growing, they don't cause a lot of problems or offer a lot of opportunities.

The second reason to discuss exponentials goes back to the 1956 discovery by physicist John Kelly that exponentials trump risk. If you can organize your risk taking to get the optimal level of exponential growth, you end up better off than you can possibly be using any other strategy. Mathematician and hedge fund innovator Edward Thorp named the strategy "fortune's formula." In a sense you conquer risk since your outcome is guaranteed to be better than that of someone who avoids risk. It's not risk if you can't lose. Kelly's result was theoretical, and we do not know how to conquer risk completely. But his work has led to sophisticated practical techniques for harnessing the power of exponentials to exploit risk.

The last reason to study exponentials is that risk-avoiding people often use them recklessly. Exponentials are powerful and dangerous, and once they're big enough to matter they never last long. When a CEO targets a compound average growth rate for earnings, she's trying to build an exponential. She will probably fail, but if she succeeds the company will soon hit a limit and the fallout will be unpredictable. When an economist justifies a government policy using projected future growth rates, he's relying on exponentials to bail out an idea that cannot float on its own. The opposite error is possible as well. Alarmists often use exponential growth rates to conjure sky-is-falling scenarios that would be laughed at without the mathematical camouflage.

Finally, we're going to discuss how risk is embedded in culture. One of the most difficult aspects of managing risk is competition from older belief systems, just as science sometimes finds itself in conflict with superstition or religion. A lot of power in the world is distributed according to claimed ability to make good decisions under uncertainty, through either superior prediction skills or a talent for managing events as they arise. This includes people from shamans to mathematical modelers, from priests to statesmen and generals. This is nice work if you can get it, since it's difficult to tell the legitimate practitioners from the charlatans. If you claim to be strong, or fast, or a good chess player, it's easy to establish the truth. But if you claim to be able to interpret the will of the gods, or to be a wise policy maker, or that your patent medicine helps ill people, or that the best chance of winning the battle is for everyone to do as you say, it takes a long time to compile evidence one way or the other. Being clever at explaining away errors and taking credit for accidental successes leads to more acclaim and power than making good risk decisions in the first place. In fact, good risk decisions usually lead to the appearance of alternating complacency and erratic actions. They are hard to defend even after the fact to people who were not involved in the decision making.

While few people would disagree with that last paragraph, I'm going to argue that it runs much deeper than is usually supposed. Bad risk management is ingrained into social institutions and popular theories. Among other things, that helps explain why it took so long after the major discoveries in the field for a book to be published that covers them thoroughly, and why so much nonsense about risk is written every day. Half of good risk management is just identifying and eliminating the bad risk management. That exercise can be extremely disruptive and can generate strong reactions because it challenges a major traditional base of power.

Payoff

What is the payoff for working through the four previous topics, as well as some more conventional risk management material? I will give you simple and logical answers to a variety of questions about risk. You'll have to decide for yourself whether the answers are true, but none of them will be airy generalities. I will not ask you to take anything on faith. The logic and evidence will be presented clearly, as will the historical development of the ideas. I believe everything in here is true, and I have tested it over many years of actual risk taking, plus observation of others. I cannot claim it is accepted widely, as it is not even known widely. But it does represent the consensus of successful modern quantitative risk takers in finance. It's how the global financial system works—and the global financial system is increasingly determining how everything works.

I have presented the material in this book over the years in articles and speeches, with mixed success. I find it easiest to communicate to professional risk takers who are good at mathematics. I hope this book will help broaden the audience to people who are not particularly fond of mathematics, and who take risk but do not focus their profession on risk. The group I have the hardest time with is risk avoiders who are good at mathematics. They seldom disagree with me and they claim to understand, but we talk at cross-purposes. I say "risk is good," and they agree, thinking I mean that risk must be accepted in order to improve expected outcomes. That makes risk a cost, something bad that you accept in order to get something good, which is not at all what I mean. In my terms, they treat all risks as dangers. I talk about making decisions and they agree, mentally imagining that means giving advice to others.

To avoid misunderstandings, I have reinforced the main points of the book with graphic material—comic strips. These are an important part of the book. If you find yourself agreeing with the text but not understanding the comics, you're probably missing the point. If you see eye to eye with me on the comics, you've absorbed the important ideas, even if you read nothing else.

I will ask you for a fair amount of trust. I have a big story to tell, with a lot of apparently disparate elements. We'll cover all of human history and the global economy and even bigger stuff. Unless you work in finance, and possibly even if you do, some of the ideas likely will be completely new to you, and strange. Some may contradict things you have accepted in the past. It may not all fit together until the last chapter. I've tried to make it interesting enough for each part to stand on its own, but this is not a collection of essays. If you will give me your attention for a few hours, I undertake to reward it.

CHAPTER

2

Red Blood and Blue Blood

25

27

28

3

Pascal's Wager and the Seven Principles of Risk Management

The modern study of risk began with an eccentric example. A series of letters between the great French mathematicians Blaise Pascal and Pierre Fermat in 1654 considered some mathematical problems related to bets on dice throws. Dice represent a very unusual kind of risk. We know for certain all possible outcomes and their associated probabilities. We can gain no useful information to predict the throw, nor to influence it. The first is by assumption, the second by rule; neither one is physically true. The result of a dice throw is unambiguous, and everyone learns it at the same time. You can search the entire natural and human world and find zero examples that resemble this kind of risk, except gambling games and controlled scientific experiments that are designed for the purpose of creating the risk. Even in gambling, the model Pascal and Fermat analyzed is only an approximation: unexpected outcomes occur, dice can be loaded, people cheat, and results are disputed. Only in the abstract play world, isolated from the real world, do the mathematical results hold.

Blaise Pascal created another work about risk that is almost as famous, but gets less attention from serious researchers in risk. It is known as Pascal's wager. He began by considering whether God existed and concluded there was no way to answer the question by reasoning. Therefore, you have to make a bet. If you bet that God exists and you are correct, you win eternal happiness; if you are incorrect, you lose whatever pleasure you could have had violating Commandments. Regardless of the probabilities involved, to believe appears to be the smart bet. Even a microscopic probability of winning infinite happiness seems worth giving up any finite amount of happiness.

Before considering Pascal's reasoning, notice that this problem is much more typical of risks that we face in life. We don't know all possible outcomes; there are many theories about God and no doubt many possible ones no one has ever thought of. We certainly can't estimate the probabilities. We might, however, be able to learn more or even influence the outcome (people have suggested a God who judges us according to our beliefs, or who exists only if enough people believe). We do not make a single, irrevocable decision; we can wrestle with the question every day of our lives—and perhaps beyond—making lots of decisions.

People often object that Pascal seems to assume that if there is a God He is the God of Roman Catholicism, and therefore we know how to get to heaven if He exists. But Pascal did not recommend applying specific religious teachings. Instead he urged readers to "be faithful, honest, humble, grateful, generous, a sincere friend, truthful," and to avoid striving for "glory and luxury." He claimed this path would reward you in this life and, possibly, afterward.

This illustrates another aspect of real risk decisions: We often don't know the stakes of the wager. Most people make at least some effort in the direction of Pascal's virtues for a combination of reasons: self-respect, belief that they contribute to earthly happiness, love of other people, fear of getting caught, desire for the good opinion of others, habit, lack of imagination, and vague belief that if there is some kind of Last Judgment or karmic *Sansara* you're likely to fare better if you're virtuous. For religious people this last reason is replaced by more definite and specific beliefs.

However, despite these reasons, most people will fail to practice at least some of the virtues some of the time, and will give in to lusts for glory and luxury—among other things—on occasion. So some kind of balancing is going on, and since some of the gains and losses are uncertain, some kind of wagering as well. But who could sort out motivations and beliefs enough to make this a mathematical problem in probability theory?

To bring this down to earth, let's consider another example with similar structure but no infinities. You are a professional asset manager, investing money other people have entrusted to you. You are trying to choose among various strategies. To some extent you can calculate the return you expect to make and how much variability there will be around that return. But you know unexpected things happen in the market. Prices can move more than they ever have in the past, prices that are supposed to move together can go in opposite directions, you may not be able to trade at all or even determine prices, institutions can suddenly fail, rules can change suddenly, assets can be expropriated, trusted intermediaries can turn out to be frauds—and those are only the things you can imagine.

You have no idea of the probabilities of these things, nor how they will affect your portfolio. Nevertheless, you have a pretty good idea that the less leverage you use, the better off you'll be if something unexpected happens. You will also likely benefit if you're holding more liquid assets, dealing with more solid counterparties, and operating on firmer legal ground. None of these things guarantee survival and in some circumstances they could even hurt. Nevertheless, it's fair to say that these things reduce danger.

The problem is how to balance well-understood, quantifiable factors with unexpected things that you cannot even describe. Is it worth a 10 percent increase in leverage to get an extra 1 percent expected return? If an illiquid bond pays 0.50 percent more per year than a similar liquid one, is it a better deal?

Note the similarities to Pascal's wager. You know some probabilities and benefits fairly well: the earthly ones in Pascal's case, the normal market returns for the asset manager. You have no idea about others: Does God exist and, if so, how will my actions affect our relationship? What might happen in a market crisis? The ones you can't quantify might be much more significant than the ones you can, even considering they have lower probabilities. Moreover, this is not a single decision; you have to decide every moment what to do.

Prior to 1987, the standard practical way to deal with this issue was to set arbitrary limits on leverage, liquidity, counterparty quality, legal certainty, and other factors. Then the portfolio manager would go out and make as much money as possible within those limits. Important decisions were made by intuition, or in the case of famous hedge fund manager George Soros, by how much his back hurt. Personal qualities and demeanor counted a lot. The clearly stated opinions of anyone with a good reputation who appeared calm and confident were weighted heavily, whereas other opinions were often ignored. The standard academic method was to list some possible unexpected events, assign probabilities and outcomes to each, and pretend that you had a fully defined gambling game. Then divide the risk level by 3 or 4 as a safety factor. These ad hoc and unsatisfactory procedures passed for risk management. But times have changed.

Principle I: Risk Duality

The first principle of modern quantitative risk management is to split the analysis into two parts. For normal, common events you have plenty of data to make reliable quantitative conclusions using historical statistics. But long-term success requires at least surviving the abnormal, unexpected, uncommon events you know will also occur. The greatest long-term success requires exploiting—not just surviving—them. So you need to take them into account as well. You must manage them even though you don't know what might happen, you don't know how your actions will influence what might happen, and you certainly can't assign probabilities.

This may seem like an obvious insight, and perhaps it is. But many people disagree. A common approach by quantitative professionals is to deal only with the first kind of analysis, based on the assumption that events you know nothing about shouldn't affect your decisions. At the other extreme, Nassim Taleb in *Fooled by Randomness* and *The Black Swan* has argued that only the second kind of analysis matters; the first is fraudulent, because long-term outcomes are dominated by unexpected, high-impact events. A more popular but less intellectual version of Nassim's argument is to make choices according to whim or tradition or gut instinct because careful analysis and planning seem to fail so often.

This idea happens to be the topic of my dissertation written in 1982 at the University of Chicago Graduate School of Business (now the Booth School of Business). I brought it with me to Wall Street, where it attracted little interest until the crash of October 19, 1987. On that day the stock market fell more than twice as much as it had on any previous day, but that was not the surprise. Quants knew that kind of fat-tail event was possible. What was unexpected was that the entire financial system realigned in a way no one had predicted—and few people even noticed.

The crash sparked a furious reassessment of historical data, which revealed that fundamental realignments were not uncommon. Marketwide ones happened once or twice a decade, and every year had a least a few smaller ones that affected certain types of securities. Qualitative managers hadn't noticed because they didn't measure and track the details carefully enough; they were more concerned with higher-level trends. A lot of ideas, including mine, were pulled out of desk drawers and offered as paradigms to deal with crises.

Principle II: Valuable Boundary

The next principle to be discovered was a complete surprise. We had assumed it would be pretty easy to define the region in which you had plenty of data—in other words, how much things could vary and still be considered normal. After all, you have plenty of data there, by definition. To make this precise, I'm going to jump ahead and steal a concept that wasn't fully fleshed out until 1992, value at risk (VaR). VaR is defined operationally. That means we specify a property VaR is supposed to have, and then try to figure out what number satisfies the property. For a 1 percent one-day VaR, the property is that one day in 100—1 percent of the time—a portfolio will lose more than the VaR amount over one day, assuming normal markets and no position changes in the portfolio. VaR can also be defined at different probability levels and over different time horizons.

The 99 days in 100 in which markets are normal and you make money or lose less than the VaR amount are used as data for mathematical optimization. The two or three trading days a year that you lose more than VaR—called "VaR breaks"—or that have abnormal markets, are analyzed separately.

To make this useful, you have to specify VaR before trading begins. If the VaR algorithm is good, losses will exceed it one day in 100, within statistical error. Moreover, the breaks should be completely unpredictable. You should have the same chance of a VaR break if yesterday was a break or if there has been no break for three years; or if VaR is high or if VaR is low. More generally, no one should be able to make money betting against you if you offered to take either side of a 99-to-1 bet that there will be a VaR break today.

The quantitative details vary, but the general idea extends beyond the specifics of VaR. It applies to any division of possible future scenarios into normal and abnormal that is useful for risk management purposes. You must be able to specify in advance the probability of a normal outcome, and you must validate your estimate rigorously.

Setting VaR seems like a reasonably easy statistics problem, but it's not. You have to quote the number every day before trading begins, even when there are data problems, and VaR is never adjusted later. For risk management, all that matters is the number in use when decisions were made, not some later correction. The statistical properties of market price changes, even in normal times, are erratic, evolving rapidly and unpredictably.

We ended up stealing methods from the people who set sports betting point spreads, and adding stuff we made up as we went along. We had to delve deeply into the back office and study methods developed by controllers and auditors. Only after years of intensive, cooperative work did we develop VaRs that could pass rigorous statistical back-tests, and on which we were willing to bet with traders. The only way you got VaR accepted on the trading floor in the early 1990s was to bet; you can imagine what traders think of a risk manager who tells them how to run their billion-dollar portfolios but won't risk $10,000 of his own money on his analysis.

One major result is we learned how little we had understood about the risk in the well-behaved center of the probability distribution on normal trading days. We had thought all our risk problems were in the tails of the distribution or on abnormal days.

There was another surprise, pleasant rather than unpleasant. It turned out that changes in portfolio VaR, once you got a good VaR system, were extremely useful information for both making money and managing risk. VaR breaks were equally useful, as signals that something had changed.

Unfortunately, when VaR filtered out of the small group of quants who had developed it, it was misinterpreted as a measure of risk or a worst-case loss. It is neither. A low-VaR portfolio is not safer than a high-VaR portfolio; it means only that there is a smaller region in which you have good data about risk. And VaR is the *least* you will lose on the worst 1 percent of your days, not the most you can lose.

Another problem is that VaR itself is often miscalculated. Regulators and auditors like numbers computed in rational, controlled systems that can be audited and whose results can be explained. They like to adjust numbers after the fact so everything is neat and consistent. Successful VaR systems are filled with ad hoc internal algorithms to detect bad or missing data and to react violently to even tiny hints inconsistent with the overall picture. These VaR systems are created by evolution, not design. They give results that are as hard to explain as market price changes. In fact, their value is that they can surprise you. You can't avoid surprises; your only choice is risk statistics that surprise you before trading starts, or market events that surprise you while you're trading. The pressure for rationality, control, auditability, and explainability has killed the value of VaR in many institutions, like a king who shoots any messenger bringing unexpected or hard-to-interpret news.

VaR is suited only to certain kinds of financial risk. The general risk management principle is to define ahead of time the set of outcomes for which you have confidence in probability estimates (usually because you have plenty of data, but possibly because you trust a theory) and, crucially, how often you will get an outcome outside that set. The effort to create this system will teach you a lot; especially it will teach you how little you knew before making the attempt to predict and validating that attempt rigorously. In my experience, any change in the set boundary will prove to be a useful input to decisions. When you get an outcome outside the set, it will be a useful alert that something is changing.

Principle III: Risk Ignition

The third principle of modern quantitative risk management was an antisurprise, which we called "risk ignition." This is an idea that traces back to John Kelly—who we met briefly in Chapter 1—in 1956. He discovered that if you take an optimal amount of risk—not more and not less—you can be certain of exponentially growing success, which will always leave you better off than any other strategy. Instead of gains and losses bobbing you up and down, you can take off like a rocket to astronomical success.

Taking less risk than is optimal is not safer; it just locks in a worse outcome. In competitive fields, doing less than the best often means failing completely. Taking more risk than is optimal also results in a worse outcome, and often leads to complete disaster.

In theory. It turned out that risk duality was the concept necessary to make risk ignition work in practice.

Consider, for example, a casino. Thousands of people are in there betting red or black in roulette, laying chips on pass or don't pass in craps, spinning slot machines, and making other wagers. None of this represents risk to the casino, as it has both sides of most bets, plus an edge such that it pays out winners less than it collects from losers. There is some unmatched risk, but it averages out very quickly.

When analyzing these games, most quantitative people focus on the house edge, the fraction of each dollar bet the casino gets on average. But a casino cares about something different: the hold, the fraction of chips customers buy that the casino ends up winning. The hold depends on the edge, of course, but also on betting speed and bettor behavior. Casinos offer games with wide variation of edge, but strikingly similar holds (with some adjustment for the cost of offering the game).

You might think casinos would try to maximize hold, but that's not true. If the hold is too big, customers buy fewer chips, and eventually stop coming. There is an optimal level of hold that makes the casino's business the most valuable: low enough for high volume and growth, high enough to make a profit. For most commercial gambling operations, the problem is that the hold is too big. That's why casinos give customers back about 75 percent of their losses in the form of free or discounted services, including food, lodging, entertainment, and forgiven debts. Internet sites offer rake-backs. State lotteries offer some low prizes. They advertise only the maximum prizes—that's why people buy tickets—but if the state paid everything out in million-dollar-plus prizes, the hold would be too big and people would stop playing. The key is that people rebet most of the lower prizes they win, so the net outflow to the lottery is not the sum of all prizes awarded but only the sum of prizes too large to rebet. But lottery players enjoy the game more when they get low prizes along the way to rebet, even though they lose the same money in the end.

Why don't casinos reduce the hold by reducing the house edge in games? Actually they do sometimes, offering better rules for the customers as a promotion. But the tactic is not generally effective, because edge does not affect hold much. People play until they lose a certain amount, and with a smaller edge, they just play longer. The casino wants to optimize the gaming experience so that people play long enough to go away satisfied, but not so long that they get fatigued and the casino's expenses mount. Another issue is that at small-enough edges the random variation in outcomes can start to matter, at least in higher-stakes games. In addition, low edges make it easier for "advantage gamblers" like blackjack card counters to turn the tables on the casino.

The parallels to more general risk taking are clear. The casino does not focus on the risks of individual bets, but on the long-term outcome that is effectively guaranteed by the laws of probability. It does not try to maximize that outcome, but to set it at an optimal level. If it sets it too high, so customers lose too much money, it loses business. If it sets it too low, it is less profitable than the competition, which can also lead to failure. If it sets it at the right level, it can have a steadily growing, profitable business. The value of that business is so much larger than any bet or short-term profit that it makes sense to focus on maximizing the probability of success rather than worrying about lesser gains and losses.

There is an important caveat, however. Nassim Taleb gives as an example the three biggest losses of a casino one year. They were:

1. The owner's daughter was kidnapped and held for ransom.
2. A long-time employee, for no discernible reason, stuck mandatory tax reporting forms under his desk for many years instead of submitting them to the government, resulting in a large fine.
3. A tiger mauled one of the casino's star performers.

Risk ignition works only inside the VaR limit, for the predictable, expected, quantifiable risks. You can optimize it perfectly and still fail due to unexpected events.

Risk ignition is not simply a strategy pursued by a few hedge funds and quant proprietary traders. It drives the important changes in the world. It creates self-sustaining exponential growth, which in the long run matters much more than efforts that do not lead to ignition.

By the way, you're going to read a lot about casinos and other types of commercial gambling in this book. I get criticized for this. Editors, referees, and well-meaning friends tell me I alienate readers with such frivolous examples. They miss the point. Casinos are not examples, frivolous or otherwise. To understand risk, you have to study how real people take real risk. That includes casino owners and customers, as well as financial traders, among many others. You can't just read about them or use cardboard models based on theory; you have to go to the tables and the trading floor to figure out what really happens. Useful work is also done by psychologists and behavioral researchers in controlled experimental situations. No one should pontificate about risk who has not spent a lot of time observing actual risk takers in action.

Enough rant. Getting back to our story, quants had been trying to ignite risk for years, and it always seemed to fail. Only when we learned to set a VaR limit and make provisions for events outside it could strategies survive long enough to benefit from ignition. Before this discovery, hedge funds had been around since 1949. Most of them had failed, but the successful ones had made their owners moderately wealthy. Suddenly we got a slew of hedge fund billionaires, and we produced a few new ones every year since. These people weren't smarter than the previous generation of managers; they followed the same well-known, trivially simple strategies. But now they knew how to manage, and to ignite, risk. Financial institutions went from earning 15 percent of corporate profits to over 40 percent, and doubled their share of gross domestic product. Financial institutions didn't change their business models or discover new markets; the increase was due to changes in risk management. And, despite popular opinion, the gain did not come at the expense of the rest of the economy but added to overall economic welfare.

Principle IV: Money

In conventional analysis of risk, you can gamble for any stakes, monetary or nonmonetary. The study of risk is unrelated to the study of money. But as we saw in Chapter 1, the two are intimately linked. You can't ignite risk without money and you can't understand money without understanding risk.

The first point of similarity is there is a duality of money that corresponds to the duality of risk. We can earn trust, repay loyalty, reciprocate affection, and lend a hand—but not with or for money. Money is applied to only a subset of human exchanges. Inside the money economy, everything can be measured to a common scale— "Every man has his price." Outside the money economy, things are not as simple or consistent. We cannot easily predict beyond the VaR boundary; we cannot easily plan beyond the money boundary. Nevertheless, these regimes are important, often overwhelmingly so—"Life is what happens while you're making other plans."

People often underestimate the importance of nonmoney exchange. I'm not talking just about things money cannot buy—at least by popular saying—like love and happiness. We don't auction off military medals or admission to elite colleges. You apply for jobs; you don't buy them. Nonmonetary gifts, charity, bequests, and volunteer organizations represent a substantial portion of the economy. No doubt money can help you be a celebrity, or date one, but it takes some indirection. Similarly, an expensive lawyer might help you beat a criminal charge and an expensive lobbyist might promote your political views, but neither object can be obtained by money alone.

Money is even less important in abnormal times. If you are thirsty in a desert, the price of water does not have much meaning. If there is a financial liquidity crisis, the money value of your levered investment is equally irrelevant.

As with risk, there is a region in which you can do precise computations in money, and the boundary is hard to define. If you do make the effort to measure it precisely and keep track of when things get outside it, you will gain great insight. If you optimize your money decisions carefully, you can ignite the wealth-creating process, but success also depends on arranging things properly for when money fails to work: panics, bank holidays, disasters, liquidity crises, expropriations, hyperinflations, and so on.

To see the connection between risk and money, consider trying to cross over a difficult mountain range. Obviously this is a risky activity, but the risk is hard to manage. You will have to take a series of chances, and it's hard to know much about each one until you reach it. You probably have to win all, or almost all, of your risks to succeed. There are plenty of dangers as well as risks.

Risk ignition depends on breaking the task into a large number of subtasks, with as little correlation among them as possible. Success should be possible even if you lose some, or even most, of your risks.

Suppose instead of crossing the mountain range yourself, you want to build a road over it. This task is more amenable to risk management. You can break it into many subtasks, each of which can be attacked in multiple ways. Success in one task will aid others. For example, if you complete a road through the foothills, you can establish a base camp and cache supplies that will make it much more efficient for surveyors and workers to tackle the next set of tasks. This kind of organization will help you both reduce dangers and make dangers productive. Another important feature is there is a continuum of outcomes, not simply success or failure. The lone climber will either get across or not. The road builder might fail completely, build a long and difficult road, build a short and easy road, or perhaps build a network of roads to support multiple uses.

Money is an important tool for arranging projects in forms that allow risk ignition. Economists tend to emphasize two effects of money: it encourages specialization and it supports spontaneous organization of people and resources. Risk managers discovered two features that are even more important. Money measures constraints and goals in the same units, meaning that partial successes in the goal reduce constraints on future activity. The more you win, the more you can bet. That isn't true if winnings are qualitatively different from, and not exchangeable with, the things wagered. Also, money captures the value of any degree of success. We will see later that those are precisely the two things that make risk ignition possible.

We'll also see that those two things are essential for the creation of true money, defined as a single instrument that simultaneously functions as a medium of exchange, a store of value, and a numeraire or standard of value. Economists tend to emphasize the first two but we had token money and commodity money as mediums of exchange, and bulk metal as a store of value, for thousands of years before true money added the numeraire function and caused an explosion in value creation. We have many things that function as partial money today, credit cards as mediums of exchange, financial securities as stores of value, special drawing rights (a unit of account for transactions between central banks that is defined by reference to a basket of currencies) and consumer price indexes (a unit of account used by economists that is defined by reference to a basket of goods) as numeraires; but the forms of money that stimulate the economy are those that equate constraints and goals of important risk-taking activities. Although few people seemed to have noticed, at the moment financial derivatives are the most important form of money used in advanced economies.

Outside the VaR Boundary

The remaining principles of modern quantitative risk management concern risk outside the VaR limit. How do you exploit risk for profit when you don't know the possible outcomes or probabilities?

You already know the answer, but to see it you have to go back to Pascal's wager. There are two tricky issues that Pascal finessed.

The first concerns the units in which we measure things. Early probability theorists assumed that all gambles should be evaluated by their expected values, and they unhesitatingly accused anyone who turned down a positive expected value wager of irrationality. *Expected value* has nothing to do with what you expect; it's a mathematical term that means multiply all outcomes by their probabilities and add them up. For example, if you flip a fair coin with which heads you win $100 and tails you pay $50, your expected value is $0.5 \times $100 + 0.5 \times (-$50) = $50 - $25 = 25.

After a few decades, it dawned on some people that it's not necessarily wise to accept a coin flip with which heads you triple your wealth and tails you lose everything. This has a positive expected value equal to half your wealth, but for most people the pain of losing everything would exceed the pleasure of tripling their wealth.

The fix for this was something called *utility theory*. It was assumed that there was some "utility" you could assign to any outcome, and gambles should be evaluated on the basis of expected utility. If you assign +1 utility to your current state, +2 to tripling your wealth, and –2 to losing everything, the expected utility of the aforementioned gamble is $0.5 \times 2 + 0.5 \times (-2) = 0$, less than the +1 you get by declining the bet.

Utility theorists usually assumed that as you get richer, the additional utility from each dollar you get declines. That assumption happens to be necessary for a lot of conventional economic theory to work. A consequence of the assumption, called *declining marginal utility*, is that all risk is bad. You would never accept a gamble with zero expected value in dollar terms; it would have negative expected utility. You have to be compensated with positive expected return in order to accept the risk. Although this concept was invented purely to salvage a mathematical assertion from obvious error and was never empirically verified as the way people do act, nor theoretically justified as the way people should act, it is accepted as unquestioned truth by many quantitatively trained people.

Some modern researchers have expanded utility theory until it gives at least a reasonable approximation to the world. There are six important extensions:

1. Allow the current set of possessions to be an argument of the utility function. People indisputably act differently with

respect to things they own than things they do not own; and this is not only not irrational, it is an evolutionary essential, as discussed in Chapter 8.

2. Include utility from conforming to social norms, rewarding those others who act as they should, and punishing those others who transgress.

3. Make utility depend on past and anticipated future consumption as well as current consumption. The technical term for this is utility that is not *time separable.*

4. Make utility of a gamble depend on all possible outcomes, not just the expected utility of outcome.

5. Do not collapse all consumption into a single numeraire. People treat money differently than other goods. Chapter 5 shows that it is common and rational to prefer A to B but be willing to pay a higher price for B than A.

6. Recognize that people have multiple natures with different utility functions, and also that people do not always know how they will feel about future scenarios.

Unfortunately, when you include these extensions, utility theory becomes mathematically intractable, except in special cases. It still has a lot of value in forcing rigorous specification of models. But it can't tell you much about the world. Almost any behavior can be rational utility maximization. So you have to get out in the field or laboratory to observe; you cannot label things rational or irrational from the ivory tower.

There are other researchers who reject utility maximization altogether and claim that behavior is better explained by heuristics and "satisficing," among other things. I respect many of the people doing this work, but basically disagree. If someone does something with predictable consequences, I think it makes sense to say she wanted the consequences, then work out what set of beliefs and preferences supports that desire. Whether those beliefs and preferences represent her true internal psychological state is not the point. Empirically, I think it's a methodological discipline that leads to more productive research.

Pascal was working before the invention of utility theory. He got around the problem by doing the calculation in "lives." This is called a *change of numeraire* as we discussed in Chapter 1. We'll see in Chapter 18 that this is a powerful technique first discovered for pricing derivatives that led to a deep reappraisal of the nature of probability. If there is no God, you have one life; if there is a God, you have the potential for infinite lives. If believing in God increased your happiness to any degree in the infinite lives in heaven, that had to outweigh any finite loss of happiness in your one life. However, Pascal emphasized the point that you don't know now how you will feel about possible outcomes. He claims that virtue will make you happier than vice, but he doesn't assume you know this from the start. For utility theory to work, you must know in advance not just the possible outcomes, but precisely how you feel about each one to the point that you can rank them unambiguously. Pascal's problem is more realistic in that uncertainty in how you will feel about things is an important part of your decision problem.

The second subtlety is the identity of the decision maker. Conventional analysis assumes that each individual is a utility maximizer. But Pascal, even without the benefit of modern cognitive science, knew that we had multiple natures. In fact, that is the crux of his wager. Parts of your brain are tempted by various pleasures of the flesh, and other parts take longer views. Suppose you do as Pascal recommends and tame your lusts and passions. He claims you not only have a better shot at heaven, but you will be happier in this life. Supposing that is true, who exactly is happier? Since your nature has changed, are you really the same person? Or does it make more sense to say your cerebral and spiritual sides are happier while your earthier natures are frustrated? It's even harder to balance your feelings now and on earth with the interests of your eternal soul (if any) in some unknowable future existence.

We can take this in another direction as well. Suppose you work for a company and are evaluating a proposal. Most of us automatically adopt the viewpoint of the company and think in those terms. We don't forget our self-interest; we may even let it override our duty to our employer. But unless we have no team spirit at all, we feel some pull to do our part in the organization rather than let our personal desires dictate everything. Only when we are on the fence do we think about this as weighing one interest against the other. Most of the time we unthinkingly take the view of the company: "We have to file these forms." "This will cost us too much money." "We should look into that idea." When making a decision about religion, many people would consider it from the point of view of a religious group as a whole and get some satisfaction from joining and nourishing something good. Similarly, people make decisions on the basis of what's best for their family, their country, their team, and other abstractions and multiperson entities.

The two effects can be combined. At certain kinds of parties, everyone displays their irresponsible, fun-loving natures. These can reinforce each other, and help partygoers suppress more serious and cautious sides of their personalities. Someone who doesn't

participate can be a so-called buzz killer or party pooper, bringing everyone else down. Similar things happen in mobs, monasteries, and mosh pits. To bring one side of our nature to the fore, it helps to be around other people doing the same thing. You can think of the decision-making entity in these cases as composed of part of the natures of many individuals.

This is a major complication in risk analysis. There are typically many levels of consideration, both within and among people. That is true both for evaluating outcomes and for making decisions. Rather than thinking of a single decision maker choosing to maximize his own utility, it's more helpful to think of a committee making a decision in order to further varied interests of a community. Actions that appear irrational in the first case are often easily explainable in the second.

These two issues rise in importance when we go outside the VaR boundary. We know how we feel about normal, everyday events, and figure out some structure of decision making. Either that or we fight a lot—mentally within ourselves or outwardly with others, or both. If you're offered a piece of cheesecake, your glutton nature works it out with your longer-term desires for good health and a good figure. Most of us have some kind of stable compromise process there. But what if you get an entirely unexpected offer? A new drug that might make you young and healthy or might kill you? An offer to betray your best friend in exchange for a life of luxury? A chance to sacrifice your life for your country? These are the kinds of decisions that call into question who you really are and what you really want. No choice will satisfy all of you, nor all the social entities you care about. And you may find yourself unable to carry out what you think you have decided. While the examples are overdramatic, you can't get through life without facing something like them. If you refuse to think about them in advance, you cannot manage risk. However, mentioning them explicitly can fracture fragile organizations and upset people whose internal natures are in uneasy alliance. This is one reason true risk management is so disruptive. But it's better to disrupt in quiet times when you may be able to rebuild stronger people and organizations than to fall apart—literally—in a crisis.

The secret to managing risk outside the VaR boundary is to make sure it is good risk, and to set up the right structure of decision making. That means we have to jettison utility theory, at least in its simplest form, because it teaches that all risk is bad. And we have to explicitly consider all aspects of all entities for which we are managing risk.

Principle V: Evolution

What are some examples of good risk? Evolution, for one. Random variation leads to more wonderful creations than anything any human ever designed on purpose. But there are two important caveats. Mutation is almost always bad for the individual, but the optimal amount is good for the population. However, the population is not fixed; it changes over time both in composition of individuals and in genetic characteristics. And a deeper look at evolution reveals that it operates on many levels, from individual selfish genes to (possibly) Gaia, the web of all life on Earth. So while the randomness can be good, we need to ask if it is good for the entities we care about.

The second caveat is that random variation is only half of evolution; the other half is natural selection. Suppose we are facing the classic corporate finance capital budgeting problem. We have a list of projects our company might pursue and we have to choose which ones will be accepted. In the classic formulation when faced with two projects of equal expected present value, we choose the less risky one. But risk creates diversity, which makes it more likely the company can survive unexpected events. Even better, the diverse company that has been refined by a series of crises will have evolved into a better-constructed entity, more fit for future challenges.

I intend to use scientific analogies like this to describe the remaining risk management principles. This form can be abused by taking a popular simplification of a scientific idea and applying it thoughtlessly as a metaphor or fanatically as a new religion. At the other extreme, serious researchers sometimes try to apply the precise mechanisms or equations from one field to another. The first approach is almost never fruitful and often crazy. The second is called *econophysics* when applied to finance, even if the scientific field lending techniques is not physics. Borrowings from signal processing and natural language processing have been spectacularly successful in finance, but the jury is still out on whether other fields can produce worthwhile insights. Econophysics offers a lot of promise and has had some minor successes, but more frustration and failure than progress.

I'm doing something different. The idea that risk can be analyzed using probability distributions and utility functions is embedded deeply in economics. The dice throw is still the fundamental model of risk. Other fields, including evolution, have more useful models of randomness that give more insight in regard to risk management. To some extent, these models can be expressed in standard probability terms, with *fitness* from biology taking the place of *utility* from economics. That works at times, but it does not capture the full sweep of biological evolution, nor is it enough to understand risk management. Economics has clung to the seventeenth-century mathematical analysis of gambling games with all its otherworldly unreality, and has been reluctant to accept insights from different models of risk that arose from subsequent scientific investigation.

For example, when I present the aforementioned argument for preferring certain kinds of risky projects to safe ones, economists often object that I should be encouraging diversity instead of randomness. In other words, they say a company should make sure its portfolio of projects contains a range of types—for example, some that will do well in good economic times and some that can succeed even in bad economic times, and some that have low probability of high success while others have higher probability of more moderate success.

This might be compared to directed evolution, or breeding. It can help only along the dimensions you foresee. That can make it a useful idea within the VaR boundary, but not outside. It operates only on a single level, and, like inbreeding, can lead to unintended bad consequences. Fundamentally, it does not harness the power of evolution.

At best, it is a weak imitation. Therefore, it's not enough for a risk manager to understand a toy mathematical example of diversity and selection. She must have a deep appreciation for the miracle of evolution and the essential role of good randomness within it.

It's not much of a stretch to see a company as an evolving entity, but how about a portfolio of securities? The principle is the same. Conventional economic reasoning says that if two stocks have similar expected future cash flows and similar dependence on the market, we prefer the one that is less volatile. But might we not see some advantage to stock in volatile company A, which has survived many crises, over stock in safe, untested company B? Perhaps A's stresses have allowed evolution of the characteristics that will succeed in the future, whereas B is narrowly positioned for the conditions of the past. In the future, perhaps A's volatility will allow it to move faster into opportunities and away from dead ends, and to evolve as conditions change.

I'm not arguing that stock A is always better than stock B, only that we have to consider the type of volatility. On one hand, A might be mismanaged, or it may have a shakier business model or a weaker balance sheet. On the other hand, it might be more innovative than B. We will see later how to identify the type of randomness that helps survive extra-VaR events and leads to continual improvements as a result of selection.

Can Darwin help us with Pascal's wager? Does it make sense to add a little randomness to your theological beliefs? I think so. Your beliefs are shaped by teachings and by interactions with other people. If those are narrow, you're less likely to find the key to your heaven, if it exists. But I don't think it's enough to intentionally broaden those things. That's the rational approach, and we're trying to get evolution to work for us beyond the rational boundary. To take advantage of evolution you need to add some randomness to your learning and experiences. Religious scholar Greg Barton noted that the more you read, the less certainty you find. The people with the most narrow and rigid views have generally read the least.

The next step is selection. You're not trying to merge a hundred random beliefs into your personal doctrine, but to evolve as a person. I don't know whether it's literally true that there are no atheists in foxholes, but I do know that intense experiences can clear away weak or overly simplistic beliefs. Everyone imagines themselves as the hero in a movie, but what would you really do when the shooting starts? It may not be worth going to war to find out, but if you do find out it might change some of your fundamental beliefs. At least people who have found out tell me it does. If there is a Last Judgment of some sort, it might help to have knocked around a bit on Earth before you face it. And if this life is all there is, why not live it by drinking from many wells of experience? Rolling the dice does not have to reduce your utility.

Principle VI: Superposition

The traditional analysis of randomness had one embarrassing weakness until the early 1900s. No one could demonstrate that randomness existed. A coin flipped in the air obeys the laws of physics; it seems random only because it's complicated to compute whether it will land heads or tails. We may not know what the top card on a deck is, but that doesn't make it random. If randomness was just ignorance, as some people argued, then it should obey the rules of psychology, not the rules of mathematics. To avoid bringing subjectivity into the calculation, other people invented elaborate constructs of randomness that frequently led to contradictions.

About a century ago, physicists discovered that something like true randomness existed on a microscopic scale. Unfortunately, it did not behave at all the way a coin flip did. If I hide a ball under a cup, you may not know where it is, but it is under one and only one cup. However, a subatomic particle acts as if it's under all the cups at once, until you lift one. (This is a gross simplification, but sufficient to understand the risk model, just not enough to understand the physics.) This phenomenon is called superposition, and it allows outcomes that are impossible if the particle remained in any single fixed location. For example, with superposition you could pick up all the cups one at a time without finding the ball, even if you know the ball is always under a cup.

There is an important macroscopic analogy. Consider a company that measures everything in money and puts very tight cost controls in place. This policy will impose some uniformity on decision making throughout the organization. The organization will run efficiently, but only according to the prevailing set of prices. Another company pays less attention to costs. It will be able to undertake projects that are not optimal under any one set of prices, but have better overall prospects. Different people in different parts of the company will face different constraint sets, so there will be diversity of approaches. Too much of this might lead to waste, but not enough can stifle growth. The only reason a company exists in the first place, instead of all physical assets being leased and all employees being independent contractors, is that some activities run better without money exchange at each stage. Overly tight cost controls defeat that.

The same is true of the economy as a whole. If everything is priced in money, marked to market and subject to liquid trading, you get a narrowly efficient result. Because the result is highly specialized to a set of prices and uniform throughout the economy, even a small change in prices can cause a large dislocation. In a less integrated and controlled economy, lots of innovation will be sparked by people encountering overlooked and underpriced assets, and by other people facing unusual price structures. A lot of this activity will represent waste, but it does mean that when prices change there will be economic players positioned to take advantage.

At this level, it sounds similar to the randomness we want to preserve or create in order to power evolution. But superposition obeys different mathematical rules and has a different place in the risk manager's tool kit.

Principle VII: Game Theory

Another beautiful addition to the theory of randomness was the development of game theory. This is the mathematical study of uncertainty caused by rational actions of others rather than natural randomness. One early game-theory result is that the most rational action is often to flip a coin. Any decision arrived at through any intellectual process is provably inferior to a random decision. Another result is that knowledge and freedom of action can be harmful. In a so-called *truel*, a three-person analog of a duel, the most skillful person often has the least chance of winning.

Game theory sent researchers into the laboratory and the world to gather data about how people actually behave, and what the results are. This is one of the most exciting and productive areas of scientific research today. For the first time we have real data to force some rigor on the study of behavior: whether in biology, evolutionary theory, anthropology, psychology, sociology, political theory, or economics. Randomness turns up in all sorts of unexpected ways in modern game theory.

Game theory results are related to the study of risk because traditional economic analysis distinguished sharply between risk, which always reduced expected utility, and freedom of action, which always increased expected utility. That is, if a future event is uncertain, that's bad if some natural process you can't predict or control determines the event, but good if you get to choose the event. Game theory told us that natural risk can be good, and control can be bad.

A little thought shows that all practical risk problems have all three dimensions: the outcome will be influenced by you, by nature, and by others. You must have some control over a situation, or it's pointless to calculate anything. In fact, by my definition, if you have no control, it isn't risk to you. You never know everything for certain; there will be some unknown, uncontrollable factors that are random, at least from your point of view. Moreover, outcomes always depend on other people. Even if you do something that affects no one else, someone might decide to outlaw it, or to tax it, or to subsidize it. These types of risk are thoroughly mixed—it's usually not possible to increase the good ones and decrease the bad ones. If you take risk, you take all kinds of risk. If you avoid risk, you still take all kinds of risk, just in different ways.

One important practical example of how injecting game theory risk into a situation can be good was described by F. A. Hayek:

> In our age, with its passion for conscious control of everything, it may appear paradoxical to claim as a virtue . . . [to] know less . . . and that a method . . . should be deemed superior because of our ignorance of its precise results. Yet this consideration is in fact the rationale of the great liberal principle of the Rule of Law. And the apparent paradox dissolves rapidly when we follow the argument a little further. To be impartial means to have no answer to certain questions which, if we have to decide them, we decide by tossing a coin.
>
> Friedrich A. Von Hayek. *The Road to Serfdom,*
> University of Chicago Press: Chicago, 1945

In other words, a legislator or judge can do a better job if she deals only with general principles without knowing in advance the precise effects of laws or decisions. That is why justice is blind: she hears only the facts of the case; she does not see anything else to make her prefer plaintiff or defendant. Her decision is to be based on principles, not predictions of effects. When this is not possible, we often resort to tossing a coin, as in the federal lotteries run to distribute green cards, or formerly run to determine who got drafted. Game theory is why, as lawyers know, hard cases make bad law. In difficult cases, clear legal principles collide with sensibilities. The proper legal decision leads to an unsatisfying result—an evildoer goes free, someone suffers for trying to do good, or the shrewd scoundrel wins over the simple honest person. When judges and legislators bend the law to force the right result, the law is worse for it, even if one decision is improved. The difficult task is to figure out the deeper principle underlying the injustice, which cannot be done by focusing on the effects in one case, but only by broader game theory thinking.

Game theory should influence thinking about risk in a different way than evolution and quantum physics did. Game theory reverses the causality. Instead of risk arising in nature and analysts trying to make predictions in spite of it, risk is something deliberately created by people or implicitly created by social systems for useful purposes. It's the difference between lightning and the electricity that comes through a wire to light your home. They obey the same physical laws, but for most practical purposes are unrelated phenomena.

One example of game theory randomness is the decision of a poker player to make a bet. In some sense this is a random decision, as it depends on cards dealt and unpredictable human decisions. But it's different from a coin flip. Suppose you observe the player for a long time and build a model of the probability distribution of cards she is likely to be holding, given the cards you see and the betting action. If she is a good player, you would have trouble building the model, of course, but let's assume you do a perfect job. You will still lose money to her on average if you call when your model says the odds are in your favor. The reason is that her calculation takes your decisions, including your model, into account. She can build in an advantage no matter how good your model is. This is a mathematical result that can be proven, and it is true in practice as well. The only way you can overcome it is to raise at least some of the time, offering her bets of your own. This is elementary game theory but quite different from a roulette wheel, where you win in the long run by making bets when the odds are in your favor. It is true that you can define a probability distribution for her hands, but if you bet on the basis of it, you lose.

A financial example of the fallacy of confusing game theory randomness with coin flip randomness is Black Wednesday, the 1994 attempt of the British government to keep the value of the pound sterling above 2.778 German deutsche marks. The British treasury spent £27 billion buying sterling at that rate, and had essentially unlimited borrowing ability. Yet hedge funds led by George Soros and Stanley Druckenmiller at the Quantum Fund forced the price down to 2.4 deutsche marks with far smaller resources.

Treasury officials were confident due to the resource advantage they held, and also due to their ability to raise interest rates, increasing the attractiveness of the pound to investors. They were treating this like a contest in which the stronger side wins. But the hedge funds were treating it like a bet. As Druckenmiller later explained, he knew there was a chance the pound would not go down, but also there was virtually no chance it would go up. All the economic fundamentals and market pressure were downward; the only thing holding the pound at 2.778 was buying by the British treasury. That made it a heads-I-win-tails-I-break-even bet. Not only is that irresistible to any red-blooded investor, but it makes it easy to borrow large amounts of money to increase the size of bets. If there's little downside, a lender has little risk. The more investors piled in, the more attractive the bet became.

The British government not only spent the £27 billion buying pounds with deutsche marks, losing £3.3 billion in the process, but it also took the unprecedented step of raising interest rates by 500 basis points. There is a saying from gold standard days: "Interest at 5 percent brings in gold from the moon," meaning that just having rates of 5 percent—much less raising them that much—protects the value of a currency against anything on earth. But with all its money and power, and all its willingness to inflict excruciating pain by raising rates 500 basis points during a recession, the British Treasury still had no chance. Similar mistakes have been repeated many times since by governments trying to fight the financial markets.

Instead of treating the exchange rate as a random walk, the British Treasury should have considered it as a bet. In order to win the contest, it had to be able to create a credible scenario in which speculators would have been hurt if they had failed. In the circumstances that may not have been possible, in which case the Treasury could have saved a lot of money and pride by bowing to the inevitable. On the other hand, history proves it is possible for governments to fight the financial markets and win, as Paul Volcker did in the early 1980s, forcing inflation down from 13.5 percent to 3.2 percent. This required the willingness to raise interest rates to 20 percent and face down the strongest criticism and most widespread protests in the history of the Federal Reserve, and most important, to make the markets believe he was willing to go farther still. Strong action is useless if everyone knows it represents the limit of your strength.

Modern central bankers absorbed this lesson. In *No Reserve: The Limit of Absolute Power* (AmazonCrossing, 2011), Argentinean central bank president Martin Redado writes:

> [A]lthough they had tolerated my exchange strategy, they didn't like it. Face to face with the president [of Argentina], I once again explained to her the need to provide the exchange rate with upward and downward movement, in order to keep the markets from thinking there was easy money to be made from it, as had happened in programs with semi-fixed exchange rates—like Martínez de Hoz's "little table" [in the late 1970s] or Cavallo's Convertibility [in 1991].

General Dwight Eisenhower had great respect for the tactical brilliance of the German officer corps in World War II, especially when it was on the offensive. However, he identified one flaw: a tendency to commit every available resource to every battle. The Allies could thus be confident they knew the full measure of German strength, an enormous strategic advantage. To Eisenhower there was a single three-year battle, to which he applied carefully calibrated amounts of resources at different places in stages. Even at the height of the fighting, he had more resources in reserve than committed to combat.

Another major insight from game theory comes from a paradox. The best-known game theory paradox is the "Prisoner's Dilemma," which demonstrates that people following rational strategies in the simplest possible games can arrive at a bad outcome, when a much better outcome for everyone is available. However, that better outcome can only be reached by irrational choices. That calls into question the definition of "rational."

A lesser-known but more profound paradox gives insight into the importance of understanding the identity of the decision-maker. Suppose you are in a booth with five blue buttons and one red button. You are told you can press one button. Someone else, who you cannot communicate with, is in an identical booth and can also press one button. If you both press the same button, you each get $100. If you push different buttons, neither of you gets anything.

It's immediately obvious that you should press the red button. The question is why? There is no general game theory principle that makes any distinction among the buttons. It is not rational or irrational to choose any one. Game theorists have offered several resolutions to this paradox. Some invoke a principle that argues for pushing the red button. Others claim that pushing the red button need not be the correct choice. In my opinion, however, none of these resolutions are satisfactory if you insist on viewing each player as a discrete rational entity interested only in its own welfare.

In practice, each player immediately understands that she is in partnership with the other. They will win or lose together. As soon as that happens, we stop asking, "What is the best option for me?" and ask instead, "What is the best option for the partnership?" and "What action should I take to advance that option?" The best option is clearly for both of you to make the same choice. If that choice is to push a blue button, there is only a 20 percent chance the partnership will get paid. If that choice is to press the red button, there is a 100 percent chance of getting paid. So you pick the red button.

Logically, you could make the same argument about pushing the first button, or the last button or the middle button. In this case, the red button is the most obvious choice. But suppose all the buttons are the same size, except that one blue button is bigger. Or one blue button is square while all the other buttons are round. Or one blue button is separated from all the other buttons. In these cases, you put yourself inside the other person's head and try to guess what he will pick. Your best guess of that is likely whichever button seems most obvious to you to pick. The point is that you're thinking like a team, not a self-interested individual, and you're trying to predict what the other person will do based on his psychology, not his rational self-interest derived from the payoff matrix of the game.

While this particular situation does not come up a lot, it provides a useful window into an important part of human psychology. People are very good at identifying opportunities for cooperation, and playing roles for the benefit of the team, even without communication. It was useful for a Stone Age hunter-gatherer to be able to figure out what other members of the tribe were doing, even if they were far away at the time, and how he could coordinate to contribute to the overall prosperity of the tribe, which was essential for both his survival and his evolutionary success. It probably was not useful to be able to figure out the rational response in Prisoner's Dilemma. (In fact, almost everyone who has not studied game theory goes right to the cooperative solution in Prisoner's Dilemma, without worrying that it is irrational, worrying only that the other player might betray them. They don't think about maximizing their payoff, only about avoiding being a sucker.)

How does game theory help with Pascal's wager? It tells us to step back from the decision whether to believe in God, and to focus on the strategy for making the decision. "Believe fanatically whatever you were taught as a child" is a popular strategy that most of us can reject with little thought. "Kind of believe what you were taught as a child but practice halfheartedly" may cause less damage in the world, but it's hard to see it as the ultimate meaning of life. "Get away from all the stresses and distractions of the world and search your heart" might sound more promising, as might "Reach out to as many wise and good people as you can, in person and in books, and see if something valid distills from their experiences."

I'm not going to take this further, as it gets into things I know little about. I do think it's easier to come up with answers to the question "If there is a God who arranged everything in the Universe, including how I think and feel, how would she plan for me to come up with answers?" than "Which organized religion is best?" Moreover, the game is not just with God (or, if there is no God, a game of solitaire). People play games as well. It's sometimes worthwhile thinking about another question: "If I follow what this person tells me is God's will, how will he benefit?"

CHAPTER

4

The Secret History of Wall Street: 1654–1982

We're going to switch for a bit from theory to history. If I had all the theory worked out, I could write a textbook organized in logical sequence. Instead, I'm going to intersperse theoretical discussions with accounts of the development of the ideas. Different aspects are easier to understand from different vantages.

The rocket scientists came together on Wall Street in the 1980s and began the process that eventually explained the modern concept of probability and reconstructed the global financial system. We were not individually ambitious. All we wanted was to make more money than any rational person could possibly spend, without ever putting on a tie or being polite to anyone we didn't like. We didn't have any use for the money, except for maybe some books and cool computer equipment. We didn't want to throw (or go to) fancy parties or buy political power—and we didn't spend it on cars, jewelry, or places to live, and least of all on clothes. We'd probably give the money away, but until then, it would give us the power to say "fuck you" to anyone, except that we were mostly pretty soft-spoken and civil in our expressions.

In recent years, I have received inquiries from researchers studying this period, and no doubt someone will put together a comprehensive history. I will be interested to read it, to see how others perceived the same events I'm about to describe. I suspect there will be vast differences. Nevertheless, my personal account is an important part of this book. It will give you a consistent story of how the ideas evolved. Collecting other accounts and carefully cross-checking facts would produce a richer and more accurate story, but I don't think it would give more insight about the nature of risk.

Although we collaborated in a grand project, we didn't know each other very well; in fact, we often didn't know each other at all. We didn't meet in seminar rooms or trading floors or restaurants, or in each other's homes. Mostly we communicated by dial-up computer bulletin boards, a pre-Internet form of geek interaction. These were initially set up to share data, something we all needed and that was generally unavailable in electronic form. So whatever numbers you typed in by hand you uploaded for others, and thereby gained access to their labors. But the story does not begin in 1980. To explain what we were doing I have to go more than three centuries farther back.

Pascal and Fermat

The letters between Blaise Pascal and Pierre Fermat in 1654 are merely the earliest tangible evidence of a fundamental shift in thought that occurred within a few years around this time. Among the consequences of that shift were that the analysis of gambling games became a serious subfield of mathematics, lists of raw data such as parish birth and death records were recognized as holding important information for science and public policy, financial instruments such as government annuities incorporated explicit—but not always accurate—actuarial analysis, and probability-based reasoning—what today are called Bayesian concepts—became the standard for assessing conflicting evidence in history and law.

Some historians dispute the novelty of these ideas in 1654, and find precursors in medieval and ancient texts, and also in non-Western traditions. I will sidestep that debate because the important point for me is that while some people might have thought this way before 1654, since that year the ideas have assumed increasing importance to the point that today nearly everyone thinks this way. What happened around 1654 was not a discovery that forced a change in thinking, but a change in social attitudes that required the development of a new theory. That theory proved extremely difficult to make rigorous, so the history of risk analysis is one of advances by practitioners, sometimes but not always explained later by theoreticians. Incidentally, I consider the book you are reading to be another practitioner advance.

The problem is that the field of probability was not discovered; rather, it was created by the confusion of two concepts. The first is the frequency with which certain events recur, such as the number of times out of 100 throws a coin will come up heads. The second is the degree of belief to attach to a proposition, such as how likely it is that France will win the next World Cup. We can say, "You will probably get between 40 and 60 heads," or if we are quants, "The probability is 96.47998 percent of getting between 40 and 60 heads, if the coin is fair." We can be precise because we have a good mathematical theory for coin flips and can repeat the experiment many times for confirmation. But we have no mathematical theory for predicting World Cup winners, and because the experiment cannot be repeated, it is not even clear what *probability* means.

The illogic of confusing these two concepts has been pointed out many times over the centuries, often by people who think they are the first to notice. The most familiar to modern readers is Frank Knight, who said we should use "risk" for the frequency concept and "uncertainty" for degree of belief. A century earlier, the mathematician Siméon Poisson—who gave his name to the Poisson distribution—suggested "probability" and "chance" instead. Fifty years before that, the Marquis de Condorcet wanted *facilité* (facility) and *motif de croire* (reason to believe). Rudolph Carnap came up with the uber-geeky "probability$_1$" and "probability$_2$" and also "statistical" and "inductive" probability. In the early twentieth century "propensity" and "proclivity" were used, and in the early twenty-first Donald Rumsfeld highlighted the distinction again with "known unknowns" versus "unknown unknowns." Not all of these authors distinguished frequency and degree of belief in the same way, but all agreed there were two types of probability. As you may recall from Chapter 1, to this day there are two opposed branches of theoretical statistics, frequentists or classical statisticians, whose fundamental definition of probability rests on repeatable experiments, and Bayesians, whose foundation is subjective degree of belief.

The fascinating question is why all of this indisputable logic has failed to make the slightest impression on anyone. We still use "probability" in both senses and ignore the difference. Practicing statisticians all use the same tools, even though some are forbidden by the frequentist school and others by the Bayesians. What happened in 1654 was that two unrelated concepts were fused, and the fusion gave birth to a new way of thinking about the world. Theoretical explanations that begin by splitting the concepts destroy what they attempt to explain, which is why theoretical progress has been so unsatisfactory. The issue was not resolved until the early 1990s, entirely by accident, on Wall Street.

If you like, you can consider the same change of thought as a fission rather than a fusion. Around 1654 it became common to analyze decision parameters in terms of beliefs and preferences, as discussed in Chapter 1, instead of as integrated decisions. For some reason, people suddenly decided it was rational to estimate probabilities of outcomes independent of utilities of outcome. It's clearly possible to do this with coin flips and dice rolls, but not so clear how to do it in general, or even why to do it in general. In the early days, reasoning from the example of dice, people assumed that there was a unique way to separate beliefs from preferences, which made this approach seem natural. The discovery that with non-casino risk in some circumstances there can be no way to define probabilities and preferences, and in other circumstances there can be many ways that argue for different decisions with no logical basis to choose among them, gave headaches to theorists, but was largely ignored by everyone else.

I was introduced to the philosophical issues of probability by W. V. O. Quine at Harvard in 1974. Professor Quine introduced me to Fischer Black, who gave me references to researchers such as Ian Hacking, Steven Stigler, Lorenz Krüger, and others who were rewriting the history of statistics. That project was possible because the effort to make statistics fully rigorous was completed only around 1960. Until then, the natural thought was that when we got to the bottom of things, the relationship between frequency and belief would become obvious. Instead, we had fully consistent theories of both, with no significant overlap, and no paths for further inquiry.

The failure of mathematics to resolve the issue opened up the field to philosophers, historians, and psychologists. While I was none of these, the work influenced me deeply. I decided there was a powerful and misunderstood thing—let's call it "risk"—that dominated both the way people think and the course of events. Risk was a fusion of observed frequencies and belief formation, and both the observation and the psychology were a lot more complex than most people realized. They required new empirical work to understand them.

Another consequence of the end of probability theory was that researchers like John Tukey and Fred Mosteller began emphasizing exploring data—letting the data talk to you—rather than testing hypotheses or generating confidence intervals. I took courses from Mosteller, and he introduced me to Tukey. Brad Efron was another strong influence on me, but unfortunately I have not met him yet. To bring things full circle, I discussed these issues with Fischer Black, who became a strong and well-known proponent of "exploring" models rather than analyzing them, or worse, believing them.

Poker

At the same time, I was supporting myself by playing poker. I had been a serious player since the age of 15. In the 1970s you didn't go online to play and there wasn't much poker at casinos, either, even if you happened to live in a place where gambling was legal. Making a living at poker required finding games, collecting winnings, and avoiding cheating, robbery, and arrest.

It also required some expertise at a variety of games. If you won someone's money at poker and he challenged you to backgammon, gin rummy, golf, or some other game, or wanted to bet on a sporting event or proposition (a bet made up on the spot, such as whether someone would answer the telephone at a random number pulled from the telephone book or whether there were more green or yellow candies in a bag of M&Ms), a refusal showed that you were a hustler who played only when he had an advantage rather than someone willing to bet on himself. Although I did in fact play only when I had an advantage and did it entirely for the money, gambler etiquette forbade admitting that. I did not pretend to be either an amateur or unskilled; in fact, I was invited to big games because I had a reputation as a good player. Nevertheless, the convention had to be honored. Incidentally, it was acceptable to plead lack of skill at any of the games and demand a handicap, but if you were suspected of misrepresenting your skill level it was as bad as refusing to play.

Among the gamblers, the confusion of frequency and degree of belief seemed natural. Betting on a dice throw was the same as betting on a proposition. It was no coincidence that Pascal and Fermat conflated the two ideas when studying dice players. And the two mathematicians did not concern themselves with the probability of one or the other player winning the game. Probability is not mentioned at all in the letters. The two mathematicians concerned themselves with the legal question of how to divide the stake in an interrupted game. In other words, if you are not allowed to observe the outcome of a frequentist experiment, how do you assign a degree of belief to the potential outcomes?

One of the admirable characteristics of the gambling subculture is that you are expected to be willing to bet a significant stake on any assertion you make. If you back down when challenged, you lose your status. That means anyone who shoots his mouth off about things he doesn't know about ends up disgraced or broke, usually disgraced *and* broke. It means you don't hear a lot of statements of fact, but the ones you do hear you can rely on. In a phrase, "you can bet on" them. When you spend some time in this subculture, the civilian world starts sounding like a bunch of ignorant loudmouths. Anyway, what we see is frequency and degree of belief not merely confused, but their fusion is enforced by strong social mores. If you assert a degree of belief, you should be willing to bet on it, because in the long run the frequency of your wins should guarantee you a profit. Risk doesn't really enter the picture, because a gambler is going to make enough bets over her lifetime that she will end up with close to the expected value. Anyone who refuses to bet either misrepresented her belief or is no gambler.

Advantage Gamblers

For reasons I will postpone discussing until Chapter 12 many quants who accepted the same kinds of ideas about risk as I did became disaffected in the 1970s, too disaffected to get either academic or professional jobs. In a phrase, we were disgusted at what we saw as the hypocrisy of many conventional quantitative thinkers in that they were unwilling to bet personally significant stakes on the results of their analyses. Naturally, this sent us in search of quantitative professionals who would bet on their analyses. Mostly we found them among gamblers. So the rocket scientists moved to Las Vegas.

One camp gravitated toward blackjack card counting and other advantage gambling (playing standard casino games in a way that the odds favor the player instead of the house). These people are frequentists. They make money from superior prediction of the frequency of various results of repeatable experiments. This route required no social skills; you didn't have to get a game together and get invited back, and you didn't have to collect from losers or master whatever games other people wanted to play. In later years it required more and more skill at deception to avoid casino counter-measures, but unlike the flamboyant misdirection described in Ben Mezrich's *Bringing Down the House* (Free Press, 2002) and *Busting Vegas* (Morrow, 2005), these guys preferred quiet camouflage.

Advantage gamblers were apt to sneer at the rest of us, calling us hustlers who conned people. While they would never admit to such a romantic description, they saw them-selves as undercover Robin Hoods, stealing back from casinos what casinos had stolen from everyone else. To a frequentist, there's no reason to gamble at negative expected value games, and it's hard to escape the idea that casinos fool and cheat their customers. The advantage gamblers saw poker players like me as closer to casino owners than customers—more like the sheriff of Nottingham than Robin Hood.

Generally, advantage gamblers hate casinos more than they love money. In May 2009 I was at a table in Reno with a group of them when someone rushed in to announce that a customer had shot and killed a pit boss in Atlantic City. My table erupted in raucous cheers, enough to get us kicked out of the casino. Believe me, it's hard for people who bet big to get kicked out of a casino for having too much fun. Of course, if the casino staff had known who my tablemates were, they would have kicked us out earlier and harder.

Sports Betting

Another group diverged in the opposite direction. The invention of the point spread and the unrestrained growth of organized crime had turned sports betting from the domain of local bookies, who took risk but might lay off a large imbalance through an informal network, to a highly organized, mostly illegal, national business that

was allergic to risk. It was easy for quants to identify profitable bet opportunities in this system, because the spreads were set to equalize money bet on both sides, not to reflect the true probability of winning (actually, it's not even clear what "true probability" means). The organization did not want to make money by predicting outcomes better than customers and taking risk; it wanted to have a guaranteed profit whatever the outcome.

You could make consistent money with strategies as simple as betting against the Los Angeles Lakers National Basketball Association team at home, because Los Angeles was a large, rich, and high-betting city and the Lakers were a glamorous team. Anyway, a quant with a computer and a bit of time on her hands could make some easy money with rules that were not much more complicated than Lakers + home = bet against. And with a little more effort, she could derive more profitable complicated rules.

Unlike the blackjack card counter, who was usually ejected from the casino or worse if caught, the advantage sports bettor was the organization's friend. For example, with National Football League betting, the pre-pre-opening line would be set after Sunday's games for the following week. It would be shown to some smart gamblers who would be allowed to make fixed-sized bets on it. The initial group was composed mainly of people likely to have inside information, and who were often friendly with or connected to organized crime. Based on those bets, the line would be corrected.

Early Monday morning, the pre-opening line would be shown to a larger group of bettors, who were allowed to make smaller fixed-sized bets on any games they wanted. This group was mainly quants who had come to the attention of the organization by winning consistently. After this round of betting, and the results of the Monday night game, an adjusted opening line would be posted on Tuesday, open to the public.

Therefore, a sports-betting quant could progress from independent agent to essentially a contract employee of the organization.

Some went further and signed up for salaried work to set the pre-pre-opening line and make adjustments. As the influence of organized crime waned, some quants opened their own risk-taking bookmaking operations, setting a line a bit above or below the national line and taking bets directly. Quants in this group could also go into casino management and later into online gambling and poker.

These guys were Bayesians, degree-of-belief believers. A sporting event cannot be repeated. The line will be set by the public's beliefs about the outcome or, more precisely, by the organization's and insiders' predictions about the public's beliefs. The algorithms used both to set and beat the spread paid more attention to how people bet than to how teams won. In theory, you could predict the probability of covering the spread from first principles, and make money betting when the probability was enough in your favor to cover the vigorish—the bookmaker's built-in edge. But you could equally well make money by determining which spreads were likely set too high or too low, without making any absolute evaluation of the likelihood of a team covering the spread.

This is the same distinction as between a value investor who tries to determine the underlying value of a stock versus a momentum investor who knows only that when a stock goes up it tends to continue going up. In both stock market investing and sports betting, having a good value estimate is a useful factor in an investment decision, but much more quant effort is devoted to studying how other investors/bettors act than to estimating fundamental value. This offends a lot of people—at least with respect to investing—but it shouldn't for reasons I'll get into later.

I dabbled in both wings of the quant gambling movement. I did a little card counting, both individual and team, but didn't enjoy it enough to persist. Mostly I counted to break even so I could play at the $500-a-hand blackjack table without expense. That was a great place to meet people who would invite you to high-stakes private poker games. I did not disguise my counting, but I didn't change bet sizes too aggressively, and I didn't make a consistent profit, and I acted to keep the game lively and fun. For those reasons I was tolerated by the casinos. Many counters were kicked out of casinos not for making too much money, but for playing in an obsessive, unpleasant manner that bothered the other bettors.

I also did a little sports betting. My specialty was line changes. Certain changes in the line represented new information, whereas others were just unanticipated swings in public demand. Generally the line changes are too small to overcome the built-in house edge, so I would buy bets from other gamblers. For example, suppose Green Bay has opened the week a three-and-a-half-point favorite over Chicago. A gambler has bet $10,000 on Green Bay, meaning he will win $10,000 if Green Bay wins by more than three points but will pay $11,000 if Green Bay loses or wins by one, two, or three points. A news story comes out Thursday that the Chicago quarterback, who had been questionable for the game, will play. The line moves to Green Bay +1½.

If our gambler doesn't like the bet with the new information, he can get out of it by betting $10,000 on Chicago. But this locks in a $1,000 loss, since he pays $11,000 for a loss but gets only $10,000 on a win. Plus, if Green Bay wins by exactly two or three points, he loses both bets and is out $22,000. If he transfers the bet to me and pays me $1,000, he locks in his $1,000 loss, but eliminates the risk of the $22,000 loss. If I determine the line move is from public reaction rather than fundamental change to game outcomes, I like the original bet. But my new bet is even better, since I either win $11,000 or pay $10,000.

Once again, I didn't enjoy this enough to make a living at it, and I didn't want to start or join a gambling business. I thought of myself as poker player, not an independent Robin Hood or an organization man. Intellectually, I saw the value in both frequency probability and degree of belief probability, and I was obsessed with teasing out the reason they were so powerful together. On top of that, modesty compels me to disclose I was only competent, not great, at both advantage gambling and sports betting. I was at least the equal of any poker player in those days, in my own humble opinion, but I met some counters and sports bettors who were head and shoulders above my level.

Quants to Wall Street

A lot of gambling quants moved to Wall Street in the early 1980s, representing maybe 20 of the 100 or so rocket scientists who arrived around the same time. Other rocket scientists had been floor traders or other kinds of risk takers. What we had in common were quantitative training, a similar view of the world, similar aspirations, and at least several years of experience supporting ourselves with independent risk-taking activities.

We also had in common a few books, first among which were Edward Thorp's *Beat the Dealer* (Random House, 1962) and *Beat the Market* (Random House, 1967), the latter written with Sheen Kassouf. Ed was the mathematics professor who analyzed and popularized blackjack card counting, and also beat the house at other casino games. In the mid-1960s he turned to investing and invented or perfected an extraordinary number of what are now the standard hedge fund strategies. In addition, he is crucially important as the first person to expand upon and popularize the work of John Kelly (whose work was the basis of risk ignition, as explained in Chapter 3). Let me correct a possible misapprehension. I have mentioned antisocial blackjack card counters and will expand more on the type. This is not meant to disparage anyone; it is an exaggerated stereotype useful for distinguishing attitudes toward risk. However, it is most definitely not meant to disparage Ed Thorp. There is a world of difference between inventing blackjack card counting, proving it in a mathematics journal, and exploiting it to prove you can— versus trying to make a living practicing something someone else invented. I have great affection and respect for advantage gamblers, but I will make some fun of them as well. Please do not take the jibes as applying to the original blackjack card counter.

We all wanted to do what Ed did. We wanted to figure out mathematical edges in the financial markets, then exploit them using the Kelly criterion. We wanted to do it for the money and for the challenge, but also out of curiosity. You cannot understand the economy without understanding the markets, and you cannot understand the markets without trying to beat them.

I call this the "secret" history of Wall Street because it has not been previously published. Many parts have been described individually in books and articles, but not the whole picture.

There are four parts of Wall Street, or finance in general. The first and most important is sales. All businesses involve sales, but in finance it is not something done to move the product; it *is* the product. Ever since the invention of paper money, economic activity has begun with someone creating the expectation of future value, which is just a roundabout way of saying "sales." Wall Street has its bond salesmen, stockbrokers, investment bankers, and many other species of salespeople. Many people called portfolio managers are actually salespeople, making their livings by attracting assets to their funds and collecting fees, rather than generating excess profits with those assets. Most of what you read about finance comes from the salespeople. They also tend to run the firms and shape government policies. They are the most accessible to journalists and constitute the majority of guests on CNBC and other financial television. Some are smart and some are not, but the job depends on interpersonal ability, not intelligence. With some exceptions, they haven't the slightest idea of the economic function of finance. Call what they write the official history.

Finance People

Most of the people working in finance are processing information. Every purchase and sale, every paycheck, every transfer of funds generates one or more transactions, and there are additional transactions such as generating daily interest payments for every pool of money and supporting financial trading, including high-frequency trading. This amounts to hundreds of billions of transactions each day. A hundred billion is not a large number in modern information processing terms. The challenge is that the transactions are dispersed around the globe and are aggregated in many kinds of systems, not all automated. Each one presents an opportunity for fraud or theft. They also involve people, and people are very bad at security and make lots of errors.

Although you don't read a lot about this kind of finance, it is the area in which people have the most personal experience. Chances are you know more accountants, financial computer people, bank tellers, insurance adjusters, and loan officers than you do investment bankers. And you have almost certainly argued with one or more of them about a transaction.

The third part of finance is information hoarding. From 1900 to 1970, most financial information was hoarded by banks as a source of their power and profits. Banks knew which businesses were creditworthy and were able to get their money out first when there was a problem. They knew the operating results of companies as well as the company management did. They knew what assets investors held and who was buying or selling. None of this information was available to the public, or even to corporate management or large investors. The government certainly didn't know, not even the quasi-governmental Federal Reserve Board. So everyone was forced to do business with banks, on the banks' terms.

The monopoly was broken in the 1970s, but that didn't mean information hoarding went away. Today it is done by a variety of institutions in different ways. Competition, also known as disinter-mediation, has brought costs down dramatically. For example, in the 1960s an individual would typically pay 3 percent more inter-est on a mortgage loan than he could earn on his savings account backed by mortgage loans. The difference was net revenue to the bank. It was protected by information hoarding. Only a few local institutions had the information necessary to make the loans, and individuals found it difficult to get the information neces-sary to make better financial investments than a savings account. Government regulation helped maintain the oligopoly.

Today a person will likely pay less than 1 percent more on her mortgage than she could earn buying a security backed by that mort-gage. Institutional spreads are even lower. This does not mean, how-ever, that financial workers are going hungry. The explosion in the volume of financial transactions has far more than offset the decline in net revenue per transaction.

Information hoarders are less likely to write books than sales-people are. Nevertheless, most people have some familiarity with banking due to extensive coverage by outsiders (often hostile out-siders) to complement a few good insider accounts. Unlike the other parts of finance, banking theory is taught in business schools and economics departments. If you don't know much about it, it's probably because it bores you, not because you don't know where to go for information.

Real Finance

Finally, there is a small group of people who actually do finance, which means they make bets. You find them on trading floors and in hedge funds and scattered other places. They are technical pro-fessionals who deal in risk. This is the part of finance that was revo-lutionized in the decade following 1982 by rocket scientists. Not all traders are quants today—the quals still outnumber the quants. But the basic structure of the profession is purely quantitative, whereas 30 years ago it was, with a few exceptions, purely qualitative.

I mention this partly so you can place this book within the larger literature on Wall Street. The other reason is it figures directly into the story. An independent financial quant in 1980 had two big problems: getting the data necessary to make good bets, and placing the bets on fair terms. Information hoarders had the business sewn up. You had to go to work for a big bank to get access to the data, and even then it wasn't in electronic form. And only starting from a bank trading desk could you get a trading account with the low cost and flexibility necessary for quant trading. Ed Thorp managed to do it independently, and there were a few others, but it was very difficult. You could also do it by buying a seat on a public exchange. Many took this route, but it was expensive and limited your trading activities.

Only when a critical mass of like-minded and highly computer-literate quants gathered did the situation change. We mined information and shared it on the dial-up computer bulletin boards I mentioned earlier. We typed in price series and also essential datalike market pricing conventions and trading rules. We wrote handbooks for opening accounts and protecting yourself from the tricks banks liked to play. Although the source for all this information was banks, the result was superior to anything the banks had. It was electronic and integrated, stripped of its protective jargon and inefficiencies. It was cleansed of errors.

What we did next is the subject of Chapter 9. I want to end this one by discussing why no outsiders seemed to notice what happened. Everyone knew, of course, that Wall Street was changing rapidly, and also that quants were becoming more important. What most observers failed to see was that the driving force was quants. Wall Street was not changing on its own in a manner that induced it to go out and hire more quants; quants were changing the way finance was done. This triggered a host of other changes, but it didn't rewrite the principles of sales or information processing, the most familiar parts of finance. It drastically modified information hoarding, of course, which is what most serious accounts of this period treat as the impetus for change.

Stockbrokers still call customers and pitch trade ideas, but there are a lot more investors in the market than there were in 1980, and most of them invest in ways that were uncommon back then or didn't exist at all. They may use no-load mutual funds or 401(k)s or enter trades online, probably getting most information from the Internet. The entity that fills their order in 1980 might have been an exchange specialist, who accumulated all the buy and sell orders and chose which ones to execute. Today the entity filling the order is likely to be a quant high-frequency trader. Prices in 1980 were mostly determined by large trades from stodgy institutions. Today, hyperaggressive hedge funds are far more important. All of this is wrapped in a rocket-scientist-designed web of highly levered quantitative risk management, in which paper money has ceased to be important. The main financial intermediaries are no longer private partnerships with negligible capital and commercial banks with strict limits on the types of business they could pursue. They have been replaced by some of the largest and most complex institutions ever created by humans, along with small and simple institutions all the way down to single individuals—but individuals with computers and leverage. We still call it Wall Street but no one who was actually on Wall Street in 1980 would recognize any part of it—and none of it is located on physical Wall Street.

CHAPTER 5

When Harry Met Kelly

Warning, this chapter contains a little math. It's nothing intimidating, mostly multiplication and some simple algebra, but I know a lot of people don't like it. If that describes you, I urge you to read the chapter anyway. It's one of the most important in the book. You can skip the math and get the ideas anyway.

Two of the most important discoveries about risk were made in the 1950s by Harry Markowitz and John Kelly. Markowitz's result became the basis of modern finance. Kelly's result received much less academic attention, and was rejected by many mainstream economists. From a practical standpoint, however, the situation was reversed. Markowitz's theory was crucially important, but the computer power available at the time was insufficient to translate it into practical results. When advances in computers solved that problem, the pure Markowitz portfolios proved to be unusable.

In contrast, Kelly's result proved invaluable for practical risk takers. It did not require computer power. It was not a useful abstraction for understanding the true nature of things; it was a practical formula for direct application. However, it could not achieve its full power until it was linked with Markowitz's work, something that did not happen until the late 1980s.

This chapter explains the two ideas and their interaction in a historical counterfactual. What if Kelly had been in the University of Chicago library one fateful afternoon when Harry was musing over some stock tables? What if Harry had met Kelly?

Kelly

Conventional wisdom says risk decisions should be made by sub-jective preference: your risk tolerance or your utility function. But in 1956, John Kelly published a contrary result: that there is a cal-culable amount of risk that always does best in the long run. Most people think that taking more risk increases the probability of both very good and very bad outcomes. Kelly showed that beyond a certain point, more risk only increases the probability of bad out-comes. Moreover, taking less than optimal risk actually guarantees doing worse in the long run; it only appears to be a safer course.

To see why this is true, suppose you had $1,000 to use to make 100 even-money bets in a row. You know you will win exactly 60 out of the 100, but the order of your wins will be chosen by the bettor on the other side. You have to specify your bets in advance and you are never allowed to bet more than you have.

For one example, you could bet $24 each time. You'll win 60 and lose 40 to end up with $1,480. But this is the best you can do with fixed bets. If you bet less than $24, you end up with less than $1,480. If you bet $25 or more, the other bettor will arrange for the 40 losses to come first, wiping you out so you cannot make any more bets.

Suppose instead you decide to bet 20 percent of your current bankroll each time. The nice thing about this rule is that the order of the wins and losses doesn't matter. You can always make the bet—you never go broke—and you always have the same amount at the end. The bettor on the other side can't hurt you.

Think of the outcomes as 40 losses matched by wins plus 20 unmatched wins. A loss reduces your bankroll to 80 percent; a win gets it back up to 96 percent. Each loss/win combination reduces your bankroll by your bet percentage squared (20 percent squared is 4 percent). Doing this 40 times reduces your bankroll to $195. But then come your 20 unmatched 20 percent wins, with no offset-ting losses. These bring your bankroll up to $7,490.

If you bet 10 percent instead, each of the 40 loss/win combina-tions reduces your bankroll only 1 percent (10 percent squared). Forty of them bring your bankroll down to $669, much better than when you bet 20 percent. Your 20 wins with no offset raise that amount to $4,501. Not bad, but nowhere near as good as the 20 percent bettor.

Suppose you bet 30 percent each time. Each of the 40 loss/win combinations reduces your bankroll by 9 percent. Forty of those gets you down to $23. Twenty wins with no offsets raises you back to $4,370, close to what you got by betting 10 percent. Twenty percent is the perfect amount to bet; betting a higher or lower fraction means doing worse. This is not probably or only theoretically true. This is mathematical fact. It really works, in practice as well as theory. While there are people who dislike the Kelly criterion for various reasons, no intelligent person disputes this aspect of the result.

You might think you can come up with a clever scheme to do better. For example, if you bet a penny more than Kelly each time, you end up with $0.32 more at the end, $7,490.19 instead of $7,489.87. There are cleverer schemes like betting one penny more than Kelly the first bet, then if you lose, betting two pennies more the second bet, doubling the number of pennies each bet until you win; then you follow Kelly thereafter and end up one penny better off. Whether these are truly better or not, or truly different or not, requires some theoretical hairsplitting. But there's no practical hairsplitting about the fact that there's no way to do significantly better using any strategy that's meaningfully different than the Kelly strategy.

So far we've discussed the case where you know exactly how many bets you will win and lose. But what if you only know the probability of winning? Suppose you are faced with a gamble with a 60 percent chance of doubling your money and a 40 percent chance of losing it. How much should you bet? If you make only one bet in your life, the amount is a matter of opinion, a matter of utility theory if you like. But if you expect to make many, many bets during your life, you can be reasonably confident that your long-term wins and losses will conform pretty closely to their expected values. In that case you're much like the person who knows she will win 60 out of 100 bets. You should bet 20 percent of your wealth (we'll explore what this means exactly, and give some cautions). The great thing about this rule is that it doesn't depend on who you are, or on your utility function (which you don't know anyway), or on what future opportunities will be available (as long as there are enough risks to ensure you end up close to your long-term expectation). Another nice feature is that if a group of people faces the risk, as long as they all contribute equal shares of their wealth, they'll make the same risk decisions and those decisions can be calculated. Kelly supports teamwork.

The Kelly result is a mathematical one that applies strictly only under certain conditions. But the insight that there is a right amount of risk to take is much more general. Just as important as selecting the risk level is consistent risk taking. Most people take a few very large risks, which dominate their life outcome, and avoid thousands of other risks. If they win, they brag about their courage and skill. If they lose, they blame Black Swans—Black Swans that they created with their betting strategies. Had they taken all the positive-edge risk and sized their bets properly, the law of large numbers would have virtually guaranteed success.

Harry

Sixty years ago, an economics graduate student named Harry Markowitz sat in the University of Chicago library trying to come up with a dissertation topic. He was reading an analysis of stock prices, and mused on the question, "Why don't investors put all their money in whichever stock seems best?" He hit on an answer: "Because that would be too risky." He worked out a system in which investors try to maximize expected return and minimize risk. This led to the development of modern portfolio theory (MPT), which has had extraordinary influence on the financial system (although Harry's dissertation chairman, Milton Friedman, is said to have observed that it was "nice work, but not economics").

Modern portfolio theory was a major advance, but suppose Harry had known Kelly, who was developing his ideas around the same time. Harry might have answered the question differently: "Because buying one stock virtually guarantees doing worse than buying a larger portfolio. It's not riskier; it's just worse."

I want to laser in on the difference here, because it's crucial for this chapter and this book, and it's not well understood except by risk managers. Let's say you look at all the available stocks and find the single best bet, in the sense of having the highest expected return. Let's say it's a little drug company whose stock will jump from $10 to $100 if it gets a favorable Food and Drug Administration (FDA) ruling, which it has a 20 percent chance of getting. If the company gets a negative FDA ruling, the stock will be worthless. The expected future value of the stock after the ruling is $0.2 \times \$100 + 0.8 \times \$0 = \$20$. That's an expected 100 percent return on the $10 investment.

You have $100,000 in your 401(k) for retirement. Are you going to put all of it in this stock? No. But why not?

Harry said it was because it was too risky. You should instead look around for many positive expected return opportunities. Since this particular stock has the highest expected return, that means you're going to average in lower expected return investments. Your portfolio expected return is the weighted average of your individual stock expected returns, so a diversified portfolio has to have a lower expected return than the 100 percent you can get with this one stock. But a diversified portfolio can have much lower risk than even the safest component. By spreading your money around, you might end up with a portfolio expected return of 10 percent, instead of the 100 percent you can get with one stock, but with much less probability of losing money. Instead of an 80 percent chance of losing all your money, you might have only a 20 percent chance of losing money at all, and only a tiny chance of losing more than 10 percent of your money. Harry said risk is bad, and investors will pay—by giving up some expected return—to reduce it.

Kelly agreed that you shouldn't put the entire $100,000 in the one stock, for an entirely different reason. If you lose, as you will 80 percent of the time, you lose more than $100,000. You lose access to all the other positive expected value opportunities that will arise in the future. This has nothing to do with your preferences or with risk being bad. If this is the only bet you'll ever face, Kelly has nothing to tell you. But if you plan to be investing for a while, Kelly can show you a strategy that is virtually certain to do better than putting all your money in the best stock.

For Harry, the key was diversification. You didn't put all your money in one stock because you should use money to buy lots of other stocks. For Kelly, the key was bet sizing. You shouldn't put all your money in one stock because it is overbetting. It didn't matter whether there were other stocks to invest in or not. Harry said not to put all your money in one stock because there are simultaneous investment opportunities. Kelly said not to put all your money in one stock because there are future betting opportunities.

Both these insights are valid, and both lead to important ideas underpinning finance and nonfinancial risk taking. In the world we live in, Harry's ideas got developed in mainstream finance, while Kelly's were promoted in what I have called the secret history of Wall Street. To understand the future, you have to understand the power of combining both views.

Harry told me he never met Kelly. Nonetheless, he was influential in developing Kelly's ideas. He discussed the idea in his book *Portfolio Selection* (John Wiley & Sons, 1959) although without mentioning Kelly. He wrote influential papers on the subject, crediting Kelly, in 1971, 1973, and 1991. Unfortunately, by this time certain assumptions that prevented many economists from understanding what Kelly wrote had crept into the economics literature. Modern portfolio theory required that the joint probability distribution of the prices of all assets at all points in the future be known, and that an investor has a completely specified utility function that depends only on future wealth. Among other things, that implies there is a perfect numeraire and that all your investment ideas can be specified over the same time horizon (in practice investors have theses about everything from an economic number that will be released in one minute to generational demographic shifts and the long-term success of some new technology—and everything in between—with no practical way to integrate these into a single probability distribution over any fixed time interval). If you assume these things, you don't need Kelly—but you are saddled with your assumptions. Kelly allows you to make good risk decisions based only on approximate knowledge of what a single asset will do over a single time period, with no reference to utility functions at all. Harry understood this, and even said that if Kelly's principle conflicted with utility theory, he would reject utility theory. In the end, however, he decided they were consistent, and that Kelly's work gave a maximum amount of risk any investor should consider, but that most investors would prefer to risk less than Kelly.

The preceding paragraph describes the strictest form of MPT. To be fair to the theory, it can be applied practically with much weaker assumptions. All that really matters is whether you can know the statistical properties of a portfolio well enough to care about them. I think the answer is that you can if you're talking about large portfolios of liquid securities held over periods of, say, 1 to 36 months. I think the answer is you can't if you're a high-frequency trader or deal in illiquid or highly concentrated or highly levered portfolios, or have aggressive trading strategies, or are concerned about events 10 years or more in the future. MPT can run a long-only large cap equity public mutual fund, but most hedge funds have to consider Kelly concepts as well.

I'm going to illustrate the similarities and differences between Harry and Kelly with commodity futures rather than with stocks, because stocks do messy thing like merge and liquidate. It's a complicated accounting job to evaluate a strategy over long periods of time. I could use horse racing like Kelly, but a lot of people wouldn't take that seriously. It doesn't matter; the field of application makes no difference. The mathematical underpinning is identical.

Commodity Futures

Table 5.1 shows the average returns and standard deviations of return for seven commodities from 1970 to 2010. It's easy to understand what an investment in silver means, but what about investments in perishable commodities? These returns are computed by rolling futures contracts. In January 1970, you enter into a long March futures contract in cocoa. That means you promise to accept delivery of 10 tons of cocoa of an agreed type and quality at an agreed location in March, and pay in exchange an agreed amount of money at that time. You must post cash to guarantee your promise; it might be 5 percent to 10 percent of the value of the cocoa.

You have no use for cocoa, so you won't accept delivery. Instead, at the end of February you will exit the March futures contract and enter into a May futures contract. By constantly rolling your contracts, you never have to accept delivery. However, you are paid the gains and must pay the losses as if you owned 10 tons of cocoa. If the price of cocoa goes up $10 per ton, you collect $100. If it goes down $25 per ton, you pay $250.

I have stated all returns as what you would earn investing in the commodity above what you could get in a low-risk asset like Treasury bills or bank certificates of deposit. If you prefer, you can

Table 5.1   Average Annual and Total Period Excess Returns of Selected Commodities, 1970 to 2010

Commodity	Average Annual Return	Standard Deviation	Total Return 1970–2010
Cocoa	4.9%	30.1%	10.6%
Corn	–3.5%	22.5%	–91.7%
Cotton	2.4%	22.7%	–6.4%
Hogs	1.6%	24.2%	–42.0%
Silver	2.8%	29.2%	–45.9%
Sugar	5.1%	38.4%	–62.0%
Wheat	–0.5%	25.5%	–78.3%
Portfolio	1.8%	14.3%	34.4%

think of them as the return you would earn above inflation, which comes to about the same thing.

The table shows that cocoa went up 4.9 percent more than low-risk bonds per year on average, but with a large standard deviation of 30.1 percent. Over the past 40 years, it would have turned a $1,000 investment into $1,106—a 10.6 percent excess return.

That might seem surprising. Since 4.9 percent per year times 40 years is 196 percent, why did the investment return only 10.6 percent over the period? For the same reason winning and losing an identically sized bet in the Kelly example left you worse off. If cocoa goes up 20 percent this year and down 20 percent next year, you're down 4 percent, not even. It's even worse for cotton, hogs, silver, and sugar: volatility turned positive average returns into negative returns for the period. If you want to approximate the total return of a commodity over the period, subtract half the standard deviation squared from the average return. For cocoa that's 4.9% − 30.1%^{2}/2 = 4.9% − 4.5%, or 0.4 percent. Multiply 0.4 percent by 40 years to get approximately 16 percent total return over the period. The actual answer is 10.6 percent, not 16 percent, but the approximation gets you in the ballpark.

In Markowitz's formulation, investors wouldn't pick one commodity, even if they thought it had the best prospects, because they would accept a lower expected return to get a lower standard deviation. But look at the last line in the table, which shows the result of splitting your money equally among the seven commodities. It returns 34.4 percent over the period, much better than even the best individual choice. Four of the commodities have higher average return, but the portfolio of all seven still dominates because it has less volatility drag. So Kelly would say it's not the fear of picking the wrong commodity that leads investors to diversify; it's knowing that even the right commodity will probably do worse than a portfolio.

At first glance, we just seem to have provided a reason for Markowitz's assertion that investors dislike risk. But the distinction is much deeper. Markowitz assumed people disliked risk on the grounds of utility theory, or because it was psychologically distressing, or because it made planning more difficult. All these assumptions treat risk as a cost, no different from taxes or fees.

Harry's argument leads to the idea that all investors should choose the portfolio with the maximum ratio of excess return (return above what you can get on the risk-free asset, like the returns in Table 5.1) divided by standard deviation. This is called the Sharpe ratio after pioneering finance professor and advocate William Sharpe. Conservative investors might want to put only a portion of their money in that portfolio, and the rest in low-risk bonds. Aggressive investors might want to borrow money and put more than 100 percent of their assets in the portfolio. But all investors hold the same portfolio of risky assets.

The next logical step is to realize that the sum of all individual portfolios is the market portfolio of all available assets. If all individuals hold the same portfolio of risky assets, and that portfolio is the one with the highest Sharpe ratio, then the market portfolio must have the highest possible Sharpe ratio. Investing is easy. Buy the market portfolio.

This theory has led to a lot of progress, especially in rooting out established nonsense. But overly narrow focus on it has led to a lot of error. My interest here is only to distinguish it from risk management. It is true that in the example, the portfolio of all commodities did better because it was less risky. But it is not true that at the same level of expected return investors always prefer less risk. There is an optimal amount of risk for each portfolio; both more risk and less risk lead to lower long-term returns.

The real problem with the individual commodity investments was not that they were undiversified; it was that putting 100 percent of your investment in any one was overinvesting. Table 5.2 shows how you could have done with perfect foresight, if you had invested the correct amount in each commodity. For example, if you had

Table 5.2   Total Period Excess Returns of Optimal Investments in Selected Commodities, 1970 to 2010

Commodity	Excess Return 1970–2010	Optimal Investment Amount	Optimal Investment Excess Return 1970–2010
Cocoa	10.6%	52.7%	67.0%
Corn	–91.7%	–70.2%	66.4%
Cotton	–6.4%	46.8%	25.9%
Hogs	–42.0%	27.2%	9.3%
Silver	–45.9%	32.5%	20.1%
Sugar	–62.0%	33.9%	41.1%
Wheat	–78.3%	–7.7%	0.8%
Portfolio	34.4%	85.7%	35.5%

put 52.7 percent of your money in cocoa and the rest in low-risk bonds, you would have made an excess return of 67 percent over the period from 1970 to 2010, instead of the 10.6 percent you made putting 100 percent of your money in cocoa. In sugar, you turn a −62 percent return into a +41.1 percent return, merely by keeping two-thirds of your money in the bank. But in all cases, you end up worse off if you take either less risk or more risk than the optimal amount.

The reason the portfolio of all seven commodities did so much better than the individual assets when we invested 100 percent of our money is not that diversification lowers risk and lower risk is good; it's that it just happened to produce a portfolio with near the optimal amount of risk (we see in the last line of Table 5.2 that we can improve a little by keeping 14.3 percent of our money in low-risk bonds).

Another very important point is that the average return on the individual investments is 32.9 percent, only a little less than the 35.5 percent from the portfolio, and it is achieved with much less average investment. An investor with even a little faith in her ability to pick the best commodity investment is not crazy to hold a single commodity rather than a diversified portfolio, as long as (and I emphasize how important this is) she knows how to size the bet correctly. Investors with no knowledge should always diversify but for active investors the best portfolio, in my opinion, is usually the one that can be sized most accurately, rather than the most diversified or highest Sharpe ratio or highest expected return one.

Now, suppose you had a genie on New Year's Eve 1969 who told you the portfolio of the seven commodities that would have the highest Sharpe ratio over the subsequent 40 years. I have listed it in Table 5.3.

The weights are probably not what you would have guessed from looking at the individual statistics in Table 5.1. Sugar had the highest average annual return and wheat had a negative average return, yet your optimal portfolio holds more wheat than sugar. More surprising, even with perfect foresight you don't put all your money in the commodity that will do best over the period. In fact, what you buy looks more like an equally weighted portfolio than the kind of concentrated bet you might expect from a psychic. The only big deviation from equal weights is the short (negative) investment in corn, which means you actually sell corn by rolling "short" futures contracts throughout the period (a short

Table 5.3   Weights of Highest Sharpe Ratio Combination
of Selected Commodities, 1970 to 2010

Commodity	Weight
Cocoa	14.3%
Corn	–37.1%
Cotton	14.5%
Hogs	8.0%
Silver	7.7%
Sugar	9.0%
Wheat	9.4%

futures contract is a promise to deliver a commodity in the future, the opposite of a long futures contract, which is a promise to accept delivery). The portfolio has a Sharpe ratio of 0.33, the best you can do with these seven investments. It has a nice return over the period, turning $1,000 into $2,924. Call this the Markowitz portfolio. We diversified to improve the Sharpe ratio, not because we had a long-term theory.

Note that Markowitz told us which proportions of assets to buy, but not what overall level of risk to take. We have the same Sharpe ratio whether we put 10 percent of our money into this portfolio or we leverage it 10 to 1. But those decisions make a big difference. If we put 10 percent of our money into this portfolio, we get only $1,132 back at the end. If we leverage it up 10 to 1, we end up with only $2; that is, we lose almost everything.

Suppose for our second wish, the genie tells us the optimal risk to take in this portfolio. It happens to be 3.322 to 1 leverage, meaning take positions in $3,322 total notional absolute value of commodities. At the end, after we've paid back our loan, we have $8,145 after inflation. Note that all this happened during a period of generally declining real commodity prices, when six of the seven commodities returned less than the risk-free rate and the one positive return was only 10.6 percent for the entire 40 years. Moreover, we beat the market with no work, no fundamental analysis, and no active trading. I hope you can start to see why hedge fund managers get rich. I haven't yet explained how they do it without genies, but that makes it only a little harder. Mathematics is all the genie you need.

To recap, just buying an equally weighted diversified portfolio got us $1,344, the 34.4 percent we see in the last line of Table 5.1. We need no elaborate theory for that. Harry showed us how (with perfect foresight) to increase that 118 percent, to $2,924. Kelly showed us how (also with perfect foresight) to increase that by another 179 percent, to $8,145. Harry and Kelly each answered different questions about our portfolio. Harry and Kelly are both valuable on their own but more valuable when married. The most important insight is that even with perfect foresight, risk still matters.

If Harry Knew Kelly

Let's go back to the counterfactual I suggested earlier. Suppose Harry Markowitz had known John Kelly's work in 1952, four years before Kelly published. Harry might have answered his initial question differently. Why don't investors put all their money in the single best stock? Instead of deciding it's because investors dislike risk, he might have said it's because putting all your money in one stock is overbetting.

In the real world, Markowitz created modern portfolio theory (MPT). It holds that investors care about the statistical properties of their portfolios and act to maximize expected return subject to a risk constraint. Expected return is good, risk is bad, and the investor balances the two.

A Kelly-inspired analogue might have been called investment growth theory (IGT). The claim would be that investors select a portfolio for optimal long-term growth. Investors care about investments, not portfolios, and determine how much to allocate to each based on expected return and variance. There are portfolio effects; your capital allocation decision on each investment depends on your past decisions, but these are pretty small in practice unless you are considering highly correlated assets.

In the IGT world, we would expect an investor to analyze investment opportunities one at a time. Each acceptable investment would be assigned an investment amount, a lot for the most attractive and lowest-risk opportunities, less for either marginally attractive or high-risk opportunities, and only very small amounts for the ones that are both marginally attractive and high risk. Once the investor had a single investment of some type, he would likely look for different types. An IGT investor does not gain much by buying two stocks in the same industry, or even two stocks in similar economic categories. It's far more important to hold investments with different time scales and investments with different kinds of risk. Rather than holding a few hundred stocks, an IGT investor might hold a few stocks of different types, some private equity, some venture capital, some real assets, some high frequency trading, some relative value strategies, some global macro strategies, some high grade bonds, and some distressed bonds.

The process would continue until the advantage to adding new assets was less than the costs of research and transacting. Using this method typically results in portfolios with half a dozen to several dozen assets. There are tens of thousands of assets available, so there's no reason for any two investors to hold the same or even similar portfolios. Also, since investors like bargains, they will have a tendency to stay away from the assets others have already bought.

MPT is top-down. An investor selects parameters based on risk preferences and an algorithm selects the portfolio that best satisfies them. IGT is bottom-up. An investor considers investments, makes an allocation decision, and then moves on to the next decision. The portfolio is what results from this process.

IGT is clearly a better description of the world. No investors used a top-down approach when Markowitz wrote. People have tried it since, inspired by what MPT said they should do, but it has never been popular or conspicuously successful. When it is used, it is generally only at the asset-class level rather than to select individual positions—that is, it is used to decide how much to allocate to each of stocks, bonds, real estate, commodities, and other assets, but not which stocks or which bonds to buy—and it is constrained tightly to force a result similar to preconceived ideas.

IGT also seems to be a better description of investor thought processes. Investors focus on how much capital is at risk in a position, what the expected return is, and how much variance of return can be expected. These are the three most important parameters in Kelly investing. MPT suggested that the most important question was correlation among investments, which was pretty far down on an investor's list of concerns—at least it was before Harry.

Harry also said that standard deviation mattered, not variance. Although the two might seem to be the same (standard deviation is the square root of variance), they differ in one key respect. In order to compare standard deviation to expected return, you have to specify a time horizon, whereas variance and expected return have the same ratio at any time horizon. MPT is a one-period theory; you pick the best portfolio, and then at the end of the period you trade it in for the portfolio optimized for the next period. IGT is a dynamic theory without a fixed time horizon; in fact, specifying a horizon undermines the assumptions of the theory.

Another virtue of IGT is it can handle short positions and derivatives naturally. MPT requires some kind of investment constraint (such as total dollars spent), and these can be tricky to define once you get away from long-only asset positions. In fact, in the IGT world, there is no difference between investors and issuers of securities. MPT assumes that security issuance and terms are exogenous. It doesn't try to explain them; it tells investors how best to react to them.

Both theories had trouble explaining the makeup of typical portfolios. MPT argued for much more diversification than was common in the 1950s and 1960s, while IGT, at least in naive application, recommended much more risk.

MPT's big advantage was it corresponded better to what investors and managers thought they were doing. The managers might proceed bottom-up and look mostly for investments with better-than-average expected returns rather than investments with the right correlations, and they might have no idea what their portfolio standard deviation or time horizon was, but judging managers on the ratio of return to standard deviation seemed reasonable. A manager in the 1950s might have agreed that MPT was a decent simplified model of portfolio construction, and Markowitz did market it as a product with some limited success. No one thought they were IGT investors, and until Ed Thorp, no one tried to market an IGT product.

The next advance in real-world finance was the efficient markets hypothesis (EMH). This held that all securities were priced fairly—that you shouldn't be able to build two portfolios out of public securities such that one consistently outperforms the other after adjusting for risk. In the IGT world, there's no clear meaning to *fair price*. The parallel hypothesis in IGT is that capital is allocated to securities properly.

In MPT EMH, if some good news comes out about a security, investors will buy it until its price goes up to the correct new value. The dynamics of an IGT EMH world are reversed. Say a company has good news, perhaps a successful new product or higher-than-expected profit margins. The company's expected return has increased, which means current investors want to hold more, so the price goes up. But once the price goes up, the expected future return goes back to the old value, and the current investors find themselves holding too much of the company due to its increased price. The solution is for the company to pay cash to investors, say with a dividend or share buyback. Or the company can recruit new investors to put in real new capital. That can leave prices at the wrong level, because it requires adjustments to get them to the right level. Those adjustments may be slow or may not happen at all. On the other hand, IGT EMH makes economic valuations solid, because they are based on tangible cash flows, not investors' opinions of what other investors will think tomorrow.

In my opinion, both MPT and IGT forces are at work in the market. Or to be more precise, both MPT and IGT are highly simplified mathematical models that capture different important aspects of how securities are priced. You can't dispute the MPT insights—there is overwhelming empirical evidence for them. But that evidence in no way rules out other ideas; specifically, it does not rule out IGT. Since MPT cannot explain dividends and buybacks, or concentrated portfolios, or dozens of other prominent market features, it cannot be the whole story. You don't have to swallow IGT, but man does not live by MPT alone.

Moreover, MPT is a one-period model that tells us the relative prices securities should have, but nothing about the absolute level of security prices. IGT may be inferior for explaining relative prices, but it roots the absolute level of prices in fundamental economics: issuers making real cash flow transactions, and investors making probability judgments about their holdings. When you think about the market for large-capitalization U.S. stocks, MPT seems pretty reasonable. When you think about the market for emerging market real estate, IGT makes more sense.

In the real world in which MPT was the dominant theory, the dominant model of market equilibrium was the capital asset pricing model (CAPM). It held that the expected excess return of any asset—remember *excess* means the return above a risk-free rate of interest—is equal to the asset's beta times the expected excess return of the market. This follows from MPT and EMH, with some specific assumptions about the market and investors.

Investment Growth Theory

In the parallel universe of IGT, we get a different formula. I present it here to expand consciousness, not to make a serious argument for it. It has some interesting properties, and explains some things that MPT CAPM cannot. Its assumptions are no more unrealistic than those of MPT CAPM. However, it has some problems, which I won't discuss, and it also has zero empirical support. We're in a counterfactual chapter, a looking-glass world. The IGT CAPM is here to demonstrate that the MPT CAPM can become a rut that prevents its students from seeing that there are rational, even reasonable, alternatives to the MPT CAPM worldview. While the empirical evidence for CAPM is strong for large portfolios over long periods of time, that evidence cannot tell us much about smaller portfolios and shorter time periods.

Here are both MPT and IGT CAPM equations with μ representing expected return, β the regression beta on the market portfolio, σ the standard deviation of return, ω the proportion of the value of the security to the value of the market, and subscripts s for a security, m for the market, and 0 for the risk-free asset.

$$\text{MPT} \quad \mu_s - \mu_0 = \beta_{s,m}\left(\mu_m - \mu_0\right)$$
$$\text{IGT} \quad \mu_s - \mu_0 = 2\beta_{s,m}\left(\mu_m - \mu_0\right) - \omega_s\sigma_s^2$$

The IGT CAPM results from simple assumptions and algebra. Everything is owned by somebody. We sometimes say things are owned by companies or governments, but we assume we can trace everything through to some beneficial owner who is the ultimate economic stakeholder. For that to be efficient under IGT, $\mu_m - \mu_0$ has to be equal to σ_m^2. This is an approximation that we will assume is exactly true for the model. If we add or subtract an asset, we assume this relationship is unchanged. That gives us the first formula that follows (ρ is the correlation with the market portfolio). From then on it's all algebra, and substitution of $\beta\sigma_m$ for $\rho\sigma_s$ and σ_m^2 for $\mu_m - \mu_0$.

$$\left(\mu_m - \mu_0\right) - \omega_s\left(\mu_s - \mu_0\right) = \sigma_m^2 + \omega_s^2\sigma_s^2 - 2\omega_s\rho_{s,m}\sigma_m\sigma_s$$

$$\omega_s\left(\mu_s - \mu_0\right) = -\omega_s^2\sigma_s^2 + 2\omega_s\rho_{s,m}\sigma_m\sigma_s$$

$$\mu_s - \mu_0 = 2\rho_{s,m}\sigma_m\sigma_s - \omega_s\sigma_s^2$$

$$\mu_s - \mu_0 = 2\beta_{s,m}\sigma_m^2 - \omega_s\sigma_s^2$$

$$\mu_s - \mu_0 = 2\beta_{s,m}\left(\mu_s - \mu_0\right) - \omega_s\sigma_s^2$$

Note that for the market as a whole, β and ω are both 1, so we get:

$$\mu_m - \mu_0 = 2\left(\mu_m - \mu_0\right) - \sigma_m^2$$

Since σ_m^2 equals $\mu_m - \mu_0$, we see that the equation is consistent. If you remove the market from the market, the equation holds. It is only the example of the MPT CAPM that leads you to expect that the average beta asset (which must have a beta of 1) has to have the average excess expected return (which has to equal $\mu_m - \mu_0$). In IGT CAPM, that's not true.

This equation applies to the market as a whole, and also to any Kelly optimal portfolio. One interesting feature is the more you own of something, the larger the ω, the lower the rate of return, so the higher the value. If you don't own the same asset, its ω is negative, so you demand a higher return for it, meaning you value it less. I don't claim this is the source of the persistent behavioral bias to value more the things we own than the things we don't own—which in Chapter 8 I argue is the basis of the concept of property—but it shows that the bias is not irrational. It can be derived from assumptions just as realistic as the MPT CAPM.

IGT CAPM provides an explanation for another behavioral observation. If you offer someone two gambles with similar expected value, he usually takes the one with less volatility. But if you give him a gamble and ask him how much he will sell it for, he places a higher price on the one with more volatility. In the IGT world, there is nothing irrational about this. Gambles you don't own have negative ω, so the higher the variance the higher the required expected return, so the lower the value. But gambles you own have positive ω. That means the higher the variance, the higher the value.

Instead of all investors holding the same portfolio, as in the MPT CAPM, IGT says that all investors who hold a security at all hold it at the same fraction of their total wealth. If there is good news about a company, its stock will rise as a fraction of the total wealth of the holders, so they will want to sell. But the people who don't own it value it less than the people who do. So it's rational for the company to pay dividends or buy back shares in order to accommodate the wishes of its investors. This is another persistent behavioral observation; companies pay dividends and buy back shares despite MPT CAPM arguments that they shouldn't. On the other hand, if there's bad news, this argues that investors will want to add to their holdings. This can happen only if some holders sell all their shares, which seems to reflect reality.

The other alternative when current investors want to sell shares is for new investors to be recruited to the company. In IGT CAPM this does not happen gradually; nonholders switch suddenly. They go from holding none of the investment to holding the same proportion as all the old holders did. Once again, this seems like typical investor behavior. Perhaps most compelling of all, IGT CAPM says investors should buy low and sell high, timeless investing wisdom, while MPT CAPM says investors should buy all securities in the market, those with low prices and those with high prices, and keep the same investment in the market whether prices in general are low or high. While it cannot be denied that this strategy has been a winner for investors, delivering average returns at very low cost, it's not very satisfying.

IGT CAPM is anticyclical. When there is good news about a company, its current investors do not want to hold more. Therefore, the business has to pay out its good fortune in cash dividends or stock buybacks. These are much harder to fake than earnings. If the company wants to grow, it has to recruit new investors. It cannot grow passively by having its stock price go up and thereby be a larger part of the market, so index fund investors will allocate more of their portfolio to it. MPT CAPM is neutral to growth. The expected return on a stock is determined by its correlation with the market, so the stock is an equally good buy at $1, $10, $100, or $1,000. With index investors on the sidelines—holding "stocks for the long run"—stock valuations will be determined by battles between fundamental investors, who sell stocks when the price rises above fundamental economic value, and momentum investors, who buy a stock when it is going up. The problem is that even if the fundamental investors win almost all the battles, fundamental victory means only that the stock goes to its true value. There's no natural limit to how high momentum investors can push a stock, and no limit above zero to how low momentum investors can push a stock. So even a few victories for momentum investors can push the market to an economically unjustified bubble or crash.

Another interesting difference between IGT CAPM and MPT CAPM is that IGT has investors holding more concentrated portfolios. It can't tell us exactly what individuals hold, because it's built from different principles than the MPT CAPM. But the feature that holding more of a security makes it more valuable will push investors to hold larger positions in fewer securities. However, it must be true that all these portfolios have the same Sharpe ratio; otherwise investors would swap for a higher Sharpe version.

Now the sum of all investors' portfolios is the market portfolio. The MPT CAPM argues that unless investors' portfolios are perfectly correlated, the market portfolio will have a higher Sharpe ratio than at least one investor's portfolio. Therefore, all investors either hold the market or hold something perfectly correlated with the market, which is really the same thing. IGT CAPM has to argue that something prevents all portfolios from collapsing on the market portfolio.

The reason that last argument is plausible is there are lots of concentrated portfolios with Sharpe ratios very close to the market's. This is something people don't appreciate enough. It undercuts the practical force of arguments based on portfolios with large amounts of assets averaged over long periods of time.

Suppose you have a portfolio of assets with the same standard deviation σ and the same pairwise correlation ρ with each other. If you have N assets, the standard deviation of your portfolio is:

$$\sigma\sqrt{\frac{1}{N} + \rho}$$

As N gets large, that goes to zero if $\rho = 0$, which means if you diversify your risk among enough uncorrelated bets, you can get your volatility down to zero. However, for equities, a typical value of ρ is about 0.16. Loosely speaking, that means however many stocks you add to your portfolio, you can't get its standard deviation much below 40 percent (0.40 is the square root of 0.16) of the average standard deviation of the stocks in it. If you stick to large-capitalization U.S. stocks, the correlation is even higher. That also means that if you pick stocks at random you get 90 percent of the diversification benefit of holding the entire market by buying just 20 stocks. What it doesn't say, but is true, is that if you pick stocks cleverly to have low or even negative correlation with each other, you can get the diversification benefit of the market with four to eight stocks. These are the kinds of portfolios we would expect investors to hold under IGT CAPM; and until MPT CAPM pushed investors to huge portfolios, typical portfolio sizes were eight to 40 stocks, even among professional managers. While in theory investors might have improved their Sharpe ratios slightly by holding more stocks, it's quite possible that the additional transaction costs would have offset the benefit. Also, with fewer stocks investors have more opportunity to monitor and even influence their companies. These factors can make small portfolios rational even under MPT CAPM.

There are many people who unconsciously internalized a super-duper-strong law of large numbers that basically says ρ always equals 0 so all risk can be diversified. In my experience, this is a professional disease among actuaries when thinking about finance. I don't mean actuaries don't believe the mathematics of correlation, or that they don't accept that correlation exists in the world. Actuaries understand that however many earthquake policies you write in Tokyo or San Francisco, you're not getting your risk down to zero. But when I managed a portfolio for Prudential Insurance, I had a lot of arguments with actuaries. They were smart and quantitative, but we often failed to connect intellectually because they had a deep, unquestioned faith that you always reduced risk by holding more securities. They wouldn't say it right out, but they had what I can only call a religious faith in diversification that mathematics could not compete with.

eRaider.com

I once tried to exploit the knowledge that it's possible to create efficient small portfolios. I was an early computer communications adopter, from the Defense Advanced Research Projects Agency Network (DARPANET) at school to dial-up bulletin boards, to UseNet, to CompuServe, and, in 1995, to Yahoo! and America Online. In these last four forums, I answered financial, statistical, and gambling questions. It was in 1996 that I became impressed with the power of stock bulletin boards. There was a lot of hype and nonsense, of course, but what nonparticipants couldn't see was that it was easy to filter that stuff out and, when you did, boards for some companies had a lot of useful information and discussion. A friend of mine, Martin Stoller, a popular professor at the Kellogg School of Business at Northwestern University, gradually figured out that for some companies a significant fraction of the float of the stock—the shares held by the general public, including institutions but not insiders—could be reached through the boards. Not only that, but there was a lot of tremendously valuable information—valuable because it was specific—from current and former employees, suppliers, customers, and people knowledgeable about the industry.

Martin and I came up with the idea of forming a portfolio of seven stocks with low mutual correlations, so that the combined portfolio had a lower standard deviation than the market. These would be companies with low institutional ownership, so there was little oversight of management, but active and intelligent message boards where we thought we could reach shareholders of at least 20 percent of the float. Furthermore, these companies would have obvious actions that management could take to improve shareholder value. For example, four years later when the portfolio was eventually formed, we had a company that I wanted to sell itself; another that I wanted to close its large, money-losing division and fund its fast-growing, profitable division; and another that I wanted to "de-REIT," that is, convert from a real estate investment trust (REIT) to a regular corporation.

Now, when people hear you want to make a low-risk portfolio out of seven stocks, even if they accept the mathematical argument about correlation, they say, "But if one company goes bad, it's such a big part of your portfolio. It has to be safer to have hundreds of stocks, so no single one can hurt you much." That argument could be true; that is, the smaller portfolio might have the same standard deviation but more tail risk of a large loss. It's also possible that there's more parameter uncertainty with the small portfolio. It doesn't have to be true, though, and I think it isn't, at least if you select properly.

However, my main response is: "Okay. But if one company shoots up in value, it's also a big part of your portfolio. Risk cuts both ways." And if you think you can make a company shoot up in value, it makes sense to be concentrated. So my idea was to assemble an all-star lineup of finance professors, accounting professors, business and scientific experts in the fields of the businesses, and journalists to help communicate—we even had a former Securities and Exchange Commission (SEC) commissioner. We'd open a web site and invite all shareholders to come and help improve their companies. Since we picked companies with intelligent and active boards that included large shareholders anyway, and since our mutual fund had accumulated a 5 percent share of the stock before announcing (5 percent is the most you can legally buy before filing a public notice with the SEC), and since there were no large blocks held by insiders or institutions, we should be in a commanding position. One other wrinkle was we awarded options and shares in the management company (the company that charged fees for managing the fund) to board participants for useful service. In 1996, getting stock in any Internet company was a big inducement. The remaining shares of the management company were owned by the fund. Martin and I planned to get rich by investing in our fund along with other shareholders, not by charging fees to other shareholders.

Unfortunately, it took four years to get the idea past the SEC, and I had to go all the way up to the commissioners themselves. I don't blame them; this idea touched on a lot of hot-button issues. The commissioners and staff were suspicious of a concentrated portfolio, aghast at Internet stock message boards, and nervous about activist investors. But at no time did I run into bureaucratic indifference or rigidity. I had open and productive discussions with many staff members, who also did a ton of free legal work for me. Once we did open, the SEC stood by us on several important occasions, which saved us from being either regulated or sued out of existence. Despite all that help, I do have a tiny twinge of regret that the four-year delay meant the fund opened on March 10, 2000. You may remember that day. The NASDAQ index hit its all-time high of 5,048.62. Over the next year and a half it meandered down to 1,114.11 and has never broken 3,000 since. It was a bad day to open a long-only equity mutual fund. After two years, the eRaider.com public mutual fund converted to a private hedge fund and I severed my ties with it.

I did keep the domain name, which I think is really cool. I bought it for $500 from someone who registered thousands of promising names. He wanted $25,000, but I had one of our young programmers claim eRaider was his role-playing name, and he had to have it, but his parents would kill him if he spent more than $500. That resonated with the domain holder—I think he had had similar experiences personally. When the seller found out he had been scammed by a business, he called me. He wasn't angry; he was respectful. It was a good con, he said, and he didn't get fooled often. It's refreshing to find someone whose business model is basically a scam who isn't self-righteous about it.

While the Nasdive didn't help the business, I don't think that was the reason eRaider.com failed as a public mutual fund. A much sadder piece of bad luck, also not the main reason, was that Martin was diagnosed with a brain tumor. Marty was a communications genius and the face of the company. He taught me everything I know about rhetoric. However, he raised a few eyebrows in the SEC because his father, Phil Stoller, was a famous securities swindler, the protagonist of Murray Teigh Bloom's best seller *Rogues to Riches: The Trouble with Wall Street* (Warner, 1973).

The eRaider.com portfolio did what it was supposed to do given the market: it lost less. We accomplished our goals at all companies, and forged friendly relations with six out of seven. We almost won a contested board election and we eliminated antishareholder provisions at all companies. What we failed to do was persuade anyone outside a small circle of true believers that Internet oversight was a better model of corporate governance than the current system. As Phil Goldstein, who does more contentious corporate raids, told me, "No one wants to pay for activism." Everyone cheers the activists, and then sells their shares at any price bounce that the activism produces. We had the same thing at our message boards. People encouraged us as they were dumping shares. People bought shares because we came in, then voted against us. It was a constant struggle to keep fractious coalitions together, and to keep people from violating securities laws—or at a minimum, keep ourselves from getting entangled in the violations. Too few people understood the difference between legitimate shareholder pressure about high-level corporate decisions and trying to run the business day to day, or even the difference between actions for the benefit of all shareholders and actions for personal benefit. The raids worked not through the consensus of organized investors and experts, but because we sent someone (usually me) to negotiate the old-fashioned way with managers and directors. I concluded in the end that the Internet investor base made it harder to effect improvements, not easier.

I'm not bitter about it. I had a ton of fun and could afford the loss. I met some good people and learned a lot. eRaider.com got a lot of great press, even if people were inclined to put us in stories with an astrologer, a preteen penny stock hyper, and a mutual fund that put a webcam in its trading room. Even more annoying: Every activist investor, regardless of amount of investment or serious-ness, is described in every news article as a "gadfly." Anyway, for the present purposes the eRaider.com story proves that I actually believe this small portfolio stuff.

As I said at the beginning of this section, my point is not that the IGT CAPM is better than MPT CAPM, or even whether there's any truth to it at all. For the record, I think it is a useful way to analyze absolute price levels in less liquid markets, and with some further theoretical and empirical work, it might have broader appli-cation, especially to help understand capital flows. However, in no possible way would it ever have 1 percent of the theoretical impor-tance and utility of the MPT CAPM. My point is that IGT CAPM gives an orthogonal view of security prices to the top-down, cross-sectional MPT world that Harry Markowitz created. Whether or not you like IGT, it operates in a domain that is the natural habitat of risk managers, and one that too many people with a mainstream finance or economics education ignore.

MPT Out in the World

In the real world, MPT CAPM encouraged academics and regulators to push people to highly diversified, low-cost index funds to mimic the market portfolio. This was unquestionably good for investors. Had Harry met Kelly and invented IGT instead, the natural conse-quence would be to push people toward concentrated hedge fund strategies—strategies that in the real world only rich people were allowed to use. In the real world, with all investors doing the same thing, we saw consolidation of investment management services, with huge funds managed by huge fund management companies. In the IGT world, with every investor different, you would expect to see far more small funds and companies.

Belief in MPT CAPM helped make the markets more efficient cross-sectionally; that is, returns on different asset classes over the same time periods aligned pretty well with their respective risk levels. But, at least arguably, MPT CAPM contributed toward prices diverging from fundamental value. Index fund investors don't ask what something is worth; they want to hold it in proportion to its price. Among other things, it guarantees that they are overinvested in anything overpriced, and underinvested in anything underpriced. It may be impossible to tell overpriced assets from underpriced ones, but that doesn't matter; it's a mathematical certainty the index fund investor has the worst of both worlds. (Of course, as Ken French and John Bogle independently pointed out to me, half the nonindex investors must be even more overweighted in the overpriced assets, and all the nonindex investors pay higher costs.)

Large, diversified portfolios have also been blamed for investors not providing oversight to their investments, and for feeding bubbles and crashes. The MPT focus on returns measured periodically, mainly monthly, may have led to underappreciation for both long-term economics and short-term market microstructure.

Hedge funds are much better than index funds at determining fundamental value, at providing oversight, for operating at a variety of time scales from microseconds to decades, for reining in bubbles, and at rushing in to repair after crashes. Of course, just because hedge funds can do these things it doesn't follow that all, or even most, hedge funds actually do these things. In the real world, hedge funds were suppressed by theories that said they shouldn't be able to make money and were overpriced. That suppression created a lot of opportunities for funds as prices diverged from fundamental value and public companies could be bought cheaply due to poor performance resulting from lack of investor oversight. Bubbles and crashes demonstrated the appeal of strategies that didn't always run with the herd.

What if IGT had been the dominant theory instead, and had encouraged the growth of hedge funds while discouraging index funds and other highly diversified investments? We can imagine the Securities and Exchange Commission insisting that investment managers know a lot about the securities they buy, not just buy everything available at the asking price. Other regulators might insist that professional managers provide rigorous oversight and demonstrate that their strategies didn't exacerbate bubbles and crashes. In fact, things like these have happened over the years, but not due to IGT or any other comprehensive theory. They were reactions to market events caused in part by MPT-based investment techniques. We had bubbles and crashes long before we had MPT or index funds, so they cannot be the main cause. It is undoubtedly active investors who trigger these events. The contribution of MPT is more to blind people to the possibility of these events than to add the fuel of passive investors to the fires.

In the IGT world, overall market prices might have been more stable and closer to fundamental value. Companies might have been run better. But there likely would have been less efficiency in relative pricing of securities. With more managers using more aggressive and diverse strategies, there would have been more scandals and blowups. While these would not have risen to the level of the scandals and blowups we had instead, there would have been more of them. I think these would have made most individuals feel less secure. In the world we had, I don't think any investment was safe. But people felt safe in government-guaranteed bank deposits—despite inflation—and diversified investments over the long run—despite long periods in which they underperformed and some sickening short-term crashes. Or at least they felt safer than they would have navigating among tens of thousands of small investment managers with complicated strategies.

However, I think the biggest perceived problem in the IGT world would have been a lack of basic fairness. There are problems in index funds, but people like that any individual can get the average return of the market, without much expense or effort. All the slick people trying to do better, do worse as a group. If some make money, others lose it, and neither the winners nor the losers hurt the index fund investor (but both pay more fees, expenses, and taxes than the index fund investor). This fairness helps generate the social support for the financial system. In the IGT world, people would have hated Wall Street for the reasons they used to—that it was a bunch of sharpies playing with other people's money and doing no social good—rather than the current reasons—that it wrecked the economy and used huge bailout funds to pay obscene bonuses.

In the IGT counterfactual, I imagine some brave rebel starting a fund to deliver average returns cheaply. She would have to organize offshore, and would not be able to market the investment to the public. Regulators, horrified at her plan to buy thousands of assets without worrying about the prices, without voting responsibly in corporate elections, and without even following news about her holdings, would throw up all kinds of roadblocks that only rich people could afford to avoid. Academics would make the point that she couldn't possibly believe indexing was a good idea, because she wasn't willing to take a fee based on performance; she wanted a fixed fee whether the fund made or lost money. That seems like someone interested only in selling the product, not running it well. It's also suspicious that she doesn't plan to spend any money on research. Clearly she's cutting costs to fatten her profits at the expense of investors' welfare. And her desire to sign up hundreds of thousands of investors, instead of a few dozen, would suggest a scam. How could so many investors possibly understand such a radical strategy? How could any strategy succeed in the huge size she proposed? Everyone would say she just wants to get a lot of assets in from foolish people so she can live off the fee income.

It would take many years, but people would begin to notice that the index fund produced pretty decent returns. After fees it was better than more than half the hedge funds. And it was liquid, transparent, and tax efficient. Pressure would begin to mount to expand access. Hedge fund versions of the index product would be introduced to avoid anti-index fund rules. Eventually, when the pendulum stopped, we might end up in pretty much the same place as the real world, in which Harry didn't meet Kelly.

CHAPTER 6

Exponentials, Vampires, Zombies, and Tulips

This is one of those chapters that might not seem to belong in a book on risk. It turns out, however, that you have to understand exponentials in order to understand risk. One reason is that exponentials underlie most of the big positive and negative surprises in life. Things that don't change don't cause risk and don't create dangers and opportunities. Things that move or grow at steady rates are easy to manage with deterministic rules; you don't need to consider risk. Exponentials can change from too small and too slow to notice to too big and too fast to survive, before you can react. Or, if you're lucky, they can change from too small and too slow for others to notice to big and fast enough to fulfill your wildest dreams, before others can horn in on your opportunity. So learning how to spot exponentials early is crucial for any risk taker.

The second reason is that exponentials are the best way to manage risk. If you have a single big choice—the lady or the tiger, for example—there's no management involved. As the saying goes, you pays your money and you takes your chance. To manage risk we have to chop it up into many little risks. In textbooks, you can then arrange all the little risks in carefully calibrated sizes in an optimal order to maximize your

101

expected utility. In reality, with real risk, you have to make a series of decisions without knowing exactly what the future risks will be, what all the possible outcomes are, what the probability of winning is, or how you'll feel about things after the results are in. Amazingly, the practical problem is simpler to solve than the theoretical one, and the solution is exponential.

Successful risk taking is not about winning a big bet, or even a long series of bets. Success comes from winning a sufficient fraction of a series of bets, where your gains and losses are multiplicative. That pattern of gains and losses leads to exponential growth. This appears to observers as overnight success. Rocket scientists named it "risk ignition" on Wall Street in the 1980s.

Types of Growth

The simplest growth is linear or arithmetic. If a car traveling at a constant speed goes 40 miles in one hour, then it will go 80 miles in two hours. Doubling the time doubles the distance. But if you drop a stone down a well to see how deep it is, a one-second fall before you hear a splash means the water is about 16 feet down, whereas a two-second fall means the water is 64 feet down. Doubling the time quadruples the distance. Distance goes up with the square of time. This is called polynomial growth.

I recently read a book that claimed the destructive power of hurricanes "increases exponentially with wind speed." That's not true. Hurricane power increases with the cube of wind speed—doubling the wind speed causes eight times the destruction. This is also polynomial growth, of degree three as opposed to the stone falling, which is of degree two.

If hurricane power were exponential, a first doubling of the wind speed could result in eight times the destruction, but the second doubling would increase power 64 times, the third one 512 times, and the fourth one 4,096 times. With cubic polynomial growth, in contrast, *every* doubling leads to the same eightfold increase in power.

Cubic polynomial growth is scary enough. Ten-mile-per-hour wind is a gentle breeze, 20 mph is a fresh breeze, 40 mph is a gale, 80 mph is a category 1 hurricane—like Hurricane Dolly, something that wipes out badly constructed mobile homes, breaks windows, and damages chimneys—and 160 mph is a category 5 hurricane—like Hurricane Katrina or Hurricane Andrew, something that destroys virtually everything in its path, including frame houses. Each doubling of wind speed means eight times the power, so Hurricane Katrina packs the punch of 4,096 gentle breezes. But if hurricane power were truly exponential with the same eightfold increase from 10 to 20 mph, Katrina would be more than 35 trillion times more powerful than a gentle breeze and would have outdone the effects of Noah's flood.

Not many people understand exponentials. The author of the hurricane book was in the large camp of nonquantitative people who think *exponential* means "very." I have some sympathy for this; the five syllables in *exponentially* can be drawn out for dramatic emphasis, and "exponentially fast" sounds smarter than "really, really fast."

At the other extreme are pure mathematicians who know that if you wait long enough, exponential growth always outpaces polynomial growth of any degree. That's true for numbers, but for any physical parameter, growth is limited.

If something in the material world is exponential, it will appear to move very slowly, then suddenly accelerate to hit a limit. Suppose you had a new product. You sold it to one person yesterday and sell it to four people today. If sales growth goes up with the square of time, in 227 years you will sell to everyone on earth—or to the number of people who are on earth right now, anyway. If sales growth is exponential, you'll sell to everyone on earth in 16 days. But that won't happen. Even Coca-Cola peaked around a few hundred million customers per day. Exponential growth in the real world continues only to the point where it attracts attention, almost always hitting its limit shortly afterward. To the world it would look like success out of nowhere, even if the exponential growth had been operating for many years before it got fast.

The existence of physical limits makes it idiotic to say "exponentially fast." In the physical universe, if it's fast, it has already lost its exponential character due to some limiting factor. The trick is to find the exponential stuff when it's still slow. By the time it gets fast, it's too late either to exploit it or to protect yourself from it. Your only hope is that its limit is not too far away. In fact, that's one way to think of risk management. The stuff that grows linearly or even polynomially gives you warning. You might be able to afford to wait until it gets big or fast before doing anything about it. You don't need sophisticated risk management. But you have to find the exponential stuff when it's small or slow. That's where the great opportunities and hidden dangers lie.

Consider, for example, the spread of AIDS in the United States. The AIDS virus probably infected the first human between 1884 and 1924, and the earliest confirmed AIDS death in the United States occurred in 1968. It was not until 1981 that the disease was identified and reported. That year 122 people in the United States died of AIDS. The spread was exponential, but remarkably slow, taking many decades before being noticed at all.

The scary part was that the death rate from AIDS appeared to be quadrupling every year. Since the AIDS infection had about a 10-year latency period, that suggested a million people were infected for every death and that everyone in the United States would be dead from AIDS by 2001. Of course that didn't happen; by the time the disease was noticed by doctors, the growth rate as a fraction of the infected population was already slowing. The pandemic had lost its exponential character. The growth rate as a fraction of the total population was still increasing rapidly, however.

That exponential growth was what made 122 AIDS deaths a bigger public health concern than mortality causes that claimed many more people. While all diseases in the past have leveled off before killing everyone, some have killed large fractions of the population. When something is growing exponentially, it's difficult to tell how high it will go before it hits its limit.

The first effective anti-AIDS measures were introduced in the late 1980s, around the time of the fastest increase in AIDS deaths—up 7,000 from 1988 to 1989. Six years later, in 1995, U.S. AIDS deaths peaked at about twice the 1989 level, and then begin to decline steadily. Suppose that people had waited until the growth was fast in 1989 to begin serious study of the disease and discussion of programs like needle exchanges and condom distribution. It's not unreasonable to guess that the increase from 1989 to 1995 would have been similar to the increase from 1983 to 1989. In that case, U.S. AIDS deaths would have peaked at more than one million U.S. deaths per year in 2001 instead of 50,000 in 1995, and total U.S. deaths from AIDS would have been 5,500,000 instead of 500,000. Those extra five million potential deaths illustrate the power of exponentials. You have to deal with pandemics—and all exponentials—when they're exponential, not wait until they're fast. Think of a jet airplane taking off. It rolls slowly along the ground, then a bit faster, then faster still. By the time it's moving fast it will be literally out of your reach.

Exponential growth means the rate of growth is proportional to the level; that is, the bigger it gets, the faster it grows. We know that's true of infectious diseases: each sick person is a new source of infection. The more people infected, the faster the disease spreads. That's why people took AIDS seriously long before it was a major cause of death.

In contrast, I recently read a story about the "epidemic" of fatal dog bites in the United States. Apparently the annual rate has doubled in the twenty-first century from the levels in the 1980s and 1990s, even on a per capita or per canine basis. Almost no one worries about this because the numbers are small—15 extra deaths per year—and no one thinks fatal dog bites are exponential, because the victims don't infect others. Vampire and zombie bites are a different matter, which is why there are hundreds of vampire and zombie movies and only one *Cujo*. If fatal dog bites continue to increase at 15 per year per decade, we can start worrying about it in 2200 or so.

The Negative Side

So far we have been speaking only of positive exponentials. Things can also shrink at exponential rates. Since rate of growth is proportional to level, this means the rate of shrinking is constantly going down. Moore's law—the claim that the cost of computing power falls 50 percent every 18 months—is an example of a negative exponential. If you bet on an exponential and it's positive, your gains are continuously accelerating. If you are right that it's exponential but wrong because it's a negative exponential, your losses are continually slowing. These properties make betting on exponentials attractive and betting against exponentials very dangerous.

Consider the Internet in 1990. Its growth was clearly going to be exponential. Every new Web user would make the Internet more attractive for business, which would pull in new users. More nodes made investment in servers and cables more attractive, which made nodes cheaper, which meant more nodes. What was not clear at that time was whether Internet growth would ignite to a level that would make any investment in it pay or whether it would hit some limiting factor such as willingness of people to use the new technology or a breakdown in Moore's law.

Regardless of your assessment of the likely prospects of the Internet in 1990, betting on it had much more favorable risk characteristics than betting against it. If you win, you can win very big. If you lose, your losses are limited. That doesn't mean it's always a smart bet. At some price it can be worth taking the other side. But if you make equal-sized bets on 100 exponential situations, you will make money winning one and losing 99, if the limits to the one win are high enough and you wait long enough. If you make 100 bets against exponential situations, you can lose money winning 99 bets and losing one.

The definition of an exponential, that the rate of increase is proportional to the level, applies to bubbles as well as physical phenomena. In fact, we can define a bubble as a self-fulfilling exponential. The price of something goes up, so people buy it in expectation of future increases, so the price goes up more, and so on. The usual progression begins with a true economic exponential. When that hits some sort of real limit, money continues to flow in from bubble investors. The limit on the bubble exponential is the supply of new money. In fact, there's a relationship between bubbles and money that we'll explore in the last section of this chapter.

Bubbles always pop and are vilified afterward. But critics seldom point to real economic losses; instead bubbles are blamed for not making real the paper wealth that existed at their peaks. Everyone who made money selling at the peak quietly counts their gains, while everyone who lost money buying at the peak complains that they have been defrauded, and an army of opportunists immediately arises to demand compensation from whatever unpopular group is convenient. In fact, many things are better after the bubble than before. Leaps of progress require disruption, and bubbles are the flip side of creative destruction—a sort of uninspired construction, to coin a phrase. There are costs to a bubble as well; pain inflicted on losers probably exceeds the pleasure experienced by winners, and who wins and who loses is often decided unfairly. Economic resources will be wasted. My point is that bubbles are not all bad, not that they're good.

Tulips

The most famous bubble in history is *tulpenwoede*—tulipomania—in the early 1600s in Holland. This event was popularized by the journalist Charles Mackay, who wrote *Extraordinary Popular Delusions and the Madness of Crowds* in 1841. He told of a population going wild, spending incredible amounts of money on tulip bulbs and contracts for future delivery of tulips. When the bubble popped in February 1637, there was widespread ruin and economic misery.

The first important thing to understand is that people were not paying the high prices for single flowers. Tulips grow from bulbs. Each year they produce a flower, in some cases several blossoms, in spring or early summer, depending on the climate. The flowers produce seeds, which grow into new bulbs over anywhere from six to 12 years. But bulbs also give off buds, which can grow into new bulbs in a year or two. The desirable coloration patterns that make particular tulips valuable come from a mosaic virus infection, and the infection—hence the valuable coloration—is passed along only to progeny that come from buds. The most striking patterns come from the sickest bulbs, which therefore reproduce slowly.

Professional growers were constantly on the lookout for interesting new patterns. When they found one, they would carefully nurture its buds, striving to build a stock of bulbs with stable and striking coloration that were healthy enough to thrive. When that task was complete, the next step was to popularize the new variety.

One technique, then as now, was to use celebrities. The grower would sell one bulb at a fantastic price—a reported fantastic price, anyway—to a person of rank or fashion. That person would display the plant prominently when it bloomed in May, carefully informing everyone that the plant was unique and extraordinarily valuable. The next year a few more bulbs would be made available to select purchasers for high prices. Each year the number of bulbs sold would increase, both because the original grower would release more and because early purchasers would have descendant bulbs large enough to flower. As the number of available bulbs of the new variety increased, the price would naturally fall. At some point, perhaps 20 years after introduction, the bulb would be so common as to command no premium over ordinary bulbs.

Now consider the value of the original stock of a new variety, assuming it becomes popular. It depends on four parameters: the value of the first tulip flower, the rate of decline of flower value, the rate of increase of bulb sales, and the discount rate—the value of money in the future relative to money today. Suppose, for example, the value of the first flower is $100 and that value declines by 20 percent every year. After 20 years the value of each flower falls to less than $1, which we'll call the value of an ordinary tulip, so we'll stop accreting value for the specific variety. The supply of bulbs triples each year for the first six years, as the grower draws on the initial stock, and then increases at 30 percent per year thereafter, limited by the reproduction potential of the bulbs. The discount rate is 5 percent. At initial creation, this tulip is worth over $200,000.

The first bulb sold to the celebrity represents a significant fraction of the total stock, so he can afford to pay a high price even after a substantial discount for his publicity value. Of course, purchase of a bulb for a fantastic price by a person of acknowledged taste serves to underline its value and desirability. The price of a bulb falls rapidly as the supply expands. After two years the nine flowers in existence are worth $64 each, but the value of a single bulb has fallen from $205,000 to $23,000. Four years after that comes the maximum present value of all flowers in one year—729 flowers worth $26 each. At that point a bulb is worth $362.

Obviously, this is a highly idealized example. The key point is that people paid high prices for the rights to a variety of tulip, not for a flower. Disney did not spend $300 million for a ticket to see *Pirates of the Caribbean: At World's End*; it paid that for the rights to all future distribution revenues, including ticket sales, DVD sales, pay-per-view fees, branded products, and so on. Similarly, tremendous prices for tulips were for control of a popular new variety, or at least for a significant fraction of the total stock. Tulips are—or were in the seventeenth century—exponential.

Tulip Propaganda

Mackay's account, and popular conception since, has confused two phenomena. The first is the aforementioned high prices paid for single bulbs and the second is the sudden crash in tulip prices in February 1637. My favorite example of the first is from Zbigniew Herbert, a great poet and human being but a mediocre economist. He tells of "a poor, unknown shoemaker from the Hague . . . growing an unusual variety of tulip called 'Black Tulip,'" who was visited by five men from Haarlem:

> Five gentlemen dressed in black entered the dark cubbyhole of the shoemaker. They began commercial negotiations—very strange negotiations, because the gentlemen from Haarlem

were playing the role of benefactors. Supposedly they had come there out of pure philanthropy to help the poor artisan, but at the same time they were unable to conceal how much they cared to possess the "Black Tulip."

The master of last and leather took in the situation, and tried to get the highest price. After much haggling a transaction finally took place: 1,500 florins, not a trifling sum. A moment of happiness for the poor shoemaker.

But the five men in black proceed to smash the bulb, and abuse the poor shoemaker for his stupidity. They tell him they would have paid far more for the bulb because they own the only other black tulip in existence and wish to protect its value.

They left. The shoemaker staggered, dragged himself to his attic, lay down on his bed and, covering himself with his coat, breathed his last breath.

> Zbigniew Herbert, *Still Life with a Bridle:*
> *Essays and Apocryphas*, trans. John and Bogdana Carpenter
> (New York: Ecco Press, 1993)

Tulips were introduced to Europe from Turkey, probably around 1550. They began acquiring significant commercial value in the last years of the sixteenth century and prices increased steadily until 1637. All the dramatic stories of high tulip prices refer to the period around 1610, and the payers of the high prices all made money. They did not make money because the price of the single bulb they purchased continued to increase, but because the natural rate of reproduction of the bulb exceeded the rate at which the price per bulb declined. No doubt there were people who paid high prices and lost money, either because their bulb did not attain the required level of popularity or because their bulb was not sufficiently healthy to reproduce at the rate required for profit, but these losses are not recorded.

Reading Mackay's stories today, it is obvious that they served as seventeenth-century advertising vehicles. Each one is centered on the name of the tulip: a bridegroom turns down a sumptuous dowry for a single bulb of the "Bridegroom" variety, a man sells his successful tavern for a single "Tavern" bulb, and so on. Moreover, each story emphasizes the rarity and value of the bulb, and puts the hearer in a mood to appreciate its qualities. The black tulip story begins with men "dressed in black" in a "dark cubbyhole" and ends with death, perfect to mull over as you gaze at your black tulip. The modern term for this is *product placement*. In seventeenth-century Holland, with many people illiterate and a high cost of mass communication, a good story was the cheapest and most effective form of advertising. Who knew that two centuries later a credulous journalist would take the stories as fact, and use them to write a book that still dominates popular thinking about bubbles? And, ironically, the stories that survived into the nineteenth century were the ones associated with the most successful bulbs. The early purchasers of those bulbs made lots of money. The people who lost money created stories that were forgotten. Mackay was making fun of people for their success, and missed the people who failed.

So criticism of the first phenomenon, high prices paid for tulip bulbs, is just a misunderstanding of tulip economics and advertising. There was no tulip bubble in 1610, just the normal operation of a business combining fashion and technology—high technology at the time. People still pay extremely high prices for new varieties of flowers, higher inflation-adjusted prices than those reported by Mackay, and the prices still go through cycles of boom and bust. The Dutch flower business today is larger in real per capita terms than the flower business in 1610. In fact, flower growing is the only consistently profitable agricultural business in Europe.

The second phenomenon is more interesting. Beginning in 1634, growth in tulip prices accelerated dramatically. The increase gradually spread to lower- and lower-priced bulbs, eventually reaching ordinary bulbs. The cheaper the bulb, the greater the price increase. Moreover, contracts for future delivery of partial interests in bulbs were introduced. The market collapsed suddenly on February 3, 1637—midwinter when all bulbs were in the frozen ground—with high-end bulbs falling 16 percent in price and the cheapest bulbs falling 95 percent.

Mackay reports that the crash caused widespread ruin and misery among all segments of the population. This is a myth. Mackay's source here was propaganda pamphlets printed by the government after the crash to point the finger at foolish speculators. There was no increase in bankruptcies, and the losses were mainly among moderately wealthy merchants and skilled craftsmen, what today we might call the upper middle class. In fact, net losses were relatively small, as most tulip investors had both bought and sold bulbs. Nevertheless, this event has all the earmarks of a bubble at least with respect to the cheaper bulbs. There seems to be no fundamental economic argument to support the peak prices, and the crash does not appear to be associated with any news (and in any case is too large to be explained by any plausible news).

As with most bubbles, we can explain some of the price increase. The 1635 Peace of Prague treaty gave Holland considerable security and promised to open up much of Europe to Dutch luxury goods. Once-popular bulbs that had become common in Holland might command higher prices again when exported to virgin territory. Something similar happened with movie studio film rights when home videocassette players became popular and cheap. Old movies suitable only for heavily edited runs on the Late, Late, Late Show suddenly acquired some value. Bidding wars broke out for libraries that had not even been worth preserving a few years earlier. And as with Dutch tulips, the largest proportionate price increases were for the least valuable properties.

Quantitative Tulip Modeling

Using our example, suppose the increase in market size causes tulip flower prices to depreciate at 18 percent per year instead of 20 percent. The exponential nature of tulips means that the 2 percent change in depreciation rate will increase the value of our $205,000 brand-new star bulb by 66 percent to $339,000. However, an older bulb whose price had fallen to $1.15, barely over the $1.00 value of an ordinary bulb, will surge 568 percent to $7.70. Again, these numbers are not to be taken seriously as valuations, just as illustrations of the basic mathematics of an exponential commodity. Slight changes in assumptions can make huge differences in valuations, and the cheaper the commodity, the greater the potential for increases. These facts have been observed time and again whenever people are paying for exponential growth—real or imagined.

The legitimate improvement in fundamental tulip market prospects cannot be the full story of tulipomania, however. The observed peak prices of the cheaper bulbs are difficult to justify under any set of reasonable assumptions, and no one has ever suggested remotely plausible news that could reverse the three-year bull market on one midwinter day. At some point in the process, not necessarily in 1634 but perhaps much later, the rational exponential increase turned into a bubble. People bought because prices were going up; prices went up because people bought. The minute prices stopped rising, people started to take money out and prices crashed.

Note that no real economic resources were destroyed in the crash. The same real goods existed before and after the price decline. The bubble might have caused some economic misallocation— perhaps too many tulips were planted—but this was at most a minor loss. In the history of human follies, one that results only in too many flowers has to be counted a relative success. Of course, there were winners and losers in the bubble, and we know that losses are more painful than equal-sized gains. So we can say there is a net psychological loss and that's as real and important as losses of goods. After all, goods matter only to the extent they affect how people feel. We also know that the gains and losses were not distributed fairly; professional growers and government cronies allied to extract unfair profits, imposing unfair losses on less sophisticated people without connections. So justice was also a victim.

However, we have strong evidence that the bubble led to some improved economic allocation. The tulip sales Mackay described were not paid for in money. For example, he says a "Viceroy" bulb was purchased for two lasts of wheat, four lasts of rye, four fat oxen, eight fat swine, 12 fat sheep, two hogsheads of wine, four tons of beer, two tons of butter, 1,000 pounds of cheese, a bed, a suit of clothes, and a silver drinking cup. This looks like someone converting the surplus of a farm, or perhaps the assets of an estate, into a portable and relatively liquid form, one that requires minimal maintenance and will not spoil or die. It was also a convenient form. You could live off the annuity provided by annual flower and perhaps biannual bulb sales, or you could trade it to someone else for assets to start a business or export for profit. You could carry it anywhere in your pocket for three months out of the year, and in a pot for the other nine months.

Money

Why not sell the goods for money instead? Money, which meant silver coin in Holland at the time, was not very stable. Inflation was high; prices doubled in the 20 years from 1606 to 1626. Worse, debasement was a chronic problem. This is true everywhere precious metal money is used, but it was particularly severe in Holland at this time for several reasons. The Thirty Years War required enormous expenditures, which were often financed by debasement of coins. Holland had a small, open economy, meaning that coins flowed into it from all over Europe; when people send coins, they send the lightest ones, the most debased ones. Finally, central authorities were weak in Holland, so individual state banks and independent mints were able to get away with more debasement than was tolerated in other countries.

This did not amount to a large problem for someone who wanted to sell goods and buy other goods immediately with the proceeds. But a tulip was a far better store of value. It was a reasonably good medium of exchange as well, especially as the amount of trading increased and tulip futures were introduced. It could be held indefinitely between purchases, increasing rather than decreasing in value, and it could even be held as an annuity. The futures allowed as much money to be created as was needed for transactions, and paper contracts are even easier to transport than tulips—and they can't die. The futures also made it convenient to hold a diversified portfolio of bulbs and not be exposed to price movements due to changing fashions in bulbs.

Viewed in this light, we can explain part of the increase in tulip prices as a decline in the value of silver money. Something used as money becomes monetized and acquires a value above—sometimes far above—its intrinsic use value. When a superior substitute comes along, the original substance used for money can fall back to its use value. At the same time, the new substance increases in value. More important, this can explain the apparently frenzied trading throughout the country among people with no apparent interest in or knowledge about tulips, as well as the popularity of futures contracts.

Why did the market crash suddenly? I have a theory. I can't prove it, but it is consistent with the known facts and doesn't involve anyone doing anything stupid or crazy. First separate off the expensive bulbs. They had been appreciating for 30 years, with ups and downs, but always an upward trend overall. The 1637 down was not out of line with history but it did seem to break the appreciating trend. Afterward, tulip prices continued to have ups and downs, but stayed at roughly the same level. Much later, they began to decline as other flowers rose in popularity.

We don't need a complicated theory to explain this. Tulips were introduced and grew in popularity. As a growth business, they attracted a lot of investment. At some point, it became clear that the abnormal growth had reached its limit, and tulips would become an ordinary business. In business strategy terms, tulips went from being a rising star (fast growth and high profits) to a cash cow (low growth and stable profits). This happens in every growth business eventually, and is accompanied by some market volatility as investment overshoots and pulls back. I attribute the specific decline on the day the inexpensive bulbs and futures contracts collapsed to market sympathy. Remember that the expensive bulbs fell only 16 percent; they were still valued more highly than they had been in 1635. Fundamentals were pulling the prices down and, as often happens in markets, there was a sudden adjustment triggered by minor news.

The inexpensive bulbs and futures contracts on bulbs are a different story. I've claimed that these had monetized, and their increase in value from 1635 to 1637 was based on their value as money, not on tulip market fundamentals. In the initial phase, when physical bulbs were traded, they were like precious metal money—total supply was limited. The introduction of futures contracts removed that limitation. However, no bank or clearinghouse existed to make the contracts into true paper money.

I do not believe people used futures on inexpensive tulip bulbs to speculate on tulips. I think they used them for money, transacting only with counterparties they believed to be financially solid, and holding roughly equal long and short balances so they had small net exposure to the value of tulip bulbs. Although modern financial institutions were beginning to evolve in Holland at this time, that was only for wealthy merchants. Everyone else was living in a medieval economy, starved for money and capital, and with severe restrictions on raising capital or putting it to work. Thus people were willing to make do with any available alternative money, even one as shaky as tulip futures.

I think people realized how high-risk the whole thing was, but were willing to take that risk because money was so useful. Someone who was willing to take unhedged risk—that is, who was willing to hold naked long positions in the futures—earned an exceptional rate of return. That's why tulip prices went up so much. Someone who wanted to borrow money, which meant holding a net short position, had to pay a very high effective interest rate. But these rates make sense in a country in severe capital shortage. From records of the time, it appears it was typical to earn 20 percent or 30 percent per year return on capital. Since usury—charging interest on loans—was still technically illegal, a rapidly deflating currency was a handy backdoor way to reward investors. Viewed in this way, the rapid increase in tulip prices demonstrates the wisdom of the Dutch in understanding the risk of tulip money, not foolishness, delusion, or madness.

There is another way to think about it for people who laugh at the silliness of using tulips for money. No one had any idea how to imitate the distinctive coloration patterns on valuable bulbs, this in an age where belief in alchemists' ability to turn lead into gold was commonplace, and precious metal coins were often debased or counterfeit. The Dutch had seen the recent example of Spanish conquests flooding Europe with silver, and at the height of the Age of Exploration it must have seemed conceivable that precious metal supply would increase suddenly and dramatically. The supply of valuable tulips was constrained by nature, but had the unique advantage of expanding at around 30 percent per year, which might have roughly matched the growth in the money economy. No other money ever invented had the property of expanding to support economic growth without the possibility of corrupt manipulation. Unfortunately, the money economy could not continue expanding at 30 percent for more than a couple of years. Once the rate of money supply increase exceeded the rate of economic growth, inflation resulted, that is the value of the bulbs crashed, and eventually they lost their status as money.

In this story, the market worked fine in 1635 and 1636. Contracts would have been settled in spring, when physical tulips were available. Futures traders could offset their long and short positions to clean up their balance sheets. But in the winter of 1637, people lost faith that contracts would be settled. As it happened, they weren't settled. Shortly after the crash, legal rulings invalidated many of the contracts, often on an asymmetric basis. So even someone who held offsetting long and short positions could lose money. Anyone who was net long lost money; even if he collected, he was paid in nearly worthless tulips. Anyone who was net short did very well. In some cases he was relieved of his obligation to repay, and if not, he could pay off in tulips worth about five cents on the dollar borrowed.

I can't point to a specific event that caused people to lose faith in contract settlement, but it makes sense that once it started, the market would unravel quickly. There was no central party to administer the liquidation of contracts. People with offsetting long and short contracts would rush to sell the long positions, and people with net long positions would be even more desperate. Without central clearing, you had to find and make a deal with the original counterparty to the contract. Initially, people likely tried to offset short positions as well. That would stabilize the market to some extent. But as tulip prices continued to fall, there would be no incentive to cover shorts. Tulips were turning back into tulips.

The later court decisions are evidence that it was rational to fear that the futures contracts would not be honored. But that may not have been the reason. It may have been that the value of the contracts as money had diverged too much from the physical reality of the tulips. That had to happen eventually, unless some organization had stepped in to provide a clearinghouse and broader economic backing to the contracts than tulips. We'll discuss in Chapter 10 how this is exactly what developed around 1850 in the center of North America.

I see some form of money creation, or attempted money creation, in all bubbles. In Chapter 16 we'll see the power of stock option currency in the Internet bubble. In the housing bubble that popped in 2007 all kinds of new currencies were created, as we'll see in Chapter 10.

I started this chapter talking about exponentials and may have ended it seeming like a bubble apologist. I do not like bubbles. Bubbles are bad. But no society has ever figured out how to deliver steadily growing prosperity. If stagnation is the alternative to bubbles and crashes, I vote for volatility. Anyway, I think we'll have volatility however I vote. So we have to figure out how to deal with bubbles and crashes. That includes harnessing their good sides, and they do have good sides. Bubbles have the energy to power us to better equilibriums. Crashes clear away things that would cause more pain if they were allowed to die slowly. This book is my attempt to persuade people to manage the risk of bubbles and crashes, rather than just complaining about them.

CHAPTER

7

Money

CIVILIZATIONS RISE AND FALL, LEAVING LITTLE BEHIND BUT CRUMBLING RUINS AND DEAD LANGUAGE TEXTS, REVERED FOR THEIR ANTIQUITY OR CULTURAL SIGNIFICANCE ONLY.

THEN THE ATHENIANS PERFECT SILVER COIN MONEY.

INSTEAD OF RATIONAL BEHAVIOR, LIKE CUTTING DOWN A TREE TO BUILD A TABLE, PEOPLE START GOING TO MARKET AND LOOKING AT WHAT THEY CAN BUY CHEAP AND TURN INTO SOMETHING EXPENSIVE.

BEGINS THAT GROWS TO ENCOMPASS THE ENTIRE WORLD AND IS WITH US TO THIS DAY.

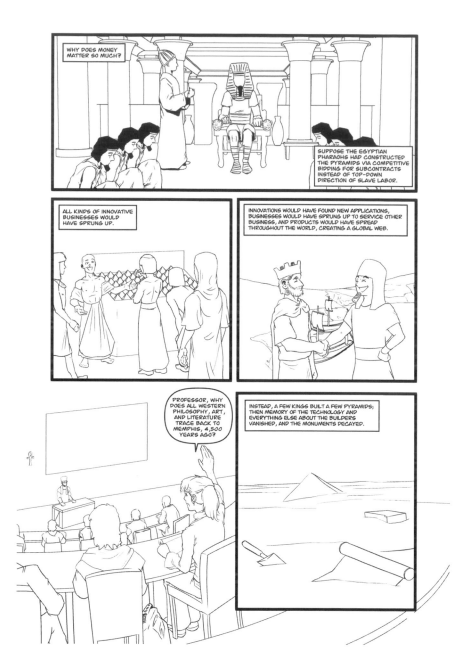

120

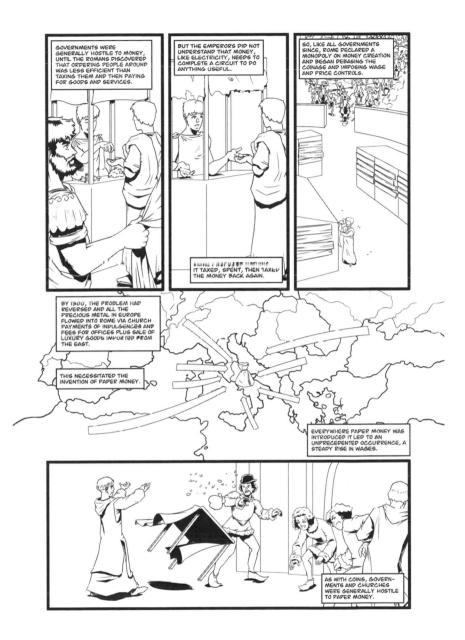

GOVERNMENTS WERE GENERALLY HOSTILE TO MONEY, UNTIL THE ROMANS DISCOVERED THAT ORDERING PEOPLE AROUND WAS LESS EFFICIENT THAN TAXING THEM AND THEN PAYING FOR GOODS AND SERVICES.

BUT THE EMPERORS DID NOT UNDERSTAND THAT MONEY, LIKE ELECTRICITY, NEEDS TO COMPLETE A CIRCUIT TO DO ANYTHING USEFUL.

SO, LIKE ALL GOVERNMENTS SINCE, ROME DECLARED A MONOPOLY ON MONEY CREATION AND BEGAN DEBASING THE COINAGE AND IMPOSING WAGE AND PRICE CONTROLS.

IT TAXED, SPENT, THEN TAXED THE MONEY BACK AGAIN.

BY 1300, THE PROBLEM HAD REVERSED AND ALL THE PRECIOUS METAL IN EUROPE FLOWED INTO ROME VIA CHURCH PAYMENTS OF INDULGENCES AND FEES FOR OFFICES PLUS SALE OF LUXURY GOODS IMPORTED FROM THE EAST.

THIS NECESSITATED THE INVENTION OF PAPER MONEY.

EVERYWHERE PAPER MONEY WAS INTRODUCED IT LED TO AN UNPRECEDENTED OCCURRENCE, A STEADY RISE IN WAGES.

AS WITH COINS, GOVERN- MENTS AND CHURCHES WERE GENERALLY HOSTILE TO PAPER MONEY.

121

IN 1775, ENGLISH COLONISTS IN AMERICA HAD A PROBLEM.

THERE'S NO ALTERNATIVE. WE MUST FIGHT A WAR FOR INDEPENDENCE!

THAT'S EASY. EVER SINCE ROMAN TIMES, YOU RAISE MONEY IN TAXES AND PAY SOLDIERS TO FIGHT FOR YOU.

BUT WE WANT TO FIGHT A WAR AGAINST TAXES.

WELL, IF YOU USE PAPER MONEY, YOU CAN ELIMINATE THE UNPOPULAR "TAXING" STEP.

THE AMERICANS ISSUED $250 MILLION OF CONTINENTAL DOLLARS, WHICH DEPRECIATED AT 50 % PER YEAR. THIS PAID FOR THE WAR AND STIMULATED AN ECONOMY THAT HAD BEEN STARVED OF MONEY BY BRITISH RULERS.

WITH THAT DEPRECIATION RATE, PEOPLE SPENT MONEY AS QUICKLY AS POSSIBLE.

WE JUST WON ANOTHER BATTLE WITH THOSE REBELLIOUS COLONISTS.

DID WE SEIZE ANY TREASURE?

NAH, JUST A BUNCH OF WORTHLESS PAPER.

WE KEEP WINNING BATTLES AND KEEP SHIPPING GOLD TO THE COLONIES. I DON'T UNDERSTAND IT.

122

A WAR WITHOUT TAXES GOT THE ATTENTION OF GOVERNMENTS ALL OVER THE WORLD, BUT THEIR EARLY EXPERIMENTS WITH PAPER MONEY WERE FAILURES. THEY DIDN'T UNDERSTAND PRECIOUS METAL COINS, MUCH LESS PAPER.

IT TOOK ABOUT A CENTURY, BUT LIKE THE ROMANS, THEY DECLARED A MONOPOLY ON MONEY CREATION, DEBASED THE MONEY BY OVERPRINTING, AND IMPOSED PERIODIC WAGE AND PRICE CONTROLS.

WITH PAPER MONEY THEY COULD ALSO FOOL AROUND WITH INTEREST RATE AND EXCHANGE RATE CONTROLS.

THE NEXT STEP IN THE EVOLUTION OF MONEY TOOK PLACE IN THE NORTHERN DRAINAGE BASIN OF THE MISSISSIPPI RIVER.

DERIVATIVES IMPROVED ON PAPER MONEY BY GIVING PRICE SIGNALS FOR ALL KINDS OF COMMODITIES AT FUTURE TIMES, INSTEAD OF A SINGLE INTEREST RATE, AND DELIVERY LOCATIONS, INSTEAD OF A SINGLE EXCHANGE RATE.

AS ALWAYS, GOVERNMENTS WERE HOSTILE TO THIS NEW FORM OF MONEY.

WHEREVER DERIVATIVES WERE INTRODUCED, THE RATE OF WAGE INCREASE EXPLODED UPWARD. MEANWHILE, PAPER MONEY WAS BEING DESTROYED BY INFLATION, GOVERNMENT MANIPULATION, AND OVERREGULATION.

MORE AND MORE OF THE ECONOMY MOVED TO A DERIVATIVES BASIS. TODAY, PAPER MONEY IS LOSING OUT EVEN FOR RETAIL TRANSACTIONS.

I'D LIKE A ONE-WAY TICKET TO LONDON.

WE DON'T ACCEPT CASH, SIR.

YOU HAVE TO. THIS IS LEGAL TENDER FOR ALL DEBTS PUBLIC AND PRIVATE. I COULD HAVE YOU ARRESTED!

BUT-- BUT YOUR NEWSPAPER AD SAYS $300!

ALL RIGHT, SIR, IF YOU INSIST. I CAN GET YOU STANDBY ON OUR FLIGHT NEXT TUESDAY FOR $10,000.

THAT'S FOR PEOPLE WHO GO TO THE INTERNET AND BID FOR FUTURE DELIVERY. THAT'S A DERIVATIVE PRICE. THE CASH PRICE IS $10,000.

OKAY, BUT CAN'T YOU GET ME THERE SOONER?

OH, YOU'LL BE BUSY UNTIL NEXT TUESDAY, SIR.

SNAP!

I'M A DOUBLE SUPER PLATINUM FLIER AND I WANT TO GO TO LONDON.

CERTAINLY, MA'AM, I'LL HAVE OUR FLIGHT HELD FOR YOU. NO CHARGE, OF COURSE.

THE DANCING BOYS ARE ON THEIR WAY TO STREW ROSE PETALS IN YOUR PATH AS YOU ARE CARRIED TO THE GATE.

MORE AND MORE TRANSACTIONS ARE MEDIATED BY DIRECT GOODS EXCHANGE, AUTOMATED CLEARING BY INTERNET BIDDING OR MATCHING, AND GOODS DELIVERED BY STATUS RATHER THAN EQUAL VALUE BY TRANSACTION. THE PROCESS IS EVEN MORE ADVANCED IN BUSINESS-TO-BUSINESS TRANSACTIONS, AND MORE AGAIN IN FINANCE.

PAPER MONEY WILL NOT DISAPPEAR OR LOSE ITS VALUE, ANY MORE THAN GOLD LOST ITS VALUE WHEN PAPER MONEY ARRIVED. BUT PAPER MONEY HAS ALREADY LOST ITS PLACE AS AN ECONOMIC DRIVER.

CHAPTER 8

The Story of Money: The Past

Most people think of money as pieces of paper issued by the government that can be used to buy things. They know there is a lot of stuff that view doesn't explain. How is the value of the money determined, and why does the value sometimes seem to change uncontrollably? What is paper money's relationship to precious metal? Why are there different monies in different countries, with relative values that also seem to change uncontrollably? How are banks and central banks and treasuries involved? Why is money covered with mystic symbols? Is money in a wallet the same thing as money in a bank?

Some people think they know all the answers to these and other questions about the basics of money. These people are called macroeconomists. These people are wrong. You don't have to take my word for it; just ask them. There are many conflicting theories of money, and none of them seem of much use in making real decisions. There are always macroeconomists who think interest rates should be higher and those who think they should be lower, and neither group has a better-than-random track record of predicting the effects of interest rate changes. If you want to guess a macroeconomist's opinion about current economic policy, you have a much better chance guessing from their political views than by reading the journal articles they write.

We are going to talk about money now because money is essential to managing risk. Once you realize that, plus a few other self-evident facts, the nature of money becomes simple. You don't need complicated theories and macroeconomic jargon. The reason people get so confused on the topic is they start by studying the highly unusual type of money that we use today, or that economic and legal theory pretend that we use. In fact, we use many kinds of money, all of which are simpler to explain than the non-interest-bearing, circulating government bonds that we call dollars or euros or yen. That kind of money is complicated due to the elaborate legal and regulatory structures built around it. So let's go back before any of the complications set in and see why money was invented.

I call this the "story" of money rather than the "history" because I don't know the history. I am using what we do know about the past to explain the present. The story is consistent with the evidence, and also is self-consistent. It illuminates the nature of money. Beyond that, there's no reason to think it's true.

Property, Exchange, and Money

Before we discuss money, we have to discuss exchange. And before we discuss exchange, we have to discuss the idea of property. Until someone owned something, nothing could be exchanged.

One of the strongest early findings of experimental game theory is that people value things they have more than identical things they don't have. For example, a classic experiment by Daniel Kahneman, Jack Knetsch, and Richard Thaler used coffee mugs with a school logo on them. These mugs sold for $6 at the campus store. A group of students was divided randomly. Half were asked how much they would pay for a mug. The other half were given mugs, and asked how much they would sell them for. Buyers offered an average of $2.87, whereas sellers demanded an average of $7.12.

This is not an isolated result from one group of college students. The effect has been demonstrated in many controlled and real-world settings, with both humans and animals, including birds and insects. There is no doubt that it is both real and important. Among other things, it explains part of loss aversion. Losing something you have is more painful than getting something equivalent is pleasurable. This is not inconsistent with utility theory, but it requires that individuals' utility function change as they acquire or lose goods. The simple version of utility theory that says all risk is bad cannot accommodate that, but sophisticated modern utility theory has no difficulty.

Why would evolution allow animals—including humans—to hold inconsistent values? The weight of the evidence is that loss aversion evolved to reduce intraspecies fighting and to allow investment. Animal behaviorists have identified many examples of competition among individuals in the same species for resources: territory, nests, pools of water, even shafts of sunlight breaking through trees. Often the property right of the first occupier is respected or, if there is a struggle, it is relatively brief and the incumbent wins far more often than can be explained by relative strength.

The mechanism for this appears to be that incumbents place a greater value on the resource than intruders do. Intruders know this, so it is usually not worth their effort to fight against an opponent with greater motivation. The stronger this effect, the less often ownership is contested, so the more valuable the property is. When property rights are secure, an individual can afford to invest in improvements like burrows and nests.

These things are clearly good for the species, but they require individuals to make inconsistent valuations, something that is suboptimal on its own. An individual who correctly balanced the value of defending the territory versus giving up and finding another would benefit from the species' expectation without paying the costs of hopeless defenses. That is, a "free rider" would often hold properties unchallenged by stronger individuals, because those individuals would expect a kamikaze defense, but it would not actually have to make such a costly effort because it would run away if challenged. If too many individuals play the prudent strategy, the expectation of defense declines and there is more fighting and less investment.

Since this is not a book on the evolution of behavior, I'm not going to go into this more deeply. I will say only that the trade-off between individual and species welfare, not to mention logic of survival on other levels from genes to environment, leads to complex, overlapping behavioral incentives. Sometime deep in the evolutionary past, or perhaps several times, species developed something analogous to what modern humans call "property." It was not enforced by police or courts, or by language or religion. It was a self-enforcing system that evolved by natural selection.

The other point I want to make is that risk is deeply embedded in the idea of property. If the outcomes of resource competitions were certain, the stronger party would just take over without a fight. Fights would be pointless because the result would be known in advance. But risk alone is not enough to prevent fights. If the risk were equal on both sides it would discourage defense as much as offense—so it would not change the balance of the decision. It would just be a cost, the way too many people like to think about risk: another weapon in the fight. Evolution turned to game theory to create an asymmetry in the fight; the incumbent feels a greater loss than just the value of the property from losing, so the incumbent fights harder, so there are fewer fights.

Once you have property, there is the potential for exchange. The most basic exchange is involuntary; one individual takes from another. We also observe gift exchange, or sharing. This mostly occurs among related individuals or with social insects, but some rudimentary forms of sharing have been documented among unrelated individuals of nonsocial species.

Paleonomics

This brings us up to early humans. We have to guess here based on modern studies of primate behavior, plus observation of surviving hunter-gatherer tribes and studies of very young children. All three kinds of evidence are indirect and possibly misleading. Modern primates and hunter-gatherers may differ from those of a million years ago, and the development of modern children may not reflect the evolution of human social conventions.

Nevertheless, there is one strong principle that stands out from all three studies, and is a plausible basis for the next advance in exchange: if it's worth fighting about, share it. This is familiar to every parent who has settled a squabble among children by dividing something in half. Judges at least as far back as Solomon have used the same procedure. It's still the basis on which wars, strikes, and lawsuits are settled. Sometimes you have to fight until enough claimants are eliminated or the resource under contention is depleted enough, but at the end the individuals remaining in the fight divide up the spoils. Hunter-gatherer tribes respect private property of low-value goods, like nuts and berries, but enforce sharing of high-value goods, like meat and honey.

Like property, sharing has its basis in risk. Things not worth the risk of a fight are owned; things worth the risk of a fight are shared. Although this rule is simple to state, in practice it gives rise to a complex set of overlapping social requirements. Not all of these are always honored. Sometimes the value of something is great enough, and the holder is strong enough, to make it worth risking a fight to not share. Sometimes a strong individual will take low-value property. There are fights. Too many violations threaten the survival of the group, whether a band sharing resources or a species respecting property. But sometimes the benefit to the individual within the group or species outweighs its stake in the group's welfare.

At this point there is a missing link. The earliest human societies we have evidence for, and the most primitive ones we can find today, have four types of exchange firmly entrenched. But among nonhumans, even our close primate relatives and social insects, there is no evidence for anything but involuntary exchange and sharing, or gift exchange.

Involuntary exchange developed from fighting. In humans it bifurcated into two distinct forms of exchange. We have involuntary exchange without contests, like taxes or embezzlement. In contrast, wars and armed robberies are more primitive versions of involuntary exchange. Every law has a component of involuntary exchange, as it requires some people to do some things, taking their time and effort, or forbids certain things, taking away freedom. I don't mean by "involuntary" that one side necessarily does not want the transaction. A person might feel that paying taxes is a social duty, or that she gets valuable services in return. She may obey laws because she feels they are right. The point is she has to pay taxes and obey laws whether she feels this way or not.

We also have exchange by contest with restrictions on fighting, and without fighting at all. This ranges from almost pure fights with a few rules, like dueling, to rules-based contests like trials and elections, to entirely symbolic games, like dice. Only a small part of wars is direct physical fighting. Negotiation, propaganda, psychological warfare, espionage, and other avenues of contention may be more important than the battles. Moreover, premodern societies and many people in modern society rely heavily on forms of gambling such as divination, astrology, and reading entrails or tea leaves to make major decisions. An exchange by contest, stripped of any element of violence, is a gambling exchange.

Gifts contain elements of both sharing and reciprocity. A gift carries with it complex social meaning, often including some expectation of repayment. When stripped of all elements except reciprocity, it becomes an equal-value exchange. "Equal value" may not be the best term; perhaps "simultaneous exchange," "symmetrical exchange," or "barter" is better. The idea is that two people voluntarily exchange goods or services and have no further claims on or obligations to each other. There is no requirement that the things exchanged have equal value by any standard.

Involuntary exchange, except in the crudest physical sense, involves complex social rules and a hierarchy. Higher-status people take more goods and make more rules. Gifts also have complex social implications and are often from inferiors to superiors (tribute) or from superiors to inferiors (largesse).

Gambling and equal-value exchange are symmetric; they can be between equals or, if they are between superiors and inferiors, the status does not matter. They are simple transactions that create limited or no future rights or obligations. As far as we know, they are both uniquely human, while involuntary exchange and sharing have deep evolutionary roots.

Most real exchanges among people have elements of all four types intermixed. Table 8.1 is useful for keeping them straight. In a symmetric exchange, both parties have the same relationship to each other. You trade with me means I trade with you. You gamble with me means I gamble with you. But if you make a gift to me or take something from me, the transaction is asymmetric. Reciprocal transactions require payback, either in tangible form or by creating social obligations. Nonreciprocal exchanges have no offset; only one party ends up with the goods.

There is also a diagonal link between gift and gambling exchange versus equal value and involuntary exchange. We prefer luxury or perfect goods for gift and gambling exchange. We give someone jewelry or a pretty sweater for a gift more often than a vacuum cleaner. A contest is more likely to offer a "shiny new convertible" for a prize than a used tractor-trailer cab. We wrap gifts in colorful paper with ribbons. In fact, we often use entirely symbolic goods for gifts and gambling. The exchange itself is often

Table 8.1   The Four Types of Human Exchange

	Reciprocal	Nonreciprocal
Symmetric	Equal value	Gambling
Asymmetric	Gift	Involuntary

more important than the goods. For equal value and involuntary exchange, the goods are the entire point, and their character doesn't matter; only their value. A mugger will take your wallet whether or not it's shiny and new, and there are active trading markets for all kinds of used, ugly, and non-luxury goods. Worn and tattered bills and dirty coins are worth the same as crisp new bills and shiny coins for transactions, although the latter are much preferred for gifts, and the only kind you'll receive cashing in your chips at a casino. Kidnappers insist on the former. Las Vegas glitters while industrial cities are ugly.

Transition

Sometime around 50,000 years ago, the Upper Paleolithic phase of human development began. Important features of this period are the emergence of long-distance exchange networks and specialized economic activity. Both of these things leave clear traces in the archeological record. There is some controversy over whether this was a sudden revolution or the result of accumulated gradual changes over 500,000 years. We don't have much evidence for exchange and specialization earlier, but that doesn't mean they didn't exist; it just means they were relatively rare or involved perishable goods.

It makes logical sense that this is the period in which gambling and equal-value exchange developed. They allow individuals from different social bands to make exchanges, without necessarily agreeing on all the complex rules that support involuntary and gift exchange, and without the necessity for future interactions.

The emergence of equal-value exchange seems to me to be a likely cause of the Upper Paleolithic advances. Neighboring tribes with some genetic relationship, perhaps due to having split from the same older tribe or else due to exchange of some members for genetic mixing, meet from time to time. If either tribe happens to have a surplus of something, it donates some to the other, creating a social obligation for the recipient tribe to reciprocate at some future meeting. This can explain the long-distance exchange networks. It also allows some specialization. If one tribe happens to have a particularly good stone quarry in its nomadic range, it could make lots of high-quality stone tools to use as gifts, perhaps collecting in return shells and dried fish from a tribe nearer to the ocean.

Specialization leads to innovation and increased production, both of which increase surplus, which allows more specialization.

As the reciprocal exchange gets more complex and impersonal, token money is a useful invention. Seashells are the most common form, but almost anything can be used. When a tribe receives a gift, it gives a token in exchange. That token can be returned when the gift is reciprocated. Tokens circulate among tribes. The older a token and the more it is associated with powerful people and generous gifts in the past, the more valuable it is. A tribe that is constantly introducing new tokens is clearly getting more than it is giving, and may find gifts getting smaller or being cut off entirely. A tribe that accumulates too many tokens may decide it's not getting its fair share of exchanges.

Token money gives way to commodity money as transactions become more impersonal and lose their gift aspects. Commodity money can be anything that has general value: salt, barley, or goats, for example. Ideally it is nonperishable, of easily determined quality, portable, divisible, and desired by everyone in essentially unlimited quantities. Nothing fits all these criteria, but precious metals come closest. However, we're still in the Stone Age, so we have to make do with less satisfactory commodities. Also, we'll likely use different things for different money purposes. Salt is nonperishable, portable, divisible, and of easily determined quality, so it makes a good medium of exchange (we still say someone is "worth his salt"). Goats are none of those things, but they make a good store of value. Barley makes a good numeraire if it represents the majority of calories in everyone's diet since everyone needs it every day.

There are two important features of early money that are obscured in modern times but remain valid. First, there arc many different types used for different types of exchanges. Today most governments have declared monopolies on money, meaning there is one legal type per country. But we'll see later that's not really true; there are many alternative forms of money circulating in disguise. Money is not something created by government mints; it is something that arises naturally among people. The government can try to suppress the home brew and make everyone use the official government-supplied product, but no government has ever been successful at that.

Even precious metal money existed in multiple forms. Gold was used for the highest-value and international transactions, silver for most merchant transactions, and copper or other base metal coins for retail. In England a few centuries ago, a gold guinea coin circulated alongside a silver pound sterling. Initially, the two coins had the same value, but were used for different transactions. The guinea was aristocratic. Luxury goods and professional services were paid for in guineas. The pound was for merchants and tradespeople. Murray Gel-Mann told me a story from 1955 when we were discussing this. He was in England and requested a dispensation from the Archbishop of Canterbury to get married without the normal waiting period. It turned out he did not need the document, so he canceled the request. He received a note from the Archbishop's secretary informing him that the Archbishop felt that "two guineas are appropriate in this matter." This was 142 years after the last guinea was minted but The Most Reverend and Right Honourable the Lord Archbishop still couldn't put his hand out for a couple of quid and two shillings—and the amazing part is everyone understands why, without necessarily being able to explain it. I doubt the Church of England still uses guineas, but guineas remain the preferred currency in English horse racing and high-stakes private gambling; also, amusingly, in sales of rams but not sales of sheep.

An equally important and related point is that only a small subset of goods can be exchanged for money, different subsets for different forms of money. We can earn trust, repay loyalty, and reciprocate affection; but not with or for money—any kind of money. Many other valuable things are awarded by merit or by competition or by birth or randomly, and cannot be bought or sold. Even goods that are available for sale for government-issued money usually require specific kinds of money. Small transactions require cash, sometimes even only coins. Larger transactions, such as real estate purchases, require bank drafts or other forms of money. Credit cards are most useful for transactions of intermediate size. Criminal and private transactions require cash. Usually the only cash you can use is that of the country the transaction takes place in. These rules are not just for transactional convenience; they really matter. Different kinds of goods circulate in different kinds of systems, mediated by different kinds of money. There is some convertibility among types of money, but it is often expensive or illegal.

These are important points because the economy is a system of interlocking risk-taking cycles, each with its own money. Since there is limited convertibility among types of money, different relative prices can persist in different cycles, just as the ratios of prices are not the same in all currencies. A strong finding from behavioral research is that people price things differently depending on whether money used. It is perfectly possible, in fact common, to value A more than B but to put a higher price on B than on A. For a related reason, it is impossible to define the rate of inflation, because the prices of different goods go up at different rates. Inflation is not a general decline in the value of money; it also changes the relative prices of goods.

We can think of each of these cycles as a game, isolated from the rest of the economy. This is the same kind of isolation required for play. Each cycle has its own numeraire. Risk has to be managed within cycles, not between them. Exponential growth is possible within a cycle, because there is money to equate constraints and goals. But you have to either take all your rewards within the cycle or at some point transfer the goods to another cycle. In effect, you have to launder your money.

What Money Does

Getting back to the Stone Age, the low quality of available money is a severe restriction on specialization. Households or small groups have to make almost all essentials for themselves. No one can afford to devote all his resources to, say, making pottery, because he can't count on buying all the materials he needs or on selling the pots for all the necessities of life. One villager might devote a portion of his time to making pots—doing all aspects of the job from gathering materials to decorating the final product—without a large investment in specialized equipment. He might trade pots for stone axes, tanned leather, wooden beams, and other useful things produced by other part-time specialists. But no one will develop the expertise of the true professional, and no activity will capture the full economy of large-scale production. Exchange will remain a small part of total economic activity.

This point is commonly made in economics texts. But there is an even more important one that is usually missed. Without good money there will be far less innovation—not because people don't have the resources to devote to research, but because risk cannot be managed. Money does not just make exchange and specialization easier; it makes constraints and goals the same. Our Neolithic potter's constraints were the amount of available resources, including time, clay, paint, tools, and devices for shaping and firing pots. His goal was to increase his household's consumption and capital assets. The only overlap of those two things are pots that are consumed by the household or used in the production of more pots, probably a small portion of the potter's output.

Imagine if there were plenty of good-quality money available. Then our ambitious potter can buy the things he needs, including paying himself a salary for his time. Money is his constraint. His goal is to make more money. He doesn't have to worry about who will supply his needs or about what the money he makes will be spent on. He can concentrate on making pots. Suppose he has a gross profit of 50 percent; that is, he can sell a pot for half again as much as the time and material cost. He can grow his business at an exponential rate of 50 percent per production cycle (the time between first making a cash outlay for materials and when cash is received for the pot). Of course, he will soon hit constraints at that rate: his suppliers will run out of material to sell him (including the possibility he will run out of time to make pots) or perhaps his customers will have all the pots they need.

At this point a third feature of money comes into play, like the first one that is found in economics texts. The price of the bottleneck material will go up (possibly the salary of potters) and the price of pots will decline. These price signals will radiate—calling in suppliers and customers from the entire world, and stimulating innovation everywhere. These same price changes will cause the potter's exponential growth rate to decline.

There is a fourth step as well. As the potter's scale of operation grows, even at a reduced rate, he will be able to make it more efficient. He can build bigger and better equipment. He can hire people and further specialize the process. He can devote resources to research and development. The knowledge also spreads out as others learn of his improvements and his skilled workers set up businesses of their own. Higher profits for suppliers lead to faster growth and more innovation there, and cheaper pots do the same for his customers. Finally, the larger trade networks necessary for supply and distribution create many other fruitful links.

Risk

So far we have not discussed risk. Let's go back to that second step, when the potter's growth rate was 50 percent. It won't be the case that the potter knows the gross profit margin at the beginning of the business, and it will change over time. It will not be a steady 50 percent per pot. Some pots will be failures—100 percent loss. Others may fetch three or five times their cost. There will be unpredictable interruptions in supply and demand, and unexpected surges in both of those as well. Without money, the potter cannot manage these risks, which means he cannot take advantage of exponential growth. He can only guess what scale of operation is optimal. If he guesses wrong, or perhaps even if he guesses right, the entire enterprise collapses. He needs money to "carry over" good luck. If he happens to have a successful period, he can grow the operation at a prudent rate and bank some surplus. In bad times, he can scale back the operation and dip into surplus. Without money, he will have to make much more violent and inefficient changes in scale, and he will be unable to compute the proper strategy. The business might not survive, even though it has the potential for a 50 percent growth rate, or it might be run so conservatively that it never grows or innovates.

What does the potter need to carry over luck? For one, he needs a store of value. Unsold pots are his only option without money, and they take a lot of room to store and have zero yield. He needs to be able to use that store to buy supplies when demand returns. Pots are not a good medium of exchange, and without money, he cannot sell them for a medium of exchange. But his biggest problem is that without a numeraire he cannot relate supply to demand, the price of pots to the price of clay, or even the price of one input versus another. So he cannot be a Kelly bettor.

We can see the same picture on a larger canvas by fast-forwarding to the early Bronze Age in Egypt, 5,000 years ago. The Egyptian pharaohs wanted to build pyramids. We don't know exactly how they did it, but it seems to have been a top-down operation. The builders, whether slaves or volunteers, were told what to do. If they were paid, it was in goods, not money.

The technological achievement of the pyramids is extremely impressive. There are aspects of their construction still not understood today. They required elaborate social organization. The same thing is true of late Neolithic and early Bronze Age monuments throughout the world. Yet the pyramids and other spectacular ancient achievements were dead ends. They did not lead to new industries or technological spin-offs. They did not stimulate the economy. Whatever was learned in constructing them was forgotten.

Imagine if instead the pharaohs had mined some copper and made it into coins, then taken competitive bids for different phases of the project. Lots of ambitious people in Egypt would have been thinking about ways to quarry and transport stone, or work it into shape, or position it in the structure. Some smarter ambitious people would have figured out that all those copper coins earned by pyramid contractors and their workers would be spent on the necessities people didn't have time to produce, and whatever was left over would be spent on investments or luxuries. Every red-blooded Egyptian would have ramped up production of whatever she did best. Egypt would have drawn in the best people and goods from neighboring countries. Innovation would have exploded. The new technologies would have been applied to all other aspects of economic life. Demand would have been further increased as exporters bought up goods to trade in other countries for more material. The flow of exports and coins would have ignited similar bursts of prosperity everywhere. Exponential growth would have been the order of the day.

Or maybe not. Maybe subcontracting the pyramids would not have caused a social revolution. Maybe there were other technological and social conditions necessary for this kind of takeoff. Maybe it isn't money that brings about the revolution; maybe the revolution causes the creation of money. What we do know is that when the Athenians actually did perfect silver coin money 2,500 years ago, there was precisely this kind of ignition, and we know that money is essential to the phenomenon, whether it is cause or effect. The economic web created in Athens expanded to cover the entire world. While it has been shut down in some times and places, it has never lost all connections or been shut down completely. Today, we still participate in the same network of commerce that Socrates did, but have no similar connection with any contemporaneous or older culture.

For the 2,500 years between the beginning of the Bronze Age and classical Athens, many great cultures had their days in the sun. They rose to a certain level of achievement, then fell. For the most part their languages and technologies died with them. They left us artifacts admired for their antiquity or cultural significance—usually claimed by a later, culturally unrelated group as a founding myth— but little of direct value. How many texts more than 2,500 years old do people read for pleasure or nonhistorical instruction? Contrast that to the wealth of Greek philosophy, science, mathematics, art, and literature, and that of many subsequent cultures that had the advantage of money.

Government and Paper

The next chapter in our story concerns the Romans, the first civilization in which the government noticed the power of money. The emperors figured out that it was more efficient to tax people and then pay them to do what you wanted than to order things done. This worked fine at first. The Romans paid soldiers to loot places just outside the Empire. The money found its way back to Rome in taxes. Rome spent the money for goods from all over the Empire.

Unfortunately, like all governments since, the emperors didn't understand that money, like electricity, does work only when it circulates. Rome produced nothing. As the Empire grew, there was less and less to loot, and more and more border to protect from impoverished and angry barbarians. Things went from cash-flow positive to cash-flow negative. Rome continued to tax and spend, but without the external contribution there was no more circulation. If you tax someone, buy her goods with the money, then tax the money back to buy more of her goods, the whole thing stops working. You no longer have money. It is not a store of value—the government taxes it away. It is not a medium of exchange; no one wants it because the government taxes it away. It could still be a numeraire, except in rcsponse to the first two problems, also like all governments since, the Romans debased the currency and imposed wage and price controls.

The fall of the western Roman empire in 476 A.D. solved the problem. Two surviving institutions played a big role in the next development. The Roman Catholic Church expanded throughout Europe, establishing monasteries, convents, and cathedrals. These served as centers of production, learning, trade, and credit. The eastern Roman Empire was represented in Italy by Venice, which along with other northern Italian cities developed trade networks supplying Eastern luxury goods to Europe.

As the church and Italian commercial cities grew in power, the old Roman problem reversed. The church collected various fees throughout Europe, and northern Italy supplied all the luxury goods. The rest of Europe produced little that anyone wanted. So all the gold and silver flowed into Italy. Circulation stopped.

The solution was paper money. It was not the first time some-one had tried to use paper or some other perishable and intrinsi-cally worthless commodity as money. The earlier efforts were token money or receipts. They could function as a medium of exchange only through legal enforcement by a strong authority. They were not stores of value, although in some cases they could be converted into one. They were not numeraires, people continued to quote prices in terms of precious metal.

The key to the new paper money was that it was backed by a debt, the promise of future value. Earlier paper money was backed either by precious metal or by nothing. The new idea was tremen-dously simulative because now economic activity was originated by persuasive people with ideas rather than people with gold or silver. The only limits on economic development were physical resources and public confidence. As a result, wherever paper money was introduced it created an unprecedented phenomenon: steadily ris-ing wages. Before silver coin money, there basically were no wages in the modern sense. After coins were introduced, wages might go up a bit when labor was scarce and opportunities good, but they would go back down when the reverse conditions applied. From the first paper money, the world has enjoyed a steady upward trend in wage rates. There are cyclical upturns and downturns, but the long-term climb has never been interrupted. The basic reason is that in a precious metal system only the wealthy can supply capital for new projects, so the wealthy can extract all the rewards above subsist-ence wages. The price of labor is set by supply and demand, and with a fixed amount of available money, workers always expand to fill the demand. It may take a while, but you can't have a long-term increase in wages. With paper money, anyone can start a project, which can lead to demand for labor rising faster than the popula-tion can increase.

Since this is a story instead of a history, I will dispense with a lot of tedious detail. Paper money was created in the face of strong official disapproval. Its advantages were great enough that it was allowed to survive, but in overcomplicated forms. This resulted partly from attempts to obscure its purpose, partly from supersti-tion, and partly through accidents of early history. Subsequent generations of thinkers have layered on more nonsense, gener-ally to promote some political opinion or other. The basic idea is quite simple. That is all I will describe here. Everything else, such as paper money's relationship to precious metal money, banking theory, and legal tender rules, is irrelevant.

Paper money is created by some institution that we will call a "bank." This institution does not need reserves of gold and silver. It does not need equity capital. It does not need a building, certainly not a bunch of marble columns in a prime downtown location or a steel-and-glass tower. It does need to make loans. It does not lend precious metal; it lends pieces of paper. The borrowers exchange those pieces of paper for goods and services for their business. Then they sell the products of their business for paper, and use that to repay the loan with interest. The use of physical paper is not important; it is merely a record-keeping device. The same system can be used with accounting entries only (this is how debit cards work). Do not think only of official banks. There are many other types of formal and informal credit webs that mediate economic activity. Most of these are invisible to economic statistics, yet they power far more economic innovation, and lift far more people to financial security, than official bank loans that are used mostly to grease the wheels of established businesses and serve people who already have money. There's a lot of truth to the adage that (official) banks are institutions that lend money to people who don't need it.

There is an obvious vulnerability to the system: what if people lose confidence in the paper money? That can happen for a number of reasons. For example, people could notice borrowers having trouble repaying their loans; demand for money in general could decline; or another institution could fail, causing a panic. Sometimes it happens for no reason at all. The bank can try to reassure the public. It can hold a lot of reserve capital to cover losses; it can make only sound, short-term loans on liquid collateral; it can offer to sell gold and silver for its paper money. But these are optional reassurances only; none are fundamental economic functions of a money creator.

When people lose confidence in paper money, they begin to accept it at a discount. It might take $105 of paper money to buy what you can buy with $100 of silver. This creates two important options. Anyone holding paper money from this bank can try to spend it at a discount, or deposit it in the bank. Because the money is acquired at a discount and will be paid back at full value if the bank survives, the latter option effectively pays interest—or increases the nominal rate of interest paid—on the money. The discount will rise to the level that this additional effective interest will compensate for the increase in perceived risk. At some levels of discount, say 50 percent, it can pay to deposit the money even if the bank does fail. The repayments that do come in, through the sale of seized collateral, might pay off the money at 60 or 70 cents on the dollar. If a holder elects instead to spend the money, all he cares about is the discount he applies when he accepts it compared to the discount at which he can spend it. As long as the money circulates rapidly, the loss can be a small fraction of each transaction, even if the money depreciates all the way to zero.

The other important option is for bank borrowers to pay their loans back at a discount. For example, suppose someone borrows $1,000 to buy a shipment of flour, planning to put it into smaller bags and sell it for $2,000. But some of the flour is spoiled and demand is less than anticipated. It looks like he can get only $600 for his flour and will default on his loan. If the bank's money is accepted at a 50 percent discount, however, he can sell his $600 of flour for $1,200 of bank paper money, pay back his loan with interest, and pocket a profit. This puts another floor level to support the value of the bank's money—what it's worth to borrowers. The bigger the discount on the money, the easier it is for borrowers to repay, so the better the chance that the bank survives and makes all the money good.

It's obvious why someone would want to start a bank and why people would borrow from it. But why do people accept the paper money for valuable goods and services? Remember, one thing that distinguishes equal-value exchange from the other three types of human exchange is that not everything is for sale. And what is for sale depends on the money being offered. No one would sell land for dubious paper money, for example. Land is a store of value. It's safer to lend someone the money to buy the land from you, and take the land back if she doesn't pay.

Suppose, however, you have a perishable commodity and no other potential purchasers. In that case you probably prefer even dubious paper money at an appropriate discount to lending the purchaser the money yourself. The paper money is better than nothing; it might buy something, or it can be deposited in the bank in the hope the bank survives. That's a diversified risk, compared to the undiversified risk of trusting one buyer. It's right-way risk as well. If the bank fails, the market for all goods is probably bad, whether the bad market caused the bank failure or the bank failure caused the bad market. In that case the perishable goods probably have little value anyway. If you sell the goods on credit, the economy can be good and the buyer still might not repay you. Moreover, with paper money, it's the bank's problem to evaluate the credit of the borrower and chase him down for payment. People with unused resources—an unoccupied rental house, a ship without cargo, or just an unemployed person—may prefer to transact for paper money than to earn nothing at all.

Why would a person accept dubious paper money instead of just lowering the price and insisting on metal coins? It's easier to answer that question in the aggregate than individually. If everyone insists on coins, the money supply is low. Only the wealthy can take economic risks. Poor people with good ideas cannot pursue their ideas. There are lots of slack or underutilized resources, possibly including unemployed people. Paper money stimulates overall economic activity. New businesses open, higher wages are paid, people specialize more and take more risks, and more goods are produced. This creates additional supply and demand, and more transactions than can be completed with coins, since the quantity of coins has not increased. Conceivably, an individual merchant could try to be a free rider and run his business only with coins, no paper money or credit. In good times, this will cost the free rider more in lost business than it saves in credit losses, because the paper money is good anyway. In bad times, lots of people will in fact pursue this strategy because there are enough coins to support the level of transactions, and the paper money may not be good.

Now consider a merchant with goods such as hats. Hats are not stores of value like land, but they are not perishable, either. She will be happy to sell a hat for gold or silver, but will also consider good paper money, or extending credit to customers who appear to be creditworthy. Her choice among insisting on metal, taking paper, giving credit, or refusing the sale will depend on the goods in question, the customer, the bank issuing the paper money, and the state of her business.

Paper versus Metal

The biggest misunderstanding about paper money is the idea that it is a promise for gold or silver, and that it serves the same function as precious metal coins. It's an entirely different thing. Rules requiring it to relate to gold and silver are passed in order to destroy true paper money, to turn it into a mere token or a convenient substitute when precious metal is in short supply.

Silver coin money measures the relative value of everything for sale at the moment. You can go into the marketplace, note the prices of everything, and figure out what is cheap that you can turn into something expensive. You don't worry about where the cheap stuff came from or who will buy the expensive stuff; all you care about is the relative price. Silver is entirely irrelevant. It could be worth a hundred times as much or one-hundredth as much; all that matters is the relative prices. There is only one silver, not lots of different kinds issued by different banks. This is the economic driver that created Western civilization

Paper money creates a much more nuanced set of price signals. There are things you can barter, things you can buy or sell for silver, and things you can buy or sell for paper money. That last is really many sets, as the money of different banks will be good in different degrees in different places and for different things. Each type of paper money has its own interest rate, which is measured by both the interest the bank pays on deposits (if any) and the discount at which the money is accepted (if any). This is a new type of price signal, absent from precious metal. Also, there are exchange rates for different paper monies, another important new signal.

A typical village might have a hard economy based on precious metal and solid credit. This would meet the needs of local aristocracy, large landowners, and government and church officials. Alongside it could be a soft economy based on paper money and risky credit. In bad times, the soft economy might disappear or deal only in surplus goods and slack resources. But the soft economy can fund any new idea from any persuasive person. Its larger pool of talent, plus the fact that poor people have more incentive to change things than rich people have, means that the soft economy will support most of the innovation. Successful innovation leads to economic growth, which makes the paper money good both because loans pay off and because there is strong demand for money. This leads to a new round of good times.

A merchant in this village will deal with both worlds. She will keep a sharp eye on the paper money interest rate. When it is low, she will borrow and expand and accept paper money even for goods that could be sold for coin. When it is high, she will repay loans and cut back, and spend whatever paper money she has. She would like to stop accepting paper money altogether, but that conflicts with her desire to sell down inventory and repay debt.

One consequence of bad times is that the local bank's paper money will start to spread out to surrounding regions where the economy is better. Those places will be slower to notice the credit problems of the bank, and demand for money will still be high. However, the neighboring villages will also discount nonlocal money on principle, knowing that they don't have the best information. As they see more and more money from one village bank— lots of buying and little selling—they will discount the paper. This will provide a signal to places with hot economies to swoop in and buy cheap goods in the place having troubles. Similarly, when a village bank's money is in strong demand, people will rush from other places to sell there.

All of this is elementary microeconomics. The aspect that's insufficiently understood is that it occurs on a very local level. Several different economies can coexist in one place. Most of these local credit webs, including the most innovative ones, will not use anything a traditional economist would recognize as money. Different types of money are used for different kinds of goods and services. People react to a host of subtle signals. When you try to aggregate this behavior and study it as macroeconomics, it breaks down. The entire virtue of paper money is how many types there are, and how easy it is to create more. If you treat it as a single form of money, like silver coins, you miss everything.

As far back as we can trace things, people have created webs of credit to support economic activity. These had to be closed and small-scale, usually limited to relatives or a small number of partners. Paper money opens up these webs into networks that anyone can join and that can link up with each other. It was the open-source movement of its day.

As with silver coin money, governments were initially hostile to paper money. One major block was the biblical prohibition against usury, which was a necessary component of loan-backed money. The larger problem is that governments favor the interests of rich and powerful people, and they had little need for paper money. While it's true that the new kind of money increased economic growth, it increased wage rates much more than asset prices, so the rich and powerful were relatively less well off, even if they gained in absolute terms. Where banks were not forbidden altogether, they were fenced in by rules limiting growth and types of lending, and mandating lots of gold and silver reserves—up to 100 percent reserves in some places, which destroys the whole idea. There was an obsession with preventing bank failures—which reached pathological extreme in the absurd idea of "too big to fail"—which led to regulations designed to suppress risk taking and punish risk takers. Of course some kind of license had to be bought from the government, and it was usually necessary to appoint people from the local elite to paid board positions.

1776 and All That

That all changed in 1776. Ever since Roman times, the way you fought a war was to raise money from taxes, then pay soldiers to fight it for you. You could fight a war for any stupid reason you liked (in fact, in most wars one or both sides claimed to be fighting for peace), except one: you couldn't fight a war against taxes. But that's exactly what the American Congress wanted to do. Fortunately, there were experienced businesspeople represented and they knew paper money could eliminate the unpopular "taxing" step. They issued $250 million of continental dollars, which depreciated at about 50 percent per year. That paid for a successful war.

Why did people accept the low-quality money? Patriotism was a factor in some cases, no doubt, as was duress. If soldiers showed up to your farm to buy supplies for the troops at Valley Forge, you weren't given a choice of currency for payment. Also, wartime creates a lot of temporarily and locally slack resources: crops you can't get to market, animals you cannot afford to feed, gunpowder that will be seized by the British if you don't sell it to the Americans today. Converting these to easily portable and concealable cash is attractive, even if the cash will have depreciated a percent or two when you spend it next week. Moreover, the American economy was doing great, supplying both armies in addition to its normal activities. All sorts of trade restrictions were lifted and taxes eliminated. A strong economy creates a demand for money, and there had not been enough silver and gold to support even the prewar level of activity.

There's another way to answer the question of why people accepted continental dollars. I live in New York City, which means at the moment I pay 8.875 percent sales tax every time I use my money to buy something. If I use money to pay a wage or return on investment, I pay a much higher rate, and there are many other taxes embedded in the prices of the things I buy. But let's just use the 8.875 percent. Suppose the government prints $1 and uses it to buy goods or services. Every time that dollar changes hands, it loses 8.875 percent of its value. The first time it is spent, $0.09 goes to the government and $0.91 worth of goods and services are tendered. When the $0.91 is spent, $0.08 goes to the government and $0.83 is left. After seven transactions, the dollar has lost the amount that continental dollars lost in a year. If we take the velocity of money at 20, those seven transactions occurred in about four months.

Those numbers are highly uncertain. You can make reasonable cases for any depreciation rate from 50 percent per year, the same as continental dollars, to 50 percent per month. And this doesn't include the additional depreciation from inflation. My point is not that taxes are too high; it's that 50 percent annual depreciation rates or even higher don't stop people from accepting and using the money. Most people barely notice the sales tax. In times of hyperinflation, you spend or invest money as quickly as possible. In countries with high transaction taxes, you try to structure things to avoid intermediate transactions. In extreme cases people sometimes burn a few bills or wallpaper a room for political theater, but mostly people just use the money, whatever the depreciation.

What inflation and transaction taxes do is encourage shifting of the economy to alternative forms of money. The official money economy does not disappear; it just declines in importance. But all this is getting ahead of our story.

A war without taxes got the immediate attention of governments throughout the world. Few of their officials had the business experience of the American leaders, and their early experiments were not successful. In the new United States, by contrast, the experience of the continental dollars left complex attitudes toward paper money. On one hand, their use had won the war. Nobody lost a fortune holding them, as people knew to spend them as fast as possible. While they were finally paid off at one cent on the dollar, only the dollars issued at the beginning of the war had been accepted at face value. Those had changed hands so many times that the $0.99 loss represented only a small sales tax split among so many transactions. Continentals accepted more recently, with fewer transactions to amortize the loss over, had been accepted at lower values, perhaps three or five cents, so the percentage loss was much less. Continentals had probably stimulated more economic growth than the value of the resources tendered for them.

On the other hand, it was distasteful for an honest government to renege on promises. Federalists like Alexander Hamilton liked hard money, whereas Democratic-Republicans like Thomas Jefferson disliked the power paper money gave the government. As so often seems to be the case with the Founding Fathers, they hit on the right solution. Keep the government far from the money-creating process, and let banks flourish.

Then came Andrew Dexter.

Andrew Dexter

Andy has the honor of being America's first great overleveraged real estate developer. He had great vision. He built the Boston Exchange Coffee House. This was not a Colonial Starbucks; it was a 200-room hotel, financial exchange, and business office. It cost $500,000 and was among the tallest buildings in the New World. Unfortunately, it was more than twice as tall as any available ladders, so when a fire broke out on the seventh floor there was no way to prevent it from burning to the ground. Dexter also founded the city of Montgomery, Alabama, boldly reserving a plot for the state capitol building although Alabama was not a state and Mobile had been the capital of the French territory for over a century while Montgomery was a brand-new town. Years later, the Alabama state capitol was indeed built on that site.

The thing is, Andy never had any money to support these big ideas. But he did have another big idea instead. He gained control of two banks, the Bank of Detroit and the Farmers Exchange Bank of Gloucester, Rhode Island. Detroit was a newly incorporated frontier outpost at the time, near the site of a recent major Indian battle. Oh, and it had just burned to the ground. There were no roads to Gloucester; you had to walk through the woods to get there. The two banks were 600 miles apart (800 if you don't go through Canada).

What if you print $100,000 worth of Bank of Detroit notes? The Bank of Gloucester can print the same. If you spend the money at places in between, it will take years to work its way back to the issuing banks, and most of it will probably never get there. So you have a long-term, no-collateral, no-doc, no-income-verification, negative interest rate loan, just what every ambitious real estate speculator needs.

Why did people accept the paper money? What about all that high-sounding stuff about subtle price signals and suspicion of non-local money? See, there was a defect in the system. In all the centuries of paper money, no one had thought of it before Andy. While it's true people were suspicious of money from neighboring villages, and very suspicious of money from a hundred miles away, and also very suspicious of money in excessive supply, if the money came from far enough away and was available in large enough supply, the suspicions vanished. Why? If the money had made it all the way from Detroit to, say, Boston, it must be good. All those people who passed it hand to hand couldn't be wrong. If the money were bad, you surely would have heard about it. And if $10,000 diffused its way to Boston, there must be millions in Detroit; those guys must be really, really rich. This kind of money was acceptable everywhere—except Detroit and Gloucester, of course, where people knew how tiny the banks were—and therefore commanded a premium, as it could be used for long-distance transactions and was a big advantage for travelers. The more it was accepted this way, the more people trusted it.

The whole thing might have worked, and for all we know similar schemes did work for others, except for cost overruns and construction delays at the Boston Exchange Coffee House, followed by disappointing revenue after it was completed. The Farmers Exchange Bank couldn't make good on money presented for redemption, and it couldn't point to any collateral to support eventual payment. So Andy had his first bankruptcy and people lost faith in the simple theory of paper money. Today most economists chuckle condescendingly at the foolishness of believing that banks do not need capital, and that paper money provides important local price signals and winds down naturally.

Laws were passed to tighten bank regulation. However, the real problem of this affair was lack of transparency, not lack of capital or regulation. The new restrictions reduced the supply of banks and paper money, and kept both firmly in the hands of wealthy people with political connections, as was the case in Europe. Nevertheless, whenever Americans got far enough away from authority, they opened wildcat or soft money banks using the old principles. Counterfeiters were folk heroes up to the time of the Civil War, just as bank robbers became folk heroes afterward and again during the Great Depression.

As governments became more accustomed to paper money, most of them took it over and declared a monopoly on money creation. This took place in the United States during and shortly after the Civil War. Governments understood paper money even less than they understood silver coin money. So they played their old tricks of debasement—which is absurdly easy with paper money; you just print more, or make extravagant, unfunded promises that you can keep only by printing even more—and wage and price controls. Paper money did give them two other things to monkey with: interest rates and exchange rates.

Of course, this destroyed all the subtle, local price signals that were the reason for paper money in the first place. Governments thought of paper money as precious metal money that was cheaper to manufacture, but that everyone should pretend is the real thing. This is exactly what governments thought when they were debasing precious metal money. The result was a kind of token money. People accept it only because other people accept it, and only if the government doesn't print too much. It does function as a medium of exchange, but only for small and criminal transactions. No one takes it seriously as a store of value. It can't be a numeraire, because it has no value of its own. I can say this costs $2 and that costs $1, but all I've really said is that this is worth two of that. To assign an absolute value, you have to ask what year I'm talking about, in which case you can try to relate the statement to some basket of goods like the one underlying the consumer price index, so the basket is your real numeraire. If you show a graph of value over time, you cannot use just dollars; you have to use inflation-adjusted dollars. Even that is accurate only for a fixed basket of goods, as prices of different goods change at different rates.

A Short Digression into Politics and Religion

I don't think my political or religious beliefs have anything to do with this book. I also don't think they are profound or interesting to other people. I claim no expertise in either. My life has been comfortable enough that both politics and religion are abstract speculations for me. I have never been called upon to risk anything for either one. As you have probably gathered, I have little respect for opinions that the holder has not bet on.

Nevertheless, I am including this short section. It's purely defensive. I have written mostly negative things about governments, and it's going to get worse. I do not want to give the impression that I am antigovernment. Also, I've spoken in terms some people might consider disrespectful about religion. I'm also not antireligion. It was Blaise Pascal, a deeply—even fanatically—religious man who threw a religious challenge into the study of risk. Ever since, it has been an issue you cannot avoid if you want to write seriously on the topic.

You are free to skip this section. Of course, you're free to skip any section, or not to read the book in the first place. But for all the other sections, I take responsibility for including useful and interesting material. This section is different. The material here is only for people who might otherwise dismiss my arguments as disguised political or religious rantings. There's no disguise—my interest and expertise start and end with risk. To the extent risk reflects on other things, including politics and religion, I leave it to others to consider the implications. I have my own opinions on the implications, or this would be a very short section, but there's no reason you should take them more seriously than those of any other random amateur.

The expertise I do claim is in risk and quantitative modeling. Since I was a teenager, I have been supporting myself by taking risk, engaged with other professional risk takers, and thinking hard about quantitative risk. For the past 20 years I have issued daily quantitative predictions that no one has bet against successfully. I have seen some of the highest-IQ people in the world develop quantitative models with unlimited budgets, and have tested those models against objective reality. I know what works and what doesn't. I have presented my views in any open forum in which I could get attention, and debated with anyone who held contrary views.

I think that makes me with respect to finance and economics like a guy who set point spreads in Las Vegas successfully for many years and also was a successful independent bettor with respect to sports. The guy may not know how to play the sport or have any understanding of the game. You wouldn't necessarily accept his opinion about how the game should be played. But if he tells you the NBA basketball New York Knicks have a 60 percent chance of making the playoffs, you should pay attention. In fact, unless you have similar expertise or inside information, you can't have any good reason to doubt him—unless you think he's lying about either his expertise or his assessment of the odds. So on the direct topics of risk and quantitative modeling, if you don't believe me, you're calling me a liar. That's okay. I'm not touchy. But if you do that, don't delude yourself that you have refuted my argument. It's like contradicting the evidence of an eyewitness. You're not arguing with the witness; you're calling her a liar.

On the other hand, when I write about political or religious or other implications of what I know, I'm going beyond my direct observation and entering the realm of speculation. You have every right to yell out, "Objection, your honor—that calls for speculation." The judge will sustain you. However, since we're not in a court of law, I prefer to keep the speculations in, but to offer this section as a disclaimer so you can weigh my views before considering my claims.

I postponed this defense until this point of the book because I had to introduce enough concepts to explain my views. With respect to government, my personal golden rule is what I think defines humans: "If it's worth fighting about, share it." That may sound like a violent creed, but it's actually the rule that minimizes violence. Pacifism doesn't work, because not everyone's a pacifist. Also, I believe there are some things worth fighting for. Trying to get everyone to submit to a rule of law requires horrendous violence on the part of the government, and not even the most ruthlessly repressive organizations on earth succeeded in getting everyone to go along. The gentlest regimes do much better, but not well enough for me.

Your first thought might be: "What about the people who won't share and are willing to fight?" They are no problem at all. They are the libertarians. You leave them alone; they take care of themselves. They can be self-sufficient, self-defending hermits if they like; or they can join society under a social contract they accept voluntarily.

You have a problem only if you try to force them to do things, or if you feel the need to protect them.

The problem is the free riders, the people who won't share and won't fight. The solution is hard but obvious. You have to make them share. They'll scream about it, but they won't fight. If they get mad enough to fight, they go into the first category, they become libertarians. Then they no longer have to share, but they have no claim on anyone's protection, nor is anyone required to share with them.

The people who will share and will fight are very important. They get to run things for all the people who will share and won't fight. This is my idea of government. There are many overlapping informal networks and formal organizations that provide this service. Each one makes the rules for sharing among its constituents, and organizes whatever internal and external violence is necessary to enforce its rules and defend its members. The good ones organize sharing in a way that makes people happy and encourages productivity, innovation, and growth, while minimizing violence. The bad ones take everything for the leaders and practice extreme violence on their constituents and other organizations. When there are good ones around, life is very pleasant. When there are bad ones around, it's not my problem unless they want to force me to join or they interfere with my life, liberty, and pursuit of happiness. I'm all for free competition and may the best systems win.

In my view, the problem is not the bad systems, whether they be gangs, cults, terrorists, or governments. Such things have always been around, and I have faith that the good systems win out in the end. The problem is when governments get involved with religion or money.

I see religion as the organized expression of gift exchange, just as governments are the organized expression of involuntary exchange. When the government goes beyond enforcing the sharing necessary to minimize fighting to enforcing sharing based on ideology, things begin to break down. It doesn't matter whether the ideology is nice (take care of everyone) or naughty (take everything for the top people) or mystic (support the priests and sacrifice to the gods). When governments try to do good, as opposed to trying to prevent fighting, it always results in doing bad and increasing fighting. Note that I'm not denying the good in helping others. I'm denying the good in forcing some others to help other others. And I'm not making a moral point; I believe it is impossible to force some others to help other others. You end up helping no one and causing fights.

That means I agree with libertarians that the government should stay out of disaster relief, charity, and offensive wars, among other things. Those things are far better left to voluntary groups. All voluntary groups fall under "religion" to me, as they operate by gift exchange. Also, the government should avoid telling people what to write, say, think, do, wear, buy, sell, or ingest; it should restrict itself to telling people what to share and not to fight.

Where I part company with libertarians is I have no problem with high taxes and lots of social services. I think it takes a lot of sharing to avoid fighting. I think universal public education is the cheapest method of reducing violence ever invented. It doesn't bother me that some people take advantage of the system to be lazy. I'm lazy myself. As long as there are enough goods and services that people aren't at each other's throats, that's enough for me. I have particular scorn for libertarians who want the government to fund massive police and military services to protect them and their goods, but to spend nothing on social services because the recipients "don't deserve" the benefits. Why should any government protect some citizens from fighting, but not make them share with anyone else?

I get accused of being a coward, of giving in to blackmail and terrorism. I am a coward in the sense that I wouldn't like to fight, and I'd rather share a lot of stuff than do it. There is a limit. I wouldn't give up everything to avoid a fight, but I don't consider current U.S. tax laws as being anywhere near that limit (some of the stupider regulations come closer, but so far I've been satisfied to ignore them rather than fight them). And I don't mind rewarding people for being willing to fight; that's the only way to see if they really think they deserve something. The problem with terrorists isn't that they want something and are willing to commit violence if they don't get it; that's really pretty much everyone—we just differ in how much we have to want something before resorting to violence, or perhaps in how much we want things. The problem with terrorists (some of them, anyway) is that what they want is unreasonable and even if you gave it to them the violence wouldn't stop. It's not enough for you to be willing to fight; before I'll share with you I have to know that you will share in return, and not fight.

Both governments and religions get into trouble whenever they deal with money. Both should stay out of it completely. Governments should not monopolize the money business, should not borrow or lend, and should not try to regulate the economy. It always leads to inefficiency, corruption, and cronyism. Governments are never honest with money, and honesty is a prerequisite for business. Seriously. I don't mind high taxes, but they should not support a big government. They should be collected and spent as locally as possible, with the government only setting the rules, not making the collections or administering the outlays. Money is just as corrosive to religion.

As far as religion goes, I think it's important to have a clear strategy for dealing with those things that require faith. I don't care if you're an atheist or a traditional believer or anything in between. You pays your money and you takes your chance. We all have one life and can wager it as we please. But if you have vague and sloppy beliefs, or claim to believe one thing but act in another way, or just don't like to think about it, I think you should stay away from risk. You can't manage earthly risks without having some idea of how they fit into a cosmic scheme, any more than you could manage the department of a business without knowing what the company does.

That takes care of the organized and ancient types of exchange: involuntary and gift. I understand that the two remaining forms of exchange, equal value and gambling, seem more pedestrian than the glory of involuntary exchange and the human value of gift exchange. But trade and gambling are what separate humans from all other known species and the forms of exchange that require no organization to enforce. Traders are the ones who forge links among strangers and are the first to share and the last to fight. Equal-value exchange underlies technological and social progress. Gambling is important as well, for innovation and growth. That's why I am spending my life in those arenas.

So that's how I feel. It doesn't matter whether you agree. This is a book about risk, not about government or religion. I offer the section only to disclose sources of possible bias. Now let's get on with the history of Wall Street.

9

The Secret History of Wall Street: 1983–1987

At the end of our last episode, we had the rocket scientists arriving on Wall Street to make their fortunes. One hurdle we had to overcome was the idea of efficient markets, which was the dominant academic theory of finance at the time. The idea remains widely misunderstood, mainly because few people bother to read what efficient markets theorists actually write.

Even among professionals who read the literature, you find a lot of evasiveness and confusion about market efficiency. Someone who can't give you a clear answer about whether they believe markets are efficient—or if inefficient, the precise flavor of the inefficiency—cannot manage risk. A typical answer, like "Well, markets are pretty efficient, but I think I can exploit a few small inefficiencies on the margin," is not helpful. It says that markets are inefficient but the speaker is too timid to say it out loud. The speaker is claiming an ability to beat the market in unspecified ways. The only thing he is clear about is that his successes will not be large or important, and this is precisely the point on which we will agree with him. His failures, however, are likely to be huge. The timid, fuzzy attitude displayed in that quote is the opposite of red-blooded risk taking.

On top of this, that statement robs investment management of any possible social value or even significance. That's not a small point. Anything done only for the money will attract the worst people, who will do it in the worst way until it becomes a pure social evil. This is what people mean when they call bankers "greedy." Of course bankers are greedy; everyone is greedy. And finance would be a strange career choice for someone without an above-average interest in money. The sin is to be interested *only* in money.

If you ask the timid soul above what value his financial activities have, he is likely to reply that he makes the economy more efficient, again in small and unspecified ways. I do not believe that is generally true. The analogy I use is the Earth. If it were reduced to the size of a basketball, it would be smoother than a billiard ball. However, at a human scale, there are mountains and oceans we can exploit. Similarly, markets are efficient for large portfolios over long periods of time, but there are inefficiencies and disequilibria we can exploit at smaller scales.

The guy talking about making markets more efficient is thinking of something like rolling rocks down a mountain to power useful work. This indeed makes the Earth smoother, wearing down mountains and filling in oceans. But there's no reason to believe that's a good thing and also it bears no resemblance to what people really do. They're more likely to build a hydroelectric dam that holds water back, that is it keeps the system farther from equilibrium, not moves it closer. The value of the construction has to be the useful work done with the electricity it generates, not its effect on the smoothness of the Earth. Similarly, in finance, the main value of transactions is the profit they produce and the good that is done with that profit, not their effect on the overall economy. Most people think the opposite, that financial profits are a tax extracted from useful economic work (I don't understand how such people can work in finance).

Financial activity is as likely to move the market farther from equilibrium as closer to it, and there's no reason outside the most wildly oversimplified and unverified theories to think closer to equilibrium or more efficient is good. To carry the analogy further, a river will be exploited by lots of people with different beliefs and goals. Some will want to irrigate with the water, others will sail on it, still others will use its power to do work. Some will drink from it, others will dump waste, still others value it for recreation. If these activities are uncoordinated, there will be a disaster sooner or later: unexpectedly large or small flows, a dam or levee bursting, an emission that changes the chemistry or biology of the water. This disaster will likely harm all river users because each of them will have optimized for the previous conditions. However, in an objective sense there's no reason to think the river is better or worse for the disaster, it's just different.

Therefore, another social value of finance is in coordinating exploitative activities and designing things that can withstand disasters caused by others. That requires understanding how other financial players are making money and thinking ahead about potential conflicts. Economic efficiency is created mostly by actors in the real economy, and by self-organizing behavior that needs no Wall Street help. Finance is just another business, to be evaluated by how much it improves things for customers, what resources it consumes and the quality of jobs and quantity of profit it creates. It has no mystical value like "making the economy more efficient" and a person who makes that his justification for a huge paycheck is likely looking for an excuse, not a reason.

Efficient Markets

There is a persistent myth about efficient markets theory. It holds that ivory-tower academics invented it because it fit their simple concept of the world, and from time immemorial these academics have enforced it as an orthodoxy on practitioners who knew better and students who did not. The truth is different. Until the 1950s, almost no one believed in efficient markets, on campus or off. It was taken as obvious that professional investors knew much more than average investors, and both knew much more than monkeys throwing darts at the stock quotation page of a newspaper (younger readers can substitute monkeys pushing random keys at finance. Yahoo.com).

But then some professors and graduate students started checking. A few maverick practitioners had done this earlier, but without attracting much attention. The evidence started as a trickle but turned into a flood. Professional investors did no better than random selections, before tacking on their fees and running up expenses. They even seemed to do a bit worse, because they all bought the same things, forcing up the prices, and they all sold at the same time. Although each year some professionals did beat the market, the ones who did were no more likely than anyone else to beat the market the next year. And investors did worse than the reported fund results, because on average they got in when the market was high and out when the market was low. Published theories of how to invest stood up no better. Once you stripped them of mystic jargon, they were as reliable as horoscopes.

This is one gigantic body of evidence that has never been refuted. You can argue that some investors beat the market; in fact I will. But you can't argue that the average professional investor beats the market, nor that the total amount of money available from beating the market is significant compared to the total value of securities. In fact, it's clear that the total fees charged for investment management services far exceed the maximum potential excess profit from beating the market. Inefficiencies can make a lot of people very rich, but if the profit were spread around equally it wouldn't raise the average return by much.

Investors as a whole would be better off if everyone invested in index funds and no one tried to beat the market. Of course, we'd all be better off, and be better people, if we shared everything else equally, too. And in both cases, the gains would be short-lived. Index funds would deteriorate in quality without active investors to monitor value, and people would produce much less if they had to share their entire work product.

On top of the empirical evidence for efficient markets, there is a logical point. The sum of all investors' returns before fees and expenses is the market return. If someone makes more, someone must make less. This turns out to be more complicated than it seems. It works only if you assume everyone has the same numeraire, and that is not true. Chapter 18 goes into more detail about that. Notwithstanding the numeraire considerations, the accounting identity that the sum of all investors' holdings is the market portfolio puts a strong restriction on theories that include market inefficiencies.

Next, academics turned to studying trading strategies that hadn't been published. What if you bought every company after a good earnings announcement, or after a dividend increase, or after a new CEO came on board? What if you bought only small companies, or big companies, or companies in growing industries? Time after time it turned out that the market had priced things very precisely, so the average risk-adjusted return on these strategies was the same.

However, it's very important to understand that all of this evidence—by necessity—dealt with averaging large numbers of transactions over long periods of time. The market could look efficient in these tests and still have lots of individual transactions that were attractive—that a smart investor could discover and use to beat the market. No statistical test could prove that attractive opportunities don't exist, a point that was well understood by efficient markets workers. The statistical resolution of the tests is important. While studies differed depending on the market studied and the amount of data available, a typical study might show that prices were efficient within 0.1 percent. That's pretty impressive accuracy, given the volatility of security prices and the uncertainty of the future. But there are on the order of $100 trillion of securities to purchase, so 0.1 percent is $100 billion. That might not be enough to change your fundamental theory of economics, but it's enough to be worth trying to get.

On a more theoretical level, the studies gathered data on the frequency of occurrences in the past. There are some subtle assumptions described in Chapter 18 to go from that to a reliable degree of belief about the future. By delving deeply into those assumptions, you can discover other market-beating techniques.

Anomalies

It is true that when academics began testing strategies systematically instead of testing conventional investment advice, some anomalies turned up. Small companies did do better than standard academic theory predicted relative to large ones. Stocks that had recently gone up tended to continue up. Companies that were cheap relative to earnings and assets were better buys than expensive companies. Stocks that had either low volatility or low correlation with the market did a bit better than expected. None of these results were suppressed or ignored, but even collectively they amount to a tiny portion of total asset returns. None of these results, or anything comparable, was ever produced by someone who didn't start from the assumption of efficient markets. Only careful quantitative work starting from a clear theoretical perspective was precise enough to discover these anomalies. People who start from the assumption that prices are irrational can explain every price as "someone was stupid." If you explain everything, you explain nothing, and, worse, you never learn.

It is true that researchers tried hard to poke holes in the anomalies that popped up. That's not blind adherence to theory over reality; it's intellectual honesty. You don't know something is true until you've tried hard to falsify it, and failed. Theoreticians struggled to find efficient market explanations for anomalies. Arguably, the academic community was slow to accept their reality. In 1980, the evidence for persistent major anomalies was accepted as refuting efficient markets by maybe 25 percent of finance professors, with perhaps another 25 percent who never accepted efficient markets in the first place. By 1995, about 95 percent of finance professors had accepted the reality of anomalies. In contrast, the serious quants who left business schools to work in finance had almost all rejected efficient markets by 1980, but of course belief in market inefficiency was one reason they left academics. I don't see this as academics being too slow, or as practicing quants having foresight. The world needs both careful people and reckless experimenters. Some of the experimenters are always going to get places ahead of the careful people. That doesn't mean experimenters are smarter than anyone else; it just means if enough reckless people try enough things, some of them will get lucky.

From 1950 to 1970, almost everyone ignored the academic evidence that markets were far more efficient than anyone had ever imagined. When the evidence got overwhelming, some commentators switched overnight to the claim that efficient markets was a dogma enforced by powerful professors for years, and only said commentator was smart and brave enough to expose the myth. None of these smart and brave commentators, of course, ever refuted efficient markets by actually beating the market, or by predicting ahead of time who would beat the market, or, frankly, even by offering a coherent alternative to market efficiency. There were serious critics of efficient markets with coherent alternatives and empirical evidence. But serious critics weren't the people screaming that an efficient markets mafia was persecuting them.

Unfortunately, most people get their ideas of efficient markets from the loudmouth critics. One version is that efficient markets theory claims every investor is well informed and rational. In fact, the theory has nothing to do with how investors think or behave. There are people who worry about that—they're called "psychologists." Behavioral finance is a field that combines psychology with theories of investment. But none of the efficient markets studies were based on interviewing or observing investors. Researchers studied price movements instead. Prices can be rational and efficient even if most, or all, investors are ignorant and irrational. Efficient markets is a theory about price movements, not about investors.

The Price Is Right . . . Not!

Another misrepresentation is that efficient markets means the market price is always right. That's absurd. Of course prices aren't always right. If they were, they wouldn't change. Any idiot can see security prices change, and in fact change far more than economic fundamentals do. While the technical definitions get complicated, a simple formulation of the efficient markets hypothesis is that the market price is right on average. That may seem like a small thing, but it's much better than human experts can claim.

Therefore, if the price of oil today is $100 per barrel, that price is not necessarily wise or good, and it certainly doesn't have to be fair. What is true is that it's darn hard to make money consistently either buying at $100 or selling at $100. Where people go astray is to make long chains of reasoning starting from the assumption that $100 is the correct price in some sense. Or, if they're quants, they do the same thing by putting $100 as a model input and generating some complex output as a result. While the $100 is likely to be right on average, the average prediction based on $100 being exactly right will be exactly wrong.

If this distinction seems subtle, consider two examples. The first one is purely mathematical. I have two unbalanced coins; one has a 10 percent chance of flipping heads, and one has a 90 percent chance. I pick one of them at random and offer a security that pays $100 if the next flip of that coin is heads. The market prices it at $50, because half the time the coin will come up heads. That is, half the time I'll have the 90 percent coin and half the time I'll have the 10 percent coin. If I flip 20 times, on average 10 flips will be the 90 percent coin, and nine of them will be heads. Ten flips will be the 10 percent coin, and one of them will be heads. That's 9 + 1 = 10 heads expected out of 20 flips, so there's a 50 percent chance of heads.

Now someone figures, "If the probability of heads is 50 percent, the probability of two heads in a row must be 50 percent times 50 percent equals 25 percent. So I'll sell securities for $25 that pay $100 if there are two heads in a row." This person will lose a lot of money, because the coin will come up heads twice in a row 41 percent of the time. To see that, suppose I pick one of the two coins at random and flip it twice, then repeat the experiment 200 times.

On average, 100 pairs of flips will be with the 90 percent coin; 90 percent times 90 percent equals 81 percent, so 81 percent of them will be two heads. That's 81 heads. The other 100 flips will be with the 10 percent coin. Ten percent times 10 percent equals 1 percent, so 1 percent of them will be two heads. That's a total of $81 + 1 = 82$ sets out of 200 with two heads, or 41 percent of the time. The original market price of $50 for one head was right on average, but the computation erred by assuming it was right exactly.

As a practical example, suppose a company with 100 million shares outstanding announces it has signed a major contract. The stock price goes up $0.25 per share immediately upon the announcement. So the market seems to be saying the deal is worth $25 million to shareholders. But now the other party to the contract wants to back out, and offers a $30 million breakup fee. That would seem to be a good deal, if you believe the market is exactly right. But the market is only right on average. The contract might be worth $25 million or $100 million or negative $100 million. The fact that the other company is willing to pay $30 million to cancel it suggests it might be worth more than $25 million. In any event, company management would be crazy to use the market estimate of the price as an input to their decision. Over 1,000 contracts signed by 1,000 companies, the market is likely to predict the average value pretty well. Over one contract with one company, management has much better information than the market's opinion.

Efficient markets theory is an essential tool for identifying market inefficiencies. If you just go out and look for ideas that seem good, like buy stocks in well-run companies or buy commodities for which there seems to be rising demand and falling supply, you lose. If you look for ideas that worked well in the past, you also lose. There is an infinite number of rules that would have worked in the past, because there is an infinite number of potential rules. You can always find lots that seem to work great—it's called data mining. Finding ideas that will work in the future requires theory.

Efficiency versus Equilibrium

A crucial point in interpreting tests of efficient markets theory was described by Eugene Fama, known as the father of efficient markets: "Every test of market efficiency is a joint test of market efficiency and market equilibrium." In simpler words, you can't test whether the market is doing what it is supposed to do without first specifying what it is supposed to do. That's true for testing markets, but not for exploiting markets. Suppose you see something sell at $80 that you think should be worth $100. If markets are in equilibrium but inefficient, you can buy at $80 and make profits. If markets are efficient but out of equilibrium, you might not be able to buy more at $80, and anyway $80 is the correct price given current market structure. In this case, you figure out why people are selling at $20 less than your estimate of economic value and find a way to accommodate their needs for less than $20. These are entirely different strategies for exploiting the same apparent mispricing.

It was the frequentists, the blackjack card counters, who adopted the idea that markets are inefficient, but always in equilibrium. Prices can be wrong in an economic sense, too high or too low, but you can buy or sell as much as you want at the posted price. In that case, you make money by computing the correct price for securities. You don't worry who is on the other side of the transaction. You're transacting with some abstract thing called the "market," just as an advantage gambler is playing against the "house," not any individual. You buy the cheap securities and short the expensive ones ("short" means you bet that the price will go down). You balance your long and short portfolio so you are hedged against any general market move.

If you lose money, it can only be because prices got even more inefficient than when you bought. In that case your position is more attractive and you should add to it. Your job is to teach the market, not to learn from it. Although you profit from market inefficiency, you hate it. That's a deep emotional response. You don't want to live in a universe of messy error; you want to live in one of clean, perfect mathematical beauty. Since you don't, all you can do is try to create a more perfect universe. In addition, you have the practical consideration that when the market gets more inefficient you lose money, and when it gets more efficient you make money.

Socially, you can be a loner. You're not interested in other people's opinions, since those are what made the market inefficient in the first place. When you read something, your first impulse is to bet the opposite. If irrational people think something, they mess up the perfect, beautiful market with the wrong prices. Since you're always right, you cannot lose in the long run. Only people—specifically lenders, counterparties, investors, and regulators—can cause you to lose by terminating your positions at a loss just when they are most attractive. Your absolute worst enemies are the fellow frequentist investors who lose the faith, selling out at the worst time. These are the only people who can hit you exactly where it hurts, pushing up the price of your shorts at the same time as pushing down the price of your longs. Moreover, they reduce the trust everyone has in your strategy, which causes you more problems with lenders, counterparties, investors, and regulators. You would prefer to bet only your own money, to have no leverage or outside investors, and to use only perfect counterparties who never default or change the rules, in a totally unregulated market, running a strategy that only you have discovered and that you will take to your grave. In summary, you hate inefficiency and the people who cause it more than you love money.

A good example of a frequentist strategy is dual-class share arbitrage. Some companies have more than one class of common stock. This might come about because when the company first went public, the owner wanted to keep control either for himself or for a tight circle of insiders or family members. So he created two classes of common stock, nine million shares of Class A to be sold to the public, and one million shares of Class B that he kept for himself and trusted allies. The shares have equal financial claims on the company. Dividends must be equal in the two classes. But Class A shares get one vote in corporate elections and Class B shares get 10 votes. If the Class B shareholders stick together, they always represent a majority of the votes.

Over time, some of the Class B shares trickled out of the insider circle. Although they have superior rights, they actually sell at a slightly lower price than Class A shares because they are less liquid. Suppose it happens that Class A sells for $51 per share and Class B sells for $49 per share. You spend $4.9 million to buy 100,000 shares of Class B, and then have your broker locate and borrow 100,000 shares of Class A, which you sell for $5.1 million. You have a $200,000 profit. You own 100,000 shares of Class B stock, and owe your broker 100,000 shares of Class A stock. Your stock position nets to zero for most purposes. If the stock pays a dividend, you receive money for your Class B shares, but you have to pay it out to the owner of the Class A shares you borrowed and sold. Most of the time, if the price of Class B stock moves up or down, the price of Class A stock moves up or down the same amount, so there's no change to the value of your account.

You cannot, however, take your $200,000 profit out in cash. Your broker requires you to post margin on both the long and the short. Suppose the margin requirement is 10 percent of market value. You have to post $490,000 on your long Class B position plus $510,000 on your short Class A position. That's $1,000,000 you have to post. Your $200,000 profit is already in your account, so you have to write a check for $800,000. As long as the price difference between Class A and Class B stays at $2 per share, you have written a check for $800,000 but are collecting interest on the $1,000,000 margin deposited with your broker. You get 1.25 times the normal rate of interest.

That may seem like a small advantage, but out of such small advantages mighty fortunes are built. You have some upside as well. If there is a contested corporate election, the Class B shares suddenly become valuable, more valuable than the Class A. The price of Class B might jump to $55 while the Class A shares stay at $51. Now you can sell your Class B for $5.5 million, and cover your Class A short for $5.1 million. Your $1.0 million margin posted with your broker swelled to $1.4 million. And since you have no more stock positions, you can withdraw it in cash. Remember, you only wrote a check for $800,000 in the first place, so you have a $600,000 profit. The day after the election date of record, the prices will probably fall back to their old relationship, so you can put your position back on again.

Beating the Market

This is not the kind of thing most people have in mind when they think of "beating" the market. The idea is staggeringly simple and obvious. Execution requires meticulous care, not swaggering courage or penetrating brilliance. You have to read all the legal documents very carefully to make sure there is no circumstance in which the Class A shares are worth more than the Class B shares. For example, the company may have adopted a poison pill that requires Class A shares, but not Class B shares, to be paid a $100 per share special dividend if anyone acquires more than 15 percent of the company without the board's approval. Not all dual-class share situations involve differential voting rights; there are many varieties of deals, each with its own idiosyncratic features and pitfalls. You have to negotiate good margin terms, as well as a good interest rate on the margin balance. You have to be very careful about expenses, both brokerage fees and the bid-ask spread on security prices. Your reward is not overnight riches, but a slightly better rate of interest and an occasional small windfall.

There is a risk to this strategy, but from the point of view of a blackjack card counter, it comes from weak and foolish people, not economics. Suppose the spread between Class A and Class B stocks widens. Say Class A goes up to $53 while Class B stays at $49. You have lost $200,000 on your short and made no profit on your long. Your margin balance falls to $800,000. Your broker now wants $1,020,000 margin instead of $1,000,000, so you have to write another check, this time for $220,000. Your interest advantage has disappeared; you deposited $1,020,000 and are earning interest on the same figure. If the difference between the share prices widens further, you will be earning interest on less than the amount you deposited.

A weak person—or someone our frequentist would call weak—would close out the position at this point. After all, he's not making any money and things might get worse. But to a true believer, this is insane. The position is twice as attractive as it used to be. Yes, you've taken a mark-to-market loss, but that's money spent. You won't get it back by exiting the position. You should now double your bet.

In the disaster scenario, dual-class share arbitrage investors start exiting the position. That means they buy Class A shares and sell Class B shares. That pushes the spread even wider, requiring you to write bigger checks to your broker without earning any more interest on your margin balance. You have to report losses to your investors. Your broker gets nervous about both the strategy and your financial health, so he raises the margin requirement from 10 percent to 20 percent. You have to write even bigger checks. The more this happens, the more people pull out and the more pressure you get from your investors. If they are not locked up, your investors may even pull their money out. This leads to more demands from your broker for additional security; perhaps eventually he will insist on 100 percent margin. If you can't come up with that, the broker will liquidate your positions for you. You could end up being that unfortunate investor, the one with "the strongest weak hands." That's the investor who endures the most pain without being able to hold on for the turnaround. The weaker hands get out earlier at smaller losses, and the stronger hands reap the profits of staying the course.

This is the world of frequentists/card counters/believers in market equilibrium but not efficiency. There are many other arbitrages they exploit. I should emphasize that I'm describing an ideal type, even a caricature. Not every frequentist counts cards, and not every card counter believes in market equilibrium and inefficiency. Not everyone of this type is antisocial or hates imperfection. Nevertheless, the stereotype is rooted in observation and is useful for distinguishing different types of quants.

Dual-class share arbitrage is also practiced by the opposite camp, the degree-of-belief/sports bettors/believers in market efficiency but not equilibrium, but from an entirely different perspective. This group calls dual-class share arbitrage a *convergence trade*. They short Class A and buy Class B in the belief the spread will narrow or, as in the case of a contested election, reverse, so Class A sells for less than Class B. Of course, they read the documents carefully and negotiate good terms, but they are not as obsessive about it as the frequentist camp. They spend more energy looking at the history of the spread movements so they can guess the future. Unlike the frequentists, they care who is on the other side of the transaction. They don't believe in an abstract "market," they are betting with people and understanding those people is more important than understanding the bet. Sports bettors want to get in when the spread is wide, and out when it is narrow or negative. They are looking for larger, shorter-term profits than the card counters. They might even reverse the bet and buy Class A while shorting Class B, even if Class A is more expensive, because they are confident the spread will widen in the future.

Although they may be in the same trade, the card counters and sports bettors are betting on opposite things. The card counters have faith in the market, and fear the actions of people. The sports bettors are relying on the predictable actions of people to move the spread a certain way, and fear the market forces that might disrupt historical patterns.

Dual-class share arbitrage is not a prime example of a trade favored by people who believe in market efficiency but not equilibrium. From this perspective, the problem is not to find mispriced assets, but to find places where transactions are not taking place, or taking place away from the market price. For example, in many markets prices have momentum. Securities that recently went up in price tend to continue up; securities that recently went down in price continue to go down. The market knows what the right price is, but cannot get there right away.

There are many variants of momentum trading; the best known is called *managed futures*. It acquired this name because the strategy was first perfected by commodity futures traders, but it is applied today in all liquid asset classes. People disagree about why momentum exists, but it is much easier to explain as a disequilibrium than as a market inefficiency. The simplest story concerns the way information flows into market prices.

Suppose there is a cold snap in the northeast United States in February. As a result, crude oil refineries delay ramping up the production of gasoline in order to produce more heating oil. Spring gasoline stocks will be lower than usual. Gasoline prices at the pump will go up until production catches up sometime after Memorial Day. Crude oil prices, however, will be affected less. The cold snap creates additional demand for crude oil but it is negligible compared to total world supply, and people increase the supply of oil quickly in response to a small price increase. Refinery capacity, by contrast, is fixed in the short run; and the additional heating oil represents a much bigger fraction of available refining capacity than world crude oil. Therefore, the gasoline crack spread, the difference between gasoline and crude oil prices, will widen for May delivery and earlier.

Without any sort of financial markets, there would be a steady increase in the gasoline crack spread from February to early June, then a steady decrease back to normal. With perfect financial markets, the effect would occur suddenly in February, with futures delivery contracts for all months immediately adjusted to the new expected prices. In the real world something more complex happens. A few specialist fundamental investors notice the news first. They rush in to buy gasoline futures and short crude futures in the appropriate months. This begins before the cold snap actually occurs; these investors will trade on predictions.

Remember that the crack spread is affected by many economic factors. Predicting the cold snap means you have a positive expected value bet if you go long the spread, but it is still a bet. Fundamental investors who live by predicting the weather necessarily have undiversified portfolios and high costs of capital.

They cannot afford to stay in positions until market equilibrium is reached. Once most of the move has occurred, the remaining positive expected value is too small relative to the risk. The specialist investors will remove their capital to deploy it in what are now more attractive opportunities.

Over time, the news becomes more obvious. The cold snap occurs. The production decisions are changed. Gasoline stocks decline. By this time most of the news has been incorporated into prices. The remaining portion is swamped by many other more recent events, so it's hard to tell how much reaction is left. It may be true that everyone knows the news, but no one knows how much the price has already changed to reflect it. It's even possible there has been overreaction and the smart bet is now that the crack spread will narrow. The market knows what the correct price is, but it can't get there. The necessary information is dispersed among many different types of investors with different information sets, and it is too expensive to extract that information.

The same story can be told for every individual piece of news. There's no practical way to know which pieces have been fully incorporated into the price, and which ones have not. However, on a statistical basis, it's usually a good bet that the average bit of news has not been fully incorporated. Therefore, if the net direction of the crack spread over the last month has been up, there has been more good news than bad, so it's more likely than not that there is net positive information—information that should push the price up—not yet incorporated into the price.

What this story fails to explain is why smart investors have not already removed this effect by trading on it. There are many suggestions about that. Whether you accept them or not, it is indisputably true that when prices have gone up recently, they tend to continue up. Exploiting this effect requires careful analysis of each market to know what period to measure momentum over and to learn if there are other signals that help manage the strategy. For example, in my line change strategy in sports betting, the first thing I noticed was that line changes early in the week were usually news and were underreactions so the smart play was to bet with them, whereas changes Friday evening and later were usually driven by uninformed bettors altering the supply and demand. Those changes were good to bet against. Similarly, with gasoline crack spreads, momentum might work best certain times of year, or in certain situations.

Paths

Most of the rocket scientists on Wall Street in the 1980s went down one of these two paths, just as most of the quant gamblers I knew in the 1970s split into card counters or sports bettors. The frequentists who believed in market equilibrium formed small hedge funds, often single-manager funds. They shunned publicity and courted investors only to the minimum extent necessary to get started. They refused more investors than they accepted. As soon as possible they limited the outside investors to those who had proven long-term loyalty, or even converted to investing only their own and employees' money. They were intensely secretive, sharing information only with like-minded investors. Whatever information they needed for executing their strategies they got from documents and direct observation; they hated depending on people and reflexively bet against opinions—even their own untutored beliefs. They were happiest buying when their intuition said to sell.

The degree-of-belief probabilists who believe in market efficiency found comfortable homes in investment bank trading desks. If they formed hedge funds, they were big ones that catered to outside investors. Like the sports bettors, they wanted to work in or to run a business, not to make money as independent bettors. They were open about their approaches, which is necessary in big institutions and also necessary to raise large amounts of money. They relied on personal information networks to run strategies.

Sports-bettor types did not restrict themselves to trading and investment management. Some disequilibriums cannot be exploited by buying and selling securities. The biggest example in the 1980s was mortgage securities. The Government National Mortgage Association (GNMA) issued securities backed by 30-year fixed-rate home mortgages issued under Veterans Administration or Federal Housing Authority programs. These were backed by the full faith and credit of the U.S. government, which in those days was considered as low-risk as you could get. These securities paid significantly higher interest rates than government Treasury bonds.

Part of the reason for the additional yield spread was that Treasury bonds are redeemed at a fixed, known maturity. GNMAs were redeemed as homeowners repaid their mortgages (or defaulted on them, in which case the security holder was paid from proceeds of the foreclosure sale or by the government).

Mortgages paid off on average in about seven years, one way or the other. Some people pay off their mortgages early because times are good, but most of the repayments occur when someone moves or refinances a home. The problem for the security holder was not just uncertainty. There was adverse selection. If interest rates went down, lots of people would refinance at the lower rates, and the security holders would get back money they had to reinvest at the new lower rates. But if interest rates went up, few people would refinance, and the security holders would get back less than the expected cash flows, at a time when they wanted to take advantage of the higher rates.

Prepayment risk was much too small to justify the yield difference. It was possible to trade GNMAs actively, along with bond futures and options, to lock in highly predictable profits. At the time we called this a *statistical arbitrage*. An arbitrage is a trade with no risk and positive profit. A statistical arbitrage is a trade with controllable risk that is much smaller than the expected positive profit. A good example is a roulette wheel from the standpoint of a casino. Today, however, the term *stat arb* has been taken over by a group of strategies descended from pairs trading.

One of the things I was doing at the time was running such an active GNMA portfolio. But along with a lot of other people, I saw that the real opportunity was to issue securities that mimicked the strategy. It was a question of size and spread. I had to crisscross the country making presentations to raise less than $200 million for my strategy, and 80 percent of the profits went to the investors. The strategy profit margin was about 4 percent of invested capital above the rate on short-term Treasury bills. That's $8 million of excess profit, of which the firm I was working for—Lepercq de Neuflize—kept 20 percent or $1.6 million. There was a management fee as well, but that was used for expenses.

Suppose instead you could divide the cash flows from the GNMAs in a clever way to back a number of different securities with limited prepayment risk. Some investors like certainty, and would accept a yield a few basis points above Treasuries to get highly predictable cash flows. Some of them want the cash flows soon, whereas others want the money put to work for longer periods of time. Other investors don't care when they get their money back as long as they make a good return. It was possible to set up rules for distributing cash that kept all these people happy. You made the same 4 percent per year, but you could keep 80 percent instead of 20 percent. And you could sell a billion dollars' worth of securities more easily than you could raise $10 million of money to invest. This is the same insight that makes issuing exchange-traded funds (ETFs) a better business than running open-end mutual funds.

Doing things this way moved the market closer to equilibrium. The fair price of the GNMAs had always been higher than what the government sold them for, which meant homeowners were paying higher interest on their mortgages than economics would dictate. Investors did not really benefit from the higher yields, because they weren't able to use the securities efficiently. It was expensive to arbitrage the difference away in the money management business. The securities issuance business, in contrast, could smash through the institutional and informational barriers.

Fortunately for me, my employer at the time, Lepercq de Neuflize, was both a securities broker-dealer and a hedge fund. That meant I could perfect my ideas using real money from investors and move seamlessly into the securities issuance business. There was a host of legal and regulatory issues to resolve, but there was enough money at stake to make it worth people's whiles to resolve them. Salomon Brothers issued the first collateralized mortgage obligation, as these new securities were called, and was the largest issuer for many years. Lepercq was not the second firm with an issue to market, but we were the second-largest issuer—for one year. Even then we were one-sixth the size of Salomon. Soon we were rounding error in Salomon's production and off the industry issuance league tables. There were good reasons for that, which I won't go into here. I will indulge a short peeve. Salomon Brothers divided the cash flows in time sequence, sending the early cash flows to one security; when that was paid off, cash flowed to the next security in line, and so forth. My first design gave only scheduled principal and interest to the early-maturity tranches, and sent all prepayments to the longest-maturity tranche. I still maintain this was a much better design and should have dominated the market. I did have a few enthusiastic early adopters, but it never caught on. In a few years people were doing much more complicated structures superior to both of these, but in the early years we were limited by both legal considerations and investor willingness to listen.

Since this is not a book on quant strategies, I will stop with these three examples. Well, make it four since I already mentioned pairs trading. In this strategy you find two similar stocks that usually trade in a similar ratio to each other, say Pfizer and Merck. Although they are competitors, most possible events affect both companies the same way. From July 1, 1983, to the end of 1985, a share of Merck sold for about 2.5 times the price of a share of Pfizer (before and after the period were stock splits, which complicate the strategy but make no essential difference). The ratio varied from a low of 2.10 to a high of 2.92. If you bought Merck and shorted Pfizer when the ratio was low and reversed the trade when the ratio was high, you made consistent money over the period. This is a strategy that has both plausible market inefficiency and plausible market disequilibrium explanations. We might believe the market has trouble valuing the two stocks, or that the market knows the correct ratio but can only slowly correct the prices to it when news comes out about one company or the other.

The essential point is that by the mid-1980s we have about 100 rocket scientists, linked in a loose network, running strategies of this sort according to Kelly principles, getting rich exponentially slowly. At this time we started seeing the first of the second generation of Wall Street quants. This is the kind who are more familiar to people today, because there are tens of thousands of them all over the world, instead of only a hundred concentrated in Manhattan. Financial pay had skyrocketed, and was tempting smart quantitative people from other fields. Moreover, reduced Cold War tensions had cut military subsidies for physics research, reducing opportunities for Western-trained quants, and would soon free thousands of Russian and Eastern European quants, and later Chinese quants.

For the most part, these new quants were not risk takers by nature. Few had spent years gambling or trading for a living. Most had no interest in finance before coming to Wall Street, and of course many had not even lived in a capitalist society. In some cases their interest started and ended with financial equations. They expected to be trained in their new duties, after which they would try to advance the state of the art through incremental improvements, all for salary and bonus. They were financial engineers, in a few cases Einsteins, not rocket scientists. They did not come to beat the Street, but to praise it.

I don't mean to overgeneralize about a large, diverse group. I am not speaking about any one individual, but the aggregate stereotype of a generation. There were old-school quants among this new group, and individualists of many stripes. It's still important to distinguish the difference, however, because the effect that the new generation of quants had on events was quite different from the effect from the old generation.

Sharpe Ratios and Wealth

Returning to the old school, the two main branches found different kinds of market opportunities, distinguished by Sharpe ratio. We're going to get a bit mathematical again, but you don't need the numbers to follow the argument. The Sharpe ratio of a strategy is defined as the return of the strategy minus what you could make investing the same capital in risk-free instruments, divided by the standard deviation of the return. It is a measure of risk-adjusted return. A strategy with an annualized Sharpe ratio of 1 will make more than the risk-free rate about five years out of six. A strategy with an annualized Sharpe ratio of 2 will make more than the risk-free rate about 39 years out of 40. However, it's hard to find Sharpe ratios near or above 1 in high-capacity, liquid strategies that are inexpensive to run.

You don't need a Sharpe ratio near or at 1 to get rich. For a Kelly investor, the long-term growth of capital above the risk-free rate is approximately equal to the Sharpe ratio squared (it's actually always higher than this, substantially so for high Sharpe ratios, but that doesn't affect the points I want to make). A Sharpe ratio of 1 means growing at 100 percent per year—that is, doubling your capital. A Sharpe ratio of 2 means growing at 400 percent per year. (For the purists, the actual figures are 173 percent and 5,360 percent.) Clearly both of those strategies will have to hit some kind of short-term limit. In fact, Sharpe ratios above one are usually meaningless; it doesn't make sense to speak about the long-term growth rate of something that can't grow at that rate for long. It makes more sense to speak of individual bets with upsides and downsides measured in dollars, not dollars per unit of investment over time.

A Sharpe ratio of 0.1 produces a 1 percent excess return; a Sharpe ratio of 0.2 gives about 4 percent; a Sharpe ratio of 0.5 gives about 25 percent. Since the high Sharpe ratio strategies have limited capacity but grow so quickly that initial investment is almost irrelevant, they are appropriate for people investing their own money. Sharpe ratios around 0.5 make good hedge fund strategies.

The lower Sharpe ratios are useful for large institutions with cheap capital and high risk tolerance.

Card counters gravitated to very high Sharpe ratio strategies. When I say these have limited capacity, I don't mean there are always opportunities to invest a small amount in them. More commonly, opportunities come up unpredictably. For that reason the strategies are sometimes referred to as "event driven." They require a lot of investment in time and money to prepare. You can make this large investment to be ready to exploit the strategy, and then wait for years during which no appropriate opportunities come up. Or some legal or institutional change can remove the opportunity forever. However, if you're lucky, there could be a run of opportunities and you're rich. You can cut down the danger by preparing several high Sharpe ratio strategies in the hope that at least one will pan out with enough opportunities. But this is an even bigger investment.

If you pursue high Sharpe ratio strategies, it is crucial to bet big when opportunities arise, but equally crucial not to lose everything on any one bet. Because card counters are the kind of people who believe in models, they tended to bet full Kelly. The trouble is that the optimal Kelly bet is highly sensitive to low-probability, large losses. If your model doesn't pick these up, and no model can, you will overbet and probably go broke.

Let's go back to our Kelly example of 100 even money bets of which you will win 60 and lose 40. We computed that you should bet 20 percent of your bankroll each time and you turn $1,000 into $7,490. Now suppose that in one of the 100 losses you will lose five times your bet, not just lose your bet; and in another you will win five times your bet. Net, that might not seem to make any difference, but now if you bet 20 percent of your bankroll each time you will go broke. That single bad outcome lowers the optimal bet to 11.6 percent of your bankroll and you will end up with only $3,513, less than half what you made without the single bad outcome.

From experience, some counters learned to bet half Kelly or some other fraction. This doesn't address the problem in real life, though. It works in the casino setting, where all possible outcomes and probabilities are known. But in finance, computing the correct bet if your model as if is perfect and then cutting it in half to allow for model uncertainty is not adequate risk management.

The sports-betting types preferred the low Sharpe ratio strategies. They would have liked higher Sharpes, of course, but by accepting low Sharpes they could find plenty of opportunities with other desirable characteristics. They could use simple strategies with liquid securities, for which there was constant large capacity for bets. They could have more strategies, and each strategy could bet more frequently, and each strategy could be individually more amenable to risk management. This kind of investing is what some people now call "quant," although it is no more inherently quantitative than are high Sharpe ratio strategies.

The trouble is that combining lots of low Sharpe ratio strategies gives you a high Sharpe ratio strategy, at least if the strategy results are not highly correlated with each other. While you are not risking much of your capital on any one bet, if a lot of bets go against you at once, you're in trouble just like an overbetting high Sharpe ratio investor. Moreover, you're counting on liquidity and good market data. If these disappear, it's bad news. The high Sharpe ratio investor didn't expect liquidity or good market data in the first place, so she's prepared when they disappear. Correlation, liquidity, and data problems are exacerbated if lots of people are following similar strategies. You don't need much overlap in positions; everyone can be running conceptually different strategies but still have large net positive and large net negative positions as a group in key securities.

The other problem is that these strategies require cooperation of many people. The growth rate is slow and the capacity is large, so it makes sense to raise outside money and take a fee rather than investing your own money. The strategies require a lot of leverage, and dealing in large size with major brokers. In these circumstances, your fate is not entirely in your hands. You may have to cut positions at the wrong time, or even close up business entirely, if other people get nervous. Most of those other people have no idea what you're doing, so no idea when to get nervous, so they get nervous a lot.

As I did with gambling, I chose a middle course. I looked for moderate-capacity strategies in semiliquid securities that could command Sharpe ratios around 0.5. These required some outside investors and dealers, but nothing like the scale of the low Sharpe ratio people. Medium Sharpe ratio strategies had some ups and downs of opportunities and were hard to manage in bad markets, but were steadier and more manageable than the high Sharpe ratio strategies.

1987

In the end, none of it made any difference. All of us were wiped out on October 19, 1987. That was the day the stock market fell nearly 25 percent, far more than it had ever fallen in one day in the past. But that was not our problem. All of us were prepared for large stock market declines. We didn't expect to see 25 percent in a day, but we knew it was possible over longer periods, and we knew financial markets sometimes move two or three times as much as they ever have in the past. It was a host of other changes that happened simultaneously that got us.

Our reaction is the subject of the next chapter. I want to end this one by conveying the sense of the times. By October 1987, rocket scientists had been on Wall Street for six or seven years. We had started as brash outsiders doing things no one had ever heard of, trying to beat the Street. We had no idea if any of this would pan out. Then we had a run of uninterrupted success. Remember, we were in our twenties. We may have had more life experience of swings of fortune than some people twice our age, but it's still hard not to let success go to your head. And I don't mean just financial success. In 1980 any form of mathematics was less likely to be understood by the average Wall Streeter than !Xoon click language. By 1987, everyone on Wall Street knew there were quants and some even had a vague idea of what we did. We were a little bit cool, and we were people who had never been remotely cool before. It was even possible to get some interest at academic seminars in your practical results.

Wall Street had been changed dramatically, and appeared to be on course to be fully renovated by 1990 or so. We had changed it to the environment we liked. Some of us, the sports-bettor/degree-of-belief/market-efficiency believers, had attained high rank in major financial institutions, or ran large pools of money. Others, the card counter/frequentist/market-equilibrium believers, had just cast off the chains of outsiders and were able to prosper investing only their own money, or at least could see their way clear to attaining that nirvana. All this had been attained by our own independent efforts, using ideas we came up with on our own, with no encouragement or help from people outside our circle. Well, as we discovered, it was really by our own efforts plus a bull market. We were neither the first nor the last to confuse brains and a bull market.

All this work and success vanished overnight. We were no longer cool; instead there was a witch hunt on to find quants to blame for the meltdown. In the end, it was mostly pinned on portfolio insurance quants from the sports-bettor camp, although suspicion persisted that some secretive card-counting hedge fund managers had engineered it.

And boy, were we excited.

This was the game we had come to play. We had pushed the market, and it had pushed back. It wiped us out, but we were alive and kicking and ready for round two. There were new secrets to uncover, new opportunities to exploit. Faux quants had run scurrying for cover, leaving the field open to us. Work to revise our models began immediately. I had forgotten how quickly that happened until I was recently asked to look up an old presentation I had given at Yale a month after the crash. It had in it almost half of the ideas that would be developed and refined over the next five years. I was by no means alone; the bulletin boards were buzzing with this kind of thing.

The burning question of the day was how to run quant strategies without blowing up, even when the market did. The answer was found by a series of accidents more than any one person's brilliance, and it contained many surprises, including resolution of the 333-year-old confusion between frequency and degree of belief. Intellectually, it was the most exciting time of my life.

CHAPTER 10

The Story of Money: The Future

The replacement for paper money was born around 1850 in the northern drainage basin of the Mississippi River, what was called at the time the Northwest United States. Boards of trade appeared in the major cities and began trading futures contracts. A futures contract is a promise by one party to buy, and a promise by the other party to sell, a specified amount and quality of some commodity at a specified future time and place, for a specified price. It has three additional defining features.

First, the amount, quality, time, and place are standardized.

Second, there are actually two contracts. Each side contracts with an institution called a clearinghouse. The clearinghouse only takes pairs of offsetting contracts. If I agree to sell you 5,000 bushels of #2 soft red winter wheat delivered on March 14 to an exchange-approved silo for $5,000, I do not actually sign a contract with you. I sign a contract to sell the wheat to the clearinghouse for $5,000, and you sign a contract to buy the wheat from the clearinghouse at that price. We each post margin, say $500, with the clearinghouse to guarantee performance. The advantage of this is I don't have to know or trust you. Also, if I later want to get out of the contract, I don't have to find you and negotiate. I can agree with anyone to buy 5,000 bushels of wheat on March 14; then we both go to the clearinghouse with our offsetting contracts. I now have two contracts with the clearinghouse, one to buy from the new party and one to sell to you, but otherwise identical, so the clearinghouse tears them both up and gives me back my margin.

Third, contracts are marked to market daily. That means if the price of wheat goes up a penny, my contract is rewritten so I have to sell 5,000 bushels of wheat for $5,050 instead of $5,000. I have to pay $50 now. My position hasn't changed; I will sell the wheat on March 14 for $5,050, which, after I deduct the $50 I had to pay the clearinghouse, is the $5,000 originally agreed. You get $50 instead. When settlement comes, you have to pay $5,050 for the 5,000 bushels, but it's okay because you collected the extra $50 earlier. You and I each get our initial margin back when the contract is settled. The point of this system is it doesn't matter if either one of us fails to show up on March 14. By that time, our contracts are written at the March 14 market price, so there's no gain or loss to the clearinghouse if we default. The difference between the settlement price and $5,000 has been paid by one of us and received by the other in daily amounts over the term of the contract. The $500 initial margin we each posted was to protect the clearinghouse if one of us failed to make a daily mark-to-market payment. If that happens, the exchange can terminate the contract at the current market price and as long as wheat hasn't moved more than $0.10 per bushel in one day, cover any losses from the $500.

Farmers and Millers

It seems that every amateur, and a shocking number of professionals, who write about futures markets start with a fairy tale about a farmer selling his wheat crop to a miller, using the futures contract to lock in a price before harvest. There were no farmers involved in setting up futures markets, and they rarely participated. When they did, they were more likely to buy crops than sell them. Moreover, farmers have always been suspicious of futures markets and frequently tried to have them shut down.

Millers, and other processors, do use futures markets, but they generally sell crops, not buy them. If you want to think of a canonical trade, consider a nineteenth-century miller who wants a secure supply of wheat so he can sign large delivery contracts with customers. Of course, he goes to a nearby grain silo that can actually deliver wheat, and contracts for the exact grade and type he wants. Similarly, a farmer who wants to sell his crop goes to a local crop buyer and contracts to sell exactly what he's growing, for delivery to a place he can get the grain to, and without a firm date he might be unable to meet. In the fairy story, futures markets replace these normal, sensible commercial transactions. But a second's thought shows the futures contract is unsuited to that task.

The futures contract does something entirely different. Our miller has gone to a silo to contract for future delivery of wheat. In a typical transaction, the miller will now go to the futures exchange and sign a contract to deliver wheat in the future. That wheat does not have to be the precise type and quality he wants, and it does not have to be delivered to a place convenient to his business. It need not match exactly in quantity or timing his wheat purchases at the silo. All that matters is that the price of the futures contract has a high correlation with the price of the wheat the miller uses.

What the miller has done is borrow wheat. He gets wheat today from the silo, and promises to deliver wheat in the future to the clearinghouse. If there were good banks and paper money, he could borrow money from the bank, buy wheat, sell flour, and repay the loan. But the government has clamped down on banks with regulations that make loans scarce and expensive. Moreover, mediating the transaction through money means any change in the value of money poses a risk. Inflation makes it easier to repay the loan, but deflation makes it harder. This is a risk for both the bank and the miller, and one that is unnecessary. It's much simpler to borrow and repay wheat.

Of course, the miller has no intention of ever delivering wheat to the clearinghouse. This is no different from a cash bond or cash bank loan that the borrower intends to pay off only by borrowing more money in the future. The point of the futures contract is not delivery—it's the mark-to-market payments. The miller will enter into a contract for future delivery and, as the delivery date approaches, will get out of that contract and replace it with one for a later delivery date. Similarly, the point of a bond or bank loan is the interest payments the borrower makes over the life of his business to suppliers of debt capital. Only when the business liquidates are the lenders likely to be repaid for good; the miller will likely close out his futures positions only when he exits his business as well.

It's important to understand the miller's motivation. It is not to hedge price risk. The effect of the price of wheat on the value of his business is complex. If wheat prices go up due to an increase in demand, there will be more demand for processing, so the spread he earns should go up. That is, the price of flour relative to wheat should increase. But if wheat prices go up due to a crop failure, the reverse is true. There will be excess milling capacity and the price differential between flour and wheat will fall. There is little the miller can do with wheat futures to reduce his risk. In any event, variation in the cost of wheat is a small part of his overall business risk. He is more concerned with the prices of machinery, labor, and fuel—and he is more concerned with events like breakdowns, product sales, and employee problems than with any prices. To a first approximation, price changes will affect all millers the same way. If his prices go up, so do the prices of his competitors, so everyone will charge more for milling services. That's not completely true, of course, but a business is usually more concerned with factors that affect only it—like a quality control problem—than with factors that affect every company in the industry the same way. On top of all that, if the miller is concerned about the price of flour falling—remember, he has already contracted with the silo to buy wheat at a fixed price so he no longer cares about the price of wheat directly—he can sign a fixed price delivery contract with a buyer.

The miller's main concern is keeping his expensive machinery working both to get a return on his capital investment and to produce a predictable supply of flour. With nineteenth century technology it was slow and expensive to start and stop machinery. The miller can get much better terms by signing large supply contracts and advance shipping agreements because everyone else wants to keep their capital investments active as well. So the miller wants a secure supply of wheat far more than a predictable price.

Therefore, the futures contract is essentially a financing arrangement to the miller, not a risk reduction tool. He uses it to eliminate money from the loan. The futures exchange, the clearinghouse, and the silo all combine to provide the function of a bank, one that lends commodities rather than money. That's not to say that people never use futures contracts to hedge price risk. They can and do. But it's a secondary function. Paper money is also used to hedge price risk. If you think stock prices are going down, you might sell your stocks and keep the proceeds in cash, thereby hedging yourself against stock price declines. But no one thinks that's the main function of paper money.

The same texts that have farmers hedging with millers usually repeat the canard that futures contracts evolved from "to arrive" contracts. A typical "to arrive" contract is the seller will deliver

5,000 bushels of wheat to the buyer for $5,000 within one week of the time the first wheat shipments arrive in the local port. Notice the assumption that wheat will arrive in port. This is a price guarantee, not a delivery guarantee. There is no way to use this for financing. These kinds of arrangements have existed from ancient times, wherever there has been private enterprise and agriculture. They never had any great economic effect and they have no relationship to futures exchanges. The largest "to arrive" market in the United States was in Buffalo, New York. Remember all those stories about wild behavior in the trading pits of Buffalo? The fortunes won and lost? The dramatic attempts to corner? The scandals and lawsuits? The rich and famous people who got their starts there? No, wait, all that stuff is from futures markets in Chicago and other cities with waterways that flow into the Mississippi.

Money, New and Improved

Futures contracts, and derivatives more generally, improve on paper money. Instead of an interest rate and exchange rate for every bank, we have an interest rate and exchange rate for every commodity and everything else of economic interest. Moreover, it's not a single interest rate; there is a different rate for every future delivery time: a rate from January to March, a different rate from March to June, and so on. Now the market has a far more nuanced way to signal economic activity. Precious metal money provides a price for everything available for sale in one place and time. It has no financing component. Paper money allows transactions between present and future goods and offers a choice of future promises based on money issued by different banks with different loan portfolios. The ability to borrow against future goods and services provides financing to innovators without precious metal capital.

The key to derivative money is the spread trade. Buy March wheat in Chicago and sell March wheat in Kansas City? You've just lent transportation services from Chicago to Kansas City, assuming the price is higher in Kansas City (if the price is higher in Chicago, you've just borrowed transportation services). Buy #1 wheat and sell #2 wheat? You've just borrowed wheat cleaning services. You don't borrow money; you borrow whatever precise future goods and services you need. And you don't repay in money; you repay in whatever future goods and services you can provide. Transactions are not limited to things people can imagine. I don't know how to turn flour back into wheat, or move a crop back in time from August to March, but the Chicago Board of Trade has been quoting prices on those services for 160 years.

To start a business with precious metal money, you need to have or to find an investor with enough precious metal to buy all the assets you need to start generating cash sales. To start a business with paper money, you need to find a bank willing to supply you with pieces of paper. Neither you nor the bank need have any net worth, although in practice banks tend to maintain net worth equal to a fraction of the loans they make. Even so, the amount of capital required to start the business with paper money lent by a bank is much less than the total value of the assets required. What is essential is that the bank's lending standards are low enough to approve your loan, but high enough to make its paper money acceptable enough to acquire the assets you need.

To start a business with derivative money, you identify all assets you require and all products you will deliver in the future. Of course, there is uncertainty around these things, especially the amount and quality of products you will deliver. You don't have to finance the eternal future, just buy enough assets to get you started and sell enough product to cover the cost of the assets you need. You may not be able to find contracts for exactly what you need as inputs and exactly what you expect to deliver as outputs. That's okay as long as you can find derivatives with a high enough correlation to those things. Since you expect the business to make money, there should be more future value of product than future cost of assets required for production. In your opinion.

This is not theoretical; people are doing it today. The first pure derivative businesses were in the energy sector. (Yes, that includes Enron. But it also includes a lot of other companies, including simple ones.) Someone would decide he wanted to build or buy a power plant. He wouldn't go to a bank or venture capital fund for the money; he'd go to a derivatives dealer. Our entrepreneur would enter into a contract to receive 10 years of oil supplies to power the plant, plus another contract to sell 10 years of electricity generated by the plant—when these two swaps are combined they are called a "tolling" swap. Since the value of the electricity exceeds the value of oil, he receives cash up front. He uses the cash to buy or build the plant, and to pay other bills like wages and maintenance. At the end of the 10 years, he owns the plant free and clear, his reward for putting the deal together and overseeing successful operation for a decade. If he has failed to operate the plant successfully, he wouldn't be able to deliver the promised electricity, and the plant would be seized by his derivatives counterparty.

You might object that there is cash involved in this deal: cash to buy the plant, cash to pay wages, and other expenses. But this is more of an accounting entry than real cash. The deal is structured so cash is spent as soon as it becomes available. Cash plays no essential part in the business or its financing. In principle, the entrepreneur could sign a contract with an engineering firm to manage the physical plant, and agree to deliver electricity to the engineers in return, without ever touching cash.

A General Theory of Money

The point that derivatives are the new money is essential for understanding the modern economy. Let's go back to the three functions of money. First is to be a medium of exchange. What does that mean? Suppose A wants goods that B has, but A doesn't have anything B wants. In a barter economy A and B have to look for a C, possibly also D through Z, to make a complete circuit of exchange. But in a money economy, A pays B in money, B uses the money to buy from C, and eventually, possibly via D through Z, someone uses the money to buy something from A. A medium of exchange is just a clearing mechanism for barter.

As a clearing mechanism, paper money has some advantages over precious metal. You can create as much paper money as you want; there is never a shortage. Clearing can be virtual; you don't have to lug gold or silver around to settle accounts. Paper is lighter and easier to carry. It can be given features like serial numbers or require countersigning to protect against theft. However, paper money is easier to counterfeit and is more perishable.

The biggest advantage of paper money, before the government monopoly, is you can choose from a variety of clearing mechanisms. Some are reliable locally and others are better for longer-distance transactions. Some guarantee that the clearing circuit involves only people with solid credit, and are backed by banks with large reserves to protect against losses. Other paper money is softer, with more risk of loss. That is useful for transactions among people without solid credit, and without the luxury of excess reserves to dedicate to supporting the paper money.

Derivatives have a formal clearinghouse, which is far superior to both precious metal and paper money. The biggest vulnerability of the old-fashioned money is that the currency can flow all over the place. That opens the door to theft and counterfeiting. With paper money there's a worse problem. No one really knows what the money is worth until the circuit is complete. A bank makes a loan, the borrower spends the money, the money circulates around until it is used to buy the borrower's product, and the borrower repays the loan, making all the transactions balance. But if the borrower doesn't repay the loan, the transactions don't balance. There's no systematic accounting while the money is in circulation. People can make guesses about the money's value—maybe shrewd guesses, but nothing more.

A clearinghouse keeps all the circulation within its books. The transactions always balance, by rule. Theft or counterfeiting requires fraud at the clearinghouse, which is much easier to police than cash flowing anywhere. Anyway, mints and banks have the same ability to defraud as clearinghouses have, and have practiced it frequently in the past. If the clearinghouse itself is honest, the only way there can be a clearing problem is if a derivative counterparty does not make required mark-to-market payments. Unlike with paper money, this concern is tracked daily and the loss is limited to one day's price movement in the derivative contract minus the initial margin requirement.

The disadvantage of derivative money is it can be used only for certain standardized products, and only with other derivatives traders. You'll never use a derivative to buy a newspaper or a cup of coffee. So derivatives will not replace paper money. But paper money never replaced coins. It's just that the coins lost any connection to metal value and can be used only for the smallest and simplest transactions. Similarly, some form of paper money or electronic equivalent will probably always be with us for everyday use, but it will lose any connection to economic value and will be restricted to minor transactions. The variety of products available in derivatives, and the population of traders, is growing very rapidly and even expanding into retail transactions. Derivatives are the medium of exchange that drives the economy now, and will to an increasing extent in the future.

The next function of money is to be a store of value. This has to do with the role of money in between clearing transactions, while it is circulating. There are three reasons to hold money. The first is for transactional convenience, which relates to money's function as a medium of exchange. The second reason is for hedging. You don't know what the future will bring, so you want your wealth in a form you can convert into whatever you need. The last reason is for speculation. You think the money will buy more in the future than in the present.

Precious metal money is an expensive way to get a store of value, since you actually have to lock up the value. That is, you have to devote valuable economic resources to mining the gold and silver, but keep them out of use. However, precious metal is a very certain store of value, so certain that many hedgers and speculators continue to use it for that purpose today.

Paper money is a less certain store of value, but it doesn't require real economic resources for its production. In the past, paper money was often backed by a fractional amount of gold and silver, so there were some resources, but even then you got a lot more money per ounce of precious metal than when using coins. One advantage paper money has is that it separates the hedgers from the speculators. Hedgers hold paper money in cash; they want to be able to spend it in an emergency. In modern times, a hedger might use a government-guaranteed checking account instead. Either way, the hedger gets little or no interest. Speculators will deposit their cash in a bank, or today perhaps buy a certificate of deposit or government bond. They expect the value of the money to go up, which means the bank will be sound, so they get additional profit earning interest.

Derivatives are a better store of value, because each user can determine precisely which future goods and services either the hedger wants to hedge or the speculator wants to bet on. Moreover, the daily mark-to-market payments protect value far better than any system for paper money. The protection is not as certain as holding physical metal, but it's as close a substitute as human ingenuity has devised.

Finally, money is a numeraire. Remember A, who wanted goods that B had. If all we needed was a medium of exchange to mediate a one-time reorganization of goods, we wouldn't need a numeraire. Each person would buy and sell until she had the perfect basket of goods for her taste.

But economies are dynamic. People want to know what to do. The numeraire helps with that. When A is considering a business idea, he can evaluate it by adding up the total price of the outputs and subtracting the total price of the inputs.

Numeraires are not magic. Minting a silver coin does not create a price list of every conceivable good or service, of any conceivable quality, delivered at any conceivable time and place. All it does is give you a unit for recording transactions. That record can be used to estimate prices of hypothetical future transactions. In addition, it gives you a way to make reasonably simple contracts for future transactions, and to create accounts necessary for all but the simplest joint commercial undertakings.

In principle, you could declare a completely abstract numeraire. That's not useless, but numeraires are much more effective when tied to a medium of exchange and a store of value. For example, there is something called the "triple bottom line" movement that wants corporations to show accounts not just for the money they made or lost, but for the social and environmental consequences of their businesses—"people, planet, profits." Whether or not that's a good idea, the people and planet numbers would be only someone's opinion; you couldn't spend them. Actually, the profit number is also an opinion, but the statement of cash flows is in principle an objective number. It may have errors or approximations in it, but to the extent it's accurate, it's cash you could spend for goods and services. However, in the pre-1990 Soviet Union, businesses reported profits in rubles, but they were opinions. They did not represent real cash the business had available to it, and rubles could not be used freely for transactions.

The trouble with precious metal numeraires is that in an uncertain world no single unit of account can be accurate. You have things whose values are tightly linked and whose relative values can be well established by either economic fundamentals or frequent, open, arm's-length transactions. You have other products and services with no theory and slim data on relative value. For that reason, neither accounts that add up items from different groups nor plans that rely on items from different groups are reliable. The net amount isn't an actionable figure.

Paper money is a great improvement if there is a diversity of banks to fund different types and segments of economic activity. There is exchange rate risk, of course, but it's something that can be quantified. Even without the diversity, the numeraire is better because it represents a broader basket of economic factors: loans if the money is issued by independent banks, or taxes if the money is issued by the government. This makes financial statements more meaningful and business planning more accurate.

Derivatives go one better than even a diverse system of banks. Every derivatives-mediated transaction is actionable. If real securities, goods, or services are involved, they are usually deliverable. Cash-settled transactions are a bit more indirect, but that cash can be used to settle other derivatives transactions. Each market participant can construct a numeraire that matches closely his real economic interests.

Value and Money

But how can derivatives be money when they require money— dollars—for quotation and settlement? This is an excellent question. It's the same question as how can paper be money when it requires gold or silver as a reference value? Even with precious metal coin money we can ask how the value of the coins was set in the first place. You might think that one is easy: It was the value of the metal in alternative use as jewelry or plate. But that's not true; the coin value of gold and silver far exceeded the use value. Once precious metal became monetized, its value divorced from its physical use.

Actually, precious metal money is the hardest one to explain. Paper money has nothing to do with gold, except through misguided regulation. The value of bank-issued paper money is based on the quality of the loans backing it up—in other words, the future goods and services that are guaranteed to be available for purchase by the paper money. Goods and services other than those produced by bank borrowers may be available for purchase, but they can also be withdrawn or sold only if the money is tendered at a discount. To the extent that the bank holds reserve assets, pays interest, is supported by a central bank, or enjoys general confidence, the paper money can have additional value, but its fundamental value is loan value.

How does that relate to government-issued paper money that citizens are forced to accept by legal tender laws? Leaving the laws aside for a moment, the fundamental value is that the money can be used to pay taxes. Just as a government can issue revenue-anticipation bonds to be repaid when taxes come in, it can spend paper money that will have value because people need it to pay taxes. The differences are that the government has to pay interest on bonds, and bonds are not convenient for most purchases. As long as the stock of money that individuals hold is smaller than or comparable to total anticipated future tax obligations, the money will have value.

When government paper money has fundamental value, it acquires additional value because it is useful for transactions. This additional value can divorce entirely from fundamental value. For example, considerably more U.S. currency is held outside U.S. borders by foreigners who have no anticipated future U.S. tax obligations than is held inside the United States by citizens. And within U.S. borders an unknown but large amount of cash is held by tax evaders and other criminals who do not plan to use it for tax payments.

Despite the large amount of currency held for transactional reasons and to store value, the basic tax value is still important. If faith in the ability or willingness of the government to raise enough taxes to cover its expenditures and debt erodes, the money will be accepted only at a discount, which we call inflation. Although that inflation applies directly only to people who expect to use the money to pay taxes, the discount will be enforced by everyone who accepts the money.

Legal tender rules complicate the situation, as do wage and price controls, or the requirement to have a ration card in addition to paper money in order to buy goods. But even the most totalitarian governments in history have not been able to prevent their citizens from developing and using alternative money when the quality of official money declines enough. Laws can prop up the value of money to some extent, but they've never been a firm foundation.

Going back to gold and silver, there is no future value associated with them, no future goods or services guaranteed to be delivered for them. You can make jewelry out of the metal or exchange it for its bullion value, but typically those uses capture only a small portion of precious metal coin value. That fact gets obscured because people still bought gold and silver jewelry when those metals were used as money, and paid prices comparable to coin prices. However, if all the coins in circulation had been melted down for ornaments, the value of the resulting metal would have fallen dramatically because the supply of jewelry would have swamped demand.

No one knows how precious metal coins acquired their initial value. It would make sense if coins had initially been issued at bullion value and acquired monetization value only after long experience with their use, when people had confidence they would be accepted at the inflated values in the future. But history shows the opposite: Coins were initially created at high value, and fell to bullion value only far away from issuance or in times of economic breakdown.

Derivatives acquire their fundamental value from liquidity. Unlike more primitive forms of money, they exist in zero net supply: For every long position there is an offsetting short position. Therefore, there is no need for a pool of loans or pile of gold to support their value. The net value is zero. What is important is that the derivatives will pay off as promised. That payoff is secured by the initial margin and daily mark-to-market payments made by derivative holders. That security, in turn, depends on two things: that we can establish a daily market-clearing price for the derivative and that the price doesn't change in any day more than the amount of initial margin required. Accurate, transparent prices and smooth price changes are both features of liquidity. Futures markets often have daily price change limits; the price is not allowed to move more than a certain amount in a day. That doesn't solve the problem of large price movements, however; it only gives participants some extra time to meet large margin calls.

Using derivatives, in principle, individuals can contract to exchange future goods and services directly, with no intermediation of paper money. Some people might choose portfolios that involve current or future inflows or outflows of cash, but in that respect cash is just like any other asset. In practice, cash is the accounting unit used to price everything, just as early paper money was denominated in terms of gold or silver. However, the nature of paper money didn't change when the gold standard disappeared (that event did remove a discipline on government paper money issuance). Moreover, we see growing use of derivatives-type contracts for nonmonetary consideration. Much of the Internet bubble economy was driven by swapping so-called clicks, eyeballs, and capacity for each other, not to mention stock options, without intermediation of official government paper money.

Numeraire

The natural numeraire for a derivatives dealer is not paper money but shares in the clearinghouse. Dealers own stakes in the clearinghouse and are responsible for its debts. Over-the-counter (OTC) derivatives are not traded on public exchanges, and may or may not have clearinghouses. If there is no multidealer clearinghouse, the dealer acts as its own clearinghouse, or else uses another dealer to clear trades.

In principle, you could set up a derivatives exchange and clearinghouse with no reference to paper money at all. As with a paper money issuing bank, you would probably want to contribute some equity capital so people would trust the institution initially, but even that is only a marketing essential, not an economic one. It's also true that having cash as one of the assets derivatives are written on is handy, because you don't have contracts for every possible thing someone might want to borrow or lend. But cash is not necessary.

To a derivatives end user, the numeraire is the net product of its economic activity, or the closest approximation that can be made from available contracts. An oil refiner, for example, can use the price of refined products minus the price of crude oil as a numeraire; a shipping company can use the price of commodities at port of consumption minus the price of those same commodities at port of production. This is the key to the economic function of futures markets. When your numeraire is your net economic product, you have no risk. When your numeraire is highly correlated to your net economic product, you have small risk.

With gold and silver money, the profit of a business is the metal received for end products minus the metal paid for inputs. With paper money, it's more complicated. First, the business can choose from various types of paper money, and can use different types for different transactions. Second, there is an interest rate attached to loans; profit depends on the timing of purchases and sales, not just the net amount. Risky businesses pay higher interest rates than safe ones, so profit is adjusted for risk. Third and most important, the value of paper money changes over time. If a business does badly, but better than the average bank borrower, it can still show a profit. It uses the money it borrows to buy goods at full value for the money, but when it sells its output it may be able to accept money at a discount and use it to repay its loan. If it sells goods for 10 percent less in gold terms than the value of the inputs it bought, but the bank's money has depreciated 20 percent over the period of production, the company will show a profit. These features—choice of currency, risk-adjusted profits, and relative success criteria—allow for much more nuanced and effective economic signals than a precious metal economy can provide.

Although governments have outlawed competition in money issuance, so there is not as much variety available as there should be, there are still different currencies in different countries. Global corporations borrow, spend, and sell in whatever currencies are most advantageous. Generally that means borrowing in low interest rate currencies, contracting future fixed costs in currencies that are inflating, and contracting fixed future revenues in currencies with low inflation rates. In all cases these rules are relative to market expectation; for example, borrowing in a low interest rate currency is no bargain if the forward exchange rate premiums are high enough to offset the interest rate differential. But except in extreme cases, market expectation usually undercompensates, so doing the short-term greedy thing is often best. The effects of currency choices are quite large relative to the net income of global businesses. It is not uncommon that a company could show a large profit for a quarter if it did its books in one currency, and a large loss if it used a different currency for accounting.

Derivative money offers an explosion of specific currencies that allow companies to tailor optimal numeraires. There is an underappreciated magic to allowing diversity of numeraire. As I write this, the one year forward USD/EUR exchange rate is $1.40 for €1.00. That means you can agree today to deliver $1.40 in one year, and receive €1.00 at that time. Suppose Anne from the United States makes a bet with her Catalan friend Anaïs. If in one year it costs more than $1.40 to buy €1.00, Anaïs will pay Anne €1.00. Otherwise Anne will pay Anaïs $1.40. From Anne's point of view, if she wins, she wins €1.00, which she can sell for more than $1.40. If she loses, she loses $1.40. Anaïs uses parallel reasoning. If she wins, she wins $1.40, which she can sell for more than €1.00. If she loses, she pays €1.00. Both women have positive expected values from this bet.

This is not just a theoretical point. Anne can go to the market and sell a one-year call on the euro at $1.40; she will be paid $0.07 today for this. If Anne loses her bet, the option expires worthless, and Anne keeps $0.07 (although she must pay $1.40 to Anaïs). If Anne wins, she can take the €1.00 Anaïs pays her and deliver it into the call option she wrote. She gets $1.40 in exchange, and still has the $0.07. So from Anne's point of view, she pays $1.33 if she loses and gets $1.47 if she wins. Anaïs can write a put option instead with which she pays €0.95 if she loses and gets €1.05 if she wins.

Where does the extra value come from? No goods are created by this bet. The answer is that Anne and Anaïs have agreed to shift their consumption in different states of the world. Because they use different numeraires, they value the states differently and can arbitrage the valuation difference.

So why doesn't everybody quit working and live off of currency bets? There is a limit to the profit you can build in as a proportion of the risk you take. In this example, the profit was 5 percent of the amount risked. By using different currencies, you could get this up to about 10 percent, but no higher. It doesn't help to shorten the term of the bet so you do 365 daily bets instead of a one-year bet. It does help to repeat the bet multiple times, as over 100 years the profit rises to 50 percent of the amount risked.

What really does help is to move to derivatives money and let everyone have a custom numeraire. This creates genuine economic value. It's hard to measure how much, but derivatives clearly more than double the value of the underlying assets they trade on. That means there is more economic value added by futures markets than by all the work that goes into making and processing the underlying commodities.

Note that the additional economic value is not reflected in a higher paper money price. That's why farmers have always been suspicious of, and often actively disliked, futures markets. There is more value, but it doesn't go to producers. The only way farmers could gain from futures markets is if contracts were introduced on agricultural land and labor and if weather contracts were expanded. We already have contracts on farm products, energy, and interest rates. Farmers could then move to their natural numeraire and improve their lives dramatically. The main impediment to these developments has been government subsidies and price supports to agriculture, which dampen out the volatility needed for futures trading to be worthwhile.

The divergence between economic value and paper money price is also why many economists have trouble seeing what futures markets do. If you reduce everything to a single numeraire before you begin your analysis, futures markets are invisible. Unfortunately, despite having theories that cannot account for the existence of futures markets, much less the excitement of the trading pit and the economic stimulation derivatives cause, too many economists feel qualified to write about futures markets and to suggest regulations.

The economic value added by futures markets to end users is proportional to the volatility of prices, just like Anne's and Anaïs's profits from their currency bet. This is where speculators come in. There are basically two kinds of speculators in all financial markets: value investors and momentum investors. Value investors buy when things are cheap relative to fundamental value, and sell when they are expensive. They keep prices within shouting distance of fundamental value most of the time. Value investors also provide liquidity to the market because they buy when others sell and sell when others buy. Value investors are the one kind of speculator polite people like to talk about. They give the markets rationality and liquidity.

Momentum investors give the market volatility. They see where the market is going, and push it there faster, sometimes overshooting. Momentum investors are behind bubbles and crashes, and they suck liquidity out of the market. They are the kind you don't take home to mother. But without them, you have no market, or at best a quiet market that adds little economic value. They are also the disruptive force that can break through entrenched interests and myths, and thereby foster innovation and growth.

One silly thing you read about futures markets is that they are zero-sum. That's true in an accounting sense: Every contract has a long and a short side; every dollar anyone gets is paid by someone else. But a bank is also zero-sum. Every dollar in interest paid to depositors is paid by borrowers. Yet banks add tremendously to economic growth and value. Money creates value by circulating, not by being created magically out of nowhere. Money itself is zero-sum. It represents an asset to its owner and an equal liability to everyone else. In the case of futures markets, and derivatives in general, since each user has a different numeraire, each one can count a net profit in economic value. Insisting the markets are zero-sum is a symptom of not understanding numeraires.

An even sillier charge is that futures markets are a casino where speculators create risk that spills over and harms the real economy. Of course they are casinos where speculators create risk. That's their function. If speculators went away or stopped creating risk, the markets would collapse, and they would take their vast economic value with them.

Clearinghouses

I don't want to get too far into the minutiae of financial operations, but it is worth remarking that the derivative economy has a complex structure. Clearinghouses are composed of clearing firms, each one representing a pool of mutualized risk. Many clearing firms are members of multiple clearinghouses, whereas others are relatively tiny operations and work only with a single clearinghouse. If you enter into a public futures contract, you will post margin with a futures commission merchant (FCM). That entity will aggregate your margin and your trades with those of its other customers, and deposit some of the margin with the clearinghouse. As long as everyone does their job properly and no contract prices move farther than the required margin amount in a day, everything gets paid off in full, like a sound bank.

If someone doesn't do their job, or if prices move too much, there will be a loss imposed on someone. Whether that someone is you depends on the financial strength of the clearinghouse, the financial strength of your FCM, and the equity of the pool of contracts your FCM cleared for all its customers. People often say that no clearinghouse has ever gone broke. I'm not sure that's true. For years, I have challenged people who say it and none has yet produced an authoritative source. I think what people mean is no clearinghouse in the past 40 years or so has failed, and anything that failed before that was too small or obscure to make the national or international news.

But the real trouble with that statement is that the reason clearinghouses seldom or never go bankrupt is that they bankrupt their customers instead. The first major example was the Paris Sugar Bourse in 1905, but the story has been repeated many times since. When the clearing members get on the wrong side of a trade and lose more money than they want to lose, they change the rules. Usually they accuse the winners of trying to manipulate or corner the market, but that's just misdirection. When pushed to the extreme, they just set an off-market price for derivative settlement (off-market in the members' favor, of course). Famous victims include the Hunt brothers and the German company Metallgesellschaft. In 1962, Tino De Angelis floated a few inches of soybean oil on tanks of seawater and used them to collateralize gigantic futures positions in soybean oil and cottonseed oil. When he was discovered, his positions had to be liquidated, and the prices of the oils crashed. Members of the New York Produce Exchange were long the oils and faced huge losses. Instead, they declared that the contracts would be settled at the old high price, changing their losses into customer losses. At least the exchange had the decency to go out of business afterward. The London Metals Exchange did the same thing twice in tin contracts, and is still "the world's premier non-ferrous metals market." The New York Mercantile Exchange did it in 1976, with Maine potato contracts of all things, and boasts of being "the world's largest physical commodity futures exchange" today.

Also, the clearinghouse doesn't have to cheat or fail for investors to lose money. If your FCM gets into trouble, you could be on the hook. If another customer of your FCM gets into trouble, that's also true. Much like the days of uninsured banks issuing private banknotes, you have to be careful whose money you accept.

Now someone has to take a loss when these things occur, and there is a social argument for not bankrupting the clearinghouse itself. But as the derivatives economy matures, we have to find some kind of bankruptcy-like process where an independent administrator appointed by a court determines the contract settlement price. It needn't take years and armies of lawyers. In any event, it shouldn't be done by vote of the dealers.

Cash

One of the indelible memories of the descent into financial crisis in 2008 was bank CEOs coming on television to announce how much cash their bank held. That was scary, because no one had any idea what the number was supposed to be, or even exactly what it meant. Naive people might have thought the bank had a vault with dollar bills in it, or that the cash was on deposit with the Federal Reserve. Sophisticated people knew it was something far more complicated than that, but only a few back-office people and risk managers— and likely not the CEO making the speech—knew exactly what it was. What everyone knew was that if the guy was giving the number on CNBC his bank was in some kind of bad trouble.

Once he told you the number, it was also scary because it was so small compared to the obligations of the bank. For example, in the last financial statements Lehman Brothers filed before failing, it reported $20 billion of cash and cash equivalents. But it had $263 billion of short-term liabilities, so the cash wasn't going to make much of a dent. That's even more obvious when I tell you the $20 billion of cash wasn't Lehman's anyway; it was cash deposited by customers as margin for securities purchases. One particularly shaky $3 billion of it was short-term notes issued by a Lehman-related entity and guaranteed by Lehman, then pledged to JPMorgan as collateral. In effect, Lehman printed up its own money and gave it to another bank, but still claimed it as part of its "liquidity pool." Nothing about this was illegal or uncommon. People say Lehman was more aggressive than other banks, but that's only because they haven't looked hard at other banks.

Lehman also reported $336 billion of noncash short-term assets. That suggested Lehman's immediate fate would be determined by the quality and liquidity of its short-term assets, not by how much cash it held. As with the cash, some of those short-term assets were actually owned by Lehman's customers and/or pledged to third parties.

In addition, Lehman held $269 billion of long-term investments, including some real estate and corporate loans of questionable value and limited liquidity (yes, and some of them were customer assets and/or pledged to third parties). These were irrelevant to the crisis; their value would affect Lehman's long-term profitability, but not its short-term survival. Only Lehman's stockholders and bondholders would have cared how the investments turned out; the result would not disrupt the market either way.

The question is: Why did Lehman own $336 billion and owe $263 billion of short-term assets? In many cases these assets and liabilities were identical: Lehman might have borrowed, say, a two-year Treasury bond from one counterparty and lent it to another. Suppose the short-term assets and liabilities could have been offset so Lehman held $336 – $263 = $73 billion of cash and had no short-term liabilities. Then there would have been no failure, no crisis.

The key to the answer is that the entire financial dealer system, not just Lehman, runs on short-term repurchase agreement (repo) financing. If a firm buys an asset, it doesn't use its cash; it uses the asset to borrow the purchase price. If a firm wants to sell an asset it doesn't have, it sells it and then goes and borrows the asset in the repo market. The result is that every firm ends up with lots of its assets pledged to other firms for security, and holding a lot of other firms' assets pledged to it. It's even more complicated, because there are also a lot of off-balance-sheet derivative exposures that can trigger billions of dollars of daily cash flows back and forth. The resulting network is so large and complex that a single dealer failure, or merely the fear of a failure, can trigger a major disruption in all financial markets.

This is not the place to discuss the wisdom of that system. It has important advantages, but it is sorely in need of some adult attention. I mention it here to show that the entire financial system has switched over to derivative money. Cash, in the sense of paper money issued by the government, is meaningless. The cash Lehman held belonged to others, and could not have paid its liabilities anyway. What mattered was whether Lehman could make its mark-to-market payments under its derivative contracts and deliver enough assets in repo transactions to get enough cash to buy back the assets it had repoed at other firms. That was entirely a function of liquidity of assets and confidence in Lehman, neither of which had anything to do with little green pieces of paper.

If this sounds a little odd, consider the three tests of derivative-based money. First, did Lehman buy and sell things for cash, or did it swap future cash flows based on contingent future events? Obviously Lehman's derivative business was derivative-based, but I'm talking about all its businesses. Consider one of the simplest, dealing in U.S. Treasuries.

A cash-based business would borrow money or raise equity capital, and use it to buy an inventory of U.S. Treasuries in government auctions. When a customer called to buy a bond, the firm would sell the bond out of inventory and receive cash from the customer. If the firm didn't have the bond a customer wanted, it would say it was out of stock, and would try to locate the bond at another dealer. If a customer wanted to sell a bond, the firm would buy the bond into inventory and pay cash. If inventory got too big or, more important, if the level of cash available to buy bonds got too low, the firm would sell bonds out of inventory. This is a business everyone can understand.

What Lehman and every other dealer did was entirely different. It ran the business with as little capital as possible; it certainly didn't start by borrowing money or building up inventory. It quoted prices on all Treasury securities, whether it owned them or not. If a customer called to buy, Lehman sold him the bond. If a customer called to sell, Lehman bought the bond from him. People also called with more complicated needs, to buy or sell bonds in the future at a price agreed today, or to buy or sell some but not all the cash flows of a bond, or to buy or sell complex contracts whose payoffs depended on bond prices in the future. But in all of these deals, no cash or bonds changed hands at the time of the trade.

At the end of the day, Lehman totaled up the bonds it owned and owed, and the cash it owned and owed, and posted them to the appropriate customer accounts. For most transactions, these were virtual transactions only; no real bonds or cash moved. For some customers with cash accounts, real bonds had to be found and real cash had to be collected or paid. In that case, Lehman would do a special repo, finding someone who owned the bond who would lend it to Lehman to put in the customer's account. Some customers wanted their bonds sent to an account at a different firm. In that case, Lehman could special repo the bond from the other firm; no actual bond had to be sent. If Lehman found itself owning any real bonds—say, because a cash account customer had sold one—it immediately lent it out to someone who wanted it. These last operations were handled by the firm's repo desk, not its Treasury desk.

There were two other processes independent of this activity. Lehman's Treasury desk would look at the entire net position of the firm in Treasuries, the billions of bonds owned (but lent out) and owed, as well as all the other complex Treasury-related products. If it decided it had a net exposure it didn't want, it would offset it using a financial derivative. Second, Lehman's margin operations department looked at all the customer accounts. If any had too little equity given the riskiness of the positions, the firm issued a margin call to either increase the equity or cut the risk of positions. Note that cash had nothing to do with this—all that mattered was the total value of all the positions in the account and the total risk of all those positions.

Derivative Money

Lehman's Treasury business was not entirely virtual. In addition to the cash accounts, there were other reasons some transactions needed real, physical settlement. The firm did maintain some real, physical inventory of bonds, although these were hedged by futures contracts. For the most part, however, the Lehman Treasury desk borrowed and lent specific things in the future. Virtual cash was used to keep the accounting straight, but real cash had only a minor role. That's one feature of derivative money. By the way, if you have a brokerage account and don't know whether it's a cash account or not, it probably isn't. That means the securities you think you own aren't there; they're lent out to other investors. The cash you think is yours is listed on the brokerage firm's balance sheet as if it were its cash. If you want physical possession of either your securities or your cash, the firm has to go out looking for them in order to get them to you.

The second feature of derivative money is obvious here as well. The only capital Lehman needed for this business was enough to cover the day-to-day price changes in its net positions. It did not need inventory or inventory financing. Okay, there are government rules mandating capital levels as well, and sometimes they are higher than the minimum required by the business itself. But these capital rules were switched to so-called risk-based capital in the 1990s, meaning that the capital requirement is based on how much net exposures might move, not on the amount of liabilities the firm has or the amount of assets it controls. Moreover, "capital" is not cash. It's basically intended to be the value of the firm's assets minus its liabilities, although the actual rules are extremely complicated. So the regulation is derivative-based as well. The government may be stricter than the market—although in the financial crisis all the firms that failed the market test qualified as "well-capitalized" by the government—but it does not insist on cash-based rules.

The last feature of derivative money is that offsetting transactions with different people can be eliminated. For example, if you borrow something from one person and lend it to another, you can step out of the loop and no longer have to worry about whether the loan is paid back. Some form of clearinghouse keeps track of everything.

This was almost true in 2008. There was a lot of offset within and among firms. Public exchange-traded derivatives had clearinghouses, as did many private over-the-counter (OTC) derivatives. Firms had procedures to identify mutual offsetting positions and cancel them, and even in some cases to identify a ring of transactions that could be canceled. A few big clearing firms assumed responsibility for other firms, thereby offsetting transactions within their network. People had been working for years, with considerable success, to increase the amount of offset. But there was not enough offset, and that contributed greatly to the pain when Lehman fell. The lesson from that disaster has led to calls for more clearing, which will sever the financial industry from one of its last ties to cash.

The idea of exchange nurtured the transition out of the old Stone Age and equal-value exchange supported the Neolithic revolution. Precious metal money freed the world from a cycle of civilizations rising and falling, leaving little behind, and generated sustained progress that survived the falls of civilizations and encompassed the world. Paper money gave us steadily rising wages and made modern society possible.

Derivative money is every bit as significant. One immediate effect was to create a golden age of innovation and growth. Nineteen of the 100 wealthiest Americans of all time—based on their fractions of the contemporaneous national income—built their fortunes in the northern drainage basin of the Mississippi River between 1850 and 1880. They were not just robber barons like Rockefeller, Mellon, and Carnegie, but great inventors like McCormick, Westinghouse, and Pullman, plus innovators in other fields such as Swift, Pulitzer, Hearst, Armour, and Marshall Field. Remember, this was a sparsely populated region in 1840, with the majority of the inhabitants living in the Stone Age. It wasn't that 19 of the 100 smartest Americans of all time were living in the Minnesota woods in 1850; it was that derivatives turned ordinary inventors and businesspeople into world-changing innovators whose names are household words to this day. But the world did not notice, preferring to discuss the goings-on in New York, London, and Washington, as if those places mattered to the economy.

In fact, if you look at a list of the wealthiest Americans in history, you will be struck by how few created their wealth with coin or paper money. The first, John Jacob Astor, did it by counterfeiting wampum. Most of the other early ones primarily used barter and local credit webs. Then come the 19 just mentioned. A bit later, but also in the same region, Henry Ford made a large fortune. He did use paper money, but his key innovation was to pay his workers enough that they could afford to buy the cars they made, increasing production scale, so the price fell enough to be affordable by the workers of his suppliers, as well as the general population. This is a derivative money concept even if it was done without derivatives.

Another big group are Internet billionaires. They did it founding companies without profits, in some cases without revenues.

Look Ma, no money! They tried to take over the economy without using money, and they nearly succeeded. People write it off today as a bubble, but I think it was an opening battle in the war for derivatives to replace paper money. Only a few years later, people tried again, this time with literal derivatives—securitized loans and credit default swaps.

The last big chunk of the list that got there without money is the hedge fund billionaires. This is literal derivative trading. The top 100 list is rounded out by decidedly less colorful and innovative people, mostly bankers and heirs who inherited fortunes and multiplied them. None of these lived recently.

The End of Paper

How will derivatives replace paper money? Paper money will not lose its value, any more than gold lost its value when paper money arrived. But the scope of transactions mediated by paper money will shrink in number and size. Paper money will lose its economic importance.

One suggestion can be seen in the world today. More and more transactions are being done on the Internet through bidding and future promises. It's easy to make the leap from bidding for airline tickets and hotel rooms to full derivative trading of future services. Companies like BetFair prove there is a large supply of sophisticated speculators willing to provide liquidity. We might see airlines going back to the business of flying airplanes from place to place and not worrying about fares. The seats would be sold in bulk on a travel exchange, where travelers would buy and sell what they needed.

The reason airline tickets are a natural early transition to derivative trading is that the value of seats is unpredictable. There may be empty seats, in which case an additional passenger costs only the extra fuel and a bag of nuts. Or demand might be high enough to support two or three times the normal price. Also, travelers form complex contingent plans. You might know you have to go someplace, but not exactly when. Or you may have your vacation scheduled exactly, but have several equally attractive destinations. Some people are on very tight schedules and change plans on short notice, whereas others are willing to be flexible for a lower cost. Some people want a big seat and tender loving care, whereas others would sling a hammock in the wheel well next to a family of rabid porcupines to save a few bucks. Paper money pricing cannot allocate efficiently under these conditions.

It's not just travel and entertainment that benefit from derivative trading. People virtually build their own computers, and many other manufacturing processes can be done more efficiently this way, satisfying consumer demand precisely and allocating production tasks efficiently. Specialist companies and individuals can replace much of the work done by big companies. All they do is go to the exchange, see where their services have the most value added, make the transactions, and do the work. No one needs large amounts of capital or complex sales plans or long supply and distribution networks.

Another suggestion concerns the fact that less and less of what people value is bought and sold for money. News and opinion are delivered free on the Internet, Wikipedia provides research services that other people used to sell, and multiplayer games substitute for paid recreational activities. Open-source products available free are often better than commercial creations. Each of these cycles has its own form of money and its own form of risk management.

Even in the paid economy, more and more goods are distributed on the basis of status, such as club memberships for airlines, hotels, discount shopping stores, and so on. Status becomes a kind of money.

My final suggestion comes from Robert Shiller, who envisions derivatives for all major life decisions. Going to medical school next year? Why not sell half the median income of a cohort of medical school entrants similar to you and reduce your exposure to future changes in doctors' wages? You couldn't sell half of your personal income, because once you did, you might work less. But selling the cohort average wage protects you from things outside your control while insulating the buyer from your personal motivations. If you drop out of med school, you buy back the contract, maybe at a gain or maybe at a loss. The prices for these contracts would be powerful signals for making career choices. Also, they allow people to sell future human capital to finance all kinds of ideas. In the past, selling future human capital was called slavery. But the amount of human capital in the world exceeds the value of all other assets, and without derivatives it remains sterile capital.

Now, you wouldn't want to sell that contract for a lump sum of cash. Money is no store of value. Perhaps you want to live in Chicago, so you would buy a contract that pays half the living expenses of a Chicago resident who is in the 95th percentile for income. What you've done is hedged your life revenues and expenses. An important point is that you no longer care about the value of money. If there's a lot of inflation, you'll pay more on your doctor-wage contract but get more from your Chicago-life contract. In fact, derivative purchase and sale may take money out of the equation altogether, except perhaps for small, incidental purchases.

These are suggestions only. I have no idea what the future will be like, except that paper money will fade to insignificant economic importance, to be replaced by derivative-like arrangements. For my purposes in this book, the question is how this affects the nature of risk taking. We turn to that question in the Chapter 12.

CHAPTER

11

Cold Blood

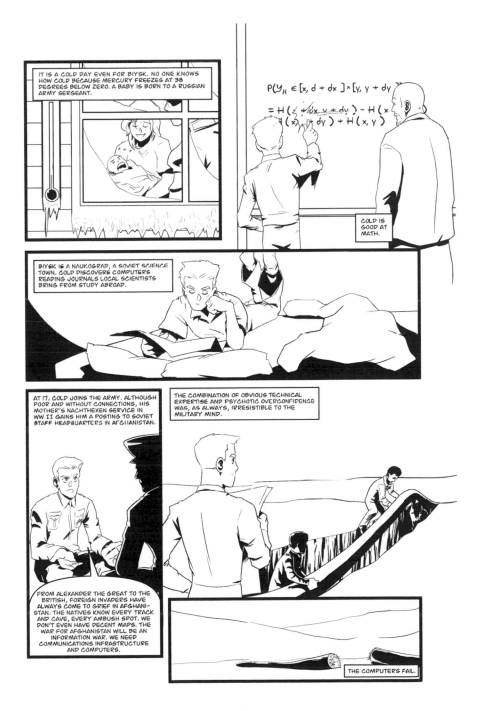

IT IS A COLD DAY EVEN FOR BIYSK. NO ONE KNOWS HOW COLD BECAUSE MERCURY FREEZES AT 38 DEGREES BELOW ZERO. A BABY IS BORN TO A RUSSIAN ARMY SERGEANT.

$$P(y_H \in [x, d + dx] \times [y, y + dy$$
$$= H(x + dx, y + dy) - H(x$$
$$(x, y + dy) + H(x, y)$$

COLD IS GOOD AT MATH.

BIYSK IS A NAUKOGRAD, A SOVIET SCIENCE TOWN. COLD DISCOVERS COMPUTERS READING JOURNALS LOCAL SCIENTISTS BRING FROM STUDY ABROAD.

AT 17, COLD JOINS THE ARMY. ALTHOUGH POOR AND WITHOUT CONNECTIONS, HIS MOTHER'S NACHTHEXEN SERVICE IN WW II GAINS HIM A POSTING TO SOVIET STAFF HEADQUARTERS IN AFGHANISTAN.

THE COMBINATION OF OBVIOUS TECHNICAL EXPERTISE AND PSYCHOTIC OVERCONFIDENCE WAS, AS ALWAYS, IRRESISTIBLE TO THE MILITARY MIND.

FROM ALEXANDER THE GREAT TO THE BRITISH, FOREIGN INVADERS HAVE ALWAYS COME TO GRIEF IN AFGHANISTAN. THE NATIVES KNOW EVERY TRACK AND CAVE, EVERY AMBUSH SPOT. WE DON'T EVEN HAVE DECENT MAPS. THE WAR FOR AFGHANISTAN WILL BE AN INFORMATION WAR. WE NEED COMMUNICATIONS INFRASTRUCTURE AND COMPUTERS.

THE COMPUTERS FAIL.

COLD LEAVES THE ARMY FOR A HIGH SPOT IN GOSPLAN.

THE SOVIET ECONOMY IS FAILING FROM RIGID TOP-DOWN PLANNING. WE NEED TO COLLECT BOTTOM-UP DATA FROM CUSTOMERS ABOUT QUALITY AND DEMAND.

WE CAN'T MAKE ALLOCATIONS AND QUOTAS IN MOSCOW. EVERY BUSINESS NEEDS A COMPUTER WITH USER-FRIENDLY, FLEXIBLE SOFTWARE TO COMMUNICATE ITS NEEDS AND OPPORTUNITIES. THE STRUGGLE FOR ECONOMIC SUPREMACY OVER THE WEST IS AN INFORMATION STRUGGLE. WE NEED COMMUNICATIONS INFRASTRUCTURE AND COMPUTERS.

THE COMBINATION OF OBVIOUS TECHNICAL EXPERTISE AND PSYCHOTIC OVERCONFIDENCE WAS, AS ALWAYS, IRRESISTIBLE TO THE BUREAUCRATIC MIND.

THE COMPUTERS FAIL.

COLD LEAVES RUSSIA FOR WALL STREET, WHERE HE FEELS AT HOME IN AN INVESTMENT BANK OWNED BY A LARGE CORPORATE PARENT.

YOU'VE GOT INVESTMENT BANKERS AND TRADERS. EACH WANTS TO GET RID OF THE OTHER.

MAYBE, BUT IT'S MORE COMPLICATED. THOSE INVESTMENT BANKERS WANT THE TRADERS TO BLOW UP, SO THEY'LL ALL BE FIRED. BUT THE OTHER INVESTMENT BANKERS WANT THE TRADERS TO MAKE SO MUCH MONEY THAT NO ONE WILL SEE ANY VALUE IN INVESTMENT BANKING. THEN THE BANKERS CAN HAVE THEIR UNIT SPUN OFF INTO A SMALL PRIVATE COMPANY THAT THEY OWN, WITH NO TRADERS.

GOT IT. LIKE BOLSHEVIKS AND MENSHEVIKS.

LIKE IN MOSCOW.

YEAH, EXACTLY. THE MENSHEVIKS WANT TO CUT A DEAL WITH THE KADETS. THOSE ARE THE TRADERS WHO WANT TO SUCCEED SO THE PARENT WILL GIVE THEM LOTS OF CAPITAL TO PLAY WITH.

DON'T TELL ME. THE TRUDOVICS ARE TRADERS WHO WANT TO LOSE SO MUCH MONEY THEY'LL BE SPUN OFF INTO A SMALL PRIVATE HEDGE FUND THEY CAN OWN, WITH NO INVESTMENT BANKERS. SO THEY'RE NEGOTIATING WITH THE BOLSHEVIKS.

210

211

CHAPTER

12

What Does a Risk Manager Do?—Inside VaR

An old joke begins with a disheveled man asking a banker type for a handout. The banker sniffs, "Why don't you get a job?"

"I have a job," replies the other man. "I watch for tornadoes."

The banker exclaims angrily, "There have never been tornadoes around here!"

"See what a good job I'm doing?"

I wish I could say there are no tornado-watching risk managers—that is, no people with the title of risk manager who stand around nodding gravely and looking worried, taking credit when nothing bad happens and saying "I told you so" when something does go wrong. These people are even worse than the tornado watcher. He at least gives a clear and rational account of what he does. It's not hard to find risk managers, even in sophisticated financial institutions, who hem and haw when asked exactly what they do. If pressed, they come up with generalities or jargon. They cannot show you tangible evidence of any of it, and if you watch what they actually do—if anything—it doesn't correspond to their claims.

Professional Standards

Financial risk management actually is a quantitative field with specific techniques and professional standards. Not everyone does it the same way, and some prominent practitioners even reject certain standard approaches in favor of alternatives. The point is they know the usual way to do things and have the ability to conform, but choose to do something different, either because it's better tailored to their institution or for some other reason. Frankly, in most cases I think the deviations make little difference in the end, and are done more to express individuality than to improve the process, but I don't insist on that view.

For example, almost all financial risk managers use value at risk (VaR) as a primary component of their processes, but a vocal minority objects to VaR on several grounds. Even the minority acknowledges the key importance of making regular daily predictions that are rigorously verified against objectively determined outcomes. Some risk managers believe counting trading profits and losses, assuming fixed positions and normal markets, is not the right measure. Others argue that the 5 percent loss point is not the right metric. Another argument is that VaR has been so misinterpreted outside the profession that it's better to scrap it for an untainted number. There are sound reasons for all of these positions, although I have always been a strong VaR proponent myself.

VaR and all the other things I'm going to describe in this chapter are orthodox financial risk management. I have no hesitation in saying that anyone who doesn't understand the orthodoxy is not a qualified professional financial risk manager, whatever her title. Qualified professionals may practice heterodox methods, although as I have indicated I'm a fan of doing things by the book—my book, in fact—unless there are very good reasons to depart from it. But even heterodox methods must conform to basic principles, or they are outside the pale of the profession. And people who use nonstandard methods because they can't or won't learn the standard ones are not professional.

To use a health care analogy, there is a wide variety of opinions among professional healers. But there are certain principles someone has to know and accept to be within the modern scientific medical profession. Someone who rejects or never learned physiology and chemistry, or refuses to accept clear evidence of double-blind, controlled experiments, is not what I would call a health care professional. The person might be a great healer, and there are certainly people who know all the principles and are terrible healers. It's also undoubtedly true that there are vast amounts of useful knowledge about healing that are outside the current professional worldview.

Nevertheless, there is a well-defined profession. Risk management is a new profession, so the boundaries are fuzzier, but the boundaries do exist.

Not everyone in a risk management department is a technical risk management specialist. One prominent example is that the chief risk officer (CRO) of a large financial institution is usually a bank executive rather than a technical expert in risk. Running a department with hundreds or thousands of employees and representing the firm in front of investors and senior regulators is something most quants can't—and don't want to—do. CROs have varying levels of technical risk knowledge. In some it is quite high. But the CRO doesn't need to know how to estimate a VaR any more than the person running a pharmaceutical company needs to know how to make drugs. She might know, but she doesn't have to.

The inverse is true as well. Not everyone who manages risk in the way I'm going to describe in this chapter is called a risk manager. Many traders and portfolio managers do their own risk management, especially in smaller organizations. I think it's a good idea to separate the responsibilities—that is, to have an independent risk manager. That's the current professional standard as well, and regulators and investors increasingly insist on it.

Front Office

I'll start with a front-office risk manager, which is what most people think of as a risk manager. A century or so ago, brokerage firms had physical front and back offices. Customers came into the front office to do business with Ivy League graduates in suits and polished shoes. The furnishings were expensive and the atmosphere was aristocratic. At the conclusion of the deal, the broker would write a trade ticket or other order document and toss it into the back office.

The back office was a different world in which accountants, clerks, and other support staff shuffled papers to execute trades and keep accounts. The furnishings were basic and the atmosphere was clerical. People might work in shirtsleeves amid piles of paper. They usually looked harassed, as they had to deal with trades that the parties disagreed on the terms of, or that one party denied altogether, or for which one party could not be found, or for which deliverable securities could not be found or any of a hundred other potential problems. Then they had to make it all add up so the customer and brokerage accounts could be maintained. In many cases, such as margin deposits with futures clearinghouses or net capital calculations for reports, everything had to add up every day, so no one went home until it was finished. The next morning brought a new pile of screw-ups.

Today the terminology has generalized, and *front office* means any revenue-producing business unit. In a large financial institution those consist of sales and trading, asset management, retail financial services, institutional financial services, lending, and investment banking. *Back office* can refer either to everything else or, more narrowly, to the clearing, settlement, accounting, and operations responsibilities of the old back office.

A front-office risk manager is employed inside each front-office business unit. In most cases, she will report up through the CRO of the firm, not through the business unit hierarchy. This change has occurred gradually over the past 15 years, to encourage independence of risk managers. Still, on a day-to-day basis, the front-office risk manager works in and for the business unit.

A front-office risk manager is usually recruited from the business, for the same reason sports coaches are usually former players. A risk manager in sales and trading is usually a former trader, a risk manager in asset management is usually a former portfolio manager, and so on. Just as great players often make poor coaches and mediocre players can be great coaches, the risk manager need not have been particularly successful in the business. What she does need is a deep understanding of the business, as well as technical risk management qualifications.

Risk managers first appeared on Wall Street in the front office. Even before they were called risk managers, someone, often the oldest trader on a desk, would take responsibility for coaching and overseeing the other traders, especially the less experienced and less disciplined ones. In the 1980s, quants were often chosen for this role, and this is how the modern profession developed. In my case,

I was running a mortgage securities department and acted as my own risk manager—something I do not recommend in general. I figured it out on the job, with a lot of collaboration from other quants doing the same thing, either as business heads or as formal risk managers. In those days there was no book; we were writing it on the job.

Trading Risk

I will describe front-office risk management of traders because that's the type I've had the most experience with. The traditional part of this job consists mainly of watching the traders for telltale signs they are taking too much or too little risk. You set limits that are tailored to the individual, position sizes they can hold on their own, sizes that need your approval, and sizes that have to be approved by the desk head. There can be different limits for different types of positions, for intraday versus overnight positions, and so on. You expect people to use their limits. If their positions are consistently much smaller than the levels allowed, you find out why. Seats at a trading desk are valuable, and traders must take risk in order to generate an adequate return on investment. Of course, people who are over their limits are a concern as well. Even the slightest hint of disguising risk, such as "putting trades in a drawer," meaning making a trade that the firm is liable for but not reporting it in the trading system, is grounds for immediate dismissal.

Experienced traders who go into front-office risk management learn how to spot traders holding losing positions out of pride or stubbornness rather than calculation, or taking profits early out of fear or greed rather than sober judgment. The risk manager gets a sense of when someone is too reckless as a result of recent big swings, either up or down. The same swings can make a different trader too cautious. You make traders explain their trades to you. You're not listening to the facts. That's not your job. You're judging behavior. Are they "talking their book," meaning pulling out every possible argument in favor of the position? That's a sign of uncertainty, not confidence. Or are they making such a weak case that they seem to unconsciously want you to forbid the trade? That happens, too. In both cases, you veto the trade. You want to hear both firm confidence in the trade and realistic awareness of the risks. Unless they are quant traders, they never tell you the real reasons for the trade, because they don't know them. But if they're good traders and in the right frame of mind, you can bet on their instincts.

Another benefit the front-office risk manager brings is longer market experience than at least the younger traders. Working on a trading desk during manias and panics and everything in between teaches important lessons. It also gives a sense of scale to events. If there's a market crash, a young trader may not know the difference between the worst event in the past few years and the worst event in history. It helps to have someone on the desk remind people of the difference. Most important, experienced front-office risk managers can pass along the accumulated wisdom of generations of traders in a visceral, personal way that no textbook can match.

Quants on the Job

When quants like me got into this game, we naturally did one more thing. We kept very careful records of everyone's bets. We figured out whether people were betting the right size. It turned out that even the best traders were bad at that. They bet more when they were wrong than when they were right. On one hand, they almost always underbet compared to the Kelly amount. You could show conclusively that the desk would be more profitable with larger average bets. On the other hand, even the most prudent traders would occasionally make large bets that were mathematically silly, that could not be justified under any reasonable theory.

My son Jacob did a study of customers at the world's largest online financial betting site, which is described in Dylan Evans's forthcoming book *Risk Intelligence.* About 90 percent of the bettors were betting randomly and losing on average due to the site's built-in edge. But 10 percent had demonstrable ability to predict price movements well enough to have a positive edge. These are very short-term bets, like will the Dow Jones Industrial Average go up or down over the next five minutes? Virtually all of the above-random bettors would have done better to make the same size bet all the time. When they bet more money than their average, they lost more often than average. When they bet less, they won more often. Some even turned winning prediction percentages into financial losses this way. Only a small minority actually made money from varying bet size, and in none of the cases was the amount statistically significant (in other words, it's plausible that their additional profit from changing bet sizes was due to random chance). Professional nonquantitative traders, even the most experienced and successful, are just as bad at bet sizing as the online financial bettors. But before quants showed up on Wall Street, no one bothered to keep track and ask the question. I know that sounds crazy, that a business built on risk taking wouldn't record decisions carefully and analyze the data for possible improvements. That's something every professional poker player learns to do at a very early stage, and blackjack card counters and sports bettors are even more rigorous about it. But Wall Street was deeply nonquantitative before 1980.

Quant front-office risk managers did other things with the data. We checked whether people traded better or worse after a series of wins or a series of losses. We checked performances in the morning and the afternoon, on Mondays versus Fridays, and in one type of trade versus another. We checked if traders would have done better to cut losses faster or slower, or to let profits run farther or shorter. We always found lots of ways to add value. Most of us made this into a game in which we kept track of the virtual money we would have made or lost second-guessing all the trades. We could buy into a trade or not, or even short it (that is, take the opposite side so we credited ourselves with gains if the trade lost money, but took losses in our virtual account if the trade made money). We could make any trade bigger or smaller for the game. Having a positive profit in the game was the only way you knew you were right. This is still a popular technique among front-office risk managers. If you're not the kind of person who likes to keep precise track of performance, yours or other people's, you won't be either happy or good as a front-office risk manager.

Quants from all three camps—frequentists, Bayesians, and the middle ground—found themselves as front-office risk managers in the late 1980s. As the field was beginning to emerge from traditional nonquantitative practice, the poker player types like me were the best at it. The sports bettor types were the best at analyzing the data to determine what should happen, but they were often lousy at communicating it in a way traders could use. You can't explain to a trader that, say, he should be willing to leave bigger positions open over a weekend because he had a greater risk-return ratio on those trades than on intraday or intraweek trades. That's like telling a basketball player he missed more free throws long than short, so in future he should aim a foot in front of the basket instead of at the basket. Your observation might be true statistically, but your advice will just mess up his whole shot. If he doesn't ignore you, he'll start by aiming where you tell him, but he'll know that he really wants it longer, and will probably end up shooting the ball over the backboard.

Poker players know how to make people make the bets they (the poker players) want. That's a basic skill of the game. Maybe you drop by Friday afternoon to discuss the positions and compliment the trader on them, relaying a piece or two of news that suggests the positions could do well by Monday. Or, with a different trader, or maybe the same trader the next week, you look horrified at the positions and tell him he'd be an idiot to hold them. Actually, those are both exaggerations; the process is not that crude or manipulative. But you learn how to work with traders to reinforce their good instincts and suppress their bad ones. You use limits and other parameters to encourage the right behavior.

This is an exaggeration in another sense as well. The risk manager need not be the smartest guy in the room, the Zen master radiating calm wisdom on the unenlightened masses. Everyone on a trading floor, to one degree or another, understands risk ideas. Everyone is trying to get the risk right. Often there is more actual risk management done by traders or other staff than by the risk manager. And risk managers learn from traders, just as coaches learn from players. The risk manager is a specialist on a team, but all team members are trying for the same goal, and all are contributing what they can, not just what their job description says. Just as the best coaching is sometimes to fold your arms on the bench and let your players play, sometimes the best risk management is to play tornado watcher.

Card-counting quants tended to overmanage. They wouldn't talk to the traders at all; they'd just make mysterious changes to limits. It's raining today? Your limit just got cut in half. Again, that's an exaggeration, but it shows the basic mind-set of a frequentist. They changed parameters and checked the effect of the change in their numbers. They'd risk manage a human trader the same way they'd risk manage a computer trading algorithm.

Let me put the breezy exaggerations aside for a moment to give a real example of the kind of quantitative analysis front-office risk managers do. I don't want to make the book too technical, but I also don't want to be misleading. One of the most basic analyses is to break a trader's performance into trades. It's actually tricky to define this properly and it's different for different kinds of traders, but ignore that for now. The *accuracy ratio* is the fraction of trades that make money. The *performance ratio* is the average gain on winning trades divided by the average loss on losing trades. If accuracy ratio times one plus performance ratio is greater than one you're making money, if it's less than one you're losing money.

In principle, there is a trade-off between these two. If you cut losers faster and let profits run longer, you'll have a lower accuracy ratio but a higher performance ratio. In practice, it very often seems to be true that the two are not closely related. The trader can pick a performance ratio, the market gives the accuracy ratio. Attempting to increase the accuracy ratio by sacrificing performance ratio seldom works. Therefore, the usual advice is to target a specific performance ratio, adjusting your trading if necessary to get to that target, but only to monitor accuracy ratio. When accuracy ratio is high, bet bigger, when it's low, bet smaller or even stop trading until the market improves for your strategy.

I know no theory that explains this result, but I have seen it confirmed many times in many different types of trading situations. It's the kind of result that requires careful analysis of trading performance and also long experience with managing trading risk. Most rules are more complicated than this one but this is the kind of thing a front office risk manager can do for a trader.

Today a professional front-office risk manager is expected to do three things. First is the traditional job—to understand the business, coach people into the right risk attitude, and watch for signs of the wrong risk attitude. Second is to keep exhaustive numbers of every decision and to analyze them constantly to find ways of improving risk decisions; also to translate that analysis into a form so it does some good, a form front-office decision makers can understand and use. Third is to communicate the risks of the business to the overall organization. This is two-way communication. The organization needs to know its aggregate risk, so it needs input from all business units. The business unit also has to understand the risk appetite of the organization. The front-office risk manager has to translate that into something meaningful in the business unit. Communication is where standardization is important.

I can also list three things a front-office risk manager is *not* expected to do, despite popular belief. She does not go around sniffing out obscure risks that didn't occur to anyone else. She does not police the traders. She does set and monitor limits, and decide whether and how much positions have to be hedged, but with the attitude of a coach telling a player to take more or fewer shots, or an engineer telling an architect how thick a beam has to be, not like a traffic cop giving out tickets. Traders who consistently violate limits or otherwise ignore advice are disciplined by the head of the desk or in extreme cases by the firmwide compliance department, not by the risk manager. And the risk manager most definitely does not fight with the desk to keep risk down. She works to help the traders take the right level of risk, as determined both by the opportunities seen by the traders and by the overall risk strategy of the desk and the firm.

Middle Office

In the early 1990s, I moved from being a front-office business head and risk manager to being a middle-office risk manager. This was a term we invented at the time; there never was a physical middle office. The basic problem of all financial institutions was that information flowed only one way, from the front office to the back office. The broker tossed the trade ticket over the wall, and never wanted to see it again. If things didn't add up, the back office was supposed to make sense of it somehow. On rare occasions, for intractable problems, a senior back-office person would approach the broker to ask him to correct an obvious mistake on his ticket. The back-office guy could expect to get yelled at. He also expected to get yelled at every time paperwork was late or wrong, even though the delays and errors were usually caused by the front office. Because front-office mistakes were headaches only for the back office, the front office never learned to do things right.

This problem was exacerbated when financial institutions started to computerize. Now a lot more data was flowing a lot faster, but it still flowed only one way. The information technology (IT) department designed computer systems to replace trade tickets. The systems never rejected a trade. If the program refused to accept clearly erroneous input (say, a stock trade with the name and ticker symbol of the stock missing), the trader went ahead and made the trade anyway and blamed the stupid computer system for the accounting mess. So the system took any input the trader cared to give—right, wrong, or missing—and in Wall Street tradition, tossed it into the back office to fix. Better to know the price and quantity of the trade without the stock symbol than not to know a trade occurred at all.

It gets worse. Financial institutions were getting bigger and more complicated. A transaction might go through many departments and several legal entities and a couple of different legal jurisdictions before it reached the back office. At each stage people tossed more garbage in. Sometimes people would fix upstream errors in a way that worked for them, but made everything worse downstream. For example, dozens of traders in a big firm might trade a certain stock on a given day. The traders might put in a lot of information, like the time of the trade, the exchange it was traded on, and so forth. These records might get sent to the equity desk, which would want to aggregate all the trades to find out whether the firm was long or short the stock, and possibly to hedge the position. The equity desk might strip off all the descriptive information in the trade records and replace the many records with a single aggregate trade for the net amount, including its own hedge trade. That made sense to the equity desk, because the aggregate position was all it cared about. But when the equity desk sent the data downstream, all the specific information the back office needed had been removed. So the back office had two sets of information—the original trades and the aggregated trades. Each set had some of the information necessary to make the firm accounts add up, but the two sets could not be reconciled. In other cases, users would fill in missing information with guesses, which should be a capital offense, and I'm a guy who doesn't believe in capital punishment. Downstream users had no idea what information was solid and what information was guesswork.

This situation caused everyone in the firm to build their own systems, grabbing whatever data they needed from other systems. No one could keep track of what went where, and no one could know the source of data they were looking at. Things got split and merged in ways that double-counted some transactions and missed others. Front-office people, investors, and regulators never noticed, because computers are good at making things look as if they add up and are under control. Neat reports went out, usually on time. But the numbers were one part reality and nine parts fantasy.

Some places were better than others. Investment bank internal numbers were a joke. Commercial bank numbers were merely bad. Commercial banks had larger back-office staffs, less arrogant front-office staffs, simpler business models, easier accounting rules, and smarter regulators. They also had a deep credit risk culture, a culture that had developed from decades of having 10 times your net worth lent out to others. Banks that can't keep track of things go broke. In fairness to the investment banks, they had a less hierarchical structure and traditionally trusted partners to oversee risk in their individual businesses. The investment bank culture did not require detailed numbers aggregated through as many layers as a typical commercial bank.

One diversified financial institution that made a serious effort to get things right was JPMorgan. Morgan was a commercial bank, but it was aggressive in trading and investment banking. (It could not underwrite securities due to Glass-Steagall, but when that law was passed in 1932, JPMorgan split its underwriting business off under the name Morgan Stanley.) I spent the early 1990s doing a variety of risk management jobs for JPMorgan, including teaching in its training program for new hires, which turned out to be more effective than anything else I did for the firm. I still meet people who remember me from those classes and tell me it changed the way they treated risk. Perhaps they're just being nice, but I've done a lot of teaching and don't get the same kind of feedback nearly as often from other students. I was giving them important stuff that in those days only I and maybe 100 other people in the world knew.

Teaching risk management—also bond trading, mortgage trading, derivative pricing, foreign exchange (FX), statistics, financial math, and several other courses—was my biggest contribution to the firm. The firm's biggest contribution to my education was putting me on a project with the controllers. Controllers—an ancient misspelling of the word, which you sometimes still see, is *comptroller*, but it means the same and is pronounced the same as *controller*—are internal accountants responsible for keeping track of everything. Today there is a separate specialty of *risk controllers* (not to be confused with risk managers), but in the early 1990s the same people who added up expense accounts and kept track of chairs and tables were expected to make sense of the complex data associated with derivative trading and structured product issuance. As you might expect, few of them had been trained for those highly quantitative tasks. I was supposed to rectify that, but I ended up learning a lot more from them than they learned from me.

JPMorgan's controllers had been wrestling with financial data problems on the cutting edge of finance for years, and they worked for an institution on that edge that cared about accurate numbers. They had accomplished the near impossible through energy, innovation, and teamwork. They needed a little help from me to show them some details about derivatives and trading, but they showed me a whole world of how meaningful information can be extracted from noisy data in real time. This was the first time I conceived of the idea of firmwide risk management, and the first time it seemed remotely possible. Ironically, many of my early allies in the battle for firmwide risk management believed in it precisely because they didn't comprehend the data problems involved. Only a few of us knew both how hard the task was and that it was possible. Even the most starry-eyed optimists of those early allies, however, were far better informed about the realities of financial data than the people who today imagine a systemic risk regulator for the entire financial system.

Back Office

This is when and where back-office risk management was born. Two other institutions that were important early on were Bankers Trust and Citibank. Both were commercial banks with strong traditions of financial control. Bankers Trust was even more aggressive than JPMorgan in trading and structured products. Citibank was a huge trader in FX, but otherwise more inclined to make its risk errors lending money, especially real estate and emerging market loans, than trading derivatives.

Most of the risk management jobs in finance today are in the back office. When I was a finance professor, most students wanted to get the glamorous, highly paid front-office jobs. I've always counseled the advantages of the back office to most people. The pay is lower, but the hours are less and the life quality is generally higher. Advancement comes from ability, not luck or politics or competitive success. Careers are longer and more stable than is usual in the front office. There is genuine scope for innovation and teamwork, even if no one outside the back office will ever appreciate it.

Back-office risk management means compiling what has become a huge volume of risk reports for decision makers, regulators, and investors. Risk IT people build the computer systems, risk controllers get the data right, and risk reporting specialists know how to put it together. Within risk reporting there are regulatory experts, especially in Basel II and Basel III capital rules, and people who specialize in specific types of risk: market risk, credit risk, and operational risk (the last named is everything other than market risk and credit risk; it actually is mostly concerned with dangers, not risks).

While I have done both front-office and back-office risk management, I consider myself a middle-office risk manager. As I mentioned, this is a term made up for risk managers; there are no other middle-office jobs. In my case, I started in front-office risk management, then worked with back-office risk management and got the idea of firmwide risk management. Other people came to similar ideas through different routes.

My first idea was that we had to complete the information loop. The back-office reports had to go back to the front-office people. Any errors in the reports had to be fixed, not the way the back-office people did it by changing the report, but by correcting the input error at the source. The trader had to rebook the erroneous trade. Everyone who handled data between the trading desk and the books and records of the firm also had to sign off on the report or fix whatever errors they had introduced. Not only would this get last night's data right, but it would also identify persistent problems that could be fixed. And if the trading system rejected a trade, the trader knew she had to fix it, either now or later when an erroneous report came out.

A lot of other people had that same idea. It's the first thing that occurs to an IT guy. A lot of money and energy was poured into it and people are still trying. But it failed. I saw that pretty quickly because I had the advantage of having worked in both the front office and the back office. The problem was that the back-office reports were not meaningful in the front office. Even the simplest transactions pulled in information from lots of places, including from other firms in the confirmation process. No one person could sign off on the result, because no one person knew all the details. Moreover, you could get two totals—one aggregated by type of security, say, and one aggregated by country. Maybe you could find one person to sign off on one, and another person to sign off on the other. But if the two totals were inconsistent, there was no one who could track down the discrepancy. On top of this, the systems were so bad, even at JPMorgan, that the reports were always wrong and had multiple errors that couldn't be disentangled and assigned to one responsible party. Not to mention that the front-office people were careless and lazy, and knew they wouldn't be disciplined for blowing off the back office.

Some IT visionaries saw creative solutions involving middleware and messaging systems and financial product markup language and other expensive technical solutions. That also failed. One reason is the businesses were changing so fast that even if you got something working for a while, it didn't keep working. But the bigger reason was that the basic problem was organizational, not technical.

Middle Office Again

The idea of the middle office is to create two information loops in the bank. The front office sends data to the middle-office risk manager, who processes it and sends it back to the front office. The key difference from my first idea is the middle office puts it in a form the front office can understand—and also that the front office can use to determine which source data to correct. Eventually, the middle office gets it right. At that point, it sends the data to the back office. The back office produces its reports and sends them to the middle office. Again, these reports make sense to the middle office, so it knows how to correct any input errors to get the back-office report correct. This idea actually worked.

The middle office did not replace the front-to-back-office data flow. There weren't enough middle-office people for that and it would have slowed things down too much. The middle office concerned itself only with information that was important for firmwide risk. Although this is a tiny subset of the amount of information flowing around a financial firm, it forces everyone to get things right. Everything affects risk. Any sorts of data errors can result in inconsistencies either in the risk data or between the risk data and what actually happens in the world. Either way, the errors are discovered and fixed.

That's what the middle-office did, but that's not why we built one. The middle office was built by risk people who wanted to tackle the problem of firmwide risk. That was the bottom-up pressure. There was also top-down pressure from CEOs who wanted to get meaningful data about the daily risks of their businesses. Front-office information was different for each business unit, and most CEOs understood only a few of the businesses. Even if that were not true and the CEO understood all businesses, no CEO had time to digest specialized risk reports on every business. Plus it was possible to understand each business in isolation and still miss gigantic risks that resulted from interactions among businesses, like everyone making the same bet in different ways.

Once we built a middle office, regulators discovered it. Their interests were similar to those of CEOs. So the middle office took over the job of communicating with regulators. The regulatory reports were still produced in the back office, but the middle office designed and explained them. The Basel II and later Basel III capital accords are based on middle-office concepts and data.

Investors never showed much interest in middle-office reports, which I find curious since that's the information you need to evaluate the risk of an investment in a bank. Financial statements of large, diversified financial firms have little meaning. However, the Securities and Exchange Commission in 1998 ordered financial firms to include risk information in their annual and quarterly reports, and suggested disclosing value at risk as one of the allowed methods. But I've never met an equity analyst, credit analyst, or investor who uses the VaR data reported in financial statement notes.

The first thing a middle-office risk manager does is issue daily VaRs for every business unit and subunit. These predictions are tested against the actual profit or loss on the positions at the time of VaR computations. It's usually two or three days before you have final profit and loss numbers for comparison.

The inputs for the VaR computations come from the front office. If the inputs are delayed, you fill in guesses. If the inputs are wrong, you correct them with the best guesses you can make. You have to build cushion in your VaR algorithm for missing inputs and input errors. You don't make a large cushion based on conservative guesses; you have to get the right number of VaR breaks—not too many, not too few—so you have to calibrate your cushion just like any other input. You're constantly tweaking your algorithms to improve the performance of the VaR.

Looking Backward

This brings up the issue of backward-looking risk management. This has become a common charge against risk managers. The idea is that in periods of low market volatility, such as from 2004 to early 2006, you issue low estimates of risk. The result is that when market volatility goes up, the firm is holding positions scaled assuming a lower level of risk. The positions are too big and it's difficult to reduce them during a market crisis. Ironically, the conventional solution is supposed to be even more backward looking, to consider the risk of your positions in scenarios from the more distant past.

Both the problem and the solution are more complicated than that. The reason risk estimates were low in 2006 was not just that current market volatility was low. All sorts of other measures of risk were low as well. For example, one forward-looking measure of risk is how much traders charge to insure against future losses in the stock market. The Chicago Board Options Exchange Volatility Index (a market index called the VIX, sometimes referred to as the "fear indicator") can be used for this. Another important indicator is whether asset prices are moving with some independence, as they normally do in calm times, or herding together, as they often do before and during a storm. Any unusual divergences are signs that risk may be picking up. Sharp changes in asset prices without an obvious underlying cause or erratic trading volumes can be clues of an approaching tsunami. You look at whether the real economy is preparing for a downturn, say by paring inventory or locking in long-term debt. There are qualitative factors as well. Is the world tense and nervous? Is there a foreseeable series of events that could lead to a crisis? Is there a buildup of debt or anything else that could amplify problems in a downturn?

Although some of these measures are forward looking, they are all historical in the sense that the data measurement happened in the past. The VIX measures what traders five minutes ago thought about the future; it does not measure the future itself. The amount and type of debt outstanding in the economy help you guess how a future crisis may play out, but the number itself is in the past. And one key insight that people too often forget is that when the crisis starts, the numbers you were looking at today will have changed. For example, looking at the accounting statements of a solid company tells you little about the chance it will default, nor about what recovery you can expect in the event of default. The reason is that if a company defaults, a lot of other stuff will have had to happen first. The balance sheet at that time, just before default, will not look anything like today's balance sheet, whether because of accounting fraud or as the result of a series of unfortunate events. Accounting statements are useful for predicting default of shaky companies, however.

Why does anything in the past tell you about the future? In science the answer is that past data help you discover physical laws, and physical laws seem to be constant, at least on the scale relevant to humans. But no one has discovered comparable laws in human affairs like economics. There are observed empirical regularities, but they are not precise, and they don't always work.

There are two different ways you could try to exploit the observed empirical regularities. You could make very aggressive, precise predictions based on complicated analysis of short-term data. You would get clear, actionable results, but you would be wrong a lot. Or you could make cautious, broad predictions based on robust analysis of long-term data. You would be right more often, but your prediction would be less useful for decision making. Neither of these approaches works perfectly, but done right they work better together than either one works alone.

The key insight of Wall Street quants in the late 1980s was how to combine both types of predictions. You use the precise short-term prediction to decide what to do, and the robust long-term prediction for plan B—what to do when the first method is wrong. VaR is one of the aggressive, precise predictions. It's not a useful number to know, but it serves as an important calibration test of your methodology. If your VaR cannot pass a back-test—that is, if you don't get the right number of VaR breaks or if they are distributed in nonrandom patterns in time or happen mostly at high or low values of VaR—then you cannot rely on any aggressive predictions. As a surprise bonus, we discovered that when VaR changes unexpectedly or you get a VaR break (a day when you lose more than the VaR amount), it's often a useful warning to reduce faith in all aggressive predictions for a while.

The more cautious predictions are based on long-term history, general principles, and imagination. It is small harm if you assign a nonzero probability to a scenario that is in fact impossible. You might give up a little profit, but that's survivable. It can be fatal to assign a zero probability to a scenario that is in fact possible. That's why you include anything you think is even remotely possible in your cautious predictions. You don't try to assign probabilities; you don't have the data for that, by definition. You just try to sort out the possible from the impossible. The risk management rule is: if it's likely, exploit it; if it's plausible, hedge it; if it's possible, prepare for it; if it's impossible, you just bet everything you have or ever will have on that assessment.

Risk Control

Getting back to your middle-office risk management job, you're reporting the VaR back to the front office, along with other statistics about their positions and performance. You highlight any discrepancies that suggest the business may not be under risk control. The precise standards for risk control depend on the business. In many financial businesses you typically ask three things: Can the business estimate the daily volatility of its profit and loss accurately? Can the business tell you its profit and loss accurately conditional on what market prices do during the day? And are the estimated numbers coming out of the business consistent with the actual cash flows from arm's-length transactions with third parties? Not all businesses can answer yes to all three questions, and most businesses have some other questions as well, but these are still the basics. Each one of these things can be measured precisely and objectively.

If you are starting a middle office from scratch, or taking over in a place with poor risk management, you will find most businesses are not anywhere close to being under risk control. The VaRs you compute for these businesses will be inflated by missing and erroneous data. The measured ex post risk will not correspond to the business's ex ante estimates, the ex post profit and loss will not respond to market factors as the business predicted ex ante, and the ex post cash flows will not match the business's ex ante accounting claims. These facts do not necessarily mean the business itself is not under control. It may be run very well and the head of the business may have a good handle on risk. The accounting numbers the business supplies may be perfectly consistent with all the rules. But there is no way an outsider can understand the business risks, and no way the business risks can be integrated into a firmwide risk strategy. And it's more likely that the business is not under control, even by its own people. Bad numbers can be just bad numbers, but usually they evidence a bad reality.

One way or another, you have to bring the businesses under risk control or shut them down. There is no third option. You can change the definition of risk control for some businesses. For example, some trading strategies and opportunistic businesses may not be able to predict their daily volatility. Some days they have lots of opportunities and take lots of risks, whereas other days they don't. But you have to find some measure of risk that they can predict. Otherwise you can't tell them to cut risk 10 percent or increase risk 30 percent, and have hard statistical reason to believe your instructions are meaningful in terms of effect on firmwide risk. It is a too-common occurrence that the risk manager orders a change in risk levels and the business offsets that change by claiming more or fewer opportunities or a higher or lower expected return. You need to be able to measure something in an objective, statistically verifiable way before you can use it as a control. Other businesses might not be able to relate their profit and loss to market movements. But they have to relate them to something, or you can't know how the business is really doing. It may not be a perfect match, but it has to be good enough that their residual risk—that is, the difference between their actual profit and loss and the prediction they made based on market moves—is statistically independent of any market factor and any other business's residual risk.

These are hard jobs that require frequent adjustment. A middle-office risk manager is constantly poring over numbers trying to improve predictions and controls. She must insist on the highest standard of rigorous validation, or the entire exercise is meaningless. If you're the kind of person who thinks something is probably true because it sounds right, or theoretically should be true, or always worked in the past, or someone smart told you, or it's so simple they must have got it right—then you cannot be a middle-office risk manager. For that job you must trust only hard statistical evidence of clear predictions made before the fact, validated against objective, accurate data after the fact.

Beyond Profit and Loss

In all my examples, I've discussed daily profit and loss as something to predict. That's due to my background in managing financial businesses in which most of the risk was in strategies liquid enough to be priced every day, and not so high-frequency that a day was not a meaningful reporting interval. But a middle-office risk manager can use a VaR for any variable related to firm performance that can be measured objectively, and measured over a time scale that allows for statistical verification. It's more important that the variable be objective and measured frequently enough than that it be the most relevant measure of the firm's business.

For example, a middle-office risk manager of a hospital might want to develop a VaR on how many patients in the hospital at midnight die before the following midnight. This is not something the hospital wants to minimize; the way to do that is not to admit any sick people. It's also not the best measure of the hospital's performance. A bad hospital might not get any seriously ill patients and a great one might get more than its share. Moreover, there are bad things a hospital can do that don't kill anyone, and good things it can do that don't save lives. But deaths are related to the hospital's business, and they are objective, and they can be measured daily.

If you tried to implement this VaR, even at a well-run hospital, my prediction is you would find all kinds of system barriers to compiling the information you need both to make and test the predictions. Patients might not be systematically tracked after discharge. There probably are multiple systems for different types of patients, and there are system or privacy issues in linking them up. Important data will be missing or erroneous. Other important data will be available, but too late to use in the VaR computation. Producing the VaR and back-testing it rigorously will improve your knowledge about the information you do receive, and also improve your systems.

I further predict that changes in the level of your VaR, and also days when you get more deaths than the VaR estimate, will turn out to be very useful indicators that help you manage the hospital's risk. Maybe certain types of patients or certain doctors or staff are more dangerous than you realized. Maybe deaths are correlated to something that never occurred to you.

A good idea in general, but inappropriate in this case, is to allow employees to bet on VaR breaks. They can either pay $1 and get $19 if there is a VaR break or put up $19 to get $1 if there is not. All kinds of information that you could never collect from formal information systems is revealed when you offer even small monetary rewards. I am dead (sorry) serious about this. It's not an irreverent suggestion to show what a freethinker I am, nor a backdoor way to lobby for gambling. It is a useful way to collect information that costs very little and that employees enjoy, and certainly enjoy a lot more than filling out paperwork for the relatively useless official information.

I know nothing about running a hospital, so it's quite likely there is a better measure to use. But any reasonable measure is far better than none. Organizations depend on complex information flows. Unless there is constant, rigorous testing of that information, its quality will be very poor. That lack of quality will be obscured by . . . the poor quality of the data. The poor quality will be further obscured by systems and people that force the data to be consistent, like dictators who repress all dissent. If you can't use the data to make simple predictions—every day, on time—about something objective and central to the institution's function, you're a fool to use the data for anything at all. Bad data leads to inefficiency and uncontrollable risks. Even if it didn't, given the vast sums spent on processing data, it's worth spending a little effort to make it good.

Numbers

I'm one of those people who always add things up: restaurant checks, bank statements, W-2 forms, whatever. The numbers are frequently wrong. Most people don't know that, because they don't check. If a person has to enter a number, say a waitress or retail salesperson, they make errors at a rate of about 1 percent to 5 percent. If a person has to do a simple calculation, like adding up a check or figuring sales tax, the error rate is about 5 percent to 20 percent. For example, I always add up the prices of the items I buy in the supermarket as I pick them out. In the days before supermarket scanners, if I had a full cart, the total at the checkout was wrong more often than not. With, say, 50 numbers to punch into a machine, the average checkout clerk made about one error.

That figure sounds reasonable to most people. The misconception is that "official" numbers from big institutions printed by computer are more likely to be correct. I have found similar error rates with brokerage statements, mortgage computations, and minor IRS tax tables, just to name a few. In the early days of adjustable-rate mortgages, the error rate on interest computation was greater than 50 percent, and it's not zero today. Another frequent error is in the correct principal and interest amount due when someone pays off a mortgage early. It's more often wrong than right in my experience. No one actually reads the thick pile of documents with dozens of signatures that make up the legal mortgage file; a clerk types numbers into a computer system. The computer system assumptions may not correspond to the documents. If the errors are big, they usually get caught either by the lender or by the borrower. But small errors are common, and they can add up to large totals. I traded nongovernment mortgage securities in the 1980s, and I remember no deal in which all the cash flows were properly allocated to all investors. Earlier, when I traded bonds, we used a desktop calculator called a Monroe Bond Calculator to compute the actual settlement cash on a transaction. People often set their calculators incorrectly for the bond in question, and the calculator itself made some errors. On a $10 million trade, the errors were on the order of a few hundred dollars. The bond salespeople on the other side didn't care; they never saw the settlement. The back-office people in the bank that bought or sold the bond never argued with me; it wasn't their money. Only a few cranks cared enough to do it right. In a different domain, the 2000 U.S. Presidential election publicized the huge error rate in counting votes, which incidentally has not gone down at all despite considerable money and effort devoted to the task. This was no surprise to risk managers.

These errors compound in large, complicated systems. The only reason the numbers don't become completely useless is that there is some reality checking. For example, a firm's accounting system computes how much cash it is supposed to have. This number will not be correct, due to errors in the firm's systems. Also, the reported cash balances in the firm's bank accounts will not be right. Obviously, the two totals will not match, either, except by extreme coincidence. In a big firm, the difference will typically be millions of dollars. But the firm will not allow the difference to expand indefinitely. It has people constantly trying to reconcile things. Suppose the firm overall is missing $5 million of cash. Its reconciliation people will naturally focus on finding that cash—that is, correcting the mistakes in the firm that cause it to overstate its cash balances, and the errors in the bank accounts that cause them to understate the firm's balances. These selective corrections will make the discrepancy shrink, but on average they will not make either total more accurate. The cash-in-bank-accounts number the firm reports on its official financial statement will have evolved to be within tolerable agreement with its bank statements. It cannot be wildly inconsistent with reality, but it will not be in any sense accurate.

What's true of cash in bank accounts is even more true of pretty much every large, complex data system. At least cash can be checked directly with independent systems, unlike things like earnings or gross domestic product. There are enough input and processing errors that the results would be meaningless except that the outputs are checked against some kind of reality. The output you see appears to be the result of aggregating inputs, but it's not. It's really a product of evolution, of selective error correction until the result is within bounds acceptable to the system owner. To know whether you should rely on a number from a complex system, don't ask about the inputs or the processes; ask what it is checked against. If the answer is that the number is not checked against anything, or only against other outputs of the same system, it's worthless. If the number is checked against independent systems, it may have some value, but you have to be careful. If the number is checked rigorously against objective reality, then you can trust it.

The Banks of the Charles

I'm now going to take a chance. If you're still reading this far into the book, maybe you will give me the benefit of the doubt for these next four sections. I know I will sound like a crackpot, but I believe deeply in what I'm about to say. It explains why I fled to the company of gamblers rather than get a job, and why I came back eager to beat the Street, not to join the Street. It's also the reason that risk management is so important—and so revolutionary.

I'm going to start with my freshman year in college. I was supporting myself by playing poker and by working at various mathematical analysis and computer odd jobs. The first such job was for a small computer company in Cambridge that had agreed to provide player rankings for a well-known tennis association. I got a call from the company CEO one Thursday afternoon. He explained he needed someone to come in and "finish up" the project because the association was having its annual banquet the next day, and needed the rankings to give out awards.

I showed up at the company around 5:00 P.M. The CEO showed me cardboard boxes full of tennis score reports that had been sent in throughout the season. None had been opened. He told me he needed the rankings by tomorrow, and left for the night. I was alone in the offices.

I started going through the score sheets and immediately hit upon problems. Some were illegible, and some listed what seemed to be impossible results. Names were often just a first initial and a last name, or sometimes even less than that. Was "T. Smith" Tom Smith or Trisha Smith? Or a one-time player? This was 1974, so there was no Google to consult for information on players. Even with perfect data, there would be a lot of questions. Do you weight results in the first round of a tournament the same as results in the final round? If not, how do you adjust? How do you rank a player who won 70 out of 100 matches versus a player who won 19 out of 20 with the same level of opponents? Do you give extra credit for wins by large amounts or is a win a win?

Since no one was around to ask, I just entered all the data into the computer, guessing as necessary, and did some pro forma rankings based on different assumptions. I worked all night. Around 9:00 the next morning, the CEO showed up. I had pages of output to go over with him, after which we would have to call the tennis association for some additional information, plus make some decisions about rankings. He cut me short and said he would take care of everything. I later discovered he just sent the first pages of my output, with the rankings under one set of assumptions. As far as I know, no one complained.

In itself, this story is not particularly surprising or horrifying. People and companies do sloppy jobs sometimes—and usually get away with it. Mixing up the rankings is not a life-and-death issue, although it probably was deeply unfair to some competitors who might have cared a lot. And I'm certainly not trying to generate any moral outrage against the CEO. I don't think I'm a lot better than him; after all, I cashed the check and kept my mouth shut about it—until now anyway, and I doubt anyone still cares. I refused to work for that company from then on, but I had plenty of work. If I'd needed the money, I probably would have helped them out of another jam like that one.

A few months later I was working for another company. This one had agreed to count election ballots for a national association. They had screwed up the counting so badly the previous year, 1973, that it had ended up in court. For some inexplicable reason, the settlement was that the company would count the ballots for free in 1974.

I got called in after the company had sent the election results. The association had replied that it didn't believe the totals. It had photocopied 200 ballots, and those results differed so much from the totals the company had sent that the association's hired statistician disputed the company's results. The company asked me to review the statistical analysis.

Looking through the photocopied ballot sample, I noticed that the ballots had serial numbers and the sample, while not sequential, was also far from random. The election had been done by mail, and it looked as if the sample had been taken mostly from the lower-numbered ballots. If the ballots had been sent out by state, that could make a big difference, as it could mean the entire sample was from Alabama, which might vote differently from Wyoming. But if the ballots had been sent out randomly, or by membership number or alphabetical order of voter name, the sample might be representative of the whole.

I asked to see the original ballots that had been used to keypunch—that was the 1974 technology—the computer cards used to tally the votes. Those turned out not to exist. On closer questioning, it developed that the company had known about the sample, and had gotten copies of the sampled ballots. Those were in fact what I was looking at; the association had not sent copies of what its statistician had analyzed. Those were also the only ballots the company had counted, but it still managed to count them wrong. No one knew—or would admit to knowing—where the actual ballots were. Nevertheless, by the point all that became clear to me, I had given them enough statistical advice to contest the association's claim. The reported results, based on a flawed counting of 200 nonrandomly selected ballots, stood.

These were two of the more outrageous examples of bad numbers, but there were a lot of bad numbers given out and a very small number of people who cared. Even the people working on projects with me were mostly able to ignore the meaninglessness of what they did. One guy used bad data or he made up data, but figured it didn't make any difference to the project. Another guy ran computer code with bugs, but lied rather than admit the error and redo things. Someone else misrepresented the results to the customer, without knowing one way or the other whether they were accurate. And everyone went home at 5:00 P.M. and cashed their paychecks. They say if you work in a kitchen you'll never eat at a restaurant. Well, I never worked in a restaurant kitchen, but I'll never believe a number unless it's something I can validate.

Waste

I discussed this at the time with Fischer Black, who had similar experiences. We worked on an informal project to estimate how much of the work done in the world was wasted. The conclusion was about 95 percent. The reason most people don't notice is they consider only the waste at their level. If a truck driver carries a load of goods from a warehouse to a store 400 miles away, he figures he did work. After all, he got paid $300 for it. But how much of that is useful work? Some of the items carried are defective, others will never be sold, and still others will be sold but not provide any satisfaction to the user. Some will be sold but used in other businesses that fail. Some will end up being moved other places, perhaps back to the warehouse. Some will be sold, but could have been sold for the same price or more at the original location.

All of this is disguised by accounting rules that treat every expenditure as a creation of value. The numbers all add up as if the truck driver did $300 worth of work. But it's fantasy. If we could really measure things right, we might find out that the average value of the 100 trips the truck driver made a year was about $300, but that 5 percent of the goods carried represented the entire $30,000 of value, and for the remaining 95 percent of goods the transportation added zero net value. Of course, we couldn't do any more than guess that 5 percent was the right figure, but it seemed reasonable in light of the calculations we could do. This makes clear how silly it is to claim that so-called real work matters while finance and government and other organizing activities are useless. The only reasons the fraction of useful work is as high as 5 percent are finance and social infrastructure and technology. Those are the things that have the potential to let everyone live twice as well with half the work. Those are the things of great social value. The only other way to increase the fraction of useful work is to simplify activities. Hunter-gatherers probably have less waste, but also far less productivity. One of the spurious appeals of socialism is noticing the amount of waste and thinking that it could be eliminated by top-down decree. If there is useful work to be done and unemployed people willing to do it, it seems like a waste not to connect them. If there were one person and one job, or even 100 people and 100 jobs, that would be clearly true. But on any scale larger than that, it is not true. Refusing to accept waste in one area leads to much greater waste in others.

Years later, my eRaider.com partner Martin Stoller made a similar point that he called "the myth of efficient government." He didn't mean the government was inefficient in the sense of wasting money or hiring too many people or requiring useless paperwork.

He meant that most people imagine the government and other large institutions in terms of much smaller scale. If a local property tax collector says there are 2,000 residences in a town with a total assessed valuation of $200 million, those numbers may be off by some percentage, but they bear some relation to reality. Therefore, you can predict the effect of changes in the property tax rate, or estimate the cost of a regulation to install additional smoke detectors.

When the federal government says there are 100 million residences in the county with a total assessed valuation of $20 trillion, those numbers are completely meaningless, divorced from any reality. There are so many definitional issues and measurement problems associated with determining them that any decision or prediction based on them might as well be a coin flip. If your mental image is a town with a few different types of residences that one person could personally observe all of in the course of a few days, your picture is wildly off-scale.

It is similarly misleading to consider the effect of some legal or regulatory change as if it happened in a town. Say the federal government imposes a tax on carbon emissions. An economist might predict that will reduce emissions, but that's thinking small. The actual rules and tax collection will go through dozens of layers of regulators with unpredictable consequences at each stage. The change will induce all kinds of other changes in people's behavior. The effects are entirely unpredictable in terms of money collected or effect on emissions. The point is that it is a myth to think of any large institution as a rational actor processing reliable inputs in a predictable way to decide on reasonable actions with predictable effects. None of that is true. If you think the world works pretty much the way it seems, you're wrong. If you think aggregated statistics tell you anything useful about the world, you're wrong. If you think you know the effect of large-scale changes, you're wrong. Only when you admit these things can you begin to figure out what works and what doesn't.

I did a lot of academic projects as well, and they weren't a lot better. The people I worked for liked running models and solving equations; they hated sifting through data to cleanse it of errors and understand exactly what it meant. They took all kinds of garbage data, and it never occurred to them to validate. Not one of them would have bet real money on his results—the very question was offensive. This was stuff for academic publication, not real. Around this time there was an extensive literature in economics on how the number of firms in an industry was positively correlated to the frequency of price changes. This was alleged to prove that firms used sticky pricing to coordinate their pricing decisions, a form of price-fixing, and the fewer firms in the industry the more successful they were at it. Then someone discovered that the data used to determine whether a price had changed was based on a government sample of firms, and the more firms in an industry, the more firms were sampled. Since if any firm changed prices the average changed, surveying more firms produced more apparent price changes. When you adjusted for this, the entire reported effect went away. But the publications were not rescinded, and the PhDs were not taken away; people just ignored the problem and went on to the next batch of data whose flaws had not been discovered yet. I considered this a major scandal that should have led to significant changes in how economics was done. But no one else cared. Worst of all, the reason no one else cared was they never really believed their results in the first place.

Now, not all economists, and certainly not all academics, think this way. For one more or less random example, I worked on a simulation of fires in residential buildings. The project included firefighters, arson investigators, survivors of fires, and engineers as well as physicists and mathematical analysts. We burned down real houses for data (legally). I found this immensely satisfying, although in all my time on the project we did not come up with any practical recommendations. It was satisfying because it was real, and I would bet on the results.

The problem is that a lot of people avoid validation, and they are tolerated by the rest. These charlatans expend effort only to confirm hypotheses, not to falsify them. It is the latter effort, seeking out alternative points of view and doing your best to come up with tests to prove your hypothesis wrong, that leads to important knowledge. They are untroubled by the philosophical puzzle of how long-term frequency is connected to degree of belief, because it never occurs to them to believe what they write. They probably are too thin-blooded to bet on anything, and if they had to bet, the last thing would be on their own results.

The Banks of the Potomac

This is all background to the summer I spent working on the U.S. government standby gas-rationing plan. One of my jobs was to figure out how much fuel would be needed to harvest crops and get food to market. I'm a city boy, so I needed to ask whether tractors run on diesel fuel or gasoline. I called the Department of Agriculture and got passed around until I found the right guy. He was out. So I called Ford Motor Company, and found an economist who had just finished modeling the U.S. tractor market. He told me 75 percent of the tractors ran on diesel and gave me a lot of supporting detail.

The Agriculture guy called me back later. I already had the answer, but I figured I'd listen to him anyway to be polite. He had also just finished a model, and told me that 25 percent of the tractors ran on diesel. I said, "You mean 25 percent run on gasoline." No, he insisted it was 25 percent diesel. I told him what the Ford guy had said and he snorted that Ford was only talking about new sales, not the existing stock. That wasn't true; I had all the supporting numbers from Ford. We discussed them at some length and he had answers to all the points I made, giving me his own supporting detail. I checked those with Ford. That guy said Agriculture was counting old tractors rusting in barns or that had been sold to Mexico in the 1950s (not true).

So I started calling farmers, and garage mechanics in agricultural areas, and fuel suppliers and refineries. The more I learned about the issue, the more I realized that no rationing plan had a hope of working. The amount and types of fuel needed and the times at which they were needed varied dramatically from place to place, crop to crop, and season to season. Moreover, people needed to know about supplies well in advance. If you really wanted to deliver the fuel necessary to service agriculture in the United States, you would need a nationwide organization with a large degree of local autonomy and massive databases, and you would have to partner with tens of thousands of businesses. Otherwise, it would be a complete disaster.

Of course, nothing like this was contemplated. The idea was that farmers would be issued ration coupons, and the government would direct supplies so that each local area would have the amount of fuel necessary to fulfill all the coupons. And it wasn't just farmers, which might have been barely possible to do right if the right people were in charge and the entire resources of the government were devoted to that one problem. Everyone was going to get ration coupons for everything deemed essential. And the whole plan was based on wild oversimplifications and terrible data.

Dietrich Dorner is a German psychology professor who has done fascinating experiments about how people manage systems. One simple one concerned a meat locker. In a virtual experiment, the subject had a dial that controlled the strength of the refrigeration. The goal was to keep the temperature within a band such that the meat would not spoil. Simple mechanical thermostats have done an excellent job of this since Cornelius Drebbel invented one in 1660. Almost all people, even with lots of explanation and practice, do a terrible job.

When the experiment starts, the refrigeration unit has been turned off, and the temperature in the locker is too high and rising. So you have to start by moving the dial to increase the refrigeration. But you have no idea how much is the right amount, so you have to guess. The crucial thing that most people cannot do is wait about five minutes to see the effect of whatever change you make. Almost everyone keeps moving the dial up because they don't see an immediate decline in the temperature. The problem with constant changes is subjects cannot develop a feel for how much difference a change in the dial makes, and how long it takes for the change to take effect. The other near-universal mistake is to wait until the temperature is at the right level before turning the refrigeration down. At that point you're going to wildly overshoot on the cold side. Of course, your reaction to that will be an overreaction on the warm side. The only people who can master this extremely simple task are ones who apply explicit quantitative reasoning and have the faith to stick with it even when it seems not to be working.

Another simple Dorner experiment is to let people manage a few variables in a simple virtual village. The experimental subjects can devote resources to health care, irrigation, house building, and other projects. Here again, almost everyone creates disasters, however much training they receive and however often they replay the game. The tendency is to correct every short-term problem without considering the long-term consequences. In a few virtual years, everyone in the village is dead and the area is an environmental wasteland. The refusal to tolerate waste leads to total waste. The refusal to let anyone suffer leads to total suffering. Top-down thinking leads to bottom-up failure.

I did something similar to this experiment my freshman year in college. My simulation was political rather than administrative. Each subject controlled a country and could allocate resources to investment, production, and military spending, and could trade or fight with other countries. The subjects were all professors and graduate students using quantitative modeling in economics or political science. The simulation was not designed to be difficult; with moderate actions the world chugged along acceptably. Everyone had complete information, both complete, accurate data and knowledge of the equations that generated the outputs depending on the inputs. But in every run, people quickly generated global thermonuclear war. Tellingly, no one was interested in exploring how rational decisions of well-intentioned people led to disaster. Instead, people claimed the simulation was rigged, without pointing to any inconsistency between their inputs and the computed outputs.

Given that humans demonstrably cannot manage simple virtual systems with complete information and power, plus lots of training and practice, you would have to be a complete idiot to expect them to manage complex real systems with noisy and out-of-date information and strictly limited power, and with no training or practice.

If the other people working on the standby gas-rationing plan had disagreed with me, I could have taken that. I'm wrong a lot; maybe I was wrong about this one. But they didn't disagree. It just never occurred to them that the plan might actually be implemented. It was all some theoretical exercise that existed on a totally different level than decisions they made for their own lives. If any one of them bought a car, he would look it over carefully and shop for the best price. But that same person was willing to take money to write a plan on which every American's food supply depended— and all the rest of the U.S. economy that is essential for survival— without checking any data or doing any experiments at all. No one even was interested in reading about the experiences of agricultural planners in communist countries.

Even worse than any of this, no one had any interest in contrary opinions. The guy in the Agriculture Department and the guy at Ford just wanted to explain away each other's results. They didn't want to see all sides of an issue, and they certainly weren't going to try to falsify their results. Their interest started and ended at being the expert on their topic. The same thing seemed true of everyone I met working on quantitative projects. Their expertise was a fortress to be defended, not a tool to explore reality.

I could understand this better if people were merely corrupt, if they did useless work for money and prestige and an easy life.

But these people worked very hard, days, nights, and weekends. They were passionate about their careers and their findings. Many of them were smart, and many had broad experience. But all that work, all those brains, and all that experience were wasted due to terrible data and no willingness to open ideas up to falsification. I would ask people to name any computation they had ever done professionally for which they had objective evidence about whether the result was accurate. Some people came up with weak or indirect validation, usually amounting to agreeing with someone else's model or even merely a general consensus. Others could not even come up with that. Incredibly, no one ever had felt the need to check. I ask the same question of job applicants today, and only a small minority of quantitative professionals can give a satisfactory answer.

Okay, I didn't meet everyone on the project. No doubt there were honest and careful people involved somewhere. But there weren't enough of them to make a difference, and they weren't in touch with each other. I came to believe that most quantitative projects, most mathematical models, and most complex aggregated data were worthless, and even the people running the projects, writing the models, or collecting the data wouldn't bet their own money on the results, and would be insulted if you proposed that they do so.

The Summer of My Discontent

It wasn't just in Cambridge and Washington. Consider accounting numbers. Until 1970 the book value of a company, its assets minus its liabilities, corresponded pretty closely to the price of its stock. Some companies were higher and some were lower, but the average price-book ratio never got too far from 1 for long. When companies went bankrupt, creditors collected something close to book value in most cases, minus about 20 percent on average for lawyers' fees. But starting in the 1970s and to an increasing degree thereafter, the relationship between book value and market value broke. The two are basically unrelated today; in fact, it's rare to find a company selling near book value. And about half the time when a company goes bankrupt, recovery for creditors is near zero. That means not only does the entire net value vanish overnight, but the assets turn out to be worth close to zero. The accounting numbers are still useful as indicators, but they have long since lost any connection to tangible economic reality, to the real prices real people pay for real things. Accounting makes it all add up nicely and neatly, but what's being added isn't real.

Now, the reason I had come to Washington was not to work on the gas-rationing plan. That was my cover story. I really wanted to play poker. Washington is one of the best poker cities because people come from all over the country—and all over the world—with their local attitudes and strategies. Today you find that to an even greater degree on the Internet, but in the 1970s Washington was not the best poker city in the world—that was probably Houston or Gardena, California—but it was the most cosmopolitan. To get really good, you had to play there.

In my academic pursuits and day jobs I knew many of the most prominent quantitative modelers in the world, and poker in Washington put me in touch with some of the most powerful non-quantitative people. There were members of Congress, cabinet members, senior civil servants, generals, and top diplomats happy to sit down in games with me. Let's just say, however, that I was not impressed. Some of these people were smart and some were honest and some were good-hearted. But none seemed to have much clue about how to do the jobs people thought they were doing. None of them had the data to do things right. None of them had any objective evidence that what they were doing had the effects they claimed. None were interested in falsification any more than the quants were.

Let me make some more qualifications. Maybe the more competent people were out making policy and running things, not playing poker with a college kid. Maybe the people I met had qualitative insights that allowed them to do good jobs without quantitative analysis or rigorous validation. But I didn't believe it then, and I don't believe it now. I think anything bigger than a small town can be run efficiently only using quantitative methods, and those methods require constant, rigorous validation and openness to all challenge. Most of all, they require people who are willing to bet on the results.

You also have to remember that this was all happening in the 1970s. More than half the world was in the grip of totalitarian horror regimes, and no country had ever emerged from communism into prosperity and freedom. None of the dictatorships admitted mistakes even after tens of millions of people died for them. The dwindling democracies all seemed to be run by paranoid lunatics or total incompetents, and also lied rather than admit mistakes. Not only did the United States build enough weapons to destroy all life on earth, but we spent more to do it than the total value of every other thing in the country except the land. That's right, half our national capital went to building weapons that would have been suicidal to use. The economy was stagnant and inflation was uncontrollable. The general fear in the 1970s was that we would make ourselves miserable and impoverished, or dead, through our own stupidity. By age 20, all my life experience confirmed this fear.

Diogenes was a Hellenistic philosopher who lived 2,400 years ago. When Plato quoted Socrates' definition of a man as a featherless biped, Diogenes plucked a chicken, brought it to Plato, and said, "I bring you a man." Plato then added "with broad, flat nails" to the definition. I knew exactly how Diogenes felt. Plato and almost all the smart or powerful people I met had no interest in falsification. Diogenes invented cynicism and went on a (sarcastic) search for an honest man. I went on a (sincere) search for honest quants, people who were good at math and willing to bet on their conclusions. More than that, I wanted people who would offer their conclusions to the world to bet on, like someone who sets the line for sports betting. And I wanted people who did this and won.

Diogenes was a banker who was kicked out of his native Sinope for defacing precious metal coins. He took a chisel and scarred a large number of coins. No one knows why he did this, although it may have been some kind of anti-Persian political protest (Sinope is in modern Turkey, so between Persia and Greece, and had a split between pro-Persian and pro-Greek parties). I enjoy the thought that I reversed the order. I started by looking for honesty, then became a banker, and am now writing a book to announce the end of paper money.

That's my rant. You probably don't agree with much of it. It's here to explain how I came to my ideas, but you don't have to travel the same route to end up at my destination. Now back to risk management.

Validation

One thing that VaR does is subject key risk information to validation. Some middle-office risk managers prefer other measures or metrics, but all competent ones believe in constant, rigorous, objective validation. Otherwise they're just pushing more bad numbers around and not doing any good for anyone. From this perspective, it's not surprising that VaR calculations turned out to contain lots of useful information. Just as the one-eyed man is king in the valley of the blind, a validated number, even if it is of little direct interest, is king in the valley of imaginary numbers.

Middle-office risk managers compute VaR, or other statistical predictions, on things other than profit and loss. Some of them invented key risk indicators (KRIs) and key performance indicators (KPIs). The idea is that whenever you measure something for risk purposes, people distort it. Even though you tell people you're not trying to minimize or maximize the measure, once people know you're looking at it, they change it. One of the reasons we selected profit and loss for VaR was that people were already trying to distort them, and financial controllers were on the job to fight the distorters. The controllers weren't always successful, but at least there were two sides in action. For KRI and KPI, you select an average of things that may be of only marginal interest . . . *and you don't tell anyone what those things are!* People don't know what to distort.

For example, you might average employees out sick, failed trades, e-mails containing the word *idiot*, caffeinated coffee consumed after 5:00 p.m., and a few other things as key risk indicators. Typically, you express each one as a number of standard deviations above or below its long-term mean so that the numbers are comparable and their average is meaningful. All that matters is that the things bear some relation to possible increasing risk and they are objectively measurable at frequent intervals. You don't care about them individually. You just hope that any change in risk levels will be reflected in changes in the indicator. For a KPI you do the same thing, except you average things associated with good performance rather than increased risk. In both cases, you estimate a VaR and see if changes in the VaR level or VaR breaks (days when the indicator moves more than the VaR amount) give you useful signals.

I have never used KRI or KPI myself; they are most popular for people who manage operational risk—defined as everything other than market risk and credit risk. I find the KRI/KPI idea intriguing, but haven't seen strong evidence that it works. Nevertheless, KRI and KPI are part of the standard middle-office risk management tool kit. I also mention them here to emphasize that VaR need not be measured on profit and loss, nor on anything meaningful at all. The important VaR idea is rigorous statistical validation, not a specific measure or metric.

Getting back to my direct experience, I don't want to suggest that every business and every VaR passes a statistical back-test. We live in the real world and you're risk managing a moving target. The middle-office risk manager must satisfy herself that the overall business is under risk control going forward, which doesn't necessarily mean it measures perfectly looking backward. She must have confidence in the numbers she's producing now, which means constantly adjusting when things come in different from expectation. With all the predictions she's making for every business, some of them will be wrong. As long as she's constantly adjusting for every error, she can have confidence in the future. To compare this to a sports bettor, she's quoting a point spread on every game. It's not enough to get the average game right, or most of the games right; a single bad spread can attract a lot of smart money and result in a big loss to her. But if she's watching the flows and adjusting the lines when appropriate, she can still run a risk-controlled business. She doesn't ask at the end of the week whether her line was correct every minute during the past week; she asks whether the errors she made were small enough to tolerate and were fixed as quickly as possible—that is, that the line always represented her best judgment at the time.

Producing VaR may sound like a big job, but as a middle-office risk manager, you're just getting started. Let's suppose you now have a reliable VaR for every business and subbusiness, and each business supplies you with risk numbers you trust. You have effected a tremendous improvement in firm systems, communication, and discipline, which may do more good than anything else you accomplish. But you've measured only the ordinary day-to-day risks of the firm and you haven't changed anything. We'll postpone the rest of the risk manager's job to Chapter 16.

CHAPTER

13

VaR of the Jungle

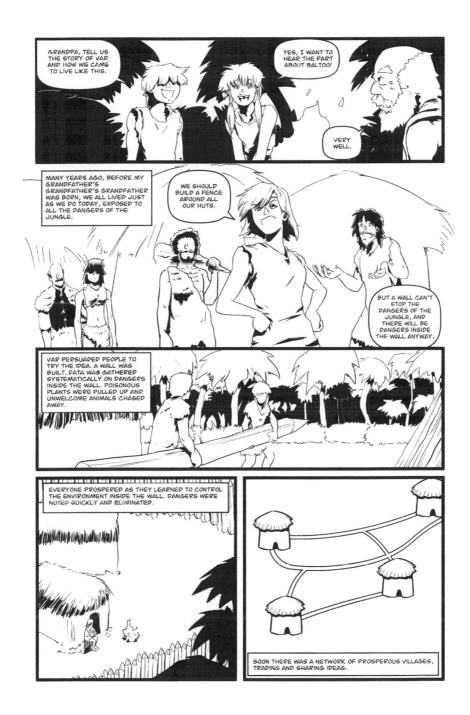

254

CHAPTER 14

The Secret History of Wall Street: 1988–1992

The stock market crashed on Monday, October 19, 1987, with stocks falling nearly 25 percent. On Tuesday, markets almost didn't open due to credit problems, and then almost failed during the day due to trading volume overload. But through luck and a thousand acts of unsung minor heroism, the financial world did not collapse. On Wednesday, the smoke was still clearing so it was hard to tell what was going on. But by Thursday the financial landscape had changed in dramatic ways. It wasn't just the stock market; the entire financial system had realigned.

Why did nobody but rocket scientists notice? Well, you had to be a quant to see it. The differences looked small without precise quantitative tools to expose them, and they didn't matter in obvious ways for nonquant strategies. For people who didn't expect to understand the market, the changes were no more unusual than a lot of other things they didn't understand. People who think computers and television sets are magic aren't going to be surprised when someone shows them a perpetual motion machine. But physicists know the difference.

Also, you had to be in the markets to see it. I don't mean you needed a job on Wall Street; I mean you had to be actively betting, and in contact with other people who were betting. Fischer Black, a Wall Street quant who did notice, famously said, "Markets look a lot less efficient from the banks of the Hudson than from the banks of the Charles." From the banks of the Charles—that is, for academics far away from the action who were not betting personally—there was nothing obvious in the reported numbers coming out of Wall Street to demonstrate the change. But from the banks of the Hudson— that is, for people on Wall Street making quantitative bets—you couldn't miss it.

Smile

One example is option smile and skew. Fischer Black, along with Myron Scholes and Robert Merton, had come up with an option pricing model in 1973 that was widely used on Wall Street. (Ed Thorp had developed a very similar model six years earlier, but he didn't publish it; he used it to make money.) Practitioners noticed that options on unusual events—say, that the stock market would rise or fall more than 20 percent over a month—tended to have higher prices than the model results. To a lesser extent, people noticed that option contracts that paid off in bad events, like a stock market crash, sold for more than options with the same model price that paid off in good events. Before October 19, 1987, this was always attributed to supply-and-demand forces. Lots of unsophisticated investors were willing to overpay to protect their portfolios, and pro- fessional traders made money selling the protection and hedging it. Selling the protection and hedging was known to be a risky strategy, but the conventional wisdom was that it had positive expected value.

By October 22, 1987, that conventional wisdom had reversed. Supply and demand did not cause irrational prices for options. It was now taken for granted that options on unusual events should sell for more, and options that paid off in bad events should sell for more than options that paid off in good events. If you graph the ratio of option price to model price by exercise price, the first effect looks like a smile. The options on either end are high and the options in the middle are low. The second effect makes the smile look like a smirk; the left side is lifted more than the right. This was called skew.

For technical reasons, adjusting for smile and skew not only requires more sophisticated pricing models, it completely changes the theoretical idea of what an option is. It actually means that an option is no longer a derivative, as its price can no longer be derived mathematically. But by 1987 the terminology was so entrenched that the definition of derivative was changed rather than change what people called options. This kind of redefinition is another reason many people didn't notice the shift. Smile and skew blew many quant strategies out of the water, but also created a host of new ones. We got two major models to account for smile and skew pretty quickly—called *local volatility* and *stochastic volatility*—but they gave opposite advice on what to do about the phenomena, and no one has resolved the two models yet or come up with anything better.

The most amazing part is that this didn't happen just in the stock market. You might expect it there. The same change happened simultaneously in option markets for foreign exchange (FX) and interest rates, even in commodity markets. There had been no major disruptions in these markets, and there weren't a lot of people who traded multiple types of options. So clearly there had been an ideological shift. I'm sure someone could demonstrate that pressure for the shift had been building for some time, and the crash just shook things up so change could occur. Lots of people were no doubt leaning in this direction, but hadn't discussed their thoughts enough to generate an explicit consensus. The crash stripped away the barriers that kept change slow, and allowed an immediate shift to the new normal. That theory may be true, but it didn't make it any less amazing to witness, nor weaken the profound implications for risk management.

One other example of sudden change was a long-standing mispricing in the mortgage market. When we first started issuing collateralized mortgage obligations (CMOs) at the beginning of the 1980s, you could make 4 percent per year profit, before expenses, by taking government mortgage securities and turning them into CMOs. Depending on the deal structure, you got some of that profit up front, some over time, and some at the back end when most of the mortgages had paid off. After expenses, that had a present value on the order of 10 percent of the value of the mortgages. That spread dropped quickly as more people got into the market. However, you would also expect that government mortgage securities would start to be priced based on their value in a CMO deal as opposed to their lower value as stand-alone securities. That is, the most attractive bonds for a CMO creator should have gone up in price while the least attractive bonds should have stayed about the same. Instead, prices rose about equally for all bonds— too much for some bonds and not enough for others.

All that had changed suddenly between October 19 and October 22, 1987. The government mortgage security curve snapped to a perfect fit of what an interest rate modeler computed. That eliminated a lot of mortgage arbitrage strategies, and compressed the spread that could be earned issuing CMOs.

The standard picture of markets is that inefficiencies are slowly arbitraged away by investors. In dual-class share arbitrage, for example, quants buy the cheap stock and sell the expensive one, forcing the two prices back together. It is usually assumed that once the prices get to the right relationship, the quants will go away as there is no more profit in the strategy, but the price will stay at its correct value. Or you might assume the price will stabilize at a small deviation from theoretical value, large enough to keep the quants holding it there, but too small to tempt more quants to come in and push it farther.

Neither story seemed to fit October 19, 1987. Instead it appeared that the arbitrages persisted as more and more people piled in to exploit them. Then all of them fixed at once. But the usual expectation is that quants profit when the arbitrage goes away. If you buy the cheap stock and short the expensive one, and then the prices converge, you make money. In 1987, the market seemed to have figured out a way first to blow up all the quants, and then move the markets in the direction the quants had been betting. If I told you I thought that was true—that the market is sentient and decided to hurt quants—you would be justified in calling me paranoid. Well, I don't think I'm paranoid, but that's still the most natural way I remember 1987.

Moreover, the market didn't just move as the quants thought it should. That happened with mortgage securities, but with options the market stayed put and all the quants moved. And there were other changes that were entirely unexpected. Some changes (not all) seemed to make sense in retrospect.

Now, I'm not claiming all this is true. The crash of 1987 remains anomalous in many respects and is not well understood. I'm telling the story as it seemed at the time, so you can understand what we did next.

Back to the Dissertation

I went back to my dissertation. In graduate school at the University of Chicago, I had worked for Professor Craig Ainsley. Craig is a Bayesian and was working on the problem of analyzing time series data—that is, data measured at time intervals like daily stock price changes or monthly rainfall—when the volatility of the series was both unknown and changing. Stock prices, for example, can spend a long period rarely moving more than half a percent in a day, and then suddenly start moving 2 percent or more on most days. Most common statistical methods assume *homoskedasticity*, that volatility is constant.

One day, a professor from California came to Chicago to give a seminar on his way to New York University for a job interview. He was working on the same problem as Craig and me, but from a frequentist point of view. Chicago seminars are notoriously rough, but this one still stands out in my memory. Craig went after the guy like it was a religious war, questioning—no, attacking—every assumption, every equation, every conclusion. Afterward he pulled me aside and said, "That guy is way ahead of us; we have to drop everything so we can publish first." I realized it was not academic ambition animating Craig; it was the battle between Bayesians and frequentists, a battle that Bayesians take much more seriously than frequentists do. This was going to be a powerful new method, and whichever camp published first would win points for a major advance. The second publication, however good, would be seen as a derivative work, a translation, not an innovation.

The frequentist professor was Rob Engle, who got the job at New York University, published first, and was awarded a Nobel Prize for the work. It wasn't just speed, however. I think Rob's work, called autoregressive conditional heteroskedasticity (ARCH), was better. Craig's work, on which I assisted, was very good as well, superior on some points to ARCH and with useful advances in Bayesian theory. But it had fewer practical applications. ARCH is a very elegant piece of mathematics, but its main claim to fame is its wide utility in practical time series analysis.

Incidentally, about 20 years later I met Rob Engle again at a dinner in New York. I was surprised that he remembered our first meeting and that he had even more extreme recollections of that seminar than I did. He did not understand why his presentation had such a hostile reception, but held no ill feelings about it or toward Craig. I'm not sure my epilogue explained anything for him.

I was always midway between the frequentist and Bayesian camps. People who think like me call ourselves data analysts, and we like nonparametric or distribution-free methods. We use a lot of rough tools, like jackknifes, bootstraps, cross-tabulations, and visualizations.

We like to let the data speak to us instead of trying to fit it in a pre-conceived model, and we like simple methods that do not require strong assumptions about either the distribution generating the data or our prior knowledge. So on my own time, for my dissertation, I was trying a third approach to the conditional heteroskedasticity problem.

A popular technique among data analysts is resampling. To predict the future, you string together randomly selected days from the past—with replacement, meaning you can pick the same past day more than once. You do this many times to generate a distribution of possible future outcomes.

Simple resampling works only when the data are independent—that is, when yesterday's move doesn't tell you anything about today's. Another name for a series with independent changes is a random walk, which of course is one of the famous models in finance. I believed, however, that financial time series were typically not random walks. One kind of common deviation from a random walk is called *autocorrelation.* That means yesterday's move tells you something about today's move—up days are followed by other up days either more (positive autocorrelation) or less (negative auto-correlation) than half the time. Both kinds of autocorrelation are observed in financial time series, but back in 1980 I believed they had to be minor. Autocorrelation is limited by arbitrage. If there is a lot of positive autocorrelation, you make money buying stocks that just went up, and a lot of negative autocorrelation means you should buy stocks that just went down; either way you arbitrage the autocorrelation away. Back in graduate school, I had a lot of faith in arbitrage to keep simple inefficiencies small. I thought it was a combination of data errors and transaction costs that made things look more autocorrelated than they really were. Incidentally, I changed my view quickly when I came to Wall Street and there was money on the line.

I was more concerned with heteroskedasticity. That's also not independent. It means if yesterday's move was big in either direction, today's move is likely to be bigger than average, although equally likely to be in the same or opposite direction. This is statistically undeniable and does not lead to an immediate arbitrage. Heteroskedasticity is easily confused with fat tails, or occasional extreme observations. With pure fat tails, the extreme days of the market would be distributed randomly in time, and returns could still be independent. With heteroskedasticity, the extreme moves would be clustered together in time. Financial data showed a bit of both, but a lot more heteroskedasticity than fat tails.

Both Rob Engle's ARCH and Craig Ainsley's Bayesian version were concerned with predicting future values of a series that demonstrated these properties. As Rob was a frequentist, he assumed there was a well-defined process underlying the data. In particular, he assumed you knew the long-term mean. This seemed like a huge and unwarranted assumption to me. If you knew the long-term mean, you knew how big your edge was, and it paid to stick with a strategy forever. Eventually it had to make money for you. You never really learned from the data. You might make your positions bigger or smaller, or even get out of the market for a while, but you never changed your mind. This is how frequentists and card counters think, and leads them to believe in market equilibrium.

Bayesians like Craig always learn from data. They start out with a "prior belief," observe the data, and update to a "posterior belief," like sports bettors with the pre-pre-opening line, pre-opening line, and so forth. That market is always efficient, and we are continually improving our knowledge of it. Unfortunately, it keeps changing so we have to run as fast as we can to stay in the same place.

Try as I might, I couldn't come up with a prior belief that worked in the market. If you had no prior belief, you never saw profitable opportunities. If you had a strong prior belief, strong enough to make money, you got wiped out in crises. That ruled out Bayesian methods for me and freed me to look for another way, a nonparametric way. That had been my inclination in the first place.

What Rob, Craig, and I were doing differed in more than technical detail. We each defined the problem differently. This is often true in statistics. The same technique can be used by three different statisticians for three entirely different reasons. Rob justified his work with arguments of long-run frequency. If the ARCH assumptions were correct and you predicted according to his instructions, in the long run you had the lowest possible average squared error (you use squared error instead of just error because squaring makes the negative errors positive so you are penalized for errors in either direction instead of having them offset). Craig proved that a consistent rational person with a given set of prior beliefs should believe the distribution he or she constructed; that is, a consistent, rational person should be willing to bet according to Craig's distribution.

I was looking for a set of parameters that, if used to make Kelly bets, produced the maximum possible growth rate. I judged my methods by whether following them made money, not whether the predictions had low mean squared error or represented consistent rational beliefs. I proved to my own satisfaction, although not to the satisfaction of my dissertation committee, that a simple resampling scheme did a better job than either frequentist or Bayesian approaches. When I say "simple," I mean that it made few assumptions. The scheme itself was a bit complicated, more complicated than I want to explain here, especially since I think I know how to do it better now. Also, in fairness to my committee, they did not reject the ideas; they requested they be more clearly related to prior work. In particular, the Bayesians thought I could recast them as a more complicated prior belief, the frequentists thought they could be captured in a parametric model, and the finance people thought they were related to other published trading schemes. Only my chairman, Ed George, seemed to think the work stood on its own, and he was one of the rare Bayesian resampling researchers. There was a behavioral finance guy on the committee as well; he seemed to like me, but I had too much math and not enough explanation to win him over. Anyway, I was given a long list of further work to do, mostly library research. I sincerely intended to do it, but when I moved to Wall Street I got too interested in other things. It's an old story.

The crash of 1987 revitalized my interest in the work. I dusted it off to see if it would have helped. Not at all. Looking back from 2011 as I write this, the crash of 1987 was the worst performance for the idea. It would have worked pretty well in succeeding crises; in particular it did an excellent job in the 2007–2009 meltdown. That's one of the reasons I say the crash of 1987 was a special event, as far as I can tell, unlike anything before or since.

Three Paths

Nevertheless, many of the ideas in my dissertation were validated by the crash. And there were lots of new ideas from other people in the air. The question was how to identify arbitrage strategies and run them so they survived crises. As usual, we split into three groups.

The frequentist card counters who ran small hedge funds or invested their own money zeroed in on the concept of capital. You had to have the right amount of capital for the set of strategies you ran. This was a theoretical calculation you could make, using observations of past frequencies plus market data. For example, suppose looking over the past you discovered that one time in a thousand, a bond rated single-A at the beginning of a year would default during the year. Then suppose you estimated, also using past frequencies, that your strategies would be down $1 million or more at their low point in one year, with probability 1 in 1,000. Thus, if you held $1 million of capital to run your strategies, you had one chance in a thousand of going broke, so your strategies were the equivalent of a single-A-rated bond. You could observe the market yield on single-A-rated bonds; that was your cost of capital.

In practice you didn't use only single-A capital. You wanted a mix of capital, just like any operating business. Some would be safe and cheap, AAA-bondlike, and some would be risky and expensive, equitylike. By constructing your capital carefully, you could design a dynamic business that could survive any crisis. If bad events wiped out your equity capital, you could continue to trade using your safer capital and the business had enough residual value to recapitalize.

The Bayesian sports bettors in big firms thought that was theoretical nonsense. They believed in earnings. Suppose, for example, you had a 10-year loan to a company and market interest rates went up. When interest rates go up, loan values go down. But a bank will not recognize a loss in this case, because it has no intention of selling the loan. The cash flows it will get from the loan have not changed, nor has the probability those cash flows will be paid. So there is no effect on earnings. To sports bettors, basing your risk behavior on market data was counterproductive. It meant you got scared when everyone else did and overconfident when everyone else did, a recipe to buy high and sell low. Risk management required steering a steady course through the wild storms of the market.

Along with the other nonparametric guys, I appreciated the elegant mathematics and clear theories of both camps, but had no faith in the results. I believed only things I saw validated every day. I focused on value—what positions were worth. Unlike the more theoretical approaches of the other two camps, I could measure my fundamental parameters daily (although not every day; in a crisis you may not get accurate quotes on positions, or markets may be closed altogether). In order to make value totally unambiguous, I defined it on normal market days only, and based it on the change in price of the positions held at the beginning of the day, ignoring any trading done during the day. Other nonparametric people were doing similar things.

Some of this development was influenced by the available data. Pure theoreticians might propose alternative measures, but we needed real data. Capital was easy to measure from account statements. Earnings were computed regularly at large institutions. And trading positions were marked to market daily. If you define something yourself, you have to undertake the expense to measure it. That is a significant cost, and it opens the method up to bias. Finally, using data people already measured meant you could analyze your ideas historically.

As I mentioned earlier, Wall Street risk-taking quants didn't waste time. The basic outlines of the main positions were settled in a month or two, and implementation began immediately. The quant trading desks began tracking and analyzing value with specific reference to market crises. We used nonparametric methods that assumed most days would be like the recent past, but with some probability they would be entirely different. We used long-term history and examples from other markets, plus some hypothetical scenarios, to fill in the distribution on bad days. We did not assume value could always be defined. For example, in one of my early attempts at implementation I assumed there were days when your loss was equal to your leverage squared, regardless of what positions you held. That may sound a little screwy, but in the crash of 1987, it seemed like the market selectively stressed all the quant strategies until they broke, and then made moves in a direction that would have reversed the losses in the strategies had they survived. There is an old saying in the market: "A stock doesn't know that you own it." In other words, the price at which you bought a stock, or the price at which you wish you had sold it, or any price in your head for any reason does not affect the stock's price movements. But in October 1987, it seemed like the market knew exactly what you owned. It really does seem that there are factors in the market that interact with traders in ways that cause this kind of thing. None of the quants thought they were long the market in October 1987, yet almost all of them lost big.

The little hedge funds were busy measuring how much capital they had at risk in various businesses. One reason was to charge each strategy the appropriate rate for the amount and type of capital it put at risk, and drop the strategies that couldn't earn more than their capital charge. Another was to make sure the capital structure of the entire fund mirrored the capital at risk in the strategies. If the fund had too little capital, or the wrong kind, it could fail; if it had too much, or the wrong kind, it could be overpaying for capital. An important component of determining capital level and type was scenario analysis. You wanted to decide in advance what you would do in foreseeable bad situations. You could cut capital allocations to some—but not all—strategies, and you could raise new capital. You had to be sure at all times that there was enough residual equity value in the fund as a whole to support the capital needed to run the strategies it could not dial down.

The third camp at big firms was modeling earnings. As long as earnings were healthy, the firm's stock price would stay high, which would provide a cushion to make the firm's bonds safe, and the firm would survive the crisis. But anything that reduced earnings too much, or created net losses, threatened a spiral that could bring down the firm. Bad earnings means low stock prices, which makes bondholders nervous so bond prices fall as well. Raising new capital is expensive; you have to sell more stocks and bonds to raise the same cash as you did before the crisis. Employees are unhappy because their stock and options have lost value; also, your bonus pool is paid out of earnings—traditionally 50 percent of net revenue—so bonuses are low. Employees who can create a lot more value than the amount you can pay them leave. That's a further hit to earnings. Prior to 2008, big financial companies didn't worry a lot about bankruptcy or liquidation. They were mostly afraid of a forced sale to another bank on disadvantageous terms.

An Unexpected Twist

None of these approaches was very productive in the end. It took an accident of history to create the right solution. Sometime in late 1989 or early 1990, the focus of risk control began to change from worrying about extreme market crises to worrying about interconnections among events and firms. The crash of 1987 was ancient history; instead people were thinking about a recent series of scandals and bankruptcies that seemed to cause damage far beyond the initial impact. Things were intertwined in ways nobody understood. Also, financial institutions were getting more complex as a result of mergers and expanding activities. That problem was most acute at two large commercial banks that competed head to head with investment banks in most businesses: JPMorgan and Bankers Trust. Citibank also felt nervous, specifically about its FX trading. At this point in the story, the investment banks were not relevant. Their trading desks were using value-type risk analysis and their business heads were thinking in earnings terms, but the firms were not leading intellectual development in either area. Hedge funds were also out of the picture; in 1990 the idea of a big financial institution learning from a small hedge fund run by an antisocial nerd was too unlikely to even be laughable.

The bankers who ran Citi, Bankers, and Morgan wanted some way to keep a handle on the trading businesses they didn't understand. They believed, mostly accurately, that each desk was run by experienced and prudent professionals. Their fear was that some market event would reveal that all the desks were on the same side of a bet without knowing it. No one had ever aggregated all the trading risks in a big financial institution before. Accounting measures were worthless. Most of the exposure came from derivatives, which are basically invisible to accountants. Even when the trading exposure was in underlying assets, how do you assess the risk of owning $1 billion of stocks and being short $1 billion of other stocks? That could be a lot of risk or a little. Also, the positions changed frequently, so by the time you got reconciled accounting information, your risk could have changed dramatically. Each firm had some large, unexpected losses that spooked executives. None had been firm-threatening in size, but if $10 million or $100 million can disappear suddenly for mysterious reasons, who's to say that tomorrow it won't be $10 billion or $100 billion?

As usual with top-down orders, the pressure was on for immediate simple answers without a lot of qualification or exposition. My camp, the value people, had the only number that could be compared across trading desks. All desks marked to market, and all could compute daily the amount their opening positions changed in price by the end of the day, on any normal market day. Capital and earnings were defined in different ways for different businesses, and most trading desks didn't measure either one, anyway. So those camps were out of the competition for providing the risk measure.

Fortunately, as it turned out, my value camp didn't have the systems to aggregate the numbers across different asset classes. Each desk based its daily marks on different market parameters, sometimes inconsistent parameters. For example, a commodity desk might mark its oil futures and gasoline futures separately, and the difference in their prices would not equal the mark another desk used as an input for a crack spread option (an option on the difference between oil and gasoline prices). That is, X minus Y did not always equal X minus Y. In any case, there were far too many market parameters and far too many complex valuation models to analyze value across all the desks.

So the value camp had the risk measure, but it was the capital camp that had the risk metric. They computed capital at risk as the amount their strategies could lose with specified probability over a specified time horizon. That's easy to define across desks, because you can test it. Every day you estimate the capital-at-risk for individual desks and strategies within desks and the sum of all desks—but using value instead of capital. You compare your computations to the actual profit and loss results and adjust your algorithm until you get the correct fraction of breaks, days when the loss is more than the estimated value.

So we grabbed their metric and applied it to our measure. Or, if you prefer, they grabbed our measure and applied their metric to it. Either way, value at risk (VaR) was born. Every day you estimate the VaR amount, and check that you lose more than that on 5 percent of days—or whatever confidence level you use—not more and not less.

It amuses me how casually people use the name VaR today without thinking that it makes no sense at all. Value isn't at risk. And the idea of specifying a probability and time horizon, and then computing a number, seems clumsy and backward. It makes sense only for capital and only when you think of the analogy of a bond.

As far as I know, nobody thought this was a good idea. Nobody invented VaR. It was a hybrid stitched together out of existing parts in order to get a quick answer to a question quants didn't think was important.

Surprise!

The first surprise we had was finding out that VaR was extremely hard to compute. Theoretical approximations based either on Gaussian distributions or on nonparametric methods failed miserably. You didn't get the right number of breaks, and the breaks were clustered in time and came disproportionately on days when VaR was low. The time clustering meant the VaR didn't have the right probability every day, even if you could get the probability right on average. For example, you might have breaks on 5 percent of days, which is what you want, but have breaks 15 percent of the time on days following another VaR break, and 2 percent of time on days more than four weeks after a VaR break. That's no good; you need VaR to be right every day. Having breaks mostly when VaR was low was dangerous. It meant bad things happened often when you said VaR was low, and seldom when you said VaR was high. People lose faith quickly if you do that.

The unvarnished fact was that none of us understood our risk in the center of the distribution. People worry all the time about tail risk—extreme events. But we didn't know much about what happened on all the other days—the normal days without extreme price movements. Moreover, most of our breaks came from system or data errors. We spent more time thinking up clever approximations and defaults for missing or obviously incorrect data than about how financial prices might move. An essential aspect of VaR is that it is never recomputed. The VaR you set at the beginning of trading is the one you test against, not some corrected value available later. For risk management all that matters is the number used for decisions.

Eventually, we got good at doing this. It wasn't any brilliant new theory; it was improvements in systems and a bunch of ad hoc methods layered on top of each other, with multiple estimation techniques at each step combined by learning algorithms. We learned a lot about systems and strategies and markets that no one ever had looked at before.

Remember that no one believed in this work. We were trying to satisfy a goofy request from headquarters with the minimum effort. It was only quant honesty—or perhaps quant stubbornness—that made us struggle to get it right. No one else understood or cared. On top of this, all the work was a sideline of our main jobs, making money and figuring out how to manage risk.

Slowly it began dawning on people that this VaR was kind of useful. Once we got good computations for it, we found it could change suddenly, and those changes were often useful warnings. Often they weren't, but it was still a valuable alert. It seems obvious in retrospect, but no one had considered that a risk measure has to surprise you if it is to be of any use at all. In finance you are always going to have surprises, and VaR surprises are cheaper than waiting and letting market price movements surprise you instead.

VaR breaks were another valuable warning. In fact, it's impossible to lose a lot of money quickly unless either VaR goes up or there is a VaR break. VaR nonbreaks were useful in another way. We found that they were much easier to model than the full set of data with break and nonbreak days combined. This echoed one of the ideas from my thesis.

I'm getting a bit ahead of the story. Once quants got faith in VaR, we started pushing it all over the place. It was the only concept that seemed natural both on the trading floor and in the executive suite. To the traders we said, "It's like a point spread." To the CEO we said, "It's like an actuarial risk projection." With the traders, we bet until they accepted that the VaR was accurate. In the boardroom, we showed statistical charts. Everyone was happy.

It got even better. What the CEOs had wanted, what JPMorgan CEO Dennis Weatherstone named the "4:15 report," was a measure of risk available immediately after the market close that covered all trading operations of the bank. The CEOs envisioned looking at the report and taking action if the risk was unacceptably high. The traders had the idea that they would report their risk upward, and as long as their profits were high enough relative to the risk, they would be allowed to continue trading, perhaps even have their limits increased.

Both ideas are unrealistic. VaR is not a measure of risk. It was never intended to be. It answers a question: "What is the amount we expect losses to exceed with 5 percent probability tomorrow, if markets are normal and we don't trade?" But nobody asked that question. The answer says nothing about what happens on the 5 percent of the days with VaR breaks, nor in abnormal markets, nor with the trading we will certainly do, nor over longer periods of time than one day. If the CEO orders VaR reduced, it's not obvious how to do it since real VaRs are the output of complex algorithms. It's also not obvious that a VaR reduction will reduce risk. Squeezing your normal results tighter might bring your abnormal results in as well, or it might do the opposite. We had no theory to argue either way, and certainly no practical experience. There's also no good theory or experience to justify the traders' use of VaR to compare to profits, or to use as a limit.

The problem is not with VaR; it's with the implied business model people were using. You can't have traders making individual bets to make money, managed by a distant CEO who manipulates the overall level of risk of the operation. It's impossible. It would be like a general telling every individual soldier exactly what to do every second. What you need instead is a chain of command, with information exchanged and decisions made at every level. VaR fits into this system perfectly. It can be computed for each strategy of each trader. The trader can think about how each strategy contributes to his total VaR. The desk head can think about how each trader's VaR contributes to the total desk VaR. And it can continue all the way up the line to the CEO, who thinks about how each business contributes to the overall firm VaR. Whatever decision the CEO makes will be passed down the chain in the same way. Each conversation is productive, because it takes place between people who understand things at the same level. But if you slice through the chain of command and have the CEO conferring with a front-line trader, the two have virtually no information to exchange that is relevant to both of them.

The story bifurcates at this point. As all this was happening, Till Guldimann of JPMorgan released a research paper in 1993 introducing VaR to the world. As far as I know, this was the first time the idea was publicized outside an inner circle on Wall Street. The next year Morgan opened a free database of correlations and volatilities to the public for use in computing VaR. This eventually grew into a business that was spun off under the name RiskMetrics. RiskMetrics was one of the leading firms selling VaR services for years, and was recently purchased by MSCI Barra. Till's publication started a chain of events that put VaR in the public domain, with good and bad results. That story belongs in Chapter 19.

At the same time, the benefits of VaR were causing Wall Street quants to question the very nature of risk. There seemed to be a frequentist domain inside the VaR boundary. You had plenty of data, so it was hard for any rational belief to deviate from observed historical frequency. Circumscribing the boundary, both in terms of loss amount and by specifying normal markets and no trading, meant you knew every possible outcome. Outside the VaR boundary there were no good data. Probability was a matter of belief. The truth turned out to be more complicated than this, but this was our starting point. The development of that idea is described in Chapter 18.

Computing VaR

I have claimed several times that it is very hard to estimate a VaR that can pass rigorous back-testing. Since this is not a technical manual for risk managers, I'm not going to go into detail. I will show a toy example that illustrates the issue. Suppose you held a simple portfolio, $1,000,000 invested in the Standard & Poor's (S&P) 500 stock index from 1930 to the present. Over that period, 19,922 days, your 1 percent one-day VaR algorithm should have produced 199 breaks. That is, on 199 days the S&P 500 should have gone down more than your VaR prediction made at the close of the previous day.

Of course, you wouldn't expect even a perfect algorithm to produce exactly 199 breaks. You could get any number from 173 breaks to 227 just due to random sampling error. Values outside that range would occur for a perfect VaR algorithm only 5 percent of the time.

One simple algorithm that occurs to people is to look back over the past, say, 1,000 days, and set the VaR level halfway between the 10th and 11th worst losses over that period. That VaR would have produced exactly 1 percent (10 out of 1,000) breaks in the past, so maybe it's a good number to use for tomorrow. This method has a name; it's called *historical simulation VaR*. It's a handy number to know; I compute it myself. But it's not a VaR. It never passes a back-test.

The method has one parameter—one number that must be set. That's the number of days you look back. A long look-back period gives more statistical accuracy if the distribution of price changes stays constant, but a short look-back period captures more up-to-date behavior. I'll use three years, the most common choice among risk managers, but you get comparable results with any other period you choose.

Over the period since 1930, 1 percent one-day historical simulation VaR with a three-year look-back period resulted in 314 breaks versus the expected 199. That cannot be passed off as random chance. The problem is that the volatility of the stock market goes up and down. Stock price changes are heteroskedastic. If you are in a calm period but have a volatile period in your look-back interval, you will have too few breaks, maybe none. But if you are in a volatile period following a calm one, you will have too many breaks. Not twice as many, 2 percent, but much more, perhaps 3 percent or 5 percent. You always end up with too many breaks, because the extra breaks in volatile periods more than offset the missing break days in calm periods.

For the same reason, your breaks will not be distributed randomly in time. Twenty-three of your 314 breaks came the day after another break. That means there was a 7.3 percent chance of a break the day after another break, not the 1 percent VaR is supposed to produce or the 1.6 percent chance on an average day. Also, 136 breaks came within 10 days of another VaR break, so you have a 6.8 percent chance of a VaR break if there's been another VaR break within the prior 10 days. But if it has been more than 25 days since the last VaR break, your chance of a break is less than 0.4 percent.

The third problem with this VaR estimate that is caused by heteroskedasticity is that the average VaR on break days is $24,100 versus an average VaR on all days of $26,500. That's because your VaR breaks occur disproportionately after calm periods than after volatile ones. That doesn't look like as dramatic a difference as the break count statistics, but it's actually more damning. It means there is more risk than average when you say there is less, and less risk than average when you say there is more. You would be better off just quoting a constant VaR number. Since a constant VaR estimate gives no information at all, and your estimate is worse than that, it's clear why historical simulation VaR is not a VaR.

Nevertheless, historical simulation VaR has become the most popular VaR number for risk reporting and regulatory purposes. Why? Because it's easy to compute and its objective. It never surprises you; in fact, it's always pretty close to yesterday's value. The fact that it can't pass a back-test doesn't matter to people who never look at back-tests. The fact that it is actively misleading, telling you it's safe when it's dangerous and telling you it's dangerous when it's safe, doesn't matter to people who only report and regulate. That only matters to people who manage risk.

One fix that might occur to you is to set the VaR halfway between the fifth and sixth worst losses instead of between the 10th and 11th worst. I picked fifth and sixth because that gives you exactly the right number of VaR breaks, 199. One problem is you have now introduced another parameter that had to be estimated. Instead of just the look-back period, we have to choose a look-back period and a rule for setting the VaR point. The more parameters you set, the more vulnerable your algorithm is to changes in the underlying statistical properties of the time series. You can always design a rule that works perfectly in the past, but the more complicated the rule, the less chance it will work in the future.

Anyway, this fix doesn't help. It gets you the correct number of VaR breaks, but it is no better on the second criterion and worse on the third. Now you have eight breaks the day after a VaR break and 80 breaks within 10 days of a VaR break, instead of the two and 20 expected if your breaks were randomly distributed in time. The average VaR on break days is $27,300 versus the $31,200 overall average VaR.

I don't care what financial time series you choose or what parameters you use; you will never find a historical simulation VaR that passes a back-test. Worse, it will be actively misleading. It will induce procyclical behavior. You will take too much risk after good times, and cut back too hard after bad times. Not only is that a recipe for business disaster, but it's exactly wrong for the economy. And worst of all, you will reinforce the natural tendency of non-quantitative people to reason from the recent past. You will be a popular risk manager, because you'll always tell people to do what they wanted to do anyway.

The second most popular VaR among regulators and auditors goes by the name *parametric VaR*. You assume price changes are drawn from some distribution and you use historical data to estimate the distribution's parameters. The most common assumption is that the underlying distribution is Gaussian—also known as a normal distribution or bell curve. This was the form introduced by RiskMetrics. RiskMetrics did not use a fixed look-back period to estimate parameters. Instead it updated the estimate each day. It took yesterday's variance estimate times 0.94 and added 0.06 times today's move squared. This is called an exponentially weighted moving average (EWMA) because each past day's information is weighted by a negative exponential function of its distance in the past. Recent days get high weight and long past days get low weight, but the algorithm never entirely forgets. A 0.94 decay EWMA is still the most popular way to estimate parametric VaR. Under a normal distribution, 2.33 times the square root of the variance is the correct 99 percent VaR point. This is also a standard assumption today.

Unfortunately, using these parameters for the S&P 500 results in 1,298 breaks, not the 199 we were supposed to get. This almost makes the historical simulation VaR's 314 breaks look respectable.

Parametric VaR has the same failing as historical simulation, heteroskedasticity, but adds another. Financial time series have fat tails, whereas the normal distribution has extremely thin tails. You always underestimate the size of extreme events when you assume a normal distribution.

As an aside, you may have thought I was exaggerating back in Chapter 12 about how unreliable numbers are. But consider these. VaR numbers are used to regulate and risk manage trillions of dollars of decisions, and are computed by some of the smartest and best-paid quants in history. Yet the most popular methods clearly fail on the simplest task, estimating VaR for a constant investment in the most liquid and best-studied financial time series. And pretty much nobody cares. Bad numbers go out, bad decisions get made, and life goes on. Many people criticize VaR, but most don't understand that the problem is sloppy computation. The VaR concept is extraordinarily valuable. The same thing is true of quantitative methods in general. They often give absurd results and lead to disaster due to incompetent implementation. The people responsible, naturally enough, claim the problem is some complex subtlety. But that's not true. The problem is basic sloppiness that the simplest validation exercises would have shown clearly. Quantitative methods are extremely powerful and useful, but only when subjected to constant, rigorous validation.

At this point, it's no surprise that parametric VaR gives far too many VaR breaks the day after a break (154, meaning the chance of a VaR break the day after a break is 11.7 percent instead of 1 percent) and in the 10 days following a break (711, so there is a 5.5 percent chance of a VaR break if there has been another VaR break within the previous 10 days). And as with historical simulation VaR, your average VaR on break days—$13,800—is less than the average VaR of $15,000.

You can get the right number of breaks by setting VaR to 7.63 times the square root of your variance estimate instead of using 2.33. Here again you have the problem of introducing a new parameter. In this case, however, we not only get the right number of breaks, but we also reduce the problem of VaR breaks clustering. With the exception of too many breaks in the first four days following a break—we get 19 when we should get eight—the VaR breaks are distributed pretty evenly in time. The reason is that parametric VaR shoots up quickly when volatility increases, while historical simulation VaR is so slow to react that by the time it has increased significantly the volatile period is usually over.

Unfortunately, the problem of having your VaR breaks on low-VaR days gets worse. Now the average VaR on break days is $22,300 versus an average VaR of $27,200.

There is some good news. It's easy to fix these problems. Take any simple VaR estimate, including either of the two just mentioned. If you get a VaR break, double your VaR estimate for the next day. Call that using a VaR scaling factor of 100 percent, since you're increasing your VaR estimate by 100 percent. Every day you have a VaR break, add one to your VaR scaling factor. Every day you don't have a VaR break, multiply your VaR scaling factor by 0.94.

You might object that that's adding two more parameters to the VaR algorithm—the increase in scaling factor on break days and the decrease in scaling factors on nonbreak days. That's true, but I didn't data mine to find perfect parameters. I just doubled on break days, and I used the RiskMetrics decay factor for nonbreak days. Any reasonable set of parameters works about equally well. The important thing is that you need a VaR estimate that reacts violently to any unusual event, and settles down moderately quickly afterward. This property is more important than other details of the estimate. There are many ways to build this property into a VaR system, including some that are optimal Bayesian rules and others that can be justified on other theoretical grounds. I don't care how you get there, but unless you do something like this, your VaR won't pass a back-test.

Another objection is that this method seems like cheating. I could always get exactly 1 percent VaR break days if I raised VaR to infinity the day after a break, and moved it down to negative infinity 99 days later. In that case I would get a VaR break exactly once every 100 days. The VaR breaks wouldn't be distributed randomly in time; they would be spaced regularly. But I could get around that by using a random number generator to make my VaR infinity on 99 percent of days and negative infinity on 1 percent of days. But there would be no way to pass the third test. All my VaR breaks would be on days when VaR was negative infinity. This illustrates the importance of insisting on all three tests. It's easy to cheat to pass any two. Incidentally, even if a VaR algorithm passes all three tests, you still should check to see if there is any factor that predicts VaR breaks. That's why I like letting people bet on VaR; betting gets people to search out factors you never would think to test.

Suppose I use a simple parametric VaR estimate, setting VaR at 2.33 times the square root of the observed variance over the previous three years, then add the VaR scaling factor just described. That gives me 188 breaks over the period, within the 95 percent confidence interval of 173 to 227 expected breaks. The breaks are distributed randomly in time. There should be two VaR breaks the day after a previous break, and there are exactly two. All of the first 10 days after a VaR break have one, two, or three breaks, except zero nine days after a break. This is all consistent with chance if the VaR algorithm is perfect.

The average VaR on break days is $27,500, which is *higher* than the average VaR of $25,100. Ideally the two should be the same, but erring on the high side is far better than erring on the low side as the first two VaR algorithms did. This means that when you say VaR is high, it really is high, higher than you say; and when you say VaR is low, it really is lower than you say. You'd prefer to get it exactly right, but at least in this case your VaR signal is directionally correct.

Now consider that this is a VaR on only one market factor. Practical VaR implementations depend on many individual market factors, from hundreds to millions, depending on the application. And it's not enough to get the VaR of each individual factor correct; you also have to think about dependencies and relationships among factors, not to mention that you will always have errors in the positions and the historical price series. Some positions will not have historical price series at all, but will have to be evaluated based on indirect models, sometimes highly complex models. Using techniques like historical simulation or parametric estimation that fail miserably on the simple one-market factor, perfect constant data case is insane. The only algorithms that work are based on simple principles—such as if anything happens inconsistent with yesterday's risk model, double whatever risk you assigned to that thing yesterday—applied in a bottom-up aggregation scheme. Algorithms like this cannot be built in controlled systems, and cannot be audited meaningfully afterward. Their outputs cannot be explained. The only reason to trust them is that they work, and nothing else does.

CHAPTER

Hot Blood and Thin Blood

279

281

What Does a Risk Manager Do?—Outside VaR

There are three standard middle-office tools for exploring the region beyond the value at risk (VaR) boundary. Most VaR breaks are ordinary days, just with bigger losses. But something like one out of 10 of them are extraordinary events: regime changes, Black Swans, crises, crashes, panics, whatever. These days are your biggest dangers and opportunities. You generally don't get a chance to think a lot while they are occurring, and in any case human instincts frequently urge exactly the wrong actions. So risk managers developed tools to use on calm days in order to prepare for the storms, and guide decisions during the storms.

Stress Tests

The first tool is stress tests. Like VaR, these are widely misunderstood outside the risk management profession. People think of them as worst-case scenarios. That would be pointless. To paraphrase John Maynard Keynes, in the worst case, we are all dead. You can postulate some plausible extreme worst case if you want, and compute the effect on your institution, but what good is the answer?

A proper middle-office risk management stress test does not postulate a situation and compute the loss; it starts from a level of loss and asks what kinds of events could cause it. The loss level is typically set at three to 10 times the VaR amount. This is the region beyond everyday experience, but not so far beyond that no one can predict what might happen. You then ask what kinds of plausible events might cause such a loss: how big a stock market crash, how severe a liquidity squeeze, how disruptive a natural disaster, how big a bankruptcy of a financial institution or sovereign default? Stress tests are intended to examine the potential for sudden events to cause damage, so you don't ask about more slowly developing crises like recessions.

The people who think stress tests are worst-case scenarios also think the institution should keep enough cash around to pay for projected stress losses. One problem with that is cash does not solve all problems. Cash in the vault is no protection against the vault being robbed. Another problem is that the level of the stress event is arbitrary. If you need $10 million to pay for a 30 percent stock market crash, why is that the right amount of cash to hold against the eventuality? Why not hold $20 million to pay for a 60 percent crash, or $5 million to pay for a 15 percent crash? By construction, you have no idea of the probability of a stress scenario occurring. It's an event beyond VaR, and you trust only the data within the VaR boundary. Magnitude without probability is useless.

What is useful is to size the relative losses from foreseeable events. For example, suppose a firm typically runs a $10 million 95 percent one-day VaR. A reasonable size for stresses is a $50 million loss. It might take a 20 percent stock market crash to cause that, or a 50 basis point decline in long-term interest rates, or the simultaneous default of three of the firm's biggest borrowers. Although no one can place accurate probability estimates on any of those, it is possible to make subjective judgments about relative likelihood. The U.S. stock market fell more than 20 percent in one day exactly once, but there wasn't much warning. U.S. long-term interest rates have fallen more than 50 basis points in a day seven times, but at the time of this writing I think most people would consider that less likely to happen tomorrow than the stock market crash. Assuming the firm's three biggest borrowers are strong credits and in different economic sectors, the simultaneous default scenario seems the least likely of the three. Notice that these judgments are made using long-term history and general knowledge, not the specific short-term data we use for everyday decisions.

The point of this judgmental probability ranking is not that the firm should worry more about stocks than bonds, and more about bonds than its loans. Worry doesn't make any difference. Anyway, you have no faith in the objective accuracy of the probability estimates. The point is it will be more productive to analyze the effects of events people think are relatively probable, because the people will have more realistic ideas of how things could happen. Asking people to plan for events they consider impossible is not productive—not because things considered impossible never happen, but because you have to be able to imagine something in order to plan for it. It's not impossible that intelligent aliens will land on Earth tomorrow, but who knows what the financial effects would be?

Anyway, the middle-office risk manager will select the four or five most plausible stresses that could cause sudden $50 million losses to the firm. To the extent possible, the stresses should be independent rather than things likely to occur together. For a financial firm a typical set might be stock market crash, credit crunch, commodity price spike, interest rate spike, and liquidity squeeze. The risk manager works through plausible scenarios of how each stress would affect other markets, not just the stress itself but the likely follow-on effects. This considers only the immediate effects, not the future effects. For example, a credit crunch means there will be more defaults. But those won't happen right away. The credit stress might begin with a major bankruptcy, but rather than guessing how many follow-on bankruptcies there will be, the risk manager estimates the effect of increased credit spreads on all the firm's positions.

The stress tests will identify potential trouble spots. Are there ways these events could inflict large damage on the firm beyond the immediate loss? Are procedures in place to deal with the event and its fallout? Would there be a shortfall in cash? Would counterparty confidence in the firm disappear? Will the firm's confidence in some of its counterparties disappear? Would clients make demands that the firm could not meet? Would the firm fall below regulatory or exchange capital minimums? Will events trigger important contractual provisions or derivative payments? Another value of the stress tests is that the changes in predicted losses over time paint a picture of the firm's changing exposures. If all stresses were initially set to a $50 million loss but the commodity spike stress will now cost the firm $75 million, that tells you something that may not be apparent from looking at the position sizes in the commodity book, or the VaR of the commodity desk.

A stress test is computed assuming the firm takes no corrective action. Over my career, countless traders have told me, "I don't care what happens to my current positions if X, because long before X I will have traded into completely different positions." That misses the point of stress testing. The middle-office risk manager is trying to test the passive defenses of the firm, the ones that don't require people to make good decisions, or even for people to make decisions at all. He assumes people do their normal day-to-day jobs correctly, but not that a trader executes a stop loss, or that the CFO sees the problem coming and raises extra cash.

Here is the most important lesson about stress tests. The risk manager knows the envisioned scenario will not occur. Whatever happens will be different from his test, and probably worse in at least one major unexpected way. The manager imagines specific scenarios only to create realistic virtual tests. He hopes the discipline of preparing for what he can foresee will help the firm survive what actually happens. The basis for that hope is that, while there is an infinite number of things that might happen, there is a small finite number of ways they are likely to work out. Running fire drills regularly can help evacuate a building quickly not just in the event of fire, but for any reason: bomb threat, toxic gases, anthrax. Imagining the most plausible disasters helps you plan specific things like emergency lights that don't depend on external power, fire doors that cannot be locked, and floor fire wardens who check for disabled or injured people. Those things might turn out to help in any emergency.

This is why the size of the stress test doesn't matter very much within a reasonable range. There's no point in planning for a fire in a wastebasket; that's too close to everyday experience to test defenses. There's also no point in planning for a fireball that engulfs the building without warning—not because it can't happen or couldn't be survived, but because no one knows what it would be like. Planning for an exploding gas line that sets nearby furniture on fire and sends out toxic fumes is rational. It doesn't really matter if you make the fire half as large or twice as large. But you certainly don't want to make it the worst fire you can imagine.

There is another, more technical use of stress tests. The middle-office risk manager at a financial firm is always concerned about the firm's exposure to movements in market prices. Usually these are thought of in a linear way, such as the firm loses $1 million for each 1 percent decline in the stock market. But there are many nonlinear exposures as well. For example, the firm might lose $12 million or $6 million instead of $10 million if the stock market goes down 10 percent. Unfortunately, while linear exposures are easy to add up among business units, nonlinear exposures can be hard to aggregate. The easiest way to describe them is often as firmwide losses in stress scenarios. When this is done, both good and bad scenarios are considered symmetrically; that is, you consider the stock market rising 30 percent as well as the stock market falling 30 percent. This use of stress tests is more a back-office risk management function than a middle-office one. It's helpful for reporting risk in a simple way but it's not an important strategic parameter. And it really shouldn't be called "stress" testing, because no stress is involved. It's a pro forma valuation.

Trans-VaR Scenarios

The next middle-office tool for exploring the trans-VaR region is scenario analysis. It bears some similarities to stress testing, but instead of a sudden shock you imagine a plausible bad sequence of events. This is a test of the firm's active defenses. The point is to make decisions ahead of time, when everyone is calm and has plenty of time, rather than in the midst of panic. Equally important is to make decisions by consensus. In an emergency, decisions are often made by the most confident or ambitious person, who may be the least qualified to make them. Sometimes it comes down to the person with the loudest voice. Even if that's not true, key people to provide input and make decisions may be unavailable when the crisis hits. So it's worth getting their thoughts ahead of time.

Scenario analyses are always run to the death. That is, you don't test up to any specified point; you just keep piling on losses until further decisions are pointless because either the firm no longer exists, or the firm has cut all possible risks to zero, or the scenario has become so implausible that people no longer know what reactions are appropriate. As a quant middle-office risk manager, I always want quantitative rules that I can program into a computer for automated warning. For example, one scenario analysis everyone runs is trading losses at the firm. You might start with a $10 million loss the first day, and double the loss each day as long as no action is taken. The executive committee might decide that after five days in a row of doubling losses, it would no longer have confidence in the business heads to manage the crisis on their own and a 20 percent cut in all firm trading limits will be enforced. That's not the only possible decision, of course. You might cut limits only for the desks that are losing money. You might order all positions taken off. You might do nothing. But whatever the decision, a quant risk manager wants it to be specific. Perhaps the rule is five or more days of consecutive net trading losses for the firm and a total loss over $300 million leads to a 20 percent across-the-board limit cut.

A common objection to scenario analysis rules is that the business units already have people and systems to take down risk as appropriate. After the $300 million loss, the adjustments will already have been made, so a firmwide cut on top of them will be an overreaction. This sounds logical but neglects an important truth. No institution has infinite capacity for losses. Firmwide decisions to cut risk will be made; if nothing else, the decisions will be made by counterparties, regulators, or bankruptcy administrators after they've pulled the firm from the CEO's cold, dead hands. The choice is not whether to cut risk in a crisis. The choice is whether to cut risk systematically and rationally according to rules developed in calm times and agreed to by the firm's managers, or to cut risk based on what seems right at the time to whomever the decision falls upon during the crisis, with whatever information that person happens to have at that moment.

Naturally, the decision made in advance is not binding. Decisions have to be made taking into full account the circumstances at the time. But it's important to have a default decision as a reference point, to know what you thought you should do when you were calm. It's also important to have all the theoretical arguments made ahead of time, so in the crisis people can concentrate on the specific facts at hand. For example, one person may believe firmly that you never cut risk in response to losses, while another insists it always makes sense to get out of losing trades and live to trade another day. That's an argument to have in calm times, and to resolve. When the crisis is at hand, everyone has to respect the resolution, and content themselves with discussing whether to override it, not out of general principles, but due to unanticipated features of the actual events. When the building is on fire is not the time for a discussion of the philosophy of fire safety.

This process is always divisive because people have multiple natures and a firm has multiple constituencies. Individuals can have trouble deciding, because parts of them want to face the risk down and other parts of them want to be cautious. They often react by not wanting to make the decision, saying, "Let's cross that bridge when we come to it." That's the opposite of good risk management. At another level of division, what's best for shareholders is not necessarily what's best for creditors, management, employees, or customers; and what's good for each of those groups is not necessarily good for the others. Again, it's easier to put off the decision than to rank the interests of the groups explicitly.

By the way, there is another advantage of scenario analyses, even if they didn't help decisions. The most painful meetings of my career are the "Well, what do you want to do about it?" sessions after big losses. No one wants to be the first to suggest cutting risk, and no one wants to be the one who blocked that decision. It is humbling and scary and emotionally searing to lose lots of money. I've done it often enough to know. Memories of euphoric days when you made lots of money are cold comfort, icy cold. I wish people who talk about how reckless financial traders don't care about losses could sit in on just one of those meetings. But the traders and managers sitting around the table are not paralyzed children; they are experienced professionals with important detailed knowledge to bring to bear on the question. If the meeting has no structure, it is both painful and often unproductive, in which case the firm did not get the maximum benefit out of the skill of its employees. When the risk manager can say, "We ran this scenario last summer and decided when these events occurred we should cut all positions 20 percent. Does anyone want to override that judgment?" it always stimulates a productive discussion. Nine times out of 10 the decision is not to override, but all sides of the issue are aired thoroughly, which was not true in the unstructured version of the meeting. And emotionally it is infinitely preferable to tackle a specific question that you're good at answering than to wander through the trackless wilderness of an unstructured discussion.

Black Holes

The third tool is entirely quantitative, searching for holes in the profit and loss distribution. Stress testing and scenario analysis concentrate on dramatic external events that could harm the firm.

But most large losses occur instead from unexpected combinations of events that are not individually unlikely. There are a number of mathematical techniques to search for these. I won't go into technical details, but one simple approach is to look at the price movements in all past days in your database, to find the ones that would cause large losses in your current portfolio if they had been scaled up to the movement size of the average day. For example, you might find a quiet day in the past when most market prices moved only about a tenth as much as their average moves. Take the price moves from that day—up and down—and multiply each one by 10. Then apply those scaled price moves to the firm's current positions. Say that gives you a loss of six times VaR. This could be a hole in the profit and loss distribution. You don't know that the scaled day is a plausible event, but you know that the relative price movements that occurred on the day are possible, and you know the total size of price moves on the day is not unusual. That's enough suspicion to investigate, with a presumption of guilt. Unless you can find a strong reason to reject the scaled day as implausible, you list it as a hole. Risk management is not guessing what will happen; it's preparing for anything that might happen. If you are prepared for an implausible day, that's okay. If you are unprepared for a plausible day, that's not okay.

Why Risk Managers Failed to Prevent the Financial Crisis

Why didn't all of these techniques prevent the financial crisis? I think I'm in as good a position as anyone to answer that question. Middle-office risk managers speak to each other a lot, and the couple of years before the crisis were particularly open, because we were all struggling with the same regulatory changes. We all wanted to know how the others did things, so we could negotiate a generally acceptable standard with regulators. Also, I've been in the financial risk business since the beginning, and am active in various formal and informal middle-office risk manager organizations. Finally, I worked in commercial banks, investment banks, and hedge funds during the period, so I have a wider group of contacts and experience than most risk managers.

My first comment is some firms took this stuff very seriously and did good jobs. All of them survived. Other firms took things less seriously, and some firms ignored the professional consensus completely, except for regulatory-minimum facades. Some of those firms failed. However, among the firms that did less-than-great jobs, the total slackers did no worse in general than the average achievers. The reason is there are lots of levels of risk management. A firm might have great front-office risk management bred in the bone and strong financial control over things that matter, without having any respect for anyone with a risk management title. That's not as good as a great modern financial risk management department in the middle office, but it's better than a mediocre or poor middle office department without strong front-office and back-office risk management. Middle-office risk management helps only if it's done really well, and taken seriously throughout the organization. That's a two-way street. Great departments earn respect, whereas poor departments lose it. In my opinion, most regulator-imposed middle-office risk management is useless. That's not because the regulations are flawed but because it's not something you can legislate. It's like passing a law that a basketball team play well.

Second, even the firms on Wall Street with the worst risk management did far better jobs than the caricatures that appear in most popular accounts and news stories. This stuff is a lot harder than it looks. No one remembers the financial institutions that failed before the crisis because they had low return on equity, so their share prices fell and they got taken over at bargain basement prices by more aggressive competitors. In 2004 that happened to JPMorgan, as it was absorbed by Bank One. During 2005 and 2006, Morgan continued to disappoint shareholders and was rumored to be a target. Once rumors start, a bank starts losing employees, who are unhappy about the value of their stock and options and don't want to face a takeover. That causes profits and the share price to fall further. It's fair to say that JPMorgan ran below the minimum possible risk for a large Wall Street institution to survive long-term from 2000 to 2004, and at the minimum from 2005 to 2007. The harm from quiet underachievers is not as dramatic or concentrated as the harm from collapses, but in aggregate it is very significant. Moreover, the firms that take too much risk do a lot of good before they implode, whereas the firms that take too little risk sag as deadweight on the economy so have nothing to offset their harm.

On the other side, Morgan Stanley was likely the next domino poised to fall after Lehman Brothers failed and Merrill Lynch was sold. So taking any more risk than Morgan Stanley took was fatal.

The differences between the risk management practices at the two Morgan organizations would be indistinguishable to know-it-all-critics who say, "Of course banks took too much risk." Both firms took risk very seriously: within the risk management departments, in the business units, and in the executive suites. Both used sophisticated analyses and spent a lot of money and energy on cash and capital reserves, contingency plans, financial insurance, hedges, and other risk mitigants. Both had talented employees dedicated to protecting the firms. Both considered the incentives created by their compensation structures carefully. I agree that overall JPMorgan was more conservative, particularly in its balance sheet and with its access to the Federal Reserve, but within the frame of the public debate over bank risk, the two firms were a hairbreadth apart. Maybe Morgan Stanley set the risk dial at 51 and JPMorgan at 49, but the critics think they both set it at 100, and want all firms to set it at zero.

The financial crisis was not caused by any one firm failing, and would not have been avoided if one firm, or even all firms, had run at lower but reasonable risk levels. The amount firms would have had to reduce risk so as to avoid the crisis would have destroyed any economic value they had. It would have made more sense to ban them completely than to make them run at such low risk that the crisis could not have occurred.

All banks, in fact all large, regulated financial institutions, either failed or would have failed but for the massive and unprecedented government bailout. That was not a function of excessive risk taking in individual banks. Individual institution risk taking had something to do with which institutions failed, but it did not cause the crisis itself. You can't make the financial system safe by making each institution safe; you can make it safe only by making the system robust to individual institution failure.

A typical Wall Street firm going into 2007 had a credit stress test event that was about 40 percent as bad as what happened. But remember, the stress event was not supposed to be a worst case. The stress tests did show the dangers to American International Group (AIG), the Federal National Mortgage Association (FNMA or Fannie Mae) and the Federal Home Loan Mortgage Corporation (FHLMC or Freddie Mac), and mortgage and municipal bond insurers. They did not show any significant danger to major commercial or investment banks. Contrary to popular belief, the stress tests included housing prices going down and large losses in structured credit, especially subprime mortgage structured credit. Firms reserved large amounts of money against these kinds of events and purchased substantial insurance. The stress tests and scenario analyses did a lot of good in helping firms prepare for and navigate the crisis.

As things got worse during the crisis, firms cut exposures and increased hedges. But here's where the big problem developed. A financial professional's instinct is always to do a spread trade. If she's afraid credit is going to get worse, she buys protection on BBB-rated securities—these are the bonds just above junk bonds on the credit rating scale. Junk bonds can default in good times and bad, but a significant increase in BBB default rates tells you there's a credit crunch. Of course, increases in default rates of higher-rated bonds—bonds with A, AA, or AAA ratings—tell you even more loudly that there's a credit crunch. But the BBB spreads start to increase first, so it's a good place to set your first line of hedging defense. If you start making money on your BBB hedge, you can use the profits to buy higher-rated protection.

The BBB protection is an insurance policy that pays off in severe credit downturns, but doesn't pay any extra for historic downturns. The professional will also sell protection on super-senior securities, to get the money to pay for the BBB protection. Selling super-senior protection will cost money only in all-time historic downturns. AAA bonds are designed to pay off even in a repeat of the Great Depression—in theory. And the super-senior bonds were bonds that had AAA-rated securities beneath them in the capital structure, so the AAAs would have to be wiped out before the super-seniors took any losses at all.

In a cash flow sense, this long BBB protection/short super-senior protection trade paid off. That is, the BBB securities had big losses, so the bought protection paid off, and the super-senior securities were safe, so the sold protection didn't have to pay. To this extent the banks got it right. Their risk management models steered them to the correct view of actual cash flows.

What almost killed the firms was the leverage the spread trade required. For example, suppose a firm bought $1 billion of BBB protection and paid for it by selling $10 billion of super-senior protection. The super-senior protection was cheaper than the BBB protection, since the super-senior was less likely to default. Because the super-senior was cheaper, you had to sell a lot more of it than you could buy BBB protection. This means a $1 billion hedge required $11 billion of notional derivative positions. In the depths of the crisis, no one cared what securities you held; all they cared about was how much leverage you had. Lots of firms went broke holding positions that would have paid off in the end had they been able to survive.

Let me be clear that I am not defending either this trade or all firms' risk management decisions. Leverage is a risk, and everyone knows it. Most firms chose to run excessive leverage going into the crisis, and increased their leverage during it—while using inadequate accounting and disclosure rules to claim publicly that they were reducing leverage. The hedges protected against some dangers, but caused others. Basically many firms bet that we were not heading into a period worse than the Great Depression *and* that markets would remain at least somewhat liquid. It was the second half of that bet that nearly killed some firms. It can be legitimately questioned, especially since events in the fall of 2007 were clear previews to the potential for a liquidity freeze. But my main point is that these decisions are hard to make in real time. Had things played out differently, the hedges might have looked brilliant. People who think a bunch of rigid rules will do a better job of risk management, or that regulators will have the judgment to second-guess firm managers, are living in a dream world. In the real world this is always going to be hard, and smart, experienced, prudent people are always going to get it wrong sometime. The only good news is that afterward they will be smarter, more experienced, and more prudent—or dead.

What can regulators do? They can isolate the essential financial infrastructure of the economy from the risk taking on Wall Street. No derivative bet should threaten an individual's small bank account, or cause ATMs to stop giving cash, or dry up the short-term credit necessary to keep goods on store shelves and factories running. But there's no reason any of those things should be attached to an institution making economic bets. It's crazy for the government to guarantee bank accounts and then let the bank take the deposited money and put it in anything other than government Treasury bills. Well, you might make a social argument for letting the banks use guaranteed deposits to make home mortgages and supply short-term business credit. You're subsidizing those lending activities, which I think is bad, but I understand why others think doing so is good. I don't feel strongly, however, because I believe both types of lending are good, and with simple, prudent standards they can be very safe. Buy why let banks make leveraged loans— loans to companies that owe a lot of money, usually as a result of a takeover—with government-guaranteed deposits? If the loan pays off, the bank keeps a huge credit spread. That's supposed to be compensation for risk, but the taxpayer took the risk, not the bank. And it's even crazier to let the bank make a huge derivatives bet that interest rates will go either up or down but either way more than people expect, or that the crack spread between crude oil and gasoline prices will widen, or that the Japanese yen will appreciate versus the Canadian dollar by more than the difference in the currencies' short-term interest rates.

Another worthwhile goal of regulators is to reduce links among financial firms. Too many unrelated businesses are owned by holding companies, and there are too many offsetting transactions among different firms. A lot of the risk in the financial system is pure sloppiness. The cleanup effort has been going on as long as I've been on Wall Street, and accelerated after 2000. It gets no attention because it's so dull, but I think with regulatory encouragement we could have things shipshape in a decade. One problem is foot-dragging by people and institutions that make a living from the inefficiencies. Another one is insufficient respect for the back office, especially for back-office computer people. That is a deep and long-standing prejudice on Wall Street. When I started, it extended to quants as well. It's changing, but too slowly. Wall Street needs some of the best and brightest computer people. It pays the right salaries to get them, but most information technology professionals prefer to work for software companies that respect their expertise, rather than financial companies that regard them as inconvenient and expensive adjuncts to the business. To a huge extent, finance is information processing, but most firms are run by former salespeople. It is not uncommon for the chief information officer or chief technology officer in a large financial institution to have a professional background outside of information processing.

Regulators could slash the volume of reports and data they demand from firms. Most of that is worthless, and it's expensive to compile. Instead they could think like middle-office risk managers:

Ask for a few key pieces of information, and validate them rigorously. Make firms supply 95 percent one-day VaR estimates for all trading businesses, before trading begins, every day. Then test those numbers and see if the firm really has the right number of VaR breaks, and that the breaks are independent in time and independent of the level of VaR. You would find out in a few months which firms were under control and which ones weren't. If I were in charge, I'd publish the VaR numbers and allow public betting. That's one of many reasons I'll never be in charge. Anyway, having a few pieces of validated data is far better than having warehouses full of fiction.

And, of course, regulators could stop bailing people out. Everyone hates bailouts because they are expensive and create moral hazard; that is, they encourage people to rely on the government to save them rather than taking precautions themselves. But there's something even worse about them. They destroy the healthy process of evolution and creative destruction. They clog up the financial system with weeds that should have been extinct years ago. Those weeds choke off resources for valuable innovations. Instead of survival of the fittest, we have survival of the biggest and, because regulations are always intensely conservative, survival of the fittest for the nineteenth century. There should be a lot of financial firm failures. They should fail fast and often. The only safe system is one that allows failure.

Managing Risk

Having disposed of current events, we can finally get to the action. The title of the chapter is: What does a risk manager do? So far the answer has been more about what a risk manager measures, or discusses, or thinks about, or plans.

Now that you've got your VaR, and used your stress tests and scenario analyses to figure out good plans for everything you can foresee, and patched all the holes in your profit and loss distribution, do you knock off and grab a beer? No, sorry, you still have to manage the risk.

This job naturally divides into two parts, inside and outside the VaR boundary. Inside the VaR boundary you have plenty of data and outcomes are limited, so conventional statistical analysis works fine. Your basic goal here is to get risk to Kelly levels, no higher and no lower. That's more complicated than the way the criterion is usually written, because Kelly is very sensitive to the possibility of low-probability bad events. That is, you're going to have to use some trans-VaR analysis to set the appropriate parameter values for total wealth and variance. If you instead use obvious measures such as the enterprise value of the firm for wealth and the day-to-day variance of outcome for variance, you will take far too much risk and will fail.

Let's postpone the question of setting the risk level for a bit in order to discuss how you exercise control. Remember that you're not a dictator, and you're not the only person in the firm who understands risk. Also, you don't have information you need to make the actual risk decisions. Some of that information is in the executive suite, and it concerns things like the long-term strategic plans of the firm and the attitudes of stakeholders. Other information is scattered in the business units. Before you can even think about setting optimal risk levels, you have to be able to set consistent risk levels. That means you need systems to aggregate business unit information into a coherent risk picture for the executive committee, and systems to translate the decisions of the executive committee into meaningful risk instructions to frontline decision makers. A middle-office risk manager who builds such a system but offers no useful advice about risk is a competent professional. A risk guru who has deep insight about risk but no patience to build machinery to aggregate risk and communicate decisions is an adviser only.

I've already described a lot about the aggregation process; it's the same process you need in order to estimate and validate VaR. You take your analysis to the executive committee and describe the risk of the firm to them, and propose improvements. There follows a discussion, with decisions at the end. Earlier I warned you that the risk manager is not the risk dictator, and that other people on the executive committee have essential information that you don't. But don't go too far in the other direction and imagine that you just present data and await instructions. An analogy is with the chief counsel. She brings information about legal matters to the executive committee and participates in discussions about what to do about them. She doesn't run the company, and within a broad range, she defers to the people who do. But she does not accept any decision that is illegal. If the committee tells her the decision and says, "Make it legal," she is a hired gun, not a corporate counsel. It's similar with the corporate controller, the chief compliance officer, the head actuary of an insurance company, and the chief science officer of a technology company. There is a responsibility to the company, but also a responsibility to the profession. This is part of what separates a professional from a technical expert.

Assuming the discussions go well enough that you're not fired or forced to resign, there has been a high-level decision about risk strategy. The qualification about being fired or resigning is a technical one only; these things do not come up except in rare, extreme cases; risk management is about communication and consensus amidst mutual respect, not grandstanding among adversaries and idiots. Now that a decision has been made, it's your job to make the risk strategy happen. One major tool is risk limits. Because your business units are under risk control, you have an objective parameter that you can measure accurately, that the business unit head can control, and that is proportional to risk levels. If risk levels in a business unit are too high, you reduce the limit. If they're too low but at the current limit, you raise the limit. If they're too low and not at the current limit, you find out why.

This process is supplemented with conversations with the front-office risk managers. You exchange risk manager–to–risk manager technical information that will help the front-office risk managers shape the risk in the business units more subtly than the top-down limit can accomplish. At the same time, the front-office managers are communicating to you risk details not yet worked into the formal validated numbers.

Of course, you track all these actions and their effects carefully. You have the plan as it sounded neat and tidy in the executive suite, the detailed and complicated precise plan that left your office, the messy and even more complicated and imprecise plan that actually got implemented, and the still messier and more complicated precise results. These are the raw material for the next round of risk decisions. But you can have your beer before starting on that.

While you're on the bar stool is a good time to think beyond the VaR boundary. I want you out of the office for this part because I have to give you the three unspeakable truths of risk management. Do not repeat any of these on company property. If you bring this book into work, black them out or tear out the pages.

Unspeakable Truth Number One: Risk Managers Should Make Sure Firms Fail

Success requires innovation, and innovation implies frequent failure. Failure isn't the problem. Slow and expensive failure is. Fail often, fail fast, and fail cheap is the formula for success. And *cheap* is not measured by initial outlay. You must plan for success to have much chance of both succeeding and exploiting the success to an adequate degree to justify the risk. That means you commit the resources and energy to do things right. But you pull the plug quickly on a failure; you don't bleed money trying to prove you were right all along. Throughout all the wars in human history, fewer soldiers have died in battle than have been massacred while fleeing battles that were fought too long, fought after any hope of victory was gone, and fought too long to maintain an orderly retreat. Other soldiers' lives have been wasted in fights to which not enough resources were committed. If you're going to fight, fight hard and give up quickly when you lose.

This applies on all levels. Healthy firms are taking all kinds of risks all the time, wasting lots of time and money. What makes them healthy is they apply ruthless selection pressure to projects and weed out the unfit quickly. That observation is disruptive and often honored in the breach more than the observance, but it's not unspeakable. What cannot even be whispered is that it applies to the firm itself. Firms should fail. Firms are created to make people happy, to do good. If they make people unhappy and do bad, they should fail. Parts of the firm will survive and prosper, employees will get better jobs, and customers and suppliers will find better firms to deal with. Trying to run a firm to zero probability of failure is disastrous and futile. It guarantees a firm that does no good in life, lives too long, and does too much bad in death.

Firm death is an event beyond the VaR boundary, a place that until now we've treated as a danger. What about the opportunities? What about the good trans-VaR risk?

Random mutation and natural selection are what make the firm evolve. The process is not gradual, however. Everyday risk contributes only a little to selection. Most of the valuable parts of a firm are forged in crises. That's not to say crises are good, but since you have them anyway, you want to put them to good use. We've discussed the things you do to survive them. Evolution is no help if you're dead. But you also want to position things so that the aspects of a firm proven unfit by the crisis are sloughed off cleanly, allowing innovations that worked well in the crisis to flourish. You can only make these arrangements ahead of time; once the crisis starts it's too late, and once the crisis is over, choices will be made by politics.

The delicate aspect of evolutionary logic is that a firm has many constituencies: shareholders, creditors, customers, management, employees, and society as well. Each has different ideas of what *fitness* means. If the shareholders get a windfall but all the employees get laid off, is that good or bad? Evolution is not democratic. It does not weigh competing interests. It weeds out the unfit ruthlessly. So whose interests should be served?

In finance, I think the answer in general is customers. In many cases, such as asset management, this is a fiduciary duty. *Fiduciary* means you act as the customer would wish, not in your own or anyone else's interests. But even for nonfiduciary businesses, the only good in finance is serving customers. In the medium run, what's good for management, employees, and shareholders is what's good for the industry. Serving clients is good for the industry. Screwing clients is bad for the industry. It's not complicated. If the customers are served but the firm collapses, it's not the best possible result, but management and employees can get good new jobs and shareholders will have net gains in their diversified portfolios. Society is better off as well. The only group left out in the cold is creditors, and that's kind of the deal with being a creditor. You get first legal claim on the assets in a failure and that's your protection, not anyone's good wishes. You ask for first lien and honest accounts, plus a high rate of interest, not for anyone to fight to the death to get you your money back.

Saying the same thing another way, I think a firm that evolves for the interests of any group except clients is pursuing an evolutionary dead end. The firms that thrive are the ones that are most valuable to their customers, not the ones that are the best places to work, or make their managers the richest, or have the highest credit ratings, or are most popular with politicians and equity analysts. The firm that evolves into an exquisitely refined environment for employee satisfaction but loses its customers will soon be extinct.

When I talk about parts of a firm dying off, I'm not talking about departments or people. I'm talking about parts of the firm culture. Firms are not organization charts of people following clear hierarchical orders. The things that happen in a firm are the result of human interactions with complex rules. These rules are products of human evolution, but an evolution in which getting food, and escaping predators, and having lots of children defined fitness—not serving customers or anything else relevant to the modern firm. Fortunately, natural evolution also gave humans strong social abilities that can be trained to serve customers or otherwise promote the long-term interests of a group. These are the abilities on which evolution must operate.

One consequence of my advice to put the customer first is that conflicts of interest between a firm and its customers are incompatible with long-term success of a financial firm. Investment bankers get fees for advising companies and underwriting their securities. I think this is a business that has to be independent. Combining it with investment management, equity analysis, and principal investing means some parts of the firm are competing with customers, both for the firm's benefit and for other customers' benefit. This conflict can be managed in good times but causes dysfunctional evolution in a crisis. I think these firms will not thrive.

This was a major part of the problem during the financial crisis. Different businesses had different customer interests, and they conflicted. The trading desks could have continued to make markets even when liquidity was low, at higher bid-ask spreads of course, but not such high spreads as to attract only desperation trading. This would have provided useful price information, which in turn could have forced accounting marks that would have shown that other bank customers were insolvent. The lending department could have extended desperately needed capital to clients during the crisis, but that would have created risks for uninsured depositors. The asset management departments could have trimmed portfolio risks by selling and shorting stocks and buying credit default protection, and equity analysts could have advised clients to dump risky assets; those actions could have threatened the survival of some of the firm's investment banking clients—even the firm itself. No organization can serve all masters. These were all intractable dilemmas, on top of which firms had to contend with self-interests like employee demands for high compensation and shareholder demands for high return on equity. Specialized institutions can go all out in service of their clients, and improve their fitness during bad times.

The recent crisis also offers examples of firms that survived at the expense of their clients. I can't think of any firm that ever lasted long after doing that. It's not necessarily that customers desert such firms, although that does happen. It's that the firm has put itself on a path with no good destinations. The basis of the unspeakable truth is that these firms harmed everyone by surviving; they should have failed.

So what does a risk manager do in normal times to let evolution work productively in the crises? She does her best to see that project success or failure is determined by the effect on customers, not employees, managers, investors, or anyone else. If someone makes extra money by abusing customers, that is a failure, not a success. If someone invents something that improves the product for customers but reduces profits marginally, that is a success, not a failure. This is the only policy that leads to good long-term results for anyone, including employees, managers, and investors. This is not business wisdom; it is risk wisdom. How a company treats its customers determines how a company evolves, and the only productive evolutionary trajectories are ones that serve customers.

Another important principle is to expose every part of the firm to natural selection. If any department gets away with performing at a level below the most competitive alternative in the market, it has no selection pressure. If the IT department spends twice as much to build a system as a software vendor charges to sell it, the problem goes far beyond the waste of money. The IT department will not evolve. It will bring down the fitness of the firm. The same is true if onshore workers are less productive per dollar spent than offshore workers, if management is paid twice the salaries they could earn other places, or if the operations department makes more mistakes than other firms. In a crisis, these will be millstones around the necks of the successful departments, the ones that should survive. There are business arguments for and against making departments compete with outsourcing or other market standards. But the risk manager is always in favor of exposing everything to selection. Let things fail one at a time in good times rather than all at once in a crisis. And if selection pressure sweeps away the entire firm, it's a favor to everyone to let it happen fast and during good times. That results in less waste, and means employees are looking for new jobs when there are jobs available. Throwing money down a black hole for years to buy the privilege of failing in a crisis instead hurts everyone. The problem in the financial crisis was not too big to fail, but that too many firms failed to fail in 2004 to 2007, and clogged up the drain in 2008.

I'm not going to cover every aspect of customer-driven natural selection, but I'll mention one more because it's been in the news a lot: compensation. This was one of the first issues Wall Street quants tackled when we went into risk management. The trick to aligning interests of risk takers and their firms is to make sure both have the same fraction of wealth at stake in the decision outcomes. One way to do that would be to force all risk decision makers in the company to hold 100 percent of their wealth in company stock. But since wealth includes the future value of human capital, for typical workers that would mean having far more than their liquid net worth tied up in company stock. For young workers the ratios could be astronomical. Another practical problem is the stock price does not represent precisely the value of the company.

The solution was to design compensation schemes with out-of-the-money indexed stock options—that is, options that could pay off big, but only if the company outperformed similar companies significantly—with long vesting and restriction periods. For example, the options might vest over five years, and if exercised the stock would have to be held for another five years. These would not be reserved for top management, whose interests are usually aligned pretty well with the company anyway, but spread deep in the organization chart, to all risk decision makers. Many low-level employees make risk decisions, and many high-level employees do not.

The other part of the solution was to reward promptly and generously in cash for performance whose value could be validated. Quants didn't want to pay people when the accounting system said they made money, but when the risk system confirmed it. For someone trading liquid instruments or zeroing out positions frequently, payment is fast. For someone creating structured products and keeping residual tranches in the firm, payment could be many years later.

The great thing about compensation schemes is they kick in automatically. You don't have to know much about the risk decisions someone is facing. As long as their interests and the firm's interests are aligned, you let them make the choice. If they make good choices, the firm makes money and they make money. If they make bad choices, the firm loses money, but makes some back because it doesn't have to pay them much. Eventually, employees improve, or quit because they're not earning enough, or get fired.

In the aftermath of the financial crisis, lots of amateurs rushed in with ideas to improve compensation schemes without hard, quantitative data on what worked and what didn't. One idea was to lock up equity awards for long periods of time. Only it turned out firms were already doing that, and were stricter about it than the proposed new laws.

So that idea was just irrelevant, not harmful. Unfortunately, the do-gooders added a major provision of staggering stupidity, one that violates the most basic principle of microeconomics: compensation for future performance.

One fundamental principle of compensation policy that is obvious to any quant is you never reward someone for future performance. For example, you don't give someone a big bonus, but tell him he can't have it if the firm fails in the next three years. Why not? Because this will cause him to make decisions assuming the firm will survive, since if the firm fails it doesn't matter what he does. You have just induced exactly the opposite behavior of what you want. It would be smarter to tell him he could have his bonus only if the firm fails in the next three years. Why? Because then he'll be racking his brains for any possible way the firm can fail, and placing bets that will pay off in that eventuality. Those bets might save the firm. All over the world governments are forcing financial firms to employ compensation schemes that encourage every financial worker to bet big that the firm and the financial system will do well. It's a classic idiocy of people who want to bring risk of failure down to zero, so they never think about what happens if there is failure. It's far better to set the failure rate at a reasonable level consistent with both innovation and stability, and think hard about what happens when there is failure.

Suppose you're going to pay someone to build a boat for you. You have some ability to observe the quality of the work, but you know the builder can make the boat better or worse in ways you will never detect. So you want to structure the contract to give her incentive to make the boat safe.

The stupid plan would be to tell her you'll pay her in five years if the boat doesn't sink. Why? She won't build an unsinkable boat; that's hard. She'll build a boat so shaky that you never take it out in bad weather. And she won't bother with safety equipment, with lifeboats and such, because if they're ever needed, she's not getting paid anyway. Say, instead, you tell her you'll pay her only if the boat sinks. Now she'll build you a boat you'll be comfortable taking out in storms, and she'll be sure that if it sinks, everything works great.

Of course, there's a problem with the second course as well. She will look for ways to make the boat sink that you won't notice before or after the fact. Frankly, that's pretty hard, so given a choice I'd sail in the second boat over the first. Best of all would be to pay the builder promptly and generously as the quality of the boat is revealed. That probably means some money at the beginning and some over time. But it's essential for you to measure the quality of the boat in a way that can be validated. Just looking at whether it sinks or not is not enough.

I'm sorry to say that your government chose to put you and your financial future on that first boat. As a professional risk manager, I advise you to learn how to swim.

Unspeakable Truth Number Two: There's Good Stuff beyond the VaR Limit

You already know that there's good stuff beyond the VaR limit, because you are a product of evolution, a process that operates beyond the VaR limit. But here I'm not talking about long-term benefits from short-term losses, nor things that are good for the population and bad for the individuals. I'm talking about using economic storms to accomplish things impossible in calm times. The secret is superposition. Superposition is a type of randomness in which a random variable takes all possible values at once.

I told you earlier about my Internet business eRaider.com to illustrate some principles of capital asset pricing theory. Now I want to consider the same events from a risk perspective.

The year is 1995 and everyone says Internet stocks are overpriced. For once, everyone is clearly right. So any red-blooded risk taker starts creating and selling Internet stocks. Of course, a lot of other people—not risk takers—created and sold Internet stocks as well. Some were technological visionaries, some were confused geeks, some were simple opportunists, and some were con artists—although *artist* implies some skill; perhaps "con fallers off of logs" would be more accurate.

What the risk takers understood was that the bubble would not continue forever. In round numbers, the NASDAQ stock index went up by a factor of 5 from 1995 to 2000, and then fell back to about the 1995 level in 2002. This understates the Internet bubble since there were some non-Internet companies in the NASDAQ. Amazon.com's 1997 initial public offering (IPO) sold shares at around $4 split-adjusted. The stock rose to $113 before falling to under $6. It's at $27 as I write this. And Amazon.com was a very solid Internet company with a good business and lots of revenue. Many of the temporarily most successful Internet companies had no earnings, no revenue, and no plans to ever get revenue.

Suppose you knew in 1995 that Internet stocks would soar and crash. I did. I don't mean I was 100 percent certain, only that soar/ crash seemed the most likely course of events. I wrote articles saying that at the time, as did lots of others. What I also said was it was harder to use that information than most people think. You could try to buy Internet stocks and hold them to the peak, then sell them and open short positions. Timing is the killer here. There were lots of gigantic up and down swings before and after the peak. If you misguessed, you could be wiped out. Even if you guessed right, you could be wiped out, unless you bet small. From the peak Amazon.com stock price of $113 to the trough two years later under $6, there were several months where the price of the stock more than doubled. Similarly, during the run-up there were months where the stock price fell more than 50 percent. If you used any kind of leverage, you might have blown up before you were proven right.

Most of the people who issued Internet stock were betting on the bubble to continue forever. That was foolish. No bubble has ever continued forever. People who knew there would be a crash mostly stayed out of the market altogether. That was a wasted opportunity.

Think superposition. There are ideas that work if Internet stocks are worth a lot. There are ideas that work if Internet stocks are worth a little. In ordinary times, you have to bet on one or the other. But in a bubble, you get a superposition opportunity. You can pursue ideas that work only if Internet stocks are worth a little and only if Internet stocks are worth a lot.

What you need is a business idea that will benefit from a run-up in Internet prices, but will succeed because the Internet crashes. Such an idea cannot work under coin-flip probability analysis. People who don't believe Internet stocks are worth much won't invest because your business needs high Internet stock values. People who think Internet stocks are worth a lot also won't invest because your business needs low Internet stock values in the future.

As mentioned earlier, I created a business with a partner, Martin Stoller. Our eRaider.com was conceived as a business that would ride the Internet bubble for funding. It didn't have a public IPO, but it used private equity and equity stock options to buy services and gain customers. Imagine hiring 36 top business experts to participate in a web site and donate their professional services for several hours per week. Asking prices would start at $100,000 a year or more. Not only that, such people would want to see expensive infrastructure before they would associate their names with a project, especially one as outrageous as eRaider.com. At a guess, it would have cost around $20 million to start eRaider.com in normal times. Martin and I managed to do it for a little over $1 million, due to the extraordinary currency value of stock options. It cost $5,000 to print up 20,000 stock certificates—because I made them look like an old-fashioned stock certificate on real banknote stock, and hired an expensive artist to add a clever engraving. I'm sorry to report that the certificates never acquired value, except as handsome pieces of art. But people were happy—no, ecstatic—to accept them like they were thousand-dollar bills. They were like counterfeiting, only legal, and honest to boot.

And it wasn't just the money. The Internet scrambled people's minds. In 1990, conservative professionals would never have been associated with a bunch of geeks running some kind of futuristic techno-business that no one quite understood. It would be embarrassing if it failed. People would ask you things like "How did you think a business could survive with no revenue?" and "Did you really think some 22-year-old hacker dropouts could challenge the largest corporations?" In the late 1990s, no one asked those questions. If you didn't have a pile of stock options from a few wacky businesses, you were considered a failure—and the wackier the businesses the better. Journalists fell all over themselves to cover eRaider.com—not because it was a genuinely interesting and original financial idea, which it was, but because its name ended in dot-com. People flocked to the site to see if the stock would take off to the moon.

So that was the easy part, starting an Internet business. The slightly harder part was thinking about businesses that people would want once the bubble popped. Martin and I deduced correctly that people would blame Wall Street equity analysts and investment bankers, and they would focus on improved corporate governance and fundamental stock valuation. Simple transparency and honesty would be refreshing. That should have done wonders for eRaider.com. Also, eRaider.com bought stocks calculated to do well when the bubble burst. That was something that confused almost everyone who wrote about us. It wasn't just unusual for an Internet company to be betting against the Internet; it was inconceivable.

Now, the idea didn't work, as I mentioned earlier. Martin and I made some bad predictions as well. We thought the Internet would survive as a more traditional place, with less advertising, less commerce, and more information exchange. We had no advertising on the site and no links to other sites, as we thought those would pull us down in the crash. We did not invest in making the site useful for anything other than exchanging information. You couldn't even invest in the mutual fund online. Those beliefs caused us to miscalculate some things that might have helped make eRaider.com work. However, I think the basic flaw was different; it was deep in the nature of the business model.

Nevertheless, eRaider.com is an illustration of how superposition can make risk work for you. It was Internet volatility that gave Martin and me a $20 million business for $1 million. That it turned out to be worth zero isn't the point. If you have to wait for ideas that make sense under one version of reality, you'll wait a long time and some big organization will probably grab the idea before you do, anyway. Success often comes from ideas that make sense under no single version of reality, but are calculated to exploit uncertainty and volatility.

You don't have to wait for another Internet bubble to try this. There are areas of uncertainty and volatility all over the place, all the time. Each one is a potential opportunity to a risk taker who understands superposition. And every middle-office risk manager encourages business ideas that can benefit from superposition. In normal times, these add little if anything to the bottom line. But when trans-VaR winds start to howl and moan, you want plenty of potential sails around to catch them and maybe give you some opportunities to offset your dangers.

This part of the job is not accomplished in meetings, or by setting limits. It uses one of the little-understood powers of a risk manager. Risk managers give people permission to fail. Before the advent of modern quantitative risk management, failure was usually evaluated after the fact. The failed risk taker would argue that the idea was sound and had been implemented skillfully. The prosecution would argue that either the initial idea or the implementation was flawed—or both were. The technical term for this form of rigorous analysis is finger-pointing.

Risk managers change the process. Now the failure is evaluated before the fact. If the risk manager looked over the idea and approved the risk, then the failure is not charged to the risk taker. People are still evaluated on performance, of course, and success is rewarded more than failure. But approved failures are tolerated and added up against successes to see if there is net value. Unapproved failures are not tolerated.

The risk manager gives people permission to fail at projects that could never be defended after the fact. An idea that depends on superposition always looks stupid if it fails, since it is based on inconsistent assumptions. Only with the stamp of risk management approval would a sensible risk taker in a big organization try to exploit superposition. The other advantage of the modern approach is that people have no incentive to pursue ideas that are not working. If there's a trial afterward, the risk taker wants to keep pushing the idea until she can prove it failed due to external events that made it impossible; also, she wants to keep it going long enough that it seems like a worthwhile idea that had a real chance of success. Risk managers want people to fail fast instead, and that requires dispensing with the trial afterward.

Unspeakable Truth Number Three:
Risk Managers Create Risk

It was game theory that proved adding artificial risk to a situation can improve outcomes. A related idea is Monte Carlo analysis, which taught that adding artificial randomness to deterministic problems can make them easier to solve. But big institutions are more comfortable with risk managers who seek only to manage the risk that arises naturally from the business, and to minimize all other risks.

This is the most unspeakable of the three truths. That the risk manager is planning for a nonzero probability of firm failure is not something people like to say, but it is something implemented in meetings and committees. It's not an idea the risk manager imposes on the firm, but something that people throughout the organization

accept. In fact, the risk manager is usually not the person best qualified to direct the effort. He is a champion for the idea, and sometimes the only one willing to say it aloud, but other people usually
do the heavy lifting.

That superposition creates trans-VaR opportunities is less well
known. It's something the risk manager usually exploits privately, by
giving the green light to projects that take advantage of it. People
know the risk manager approves some projects and vetoes others,
but they seldom ask why. If someone does ask, she is usually satisfied with "It was too risky" if the answer was no, and "It had a risk-
return trade-off within our appetite" if the answer was yes. People
don't like long discussions about risk.

Adding pure artificial risk to things is the hardest of the three
unspeakable truths to explain, and in my experience it is the least
known outside the profession.

There is a tendency in large organizations to standardize everything. Standardization increases correlation, which creates dangers.
Doing things a bit more randomly on the micro level can improve
macro-level predictability. Standardization is easy to exploit by rogue
employees and competitors. Also, standardization is an enemy of
change. Think of a guy who walks exactly the same route to work
every day. He won't notice if something is better or worse about some
alternate route. Also, when people do things one way only, they tend
to build things that make change expensive.

Consider a company that runs retail stores in many locations.
There are a number of strategies for delivering goods to the stores.
Goods could be picked up from all shipment points and brought
to a central warehouse, then redistributed from there. Or trucks
could pick up goods from the shipment point and deliver directly
to stores. Or trucks could deliver all the goods to the closest store,
then pick up a mixed load of goods from that store's warehouse
and deliver that to the next store. Or each store could have its own
trucks that it sends out to make the pickups and deliveries it needs.
The physical delivery system could be managed in a variety of ways.
All stores could send information to the center, which could schedule all deliveries, or stores could order from the central warehouse
and each other, or there could be other systems.

There is a natural tendency to pick one system and stick with
it. It's more efficient that way. People can be trained in specialized
jobs, and the best equipment for the system can be purchased. With

all equipment the same, it's easier to store spare parts and maintain things. Long experience means parameters can be optimized and potential problems identified and solved once.

But things change. Maybe the stores start carrying perishable goods. Maybe the supplies arrive in different places. Maybe fuel prices go up and information processing costs go down. Organizations with one fixed system can be slow to recognize the need for change, and can find it expensive to make the changes. People tend to assume that standardization results in fewer errors, which is probably true, but the errors can have far more impact.

Earlier in the chapter we discussed two arguments for maintaining diversity in the system. Evolution means that the better ideas will thrive and the worse ones will die off, at least if we're willing to subject the system to customer-driven selection pressure. Superposition means that things will be possible under a mixed system that are impossible under any one standardized system. But there are also pure arguments for preferring some randomness in the system. It will be more robust to disasters, as it's harder for one event to bring the entire system down. It makes it easier for the company to compete. Competitors cannot focus on the defects of the transportation system and build a business around them. It's harder for employees to game the system, either to cheat the company or to make their jobs easier at the expense of overall profitability, because the system is not as mechanical.

To use another example, companies often get predictable in the new ideas they will pursue. Movie studios make the same kind of movies based on the same kind of theories and metrics, consumer product companies market indistinguishably "new and improved" versions of products and let nimble competitors break in with end-run ideas, and software companies wed themselves to a single licensing arrangement. It is smart risk management to take fliers sometimes, even if they are completely at random.

Standardization usually reduces costs and increases efficiency, so the risk manager does not strive for complete anarchy except in the riskiest businesses where the need for innovation trumps all cost considerations. The benefit of added randomness can be quantified through careful analysis, and balanced against cost savings of standardization.

A risk manager adds randomness through personal campaigns against useless and counterproductive standardization, and by challenging people with accounts of how other organizations approach the same problem. Employee turnover can be a help here as well. Yes, turnover adds to costs. But it shakes things up and brings in new ideas.

Not every risk manager does everything in this chapter. Not all techniques are appropriate for all organizations, and risk managers differ in the relative value they place on different parts of the job. But all competent professionals are familiar with all of these ideas, and know how to implement them. They have been most highly developed on Wall Street. As risk management ideas spread both geographically and outside of finance, no doubt lots of good new ideas will develop. But I think they will be based on the same foundation that revolutionized finance: careful attention to quantitative data that is rigorously validated plus analysis of risk that goes beyond coin flips.

CHAPTER

The Story of Risk

315

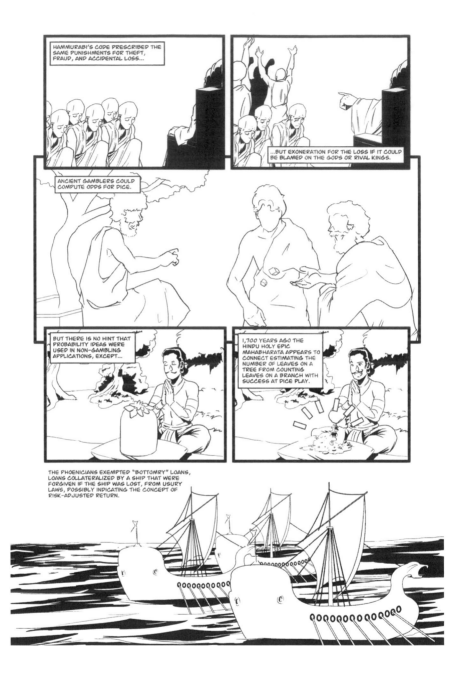

HAMMURABI'S CODE PRESCRIBED THE SAME PUNISHMENTS FOR THEFT, FRAUD, AND ACCIDENTAL LOSS...

...BUT EXONERATION FOR THE LOSS IF IT COULD BE BLAMED ON THE GODS OR RIVAL KINGS.

ANCIENT GAMBLERS COULD COMPUTE ODDS FOR DICE.

BUT THERE IS NO HINT THAT PROBABILITY IDEAS WERE USED IN NON-GAMBLING APPLICATIONS, EXCEPT...

1,700 YEARS AGO THE HINDU HOLY EPIC MAHABHARATA APPEARS TO CONNECT ESTIMATING THE NUMBER OF LEAVES ON A TREE FROM COUNTING LEAVES ON A BRANCH WITH SUCCESS AT DICE PLAY.

THE PHOENICIANS EXEMPTED "BOTTOMRY" LOANS, LOANS COLLATERALIZED BY A SHIP THAT WERE FORGIVEN IF THE SHIP WAS LOST, FROM USURY LAWS, POSSIBLY INDICATING THE CONCEPT OF RISK-ADJUSTED RETURN.

IN LESS THAN A DECADE, BEGINNING 1654, THE MODERN IDEA OF RISK IS BORN.

THE STUDY OF GAMBLING GAMES BECOMES A RECOGNIZED SUBFIELD OF SERIOUS MATHEMATICS.

PEOPLE BEGIN COMPILING AND PUBLISHING STATISTICS, AND MAKING INFERENCES FROM THEM.

PROBABILITY CONCEPTS ARE USED TO ASSESS LEGAL EVIDENCE.

ACTUARIAL REASONING IS APPLIED TO ANNUITIES AND INSURANCE CONTRACTS.

PROBABILITY ARGUMENTS ARE USED TO DEMONSTRATE THE EXISTENCE OF GOD AND OTHER THEOLOGICAL AND PHILOSOPHICAL CONTENTIONS.

RULERS AND MEN OF AFFAIRS EXPRESS POLICIES IN RISK-BASED TERMS.

THINK OF THE RICHES IF WE DECLARE WAR AND WIN!

YES, BUT WE HAVE A BETTER AVERAGE OUTCOME WITH A PEACE TREATY.

SCIENTISTS AVERAGE MEASUREMENTS.

THE MEASUREMENTS DISAGREE?

I'LL TAKE THE AVERAGE.

NO! ONE MUST BE WRONG AND IF WE AVERAGE WE'RE SURE TO INCLUDE THE BAD ONE!

THAT ARGUMENT IS SO TEN YEARS AGO!

...AND STRUCTURED FINANCE UNDERWRITERS...

...WHO BELIEVED IN MARKET EFFICIENCY BUT NOT EQUILIBRIUM.

TWO YEARS AFTER DE FINETTI'S BOOK, ABRAHAM WALD BEGAN A SERIES OF PUBLICATIONS THAT DREW ON FREQUENTIST AND BAYESIAN IDEAS AND GREW INTO DECISION THEORY, NONPARAMETRIC STATISTICS, AND DATA ANALYSIS. IT WAS A REALISTIC MIDDLE COURSE THAT AVOIDED THE STRICT ASSUMPTIONS OF THE MORE RIGOROUS SCHOOLS.

WALD'S FOLLOWERS LIKED POKER...

...AND BECAME TRADERS AND PORTFOLIO MANAGERS...

...WHO THOUGHT THEY COULD FIND BOTH INEFFICIENCIES AND DISEQUILIBRIA.

THEY ALL CAME TOGETHER ON WALL STREET IN 1987.

18

Frequency versus Degree of Belief

The events on Wall Street in the early 1990s, important as they were for the world economy, may be even more important for changing the fundamental understanding of probability and randomness. It was in the decade after 1654 when these ideas first entered intellectual and practical life and fused the concepts of frequency and degree of belief. It was in the decade of the 1990s that we finally figured out why that fusion makes sense.

Reading the 1654 letters between Fermat and Pascal, it's not obvious why they started an intellectual revolution. Probability is never mentioned, nor is randomness. The two great mathematicians struggled painfully with problems any high school student can easily solve today. Each of them came up with a different answer to the question of how to divide the stake in an interrupted game. The key of the letters is when Pascal realizes, to his enthusiastically expressed joy, that the two methods give the same answer.

Consider two gamblers playing a series of games. The first one to win seven games gets the stake. One gambler has six wins and the other five when the game is interrupted. How should the stake be divided?

Fermat noted that if the game were to continue, the result must be decided after two more games are played. Letting W represent a win for the first player (the one with six wins) and L represent a loss, the two games could come out in four ways: WW, WL, LW, and LL. In practice, in the first two of these cases, WW and WL, the second game would never be played since the contest would be over with the W. Fermat argued that the result would be unchanged if both these games were played. He then noted that the first player wins the stake in three outcomes, WW, WL, and LW, and loses in one, LL. Therefore, the first player is entitled to three-fourths of the stake.

Fermat was the lawyer, but Pascal was the one who took a legalistic approach instead of a combinatorial one. Pascal started from the rule that if the game is tied, divide the stake in half. Therefore, if the first player loses the first game, the series would be tied, and each player would be entitled to half the stake. Looking at things this way, the first game is a contest in which the first player gets the full stake if he wins, and half the stake if he loses. Thus we can think of the situation before the first game as the first player owning half the stake, and playing in a tied series for the other half. Since you split things in half in a tie, the first player is entitled to half the stake plus half of the other half, or three-quarters in total.

Note that neither argument considers the probability of the first player winning a game; probability is not mentioned at all. Fermat's argument is based on frequency. You play out all the possible games, and divide the stake according to the frequency of hypothetical future events. Pascal's argument is based on the beliefs of the two players; he assumes they agree that division of a stake in half is the fair way to resolve a tied series that is interrupted.

Statistical Games

I have noted earlier that this problem is very special for the type of randomness under consideration. The solution would not make sense if the bet concerned the weather, for example. If I bet it would rain on at least 7 of the next 13 days, and the bet is interrupted after 6 rainy and 5 sunny days, it does not necessarily make sense to award me three-fourths of the stake. If the 6 rainy days came at the beginning of the period and it has been cloudless since, you might even be the favorite at this point. In any case, an arbiter awarding the stake should at least look at the sky and listen to the weather forecast. But the problem is very special in another way as well. We're trying to resolve a game for money. Consider the same question with one player having promised to marry the other if she lost, in return for the other player promising to go to war in place of the first player's brother if he lost. Should the first player marry one quarter of the second player, while the other three-quarters of the second player goes to war along with one-quarter of the first player's brother? The only possible way to decide this case is to pick randomly, with the first player having a three-fourths chance of winning. This means continuing the game. And you don't need such far-fetched dramatic examples. Any time the stakes cannot be converted to a divisible common unit—that is, if the gamble is not for money—Pascal and Fermat have nothing useful to tell us.

To see how unusual the interrupted dice game is, consider the actual rules for deciding a baseball game that is rained out before completion. Assuming at least five innings have been completed, the team that is ahead at the time play is stopped is declared the winner if either (1) it was ahead at the beginning of the inning or (2) it would have to be ahead by the end of the inning. Otherwise the game is suspended and completed later. There is no partial division of the stake, and no consideration of the probability of either team winning. There is not always a decision at all. So there's nothing in an interrupted game that naturally suggests probability analysis. Pascal's and Fermat's logic makes sense only for a gambling game played for money, because the resolution they propose is based on gambling logic and only makes sense when both players' stakes can be measured in the same units and divided in any proportion.

Despite the narrowness of the application, the idea of fusing frequency and degree of belief stimulated a burst of creative mathematics. This culminated in Jakob Bernoulli's *Ars Conjectandi* (*The Art of Conjecturing*), written between 1684 and 1689, but not published until 1713. In this work we have the full-blown idea that precise mathematical statements of relative plausibility can be made on the basis of long-term frequencies of hypothetical random processes. Bernoulli makes the explicit claim that these hypothetical random processes should guide real decision making.

Bernoulli's favored example was an urn filled with marbles of different colors. Suppose you have an urn with 100 marbles, some red and some black. You cannot see into the urn, but you can reach in and pick out one marble. Say you pick one marble at random, put it back, pick another marble at random, put it back, and so on until you have chosen 10 marbles in all. Nine of your marbles are red, and one is black. You would like to know the probability that more than half the marbles in the urn are red.

Bernoulli knew that he couldn't answer that question. But he could answer a different one. If half or fewer of the marbles in the urn are red, what is the maximum probability that you would draw nine or more red marbles out of 10? The answer is 11 divided by 1,024 or 1.07 percent. In this case, *probability* means long-term frequency. I computed the answer, but I know that if I repeated the experiment of drawing 10 marbles a large number of times and if the urn had 50 or fewer red marbles, I would get nine or more reds out of 10 no more than 11 divided by 1,024 times. *Ars Conjectandi* contained the first proof of the law of large numbers, which says that you can get results to conform as closely as you want to average by repeating the experiment enough times. This tied mathematical computation to long-run frequency, but gave no reason to tie long-run frequency—whether observed in the past or computed according to a theory—to a specific one-time decision about an unknown future event.

Notice where randomness comes into this problem. There is none at the beginning. We have an urn with marbles in it. Some number are red. That's a deterministic number, not a random number. We deliberately introduce randomness by picking marbles at random. We do that so we can make the 1.07 percent calculation. If we took all our marbles from the top layer in the urn, the experiment would tell us nothing about marbles below the top layer. That's obvious, but it's also true that if we draw in any pattern at all, the calculation fails. So randomness is something we create in order to learn about something deterministic. It's pretty amazing. Just by stirring the marbles around so you pick at random, the marble you hold in your hand can tell you something about the marbles remaining the urn, at least 90 of which you've never seen. If the marbles were instead in a tube, looking at the first 10 marbles could never tell you anything about the 90 remaining in the tube.

We'd like to turn that 1.07 percent into a statement about the number of red marbles in the urn. There is no purely logical way to do that. Bernoulli took a frequentist approach, which was made rigorous only in the twentieth century. In modern formulation, a frequentist statistician says she can reject at the 5 percent level the null hypothesis that fewer than half the marbles in the urn are red. Five percent is a standard level of significance; we reject because 1.07 percent is less than 5 percent. The statement means that if the null hypothesis is true—that is, if there are fewer than 50 red marbles in the urn—the probability you would draw nine or more red marbles out of 10 is less than 5 percent. In principle, for this method to be valid, you have to pick your significance level before you draw the first marble.

This still doesn't say anything about the number of red marbles in the urn. However, the frequentist's argument is that if she follows this method all the time, fewer than 5 percent of the null hypotheses that she rejects will turn out to be true. There's quite a lot of theoretical machinery we need in order to justify that statement, and it may well not be true in practice, but that's not the point of this book. For the moment, accept it as valid. We have turned a long-run frequency calculation into a quantitative degree of belief, although the belief is twisted in two ways from what we originally wanted to know. First we have a statement about the probability of getting our experimental result, rather than a statement about the probability of the number of red marbles in the urn. Second, we know nothing about the accuracy of this statement in particular; we only make a claim about the long-term accuracy of lots of statements. This is how we turn an event that has already happened—drawing nine red marbles out of 10—into a hypothetical coin-flip gambling game that can be repeated indefinitely.

The main alternative to frequentist statistics today is the Bayesian view. It is named for Thomas Bayes, an eighteenth-century theorist, but it was Pierre-Simon Laplace who put forth the basic ideas. It was not until the twentieth century, however, that researchers, including Richard Cox and Bruno de Finetti, created the modern formulation.

In the Bayesian view of the urn, you must have some prior belief about the number of red marbles in the urn. For example, you might believe that any number from 0 to 100 red marbles is equally likely. Drawing the 10 marbles causes you to update your prior belief into a posterior belief. Under your prior belief, the probability of half or more of the marbles being red is 51/101 or 50.50 percent. I won't go into the details of the computation, although they are simple, but after observing nine red marbles out of 10, your posterior probability that there are 50 or more red marbles in the urn is 99.47 percent.

The Bayesians can do what the frequentists can't. They can answer the question we asked. However, to do it, they have to ask us what we thought before any marbles were drawn. And they don't just ask us what we thought the probability of 50 or more red marbles was; they ask us the exact probabilities of all numbers of red marbles from 0 to 100.

Bruno de Finetti claimed that we can always specify a prior distribution. We discussed it in Chapter 1 with his favorite example of life on Mars. Suppose we are forced to bet on whether there are exactly 90 red marbles in the urn. We name an amount of money; call it X. Someone else gets to pick whether to pay us X and receive $1 if there are exactly 90 red marbles in the urn and nothing otherwise, or to get X from us and pay $1 if there are exactly 90 red marbles in the urn. De Finetti claimed there had to be an X, and it was our subjective prior probability of there being exactly 90 marbles in the urn.

Whatever you think of that argument (and opinions among professionals are sharply divided), note that it explicitly references money. Bayesian probability theory depends on money or something moneylike to bet. It has to be moneylike, because you have to be able to divide X by the payment amount to get the probability. If the bet were, say, how many minutes of work would you do in order to get a good dinner if there were exactly 90 red marbles in the urn, the answer wouldn't tell you anything about probability, because you can't divide minutes worked by a good meal, unless you first convert both to money or some other numeraire.

It is money that fuses frequency and degree of belief. That was the aspect of the problem Fermat and Pascal first considered that allowed them to make progress. That doesn't mean statistics works only with money. It means that you have to put things in a moneylike framework for frequency arguments to equate to a degree of belief. This is why formal statistical reasoning has not replaced legal arguments or most other practical questions of uncertainty. The distinction people like Frank Knight and John Maynard Keynes draw between uncertainty problems amenable to mathematical analysis and those that cannot be calculated is precisely the distinction between issues that can be cast in moneylike terms and those that cannot. The error those two and many other writers made was to assume that formal statistics based on coin-flip probability and moneylike logic were the only possible mathematical way to treat uncertainty.

So far, my argument is not out of the mainstream of modern theoretical statistics. I place more emphasis on the moneylike nature of the connection between frequency and degree of belief than is usual, but most frequentist theorists accept the need to justify adding up the results of a large number of statistical predictions in order to use long-run frequency analysis to make decisions in individual cases. Bayesian theorists generally agree that defining subjective probability requires some correspondence among possible outcomes to establish at least relative preferences. These people have thought far more deeply about these issues than I have, and have come up with elegant and rigorous formulations. I do not despise that effort; I respect elegance and rigor. But mainstream probability theorists are wrong. They haven't taken the ideas far enough. I know this not because I am a more subtle theoretical thinker, but because I tried this stuff. I am reporting back about what works and what doesn't. I leave it to others more qualified than I am to make these observations formal and precise.

Thorp, Black, Scholes, and Merton

Finance started to diverge from statistics in the decade around 1970. We could start with Ed Thorp's first development and use of an option pricing model in the 1960s, or the publication of Fischer Black's and Myron Scholes's famous 1973 paper, "The Pricing of Options and Corporate Liabilities," or the publication of Robert Merton's paper, "Theory of Rational Option Pricing," the same year.

Popular finance books usually describe the Black-Scholes option pricing model as horrendously complex and requiring advanced mathematics. That's silly. The basic idea is simple. Some of the technical details in proving it are complicated, and the formula itself looks a bit intimidating compared to, say, $2 + 2 = 4$, but that's no reason to ignore the insight.

Suppose there is a stock that sells for $70 today and will be worth either $100 or $50 tomorrow. What is an option to buy 100 shares of the stock at $80 per share tomorrow worth? Your first thought might be zero. You can buy the stock for $70; why would you pay for the right to buy it at $80? The reason the option has value is you get to choose whether to buy tomorrow, after you know the new stock price. The option is worth $2,000 ($20 per share) if the stock goes up, and zero if the stock goes down.

Suppose you bought 40 shares of stock. These will be worth $4,000 tomorrow if the stock price goes up, and $2,000 if the stock price goes down. Either way, they're worth $2,000 more than the option. Since 40 shares of stock sell for $2,800, and they are worth the same as the option plus $2,000 (actually, that should be the present value of $2,000 since it is received tomorrow, but we'll ignore the discounting), the option must be worth $800, or $8 per share. This is an arbitrage argument. If the option sells for any price other than $8 per share, you can make riskless profits buying or selling it and hedging with the stock.

A real stock could sell for any price tomorrow, not just $50 or $100. But we can break its price movements down into ticks, say $70 to $69.95 or $70.05, then up or down a nickel from there, and so on. If the stock price can jump, it creates some technical problems for the model, but they're not very serious in practice. If we go one tick before exercise, the option is worthless if the stock is selling below $80 per share, and worth the stock price minus $80 if the stock is selling above $80.05 per share. If the stock is selling for $80, we can use the argument from the previous paragraph to price it. If the stock ticks up to $80.05, the option is worth $5. If the stock ticks down to $79.95, the option is worth zero. This is the same value as 50 shares of stock minus $3,997.50, or $2.50. Now we go two ticks before exercise and repeat the process. We know the option value at any stock price one tick in the future, so we can figure the value now. By repeating this enough times, we can find out what the option is worth today given the stock is selling for $70.

I hope you notice the similarity between this and Pascal's method for dividing the dice players' stake. Pascal started one game before the end of the match and figured the value of the stake to each player. Then he went one game earlier and treated it as a game not for the full stake, but for the value of the stake to each player conditional on who won the game. He continued backward until he got to the point where the problem was posed. Pascal and Fermat were astonished to discover that the backward induction method gave the same answer as Fermat's forward solution. The value of Thorp, Black, Scholes, and Merton's work was that the backward argument from arbitrage was identical to a forward argument based on stochastic partial differential equations, plus an equilibrium argument based on the capital asset pricing model.

In the early 1970s, the word *derivative* was invented to describe options because their price can be derived, in theory at least, from mathematical reasoning. If the option deviated from the theoretical price, again in theory, anyone could make riskless profits, also known as arbitrage. Today you usually see the word *derivative* explained as meaning the value of the derivative security depends on some underlying asset. That makes no sense. Every financial instrument price depends on something. In practice, the word today refers to a specific set of instruments: futures, forwards, options, swaps, and some more exotic instruments. Some of these are derivatives in the old sense, some in the conventional definition, and some in neither. I prefer the older meaning myself, because it makes clear that *derivative* is a way of looking at an instrument, not an inherent property of the instrument. You can regard an option as a derivative and treat its price as something you can derive mathematically from the underlying stock price, or you can regard the option price as something that trades up and down on its own, correlated to the stock price but not determined by it. Both views are valid for different purposes.

In this context, it is important to understand that the Black-Scholes-Merton option pricing model is not really a pricing model. It tells us one thing we don't know, the price of an option, in terms of another thing we don't know, the volatility of the underlying stock. Solving for the *implied volatility* (the volatility that gives the option its market price) from the price is exactly analogous to solving for the yield to maturity of a bond from its price. Both are conversions, like from Fahrenheit to Centigrade temperatures. They are mathematical transformations with no economic content.

The reason people solve for the yield to maturity of bonds is that two bonds with similar terms and credit qualities will have similar yields, but not necessarily similar prices. Thus we can take the price of a bond we do know, convert it to a yield, and apply the yield to get the price of a similar bond whose price we do not know. We can graph bond yield versus time to maturity to get a reasonably smooth yield curve. This is both a useful economic indicator and a way to interpolate yields of other bonds. We can also graph bond yield versus credit quality with similar results. And we can take the derivative of bond price with respect to yield to get a first order idea of the volatility of a bond.

The Black-Scholes-Merton model works the same way. Two options with similar terms will have similar implied volatilities, but not necessarily similar prices. So we can use implied volatilities of options we know the prices of to estimate the implied volatilities, and hence the prices, of options whose prices we do not know. We can graph option implied volatility versus time or moneyness (the ratio of the strike price of an option to the underlying price) and get the same kind of insights we get from yield curves and credit curves. We can take the derivative of option price with respect to implied volatility, known as *vega*, which some forgotten trader thought was a Greek letter. All of this is pure mathematics; it does not require any economic assumptions.

Anyway, the derivative concept in the old sense led to a fresh conflation of frequency and degree of belief. If an option price can be mathematically derived from the underlying stock price, then its price obviously does not depend on the utility function of the person evaluating it. In particular, the option has the same value to a risk-neutral investor—one who values everything at expected value—as anyone else. To a risk-neutral investor, the stock must be selling for its expected value as well. If we know the prices of options for any future expiration date and exercise price, we know the exact probability distribution a risk-neutral investor places on the stock. This is called the *risk-neutral probability distribution.* No risk-neutral investor need exist for this argument to be valid.

Continuing this argument, we can use market observation of underlying stock and option prices to estimate the risk-neutral distribution of underlying stock returns, and price any derivative at its expected value under the risk-neutral distribution. The risk-neutral distribution is distinct from the actual probability distribution. For one example, we know investors pay more for returns in bad states of the world than in good states. This means the risk-neutral probability distribution has higher probability values on market crashes than their actual chance of occurring.

The risk-neutral probability distribution represents a degree of belief, while the actual probability distribution is a frequency concept. To learn the first, I look at what investors pay for options. To estimate the second, I compile data of actual movements. Prior to the invention of risk-neutral probability distributions, probability theorists had been split into those who made practical progress by conflating frequency and degree of belief and those who refused to conflate but had no useful alternative. Now, for the first time, we had a theory that related degree of belief to frequency, but kept the two distinct.

Change of Numeraire

There is another way to view risk-neutral probabilities. Recall in the derivation of the option price, we converted the option on 100 shares of stock into ownership of 40 shares of stock minus $2,000. In effect, we expressed the option price in terms of shares of stock instead of dollars. The technical term for this is a *change of numeraire*. By stating prices in shares of stock rather than dollars—in other words, by using the stock instead of dollars as money—we make the option riskless. A share of stock is always worth one share of stock, whatever the price is in dollars. Since the option price can be stated as a fixed number of shares, at least in theory and for an instant, the option is also riskless in the stock numeraire.

This is a general technique in derivative pricing, and financial engineering in general. Picking the right numeraire can make a hard problem easy (and we saw in Chapter 1 that it can reverse the answer). It can make a problem that required estimation of probabilities into one that can be answered directly from observation. The numeraire is what connects frequency to degree of belief. And it's fundamentally a concept of money. Looking at it another way, the way to make degree of belief correspond to frequency is to measure things in the right units. Reversing that logic, the thing you choose for your numeraire fundamentally alters your interpretation of statistical evidence. That's why the nature of money is so crucial to an economy. Of lesser importance, that's why statisticians should always think about the moneylike basis of what they are analyzing.

Consider a famous paradox of probability theory, first described by Belgian mathematician Maurice Kraitchik in 1953. Kraitchik used wallets and neckties, but the problem is more often described today with envelopes. Two different amounts of money are placed in two sealed envelopes. One amount is twice the other amount. You choose one envelope at random, but don't open it. You are then offered the opportunity to switch envelopes.

Like the bet we discussed with Anne and Anaïs in Chapter 10, this appears to create expected value out of nothing. You reason, "Call the amount of money in my envelope X. Since I picked my envelope at random, there is a 50 percent chance I have the larger amount, in which case the other envelope contains X/2, and a 50 percent chance I have the smaller amount, in which case the other envelope contains 2X. Therefore the expected value of switching is 1.25X. I should switch." While this seems sound, it's hard to see how the extra 0.25X expected value got created out of nothing. Even if you accept that, from the example of the undoubtedly valid gain in the case of Anne and Anaïs, there is a problem. As soon as you switch, you can use the same argument to switch back.

There are a number of proposed solutions to the paradox, but the obvious one to a financial quant is that your positive expected value argument uses X as a numeraire. As soon as you switch envelopes, you switch the numeraire to the amount in the second envelope. That's why you keep switching envelopes back and forth.

To see the implication of using X as your numeraire, suppose I told you that the amounts in the envelopes were selected by picking an integer from 1 to 99 with equal probability, putting that number of dollars in one envelope and twice that number of dollars in the other. When you pick an envelope at random, the expected amount of money inside is $75. The expected amount of money in the other envelope is also $75. However, it's also true that the expected amount of money in the other envelope is 1.25 times the amount of money in your envelope. Read carefully. I didn't say the expected amount of money in the second envelope is 1.25 times the *expected* amount of money in your envelope. That would be clearly false, since both envelopes have the same expected amount of money.

The only reason this paradox is difficult is the English language. If you write it down in mathematical equations, it's straightforward. The two envelopes have the same expected amounts of money. However, the expected value of the ratio of the first envelope amount divided by the second envelope amount is 1.25. That's also the expected value of the ratio of the second envelope amount divided by the first envelope amount. There's nothing strange about that mathematically; it's just confusing when you state it in English.

The reason Bayesians have no problem with Kraitchik's paradox is not that they have a better theory. It's that they have a tendency to thoughtlessly assign a dollar numeraire to problems. If you use dollars as numeraire, there's no reason to switch, and no paradox. But it's not always correct to use dollars, as Anne and Anaïs prove. For another example, suppose the envelopes contained not money, but scrip to be used in an auction. All the other bidders would receive the amount in the first envelope; only you had a choice of switching. In that case you definitely improve your expected value by switching. If you win, you can buy twice as much at the auction as everyone else. If you lose, you can buy half as much. In this case, X is the correct numeraire. This, by the way, is the trick Pascal used in his famous wager. He switched the numeraire to lives, which is the crux of his argument. If you accept that your entire earthly life is the appropriate numeraire for decision making, then the rest of Pascal's case is easy to accept. Just as Archimedes claimed that with a long enough lever he could move the earth, I claim that with a big enough numeraire, I can make any faith-based action seem reasonable.

Frequentist statistics suffers from paradoxes because it doesn't insist everything be stated in moneylike terms, without which there's no logical connection between frequency and degree of belief. Bayesian statistics suffers from insisting on a single, universal numeraire, which is often not appropriate. One thing we know about money is that it can't buy everything. One thing we know about people is they have multiple natures, and groups of people are even more complicated. There are many numeraires, more than there are people. Picking the right one is key to getting meaningful statistical results.

The only statistical analyses that can be completely certain are ones that are pure mathematical results, and ones that refer to gamelike situations in which all outside considerations are excluded by rule and the numeraire is specified. These points are generally accepted among theorists, but are often missed in practice. Professional economists are well aware that numeraires matter. In fact, they spend a lot of effort thinking things like how to integrate human lives into the same equations with money, or what discount rate to apply to present harm versus future potential harm. But in my experience, few of them consider that these questions go to the nature of probability. They are not merely questions of utility, of preferences. They are essential for defining probability or belief. Professional statisticians, in contrast, know that it's possible to argue for almost any probability you want just by changing the terms of the analysis. That's why there are always statisticians on both sides of any lawsuit, and why no error in the social sciences, medicine, or public policy has ever been prevented by failure to get statistical confirmation for the side that turned out to be wrong. Statistics cannot settle arguments unless people want to agree in the first place. Only when two people agree to trade, when they agree on a relative set of actionable prices, can probabilities be defined objectively. Where many statisticians err, in my opinion, is in not seeing that these are questions of relative preferences, of prices, not of statistical methodology.

Practical statistical analysis must specify a range of application—what the numeraire is, and what it can buy. Otherwise there is no logic to connect frequency with degree of belief. And the only range of application you can trust, outside of a few that are derived directly from physical laws, is one that is validated by back-testing. Putting it another way, the only numeraire you can trust is one that can be measured in observable transactions.

Polling

This is not a book on statistical practice, but I'm conscious that everything so far is pretty abstract. So let's take one example: political polling. I picked this because it is an important practical application of statistics, and one that seems to be pure objective probability, with no reference to money. In Bernoulli's coin-flip world, political polling is the same problem as drawing marbles from an urn. You sample some random voters and use their replies to set a confidence interval on the election results.

In the real world, the problem is much harder. It is difficult to get a truly random sample, and people don't always tell the truth about whether they will vote or how they will vote. Or they can tell the truth at the time but later change their minds. And it turns out the best sample is not a purely random one; it makes sense to concentrate your subjects in swing vote groups, and to weight each response by the number of similar voters in the population. With all of these difficulties and adjustments, no one would take seriously a theoretical computation of error rate. The only reason to believe a poll result is if the researcher or organization that administered it has been right in the past. Of course, many polls do not even try to be correct, but I'm talking about the ones that do try. Also, some polls are for very specific purposes, for example to direct campaign spending to these most advantageous places. These have to be judged for their success at their purpose. I'm talking about polls for general information.

So the question is: What kind of track record—what past frequency—would persuade me to bet on future predictions—

would change my degree of belief? I don't just mean that I would take the poll results as general information; I mean that I would bet on the specific probabilistic claim. If the pollster says there is a 60 percent chance of the Democrat winning, am I willing to put up $59 to $41 on the Democrat winning or $39 to $61 on the Democrat not winning? If not, I do not believe the pollster's claim. You don't need statistics or probability theory to ask a bunch of people how they're going to vote and change your general assessment of the odds of various outcomes as a result. The claim of statistics is that we can make objective calculations that should determine subjective belief.

The gold standard of statistical validation for me is opening up your predictions for public betting. But if that's not available, we can do a virtual test if you have any track record of success. Suppose you bring me your results from the 2008 elections. What will I look at in order to see if I should believe your predictions about 2012?

First off, I'm going to need a lot of predictions. If you predicted only the Presidential election, I have no way of knowing if you're good or bad at the job. But if you made, say, 20,000 predictions covering state assemblies, governors, Congress, and the Presidential election, then we have something to go on.

If you got more than half the predictions wrong, we can stop right now. I won't bet on your new predictions. But let's say you got 19,000 (95 percent) right. Does that mean I can be 95 percent confident about your new predictions? No, because a lot of races are easy to predict. If I'm betting on the Presidential race, maybe I don't care that you got almost every state assembly election right. If I'm betting on an election where a thunderstorm is predicted on election day or a major scandal broke between the time of your poll and the election, maybe your track record isn't relevant.

What I'm going to do is assign a numeraire to your past predictions and see if you would have made a profit with them. I might, for example, build a simple model that estimates the chance of the Democratic candidate winning based on the percentage of the vote the Democratic candidate got four years earlier, using historical frequencies. Each of your predictions will count as a bet, with the payout odds determined by my simple model. I won't size the bets evenly, because for general interest polls, the more important elections are more important to get right. In a real betting setting, the more important races will attract more betting action, so if you were setting odds for a national line, it would be more important to get those right. In addition, races are correlated, so it would be double-counting to give you full credit for correctly predicting different races in the same election district, for example. To keep it simple, I will make the bet size equal to the population represented by the electoral region, although there are many other schemes.

What I have described is not a perfect numeraire for this problem. There probably is no perfect one, although opening up to actual betting is pretty close. Different people have different uses for the numbers, and would assign betting odds and amounts differently. That is, they would use different numeraires. But everyone needs something to add up among races. The total number of correct predictions is just not meaningful. However, it is probably true that most general interest numeraires would give similar estimates of your prediction accuracy. So the simple one might be reasonable.

So far I've only suggested a weighting scheme for predictions, based on a prior estimate of likelihood and importance. No one is going to argue with that. I've called the scheme a numeraire, but I only justified it as something that is probably correlated reasonably well with the weights that would be given by most people making real general decisions based on the results.

I prefer a true numeraire, something you can spend. But I think you can get most of the benefit with a pretend numeraire, if you take it seriously. That is the next step, in which I go beyond most modern probability theorists.

Your numeraire, real or pretend—but especially pretend—is not going to function well all the time. In sports betting, for example, there are runaway lines due to fixed games. There are other potential problems as well that go outside your numeraire. A single one of those can put you out of business if you are not careful.

It is not enough for a pollster just to make predictions and expect to be judged by the weighted percentage that is correct. For practical use, there has to be explicit guidance about when the prediction is reliable. Does it hold if there is bad weather on election day? If one of the candidates dies? If there is a scandalous headline the day of the election? If I am going to bet on the predictions, I need to know if it is safe to bet with a meteorologist, or one of the candidates' doctors, or a newspaper editor.

Another set of issues concerns whether results from four years ago have any relevance to tomorrow's elections. Will changes in your organization or methodology make a difference? Is there a change in the nature of elections or opinion formation or polling technology? Is it better to use data from the more recent 2010 off-year elections than the older 2008 presidential year results? These are harder to analyze than the first set of issues, but they are more important because they can affect every prediction you make.

If I'm making practical decisions based on the poll results, those decisions might involve interactions with weather, health, news, or anything else. The usual practice is to oversell the reliability of statistical results, and then use excuses after the fact if the results are wrong (and, of course, never to bet anything of real value and to insist on being paid by the client whether you are right or wrong). This is not good enough for serious work. Potential excuses must be identified before the fact. One reason is to make the prediction useful. Another reason is to prove that success is a result of skill, not luck. This is where VaR-like concepts come in.

Thus for me to bet on your poll results, you have to show me that you specified before the 2008 election in what circumstances your results would be invalid, and that you estimated the probability of such circumstances accurately. I need to be able to distinguish between exceptional circumstances and races you got wrong through the normal ups and downs of elections—in other words the races where you would have lost your shirt to informed bettors and the ones where you would have lost tolerable amounts because bets were reasonably balanced on both sides. I need to know the relative probabilities of those two things. Just as important, I need to know that you understand the difference. If I'm taking bets, I have to know when to shut down a line due to unbalanced betting, and when to trust your prediction of the odds.

Political polling is one of many areas in which the opportunities for breakthroughs are unlimited. In the period after World War II, advances in computers and applied mathematics revolutionized many fields, and not just quantitative fields. But serious thought about collection and validation of data lagged behind the improvements in data analysis and processing. As a result, advances were limited to fields in which theorists either collected their own data or were closely linked to people who collected data. Other fields developed a middle layer of statisticians or other specialists to mediate between subject-matter experts and data collectors. This middle layer was a complete failure; it ended up consuming vast resources and insulating theorists from data and data collectors from theory. In some fields both theorists and data collectors have been squeezed out entirely. The remaining workers have no knowledge of or interest in the subject area, no taste for data collection, and no skill at experimentation or observation. These experts content themselves with empty reprocessing of data collected for other reasons, and endless political bickering disguised as academic debate.

Economics is an excellent example of such a field. However, it had a bastard offshoot, the field of finance. Finance had good theory and good data, but most important, it offered huge monetary rewards to people who could connect the two in an effective middle office. Pure theorists without data and data miners without theories both went broke. Eventually the survivors figured out how to connect the two. The field exploded in profitability, knowledge, and influence. The same thing will happen in other fields as they adopt, and improve, the techniques we invented.

I predict political pollsters will make extraordinary discoveries when they insist on prespecifying a region of application for their results and on rigorously back-testing the frequency with which results outside this region occur. The effect of things like weather, news, and voting technology will become clear, and will be surprising. Commonsense, top-down mental images of elections will be exposed as deeply misleading. Both prediction and interpretation of election results will change dramatically. Election predictions good enough that you can bet on them will be available for the first time in history. These predictions will have enormous influence on policy.

Until practitioners start doing things this way, most quantitative model results, including polls, will not be reliable. The good ones will be general indications, but none will be results you can bet on. The required rigor will drive a lot of charlatans out of the quantitative prediction business. But the payoff will be great. I have seen quantitative modelers who held themselves to rigorous standards perform miracles. Everyone said you can't beat the house, but quantitative modelers beat the house in casino games—and won at poker and completely revolutionized sports betting. Everyone said you can't beat the market, but quantitative modelers beat the market—and completely revolutionized it. Everyone says you never can tell, but quantitative modelers will tell—and it will cause revolutions.

The Quant Revolution

The VaR limit is the region in which we trust the numeraire. Outside the VaR boundary, we can't aggregate the data with normal observations, because we can't translate them to a common numeraire. By itself, this is not a new idea in statistics. Standard analysis identifies outliers and analyzes them separately from the rest of the data. Sometimes outliers are data errors or rare exceptions of minor interest. Sometimes they are far more important than variation within normal data. But it is almost never fruitful to combine outliers and ordinary observations in a single analysis.

Wall Street quants took this idea further by identifying the outlier region in advance. As I have said, we were forced to do it by circumstances. No one thought of the approach as a useful way to improve statistics; it was a way to satisfy top-down demands with the tools at hand. Only when we tried to do it did we discover how hard and useful it was. After a few years, we didn't trust any statistical result that didn't have a clear numeraire and validated analysis of situations when the numeraire broke down.

For financial trading applications, the standard process is:

- Estimate a 95 percent one-day value at risk each day before trading begins. You estimate every trading day, even if systems are down or data are missing.
- Compare actual daily profit and loss (P&L) against the VaR prediction when the daily P&L becomes available.
- Test for the correct number of VaR breaks, within statistical error. Test that the breaks are independent in time and independent of the level of VaR.
- Once you have a reliable VaR system, collect data within the VaR limit.
- Investigate days when you lose more than the VaR amount, but supplement the observations with hypothetical scenarios and days in the past when your current positions would have suffered large losses.
- On the basis of the previous point's analysis, estimate a left tail of the distribution—that is, the distribution of rare big

losses. A power law fit is often appropriate. Don't try to go to the worst possible case; accept a nonzero chance of catastrophic failure.

- Also on the basis of trans-VaR scenarios, consider risk factors not measured in the P&L. These include leverage risk, liquidity risk, counterparty credit risk, model risk, fraud risk, and others.
- Try to determine the optimal Kelly bet based on the good data you have within the VaR limit, plus the hypothetical left tail you created. Try to get up to this level of risk while staying under the levels of leverage, liquidity, counterparty credit, and other risks that could destroy the firm in the identified trans-VaR scenarios. Again, you are not trying for zero probability of failure.

The third point, the VaR back-test, is the only objectively validated part of the process. That's why it is so crucial. Without it, you can't know you're doing the right thing, and you can't convince anyone else. With it, you might be doing the wrong thing, but my empirical observation is that doesn't happen often.

It will take some more development to apply this outside of finance, but I am convinced the basic principles apply to any statistical reasoning.

- Define a clear set of predictions.
- Define a clear numeraire such that it makes sense to add predictions together.
- Estimate the range of outcomes in which the numeraire can be trusted. These estimates should be frequent enough that you have 30 breaks over a period for which it is reasonable to assume parameters are fairly close to constant. There's nothing magic about 30, but it's a good rule of thumb to have 30 observations to estimate one parameter.
- Validate your estimates rigorously, especially number of breaks, time distribution of breaks, and breaks conditional on the size of the range estimate.
- Ideally, supplement this by letting people bet against your range estimate.
- Analyze the data within numeraire range using standard statistical methods.

- Analyze the data outside the numeraire range using data, judgment, and imagination. Since the numeraire is not reliable here, consider other factors that would be important in that scenario.
- Make a plan that accounts for the ordinary days and the out-of-region days—one that optimizes growth in your objective.

Once again, without the fourth step, I don't trust any statistical analysis. Someone who can't predict the ordinary events can't have much useful to say about the entire distribution. Someone who could predict ordinary events but doesn't bother is missing a valuable tool to improve knowledge. Also, he must have made up his mind he was going to be right before he started, because he didn't take the trouble to check rigorously afterward. Someone with that kind of faith in himself is not to be trusted.

This is obviously not the last word on statistical practice. It's a messy system that so far has found only one application. Messy as it is, however, I consider it the first satisfying and complete answer to the problem that began with Pascal in Fermat in 1654. It took Jakob Bernoulli 35 years to put those ideas into elegant and rigorous form. By that schedule, we should have a rigorous foundation for statistics around 2025.

CHAPTER

19

The Secret History of Wall Street: 1993–2007

I've allotted myself one chapter to cover the period in which Wall Street, and finance in general, exploded in global impact. In 1980, investment banks were small private partnerships, commercial banks had balance sheets a nineteenth-century auditor would have understood, investment banks and commercial banks were walled off from each other by Glass-Steagall, hedge funds were small and obscure, few individuals owned securities, and fewer individuals cared about anything that happened on Wall Street. Then things changed. The groundwork for change had been laid by finance professors from the 1950s to the 1970s, and the triggering event was the arrival of rocket scientists around 1980. I'm not claiming the professors and quants caused everything that happened, but we set things in motion and the changes that did happen cannot be understood without knowing their quant foundations. I'm going to try to cover the stuff that other histories leave out.

The most obvious change during this period was one of scale. Individual firms got larger, firms merged into gigantic complexes, and private firms went public to raise additional capital. The total market value of securities went up, and uncountable new varieties were introduced. Since 1980, the U.S. economy in real terms has about doubled whether you measure gross domestic product, national income, total nonfinancial corporate profits, or another major aggregate of economic activity. Financial businesses have about quadrupled in real terms over the same period whether measured by revenue, profits, or assets. Although financial employment increased only slightly faster than population growth, the aggregate statistics mask a trend of lower-wage service employees falling in numbers  while higher-wage decision-making employees like traders and portfolio managers increased dramatically. During this period, many of the most ambitious young people got MBAs and headed for Wall Street, where salaries and opportunities for innovation were skyrocketing.

At the same time, Wall Street was both expanding and contracting geographically. It was contracting in the sense that more and more financial services were delivered by global institutions headquartered in major financial centers such as New York and London. Neighborhood bankers, insurance agents, and stockbrokers declined in importance relative to people delivering the same services—or nominally the same, anyway—from Wall Street. Local and regional firms were bought up by global ones. At the same time, consciousness of finance was expanding into people's homes, televisions, computers, and brains, and expanding all over the globe as well. Financial scandals, large and small, began to compete seriously with natural disasters, politics, and celebrity scandals for newspaper headlines. There were more financial scandals, of course, and they were bigger; but the main reason they were on the front pages was people cared more about finance.

Actually, there was a second reason for the breathless coverage of financial scandals. Traditionally, people in finance shunned publicity. The only good news coverage was no news coverage. If a firm made the headlines it was due to government investigation or bankruptcy or some other scandal. Banks preferred to make money quietly, with few people outside of finance even knowing the names of the main firms. Retail banks, insurance companies, and brokerages had to advertise of course, but mostly staid ways emphasizing their solidity. When a firm did get flamboyant, as upstart (at the time) Merrill Lynch did with a 1971 World Series television ad featuring a literal bull in a china shop, it was shocking.

When finance started changing rapidly in 1980, innovators needed attention. Older professionals remembered the days when the job of a publicist was to keep any bad news out of the paper. But the younger crowd matured in an era dominated by Andrew Oldham's famous insight that bad boys got more attention than good ones. In 1963, Oldham realized the Rolling Stones could not compete with the Beatles for nice, cheerful, friendly, non-threatening pop band. So he ran the scariest and scruffiest pictures of the band he could find, and played up stories of rowdiness, violence, and drug use.

It took finance 20 years or so to catch up, but when it did, innovators realized you got more headlines jamming "junk" bonds into institutional portfolios than making a market in high-yield securities. You didn't offer to buy a large block of a company's shares, you ran a corporate "raid," "hostile" if possible. George Soros did not try to explain that his selling of the British pound improved economic allocation for everyone; he gloried in the charge that he had attacked Britain and won.

The 1970s saw major innovations of great importance to investors. Money market funds, for example, got around the long-standing rules that limited interest rates investors could earn. No-load, low-fee index mutual funds offered tremendous value compared to alternatives for most investors. The fixed commissions that had been the entire reason Wall Street was created in the 1792 Buttonwood Agreement, disappeared in 1975, paving the way for the discount brokerage firms that would dominate the market and changing the way Wall Street did research. All of these were quiet changes whose full impact was not realized for many years (although the last one is described as the "big bang," it did not get widespread publicity outside the financial pages).

The reason for seeking the bad-boy publicity is finance, for the first time, was playing to the people. Traditional intermediaries want to keep their customers far away from their suppliers. Ideally, neither one even knows who the parties on the other side are. People put their money in the bank without having a clear idea where it went after that. They had even less idea about the investments supporting their pension funds or insurance policies. Companies raised funds without much knowledge of the source of the funds. Intermediaries liked it that way; it let them get away with higher fees. The more complex intermediate layers serviced by anonymous entities with mysterious duties, the more money leaked out of the package between supplier and user of capital.

Thirty years of academic writings failed to persuade many individuals to learn enough about finance to get a better deal. It took headlines to do that, and headlines required drama, or at least dramatic metaphors. The language of public discussion of finance has changed, and today is closer to the language of political debate and sports than to the sedate banker-speak of the past. In that sense, quant innovation has to take some of the blame for Jim Cramer.

Where Did the Money Come From?

How did a few nerdy quants incite this riot? Let's answer that question by asking another one. Who paid for all this growth? Did people suddenly start saving more, or taking money that had been other places and giving it to Wall Street? No and no. Global savings rates declined. People changed the types of financial institutions that held their money, such as from bank accounts to money market funds, or using mutual funds instead of whole life insurance for retirement planning, but they didn't contribute significantly more money in total. The reason it seemed that more money came to Wall Street is that most private retirement plans changed from defined-benefit plans where the employer manages the retirement account to defined-contribution plans where the employee does. But Wall Street held the funds under both systems.

It was quants who created the money to pay for the party. You're welcome. We did it by redefining the basis of value from cash or gold in the vault to risk equations. That basically doubled the amount of capital available for everyone. Unfortunately, we didn't do as good a job as we should have. That's the main reason we had the recent financial crisis. Sorry.

Economic activity is limited by the amount of capital available. The total value of all goods in the process of production or available for sale, plus the total value of all capital assets used for production, has to be financed by somebody. Institutions can be a conduit for this, but institutions have to get the capital from somebody. Even governments that print their own money get their capital from people. If the government pays for something with tax money or borrowed money, that's obvious. If it "monetizes the debt"—basically if it prints money instead of issuing bonds—either there can be inflation, which subtracts a little bit of money from all holders of cash, or extra money can create the expectation of future tax increases, which shrinks economic value as surely as inflation. This need not be an accounting identity; printing the money could fool people into thinking there is more capital, in which case there really is more, at least for a while. Or it could cause people to overreact and result in a net subtraction of capital. My general belief is the average effect is negative, because people aren't consistently fooled and they correctly reason that debt monetization usually accelerates rather than reverses. So they will react not only to the amount of money printed, but to the increased future expectation of printing. Government capital creation has been a dream of many economists, and a nightmare for everyone else.

Quants know how to create true capital, and you don't need a printing press or sovereign powers. The keys are derivatives and securitization. It sounds like black magic. It's more or less magic, but it's not black. You get to keep your soul.

If you ask people who work in finance what social good they do, the most common answer you'll get is that they make the market more efficient. This is not true, economic efficiency is created by people working with real assets, and by self-organizing systems that need no help from Wall Street. Financial trading is more likely to impose stresses on the market, to push it farther from efficiency and equilibrium, than to relieve stress. This is why when the market does not move smoothly from one alignment to another, it snaps suddenly and usually in the opposite direction traders were pushing. Moreover, making things more efficient in the sense apologists mean is not even good. Only a wildly oversimplified model of the world holds that more efficient markets add to real welfare.

The social value of finance is the profit produced by financial activities. As I discussed in Chapter 9, it seems to me that most people believe the opposite, that financial profits are a tax on the real work that is done. But in honest finance the customers on both sides of the transaction are better off, and there is profit generated by the intermediary, real value created. That value is extremely important. It accumulates at strategic economic locations where it is invested to produce far more growth and innovation than any other kind of value.

Rocket scientists entered a system in which most financial profits were taxes on real activities, protected by information hoarding and crony regulation. We weren't altruists, but we were honest. We wanted to make money by creating value, and we did. This changed the nature of finance in a fundamental way, and unleashed a wave of growth and innovation in the world.

As we left things at the end of Chapter 14, value at risk (VaR) had been born from the accidental union of the capital camp, composed of frequentist quants mostly running small hedge funds, and the value camp, composed of nonparametric quants mostly running trading desks or other risk-taking businesses in diversified financial firms. We now need to shift focus to the third camp, the Bayesian quants holding executive or staff positions in large financial firms. These people had hitched their risk management theories to earnings, which had been left out entirely in the VaR revolution.

Recall that these are the sports bettors, the people people. Not for them the stubborn insistence of sticking to some deep underlying truth until long-run frequency rewarded them. If the football line changes, you accept it and modify your bets accordingly. There is no long run; the game will be played next Sunday, and this week's bets no longer matter after that. I admit there were some exceptions, Bayesians who went down with the ship. Even today I run into unreconstructed earnings-risk believers. These were the people blaming mark-to-market accounting for the financial crisis when the rest of the world believed—correctly in my view—that refusal to accept honest marks was the problem. In most cases, however, these were not the quants who originally developed the ideas in the late 1980s. They were people who absorbed the idea secondhand and never reconsidered, or who seized the idea because it justified what they wanted to do anyway.

The Bayesian quants stole the focus on capital from the frequentist quants. In the process, the idea was reversed. Instead of capital being held to offset risk, risk would define capital. "Risk-based capital" was born. All financial institutions, not just banks, should be required to hold capital proportionate to the riskiness of their assets. Not surprisingly, the new definition they wanted to use for risk looked a lot like the definition of earnings volatility that the sports bettors had favored previously. People people know that a few small tweaks and a change in terminology can resurrect ideas most people have given up for dead.

This new focus on bank capital was a change. Banks had long had reserve requirements. Reserves are the opposite of capital. They are liquid, high-quality assets, originally precious metal but later government bonds and deposits with the central bank. A reserve requirement is a fraction of liabilities (such as deposits, which are a liability to the bank) held as an asset (such as gold). For example, with a 10 percent reserve requirement—the current U.S. rate for checking account deposits—if someone deposits $100 of cash in a bank the bank could lend $90 of it out, but the other $10 had to be used to purchase gold or some other reserve asset. The $90 loan will likely be redeposited in the banking system, first by the borrower and later, when the borrower spends the money, by whoever received it. Then it can generate a new $90 × 0.9 = $81 loan, with $9 going to purchase reserve assets. The process can continue until the original $100 deposit has generated $1,000 in loans; and the entire $100 is held in the form of reserve assets. Lowering the reserve requirement increases the total amount of loans that can be made for a fixed initial deposit base, but it also makes the banking system less stable.

So a reserve requirement is a fraction of liabilities that must be held as a certain type of asset. A capital requirement is a fraction of assets that must be held as a certain type of liability or as equity. Liabilities and equity both go on the right-hand side of a balance sheet; assets are on the left-hand side.

With an 8 percent capital requirement, when a bank makes a $100 loan, $8 must be provided by the bank owners; only $92 can be funded from deposits or other liabilities. A reserve requirement protects the liquidity of a bank's notes; it makes it more likely they can be redeemed immediately for gold, or today, cash. A capital requirement protects the long-term value of the bank's notes. It makes it more likely they can be paid off in full eventually. A bank with $10 deposited with the Federal Reserve, worthless loans, and $100 of deposits can satisfy a 10 percent reserve requirement, but not capital requirements. It has negative $90 of capital. A bank with $100 of solid loan-term loans, no reserve assets, and $92 in deposits can satisfy an 8 percent capital requirement, but not reserve requirements. It has no reserves. The first bank has a long-term problem, whereas the second bank has a short-term problem.

Before 1980, government bank examiners did care about capital, but there was no minimum amount set. It was left to the examiner's judgment whether a bank was adequately capitalized. The problem was that in good times almost all banks had plenty of capital. When times got rough, any strict mark-to-market accounting would show that many banks were thinly capitalized, or even insolvent. But forcing them to close in that circumstance was counterproductive. Telling everyone a bank's capital had fallen to a dangerous level seemed even more counterproductive. I disagree, however; I believe transparency is best in the long run. Insolvent banks should close down and pay off depositors as their loan portfolio run off. Depositors who need cash immediately can sell their claims at a discount to either borrowers, who need it to repay loans, or to speculators. Although the United States has deposit insurance, some depositors are not protected, and no other bank creditors are. Even for the insured depositors, it is inconvenient to have an account in a failed bank. So a public announcement that a bank had inadequate capital could trigger a run on the bank, followed by the bank's failure. I think that's the right solution, but few people agree with me.

The only productive things to do when bank capital shrinks below prudent levels are to let the value of the bank's notes fall— which was impossible under the government monopoly on money— or to get the bank's owners to contribute more capital—which was a political nonstarter. An examiner might use the threat of declaring capital inadequate to force a sale to a solvent institution or some other form of capital contribution, but it was a game of chicken in which most banks had the political backing to force the examiner to chicken out.

It took an international organization to accomplish what no country could enforce upon its own banks. The Bank for International Settlements declared in 1988 that internationally active banks had to have capital equal to at least 8 percent of assets. Well, sort of. No capital was needed for government bonds, and other favored types of bank investments got "risk weights" of less than 100 percent. Also, "capital" did not actually have to be capital; banks were allowed to count certain types of liabilities as well.

One obvious problem with this approach (called Basel I) is banks have the incentive to fund the riskiest assets in each risk category or bucket. For example, most loans to corporations carried a 100 percent risk weight, so you needed to hold 8 percent of their amount in capital. That was true for short-term senior secured loans to the most creditworthy corporations, and long-term unsecured subordinated loans to companies teetering on the edge of bankruptcy. The latter carried a much higher interest rate, giving the bank a much higher return on equity.

A less obvious problem is there was no provision for derivatives and other off-balance-sheet items that contributed to much of the risk of sophisticated banks. There was an attempt to address this, but it was a minor afterthought and did not work well in practice.

By the way, since the financial crisis, there have been many calls to impose leverage limits on banks. Basel I is a leverage limit, just stated the reverse way. Leverage is defined as bank assets divided by bank capital. If you limit that to 12.5 it's the same as saying you must hold capital equal to 8 percent of your assets. And all of the leverage cap proposals bucket assets and give risk weights, and have trouble dealing with derivatives, just like Basel I. Limiting leverage is a step backward in bank regulation, both intellectually and historically, not a step forward. Of course, that's exactly what many of its proponents want.

Recall that our Bayesian sports-bettor bank executives lost out in risk management to value at risk, which combined ideas from the frequentist and nonparametric camps. Seeing the problems with Basel I, that capital was based on arbitrary rules and did not provide the right risk management incentives, the Bayesians declared that we must have "risk-based" capital. Now that idea is unquestionably correct in a world where the government has monopoly on money and also guarantees the banks. Banks need some cushion to protect against failure, and the size of that cushion has to be related to the amount of risk the bank takes.

Measuring risk is tricky, however. And VaR was lying around, already computed and looking sort of like a risk measure. The temptation was irresistible to use it as the basis of bank capital. The core idea of Basel II, which was developed from 1994 to 2005 and implemented from 2006 to 2009, was to set the capital requirement at three times the 99 percent, 10-day VaR. Of course there is a tremendous amount of additional detail, thousands of pages. The VaR rule was modified for different kinds of assets; it applies directly only to liquid assets held for sale and marked to market. But intellectually, this was the thrust of the movement. Capital was to be based on a measure of risk, and risk was to be defined as a multiplier of the amount you could lose in specified conditions with specified probability. Originally the VaR was to be subjected to a rigorous back-test, and supplemented by extensive stress testing. But those requirements got watered down or overlooked in the implementation.

In principle, using VaR as a risk measure is crazy. VaR wasn't designed to measure risk, and it can't do it. VaR is determined only by events in the center of the distribution; it ignore the tails. It covers only static portfolios in normal markets. It is not the most you can lose; it is the *least* you will lose 1 percent of the time. The parameters were wrong as well. A good rule of thumb in data analysis is that you want at least 30 observations for each parameter. A 95 percent one-day VaR produces breaks every 20 days, so 600 trading days or about two and a half years gives you 30 observations. That's a reasonable time interval over which to assume market conditions are constant. A 99 percent 10-day VaR requires 30,000 trading days— 119 years—of data for the same reliability. Even if you have that much data, most of it will be irrelevant to current conditions. Some people even suggested 99.97 percent one-year VaR, which means they would need 100,000 years of data.

In practice, however, using VaR as a risk measure had a lot to recommend it. There was no good measure of bank risk, and at least VaR was available and could be verified objectively. It forced banks to confront their central risk, which is important in itself and a prerequisite to understanding tail risk. It required major improvements in systems and controls. No one had a better idea, and no one wanted to wait around for a decade or so until one arose. It would be better to have a rational risk-based system on a flawed measure and improve it later than to do nothing because you couldn't do it perfectly. At least, that was a common attitude. Or maybe quants liked it for all the power it gave them, and all the jobs it created.

So VaR was dead wrong in theory, but defensible in practice. That solved the problem of defining the capital requirement. You also have to define what capital is, so you can see if a bank has the required level. On this issue Basel II got the theory right, but mandated an impractical system. The function of capital is to protect bank creditors if the bank's assets decline in value. The theory is that someone starts a bank and contributes equity capital, say $100. If there is an 8 percent capital requirement, that $100 of equity allows his bank to purchase assets and make loans up to a total amount of $1,250 (8 percent of $1,250 is $100). Since the bank starts with only $100, it will borrow or accept deposits of $1,150. As long as the value of the bank's assets don't fall by more than 8 percent, all deposits can be honored and all lenders repaid.

In practice, things aren't that simple. We're not dealing with a freshly started bank with only equity capital and assets. All big financial institutions are comprised of thousands of legal entities, incorporated in many different jurisdictions. Some of these are consolidated onto the holding company's balance sheet, and some are not. Each of these entities can have complex financing and ownership arrangements. Many of the bank's assets are pledged to or controlled by other entities, and there are assets not on the bank's balance sheet that are pledged to and controlled by it. Some assets have easily determined value, but many assets are valued by management estimate. Other assets are on the balance sheet at values from the distant past, some due to accounting rule, some due to valuation practices more suited to a nineteenth-century dry goods store than a twenty-first-century derivatives dealer.

In theory, and leaving out a few details, if you add up the value of all the assets and subtract all the bank's obligations, you are left with the amount of capital the bank has. In practice, however, that number bears little relation to the cushion a bank has to absorb losses on its assets. The value of the assets is subject to far too much management discretion, error, and arbitrary accounting rules to be a reliable indicator. Even if you have enough assets to cover obligations overall, individual entities and jurisdictions can have more obligations than assets, and the holding company may not be willing and able to transfer assets to cover the difference. On top of that, you can get blindsided by obligations that were not on the balance sheet and assets that were on the balance sheet but were pledged to others or not under the bank's control.

Accountants and regulators—well, all accountants and some regulators—are well aware of these issues and they do their best to adjust capital to allow for them. But the task is hopeless. The capital number might as well be fiction. Never trust a complicated computation that cannot be independently validated against some objective standard. Computing VaR is even harder than computing capital, but we trust it because it passes rigorous statistical back-testing. There are only two ways I know to get a reliable capital number. One is to define some statistical properties it is supposed to have, and test if it has them. This is sort of what an audit is supposed to do, but audits check only that the bank followed the rules, not that the resulting number reflects economic reality. Audits are basically a check on inputs, not outputs. Anyway, as long as shareholders routinely approve management's recommendation of the auditor, we cannot expect auditors to bite the hand that feeds them with vigorous falsification efforts.

The second way is to create a market instrument that tracks what you want to know. The common stock of a bank sort of represents its capital, but most of the value of the common stock is intangible, based on long-term projections of future hypothetical cash flows. That's too ethereal to count as capital. Nevertheless, I look at the stock price as a much better indicator of bank financial health than the reported capital number. It's possible to design securities that are more directly related to the tangible, short-term asset value of an institution. But neither of these approaches was adopted. The capital requirement was supposed to be validated, but wasn't, and the claimed capital amount was not even supposed to be validated.

There were a few more fateful decisions made in the mid-1990s. First was that each bank would compute the capital for itself. This decision has come in for a lot of criticism, but it was the right one. VaR is extremely hard to compute, and no outsider is going to be able to do a good job. One-size-fits-all systems are worthless. But VaR is very easy to validate. You just examine the breaks for the correct number (not too many or too few), independence in time, and independence from the level of VaR. If someone's VaR doesn't back-test, either they don't understand their central risks or they are misreporting them. Either way, regulators can insist on improvement or shut the bank down. Another advantage of this system is banks would use the same metrics for internal risk control as for regulatory reporting. This became known as the Basel *use test.* That saves money, of course, but it also meant regulators and executives could see eye to eye. Recall that one of the advantages of VaR is that it played on the trading floor and in the executive suite—it turned out to play for regulators as well.

The next decision was to emphasize variance-covariance VaR, which is computed assuming a normal distribution and known parameters. *Known* doesn't mean you know the parameters in advance, but that you estimate them from data, then compute the VaR on the assumption your estimates are perfect. There are many problems with this approach, the biggest theoretical one is the average prediction made assuming an average value is exactly right, is exactly wrong. The biggest practical one is it never back-tests well. Moreover, variance-covariance VaR tells you even less about the tails than other VaRs. However, it was the form in which JPMorgan introduced VaR to the world. Some people still think of it as the definition of VaR. JPMorgan needed it to produce a report within 15 minutes of market close, using 1990-era technology and data systems. Variance-covariance was the only practical option. For Basel II, however, many flavors of VaR were easily available and we should have insisted on one that can pass back-test.

But the most momentous decision, which seemed innocuous at the time, was to promise banks capital relief for spending all the money to create Basel II systems. It was clear from the start that only the most sophisticated banks would be able to compute Basel II capital, so simpler options were offered for other banks. The "advanced approach" banks had to be rewarded to give them an incentive to make the investment, and the obvious reward was lower capital requirements. After all, if they managed risk better, they should be allowed to hold less capital. This deal was never written down, as far as I know, but it was accepted as a working agreement by everyone involved in the project.

The effort to compute Basel II capital turned out to be far more expensive that anyone imagined. Sandy Weill of Citigroup, when presented with yet another $100 million plus budget request from the risk department, bemoaned, "Can't you build me $10 million risk management?" (Someone at the meeting, who asked not to be named, replied, "We could try wrapping it in brown paper and delivering it to regulators." In retrospect that might have been a good idea, at least someone would have profited from the debacle.) Moreover, the project turned up far more risk than anyone ever imagined. By 2000, it was clear that capital requirements of 8 percent were far too low, yet the advanced banks had been promised lower levels still. The proper solution would have been to raise the capital requirements of all banks, so the advanced banks could be awarded relief and still hold prudent amounts of capital. But there was no constituency for that. During the dot-com bubble, worrying about risk seemed silly. After the technology crash of March 2000, raising capital requirements would risk deepening the expected recession. In fact, central bankers were moving in the exact opposite direction, cutting interest rates and trying to stimulate risk taking.

Next came an accident of history. Around 2004, as the final implementation details of Basel II were being worked out, market volatility dropped to extremely low levels. Lower market volatility meant lower risk-adjusted capital requirements. In that environment, the Basel II capital requirements didn't seem unduly low. Every time implementation costs went up and new risks emerged, market volatility seemed to drop enough to compensate.

Everyone working in the process understood this clearly, and also understood that market volatility would go back up someday. But there was too much momentum to the project to stop it. The easy road was to continue along as if nothing was wrong and get Basel II implemented while volatility was still low. Then when volatility increased, advanced banks would have to hold more capital. By that time, people would understand and trust the Basel computations. They would realize that all the other banks had been holding inadequate capital all along. As a result, basic capital requirements for banks that did not use the advanced approach would be raised.

An unfortunate consequence of taking the easy road was that the rules were weakened further. All the way back in 1987, quants understood that risk measures had to be forward-looking. If nothing bad had happened in the recent past, you couldn't assume everything was safe. You had to factor in at least some probability of the market climate changing, and you had to look for telltale warning signs of approaching storms. This was doubly true for capital rules. If you based everything on the recent past, then banks would overexpose themselves in good times, and cut back doubly hard in bad times, exactly the opposite of what regulators wanted to encourage. But the only way to shoehorn Basel II capital computations in under the 8 percent bar was to jettison all the forward-looking aspects.

Well, so how did the plan work out? Not so good. Volatility started increasing in 2006, before Basel II had been installed. I often read that Basel II was responsible for banks not holding enough capital before the financial crisis, but that is not true. Banks weren't on Basel II in the first place, and in the second place the increased market volatility would have pushed up capital levels if they had been. Moreover, all major banks were holding significantly more capital than regulatory minimums, so the mandated levels weren't relevant. And no major institution failed for lack of capital; the failures were all from loss of liquidity and market confidence. A higher reserve requirement would have helped (that is, a lower leverage limit), not a higher capital requirement.

That's not to say the Basel II project bears no blame. Information was turned up in the decade before the financial crisis that no one acted upon. We all decided to continue building the ark rather than try harder to convince our neighbors a flood was coming. In the end the rains came before the ark was seaworthy. If everyone had not been harnessed into one massive international project, more independent voices might have been heard. Or maybe not. The Basel II project did create the knowledge and infrastructure for rational banking regulation in the future. At the moment no one seems interested in harnessing that knowledge and infrastructure, but as the world calms down we might get sound bank regulation, for the first time since the government took on the job.

Where Did They Put the Money?

One of the important economic functions of markets is capital formation. Capital is assets used to make more assets, most commonly, money used to make more money. If you own and live in a house, the house is an asset, but not a capital asset. If you rent it out to someone else, it becomes a capital asset. Left to their own devices, most people are content to use assets or let them lie fallow if they have no current need for them, to spend cash or to hoard it. Persuading people to rent out unused land or put cash in the stock market instead of spending it or hoarding it is part of what the finance industry does. Capital allows businesses to form and grow, and at the same time—hopefully—allows the provider of capital to achieve financial security.

It is also possible to create capital out of thin air. In the right circumstances, you can print up some paper money, lend it to an entrepreneur, and generate a productive cycle of exchange that creates a new company without ever putting up anything of value. We just saw how quants accomplished this trick on a massive scale from 1980 to 2007, doubling the available capital in the world without persuading people to give up existing assets. Assets do not have to be tangible, like houses or cars. The belief in future value is just as much an asset as a bar of gold is. John Kenneth Galbraith even pointed out that embezzlement creates capital, since both the embezzler (correctly) and the embezzlee (incorrectly) think they have the "bezzle," and act and spend accordingly. One of the exacerbating factors in financial crises is the disappearance of this bezzle, as falling asset prices cause frauds to be revealed. Bernie Madoff is just the biggest in a long line.

Whether capital is created honestly or dishonestly is important legally, but what matters to an economist is how the capital is allocated. If it is put to good use there is a net increase in wealth. That brings us to the second major function of financial markets, capital allocation. One of the silly things people who don't understand finance like to say is Wall Street should stick to raising new capital for businesses and get rid of all that casino trading that just transfers money from one speculator to another without accomplishing any economic good. That makes as much sense as saying lawyers should go around dispensing justice instead of arguing with each other all the time. Lawyers have no more idea about justice than anyone else, and financial professionals, with the exception of a few specialists, have no more idea what's a good business idea than anyone else. Moreover, no one but a child or a child-at-brain wants a lot of lawyers or finance people running around fixing everything. The only good thing about that is it would be fun to find out which profession did a worse job.

What lawyers and financial professionals do is participate in systems that allows people to accomplish goals. Lawyers resolve disputes. Not by determining and enforcing justice but by offering their services to competing parties in an organized system. Financial professionals enable capital allocation by offering their services to providers and users of capital. Now it is true that some financial professionals make direct capital allocation decisions: venture capital investors, bank loan officers, and private equity fund managers. But these people are really acting as investors. They are professionals, but they are using the same financial services as any other investor. The analogy with lawyers is that some lawyers are judges. But few people would say our justice system would be unchanged if lawyers stuck to judging things and the plaintiffs and defendants had no attorneys and weren't allowed to argue. And calling Wall Street a casino is as true and false as calling a courtroom a casino. As in casinos, risks are taken in the financial markets and in courtrooms, and in all three places there are winners and losers determined by rules.

On Wall Street, quants changed the rules so there were more winners and fewer losers. That doesn't mean there were no losers. Junk-bond-financed hostile takeovers were great for the economy and the stock market, but many lives were disrupted and portfolios damaged in the process. Venture capital financing led to an extraordinary spurt of technological progress—and the Internet bubble. But these were souped-up versions of traditional capital allocation. The entirely new idea in the period was securitization.

I read a lot of books and articles on finance, and I seldom see a discussion of securitization that doesn't use the phrase "slicing and dicing." This is a reference to a famous infomercial of the late 1960s for a product called the Veg-O-Matic. It's not a very good description of securitization. It's true that underlying assets have their cash flows cut up—sliced if you will—but they are not then sliced twice more in orthogonal directions—diced (technically, the Veg-O-Matic didn't dice either; it worked only in two dimensions). The slices are instead pasted together with other slices, more like making plywood than cutting vegetables. Logs in a sawmill are bathed before thin veneers for plywood are cut with a lathe. So "bathed and lathed" makes more sense than "sliced and diced." I can also live with "hewed and glued" or "plied and dried."

Securitization takes the institution out of finance—*disintermediation* is the technical term. Providers and users of capital are linked directly. The reason that requires financial engineering is most providers of capital want to provide a different type of capital than most users need. Providers want diversified, liquid instruments that pay off cash at predictable times. Users have specific projects that are illiquid with unpredictable cash flows.

The traditional way to solve this is to set up a financial institution. A simple example is a savings bank. The bank offers a liquid, predictable investment: savings accounts that pay regular interest. It uses these to fund long-term mortgages that have some credit risk and can be repaid at any time. This is not an efficient solution. There is no true liquidity in the investments; the bank just hopes that not too many people want their money back at once. There is some diversification: the loans are not all to one person on one house; but they are in a small geographic area with correlated housing values and incomes. On top of that, the banks were expensive, consuming half or more of the interest paid on the mortgage before paying it out to depositors, and socking the taxpayers for about

$100 billion more—which used to be considered a big bailout—when interest rates went up.

It's far better to put together a national pool of mortgages in a structure that directs cash flows to different investors at predictable times. These securities can be standardized for liquid trading, so if investors want their money back early, or want to rebalance their portfolios, it's cheap and easy to do. Borrowers pay less on home mortgages, and investors earn more on their mortgage securities than they ever got in savings accounts. This can create what economists call an agency problem, that the institution deciding who gets mortgages doesn't bear the risk, and therefore can be incented to cut corners on underwriting. However, any intermediation creates agency problems and it is no harder to address them in securitization than with institutional intermediation.

Another major area of securitization was credit derivatives. An investor who buys a bond or a bank that makes a loan is exposed to credit risk—the risk that the bond issuer or loan borrower will not repay the debt. It's clearly efficient to diversify that risk, but that's difficult with loans and bonds. You have to buy a lot of bonds or issue a lot of loans, and if you do, your portfolio will be made up of so many little investments that it will be difficult to trade. Structured credit pulled the credit risk from bonds and loans and packaged it into diversified portfolios with predictable characteristics.

These and other securitization techniques allow capital to flow directly from providers to users. Investors get better investments, and capital users get cheaper and more convenient capital.

Obviously, mortgage and credit securities were a big part of the 2007 to 2009 financial crisis. Contrary to popular belief, the root failing was not models. The primary cause of every securitization disaster, and there were many prior to 2007, is always failure to sell the entire deal in true arm's-length transactions.

When a securitization market is new, the profits for structurers are huge. You don't have to be very efficient in how you carve things up, and if there are some unpopular pieces there's plenty of money available to make their yield so high someone will buy them. But margins fall as more people get into the business. The price of the collateral gets bid up, and the price of the securities gets bid down.

At first you react by making your structures more efficient. Also, as the market expands you can do much larger deals, so you can take a smaller percentage profit. But the more successful you are, the worse the problem gets. At some point you hit an absolute bottleneck. You have a deal with one piece that you can't sell at a high-enough price to make the deal profitable. So you walk away and find a new business.

Or maybe not. Maybe you can jam the unpopular piece into some account or other. There are many variants of this, all distasteful. You find a stupid person responsible for investing a lot of money and you wine and dine or otherwise cajole him. You put the security in an account your firm is supposed to be managing for the benefit of the account owner. You sell the bonds to someone, and loan her the money to buy them. She's happy to take them because if they pay off she keeps the profits, and if they don't, she walks away from the loan. Often this person is tiptoeing the line of fraud with her investors. Or the simplest solution is to just hold on to the unsalable bonds yourself. Sometimes you do that and hedge the exposure—as if a hedge can turn a bad purchase into a good one. With the help of some accommodating accountants, you can look profitable for a while. All of these maneuvers have been done many times in many variants. They have always, always led to disaster.

The final function of financial markets is price discovery. By establishing reliable prices in public, everyone's economic planning is improved. Here the change was driven by hedge fund and bank proprietary trading or *prop* desks. Improvements in risk management led to astonishing increases in leverage. Increased leverage makes it profitable to exploit smaller market anomalies. All other things being equal, more leverage means wilder markets. But other things weren't equal. The risk management improvements more than offset the danger from increased leverage. The reason that's not widely known is most people see the quant risk management only when it fails. It's dramatic, because the type of failure is new and different. But there were more and bigger failures as a fraction of value created before the quants reengineered everything.

While only a small fraction of levered traders were quants, it was our old friends the card-counting frequentist hedge fund guys who figured out the risk management. This led to massively increased trading volumes, including high-frequency trading, which improved market efficiency and liquidity. More efficient and liquid markets mean better price discovery. That's good for the economy, and good for the investors. It is also disruptive.

How do billion-dollar prop bets and millisecond trades help long-term investors? It's sort of like the "For Want of a Nail" proverbial rhyme. If a long-term investor trades every five years, it's a help to him to see, say, monthly prices. These allow him to monitor his portfolio. When he does want to sell, he doesn't have to wait five years for another long-term investor to step up; he can get his sale executed in a month. The monthly trader would like to see daily prices for the same reason. The daily trader wants prices every 15 minutes. The 15-minute trader . . . well, you get it.

What happens to the highest-frequency trader in the market? She has a rough life. She does not see other trades between her trades. If she buys or sells at the wrong price, there's no way of knowing it until she's done many trades. She cannot monitor her positions in any meaningful way. If she wants to get out of a position, she has to wait for a slower trader to react—like the monthly investor having to wait for the five-year investor. But because she's willing to live on the frontier, everyone else has an easier life.

The same thing is true of size. The 100-share investor needs someone willing to take 1,000-share positions in order to be executed quickly and efficiently. The 1,000-share trader needs 10,000-share traders. The biggest trader in the market has a problem. If she wants to make a trade she has to do it in small batches, which can take a long time. Therefore the fastest and biggest traders demand extra profit to make up for their unfavorable positions. Competition among them keeps the extra profit down and liquidity up. In some sense that extra profit is a fee paid by long-term investors for liquidity, even if the long-term investor never deals with a big or fast counterparty. But the fee is far smaller than what used to be charged by market makers in the old system, and the liquidity is much greater.

Where Did the Money Go?

So how did these three great ideas—massive free capital, improved capital allocation, and better price discovery—lead to disaster? Not just the one big disaster in 2007, but the many others: the Drexel Burnham bankruptcy, the Bankers Trust scandal, the Kidder Peabody crash, and Long-Term Capital Management's failure, to name only four. These were among the most advanced firms in these techniques. I haven't included the collateral damage from Wall Street abuses such as the Orange County bankruptcy, nor the non–Wall Street financial firms like Enron, nor the damage over-seas as with the Asian financial crisis, nor the ones that entered more people's homes like the Internet stock collapse and the mutual fund timing scandal.

First, let me reiterate that the good from financial innovations far exceeds the damage. There were scandals and bankruptcies and disasters before quants came to Wall Street. Taking the good and bad together, the past 30 years have been the most extraordinarily good economic time for the globe in history. The horrendous times are decades of stagnation or totalitarian repression, not the exuberant and painful times of boom and bust. I know that not everyone shared in the fruits of this time, and even among those who shared the gains were unequal. I consider that a separate issue, however. The new techniques were empowering and liberating. They lifted more people out of poverty than any previous innovations in human history, and they also created more billionaires. That they didn't help everybody is just saying they weren't perfect. Saying that they didn't help everybody equally is just silly.

Second, I admit that many mistakes were made, including mistakes I made personally. I'm wrong a lot. But I don't consider this a contributing factor to the disasters. It takes lots of compounding to turn a mistake into a disaster. There will never be any shortage of mistakes, especially in innovative times. So it's the compounding you have to prevent, not the mistakes. As long as people fail fast, losses are acceptable and progress is rapid. But when people instead choose to fail slowly—and big—it's a different story.

Third, I'm going to exonerate some commonly blamed villains. Greed was not the problem. Calling someone greedy means they served their own interest when you would rather they had served yours. In some sense everyone in finance is greedy; the field isn't appealing to people who want to live the simple life with what God provides free. It's also true that there are many people in finance who are personally greedy beyond what I can respect, probably beyond the level that can coexist with their own contentment or happiness. But there are also many philanthropic and open-hearted people, and many people with simple tastes and modest lifestyles. There are all kinds, and I have not noted more greed on Wall Street than on Main Street.

An even sillier accusation is that Wall Streeters took excessive risks because they got rich if they won and didn't care if the firm failed if they lost. The largest shareholders in all Wall Street firms were the employees. Why would they buy the stock if they were playing "heads I win, tails the firm loses"? There were three Wall Street CEOs with more than a billion dollars at stake in their companies: Hank Greenberg of American International Group (AIG), Dick Fuld at Lehman Brothers, and Jimmy Cayne at Bear Stearns. So the people with the most to lose failed. In my entire Wall Street career I have been in on many risk decisions. I didn't always agree with the decisions, but there was never a meeting in which every senior person didn't think seriously and hard about the risk. And they weren't thinking of the money they would lose if things went bad; they were thinking of their pride, and their friends and employees, and customers and creditors. No one wanted to fail. True, many reckless decisions were made, but they were not made recklessly.

The biggest single reason things fell apart was that the risk takers were chased out of Wall Street. We built a system designed to be run by people with extensive experience in risk taking. We believed in finding niche opportunities, failing often and fast, milking our successes until they reached their limits, and then looking for new opportunities. We built a capital structure and market structure to support this strategy, with quantitative financial risk management at the core.

But things got big, far bigger than we ever imagined. Lots of people with no risk-taking backgrounds came to Wall Street to get rich safely. Of course risk takers came too, but their proportion shrank every year. The risk avoiders had better credentials. That's always true; one way to avoid risk is to amass credentials. They had fewer failures in their background. No risk, no failure. They dressed better and had better interpersonal skills, again classic risk-avoider behavior. Most of all, and the easiest way to tell a risk avoider, they all agreed with each other.

Not for them the flaky, untested niche idea from someone whose last four ideas flopped. They wanted to see something solid with a stable long-term track record that was endorsed by experts. Unfortunately, when they found a business like this, it was usually near or at its limit. Risk avoiders love steadily growing revenue and earnings. You can't get those taking risks. You can appear to get those by forcing exponential growth on an idea that has already hit its limit. You can keep up the pretense if everyone agrees:

accountants, economists, and regulators. But reality has an ugly way of bursting through the strongest consensus of the most respected people.

Risk takers have to be honest to survive. It's bred in the bone, and reinforced constantly. Risk avoiders think that as long as everyone is calm, the ship can't sink. The world needs risk avoiders. Risk takers are inefficient and unreliable. But you can't put risk avoiders in charge of a system built for risk takers. Or rather, you can, but the result is not pretty.

Another problem is risk avoiders like to think they can understand things. They want clearly expressed, rational reasons for everything. We already saw how they eviscerated VaR by putting it into controlled systems, preferring predictability to information content. Risk avoiders are good at explaining things after the fact, and it never seems to occur to them that their sincere explanations always leave them looking good. Risk takers don't explain well before or after the fact, and don't care about looking good. When something bad happened and someone had to go, it was always the risk taker.

The first to leave the Street were the card-counting frequentists. They started hedge funds and generally kept them small and obscure. I can't blame the risk avoiders for that; the antisocial quants would have left anyway. Next, most of the poker players went. Things got too regimented for most of them. They couldn't get support for their good ideas, and they saw too many bad ideas being inflated beyond reason. More important, it wasn't fun anymore. They had come to beat the Street, they had done it, and now lots of other people were rushing in to collect the loot. Some of the poker types went to hedge funds, but most left finance altogether.

The Bayesian sports bettors initially benefited from the wave of risk avoiders. They had the social skills to mingle with the new crowd, and their experience running businesses was respected. But even they found the heavy pressure of regulation wearing. Also, they were passed over for promotion in favor of better-credentialed people. All of the quants were computer nerds as well as math geeks, so the Bayesians found a natural home in technology start-ups in the late 1990s. By the early 2000s, it was hard to find an original vintage quant still on Wall Street. There were still a lot of risk takers on the Street, but most weren't quants, and most of the ones who were quants hadn't built the system and didn't understand it fully. But the biggest change sprang from the fact that risk takers don't form consensus, while risk avoiders do. Even if the risk takers had been in the majority, it would have been hard for them to get their disparate and unexplainable views into what had become a formal decision-making process.

The exodus continued even after almost all of the original quants were gone. The big firms kept buying hedge funds and other companies where the risk takers had fled. Regulators kept casting the net of regulation wider.

How about the future? I believe the market has told us in unmistakable terms that the global financial institution of the late 1990s to early 2000s doesn't work. That's not really surprising; they existed only for about 10 scandal- and disaster-filled years. I would like to see a system of smaller, diverse, innovative businesses—including some that would not be considered financial businesses today—offering competing ways to accomplish financial tasks. These firms might fail a lot, but none would endanger anyone but their investors and their employees. In this vision I would have a robust payment-processing and short-term credit system and a way for individuals to make basic financial transactions, including deposit accounts. All of this would be done with minimal risk, and would be completely separated from any risk-taking activities. It would be a business run by risk avoiders for risk avoiders. We could call these People's Banks, or Volcksbanks in honor of Paul Volcker, who championed this kind of thing.

My guess is that will not happen. I think the big institutions will reinvent themselves, and will keep control of the essential financial infrastructure. I hope they will do a better job next time.

CHAPTER

20

The Secret History of Wall Street: The 2007 Crisis and Beyond

WE HAVE ONLY RUMORS ABOUT FRAGMENTS OF RED'S CAREER AFTER LEAVING HOME...

GOODBYE, BLUE. DON'T LET THE BASTARDS GET YOU DOWN.

PLEASE, RED, PLEASE BE CAREFUL.

WORKING IN A THREE-PERSON ELECTRONICS START-UP IN A GARAGE.

RUNNING A DOCUMENT-LITE SHIPPING BUSINESS IN THE GOLDEN TRIANGLE.

PLAYING THE HIGH-STAKES SOUTH AMERICAN POKER CIRCUIT

ARRESTED IN MOMBASAM IN A BARROOM DRINKING GIN

PROTESTING POLITICAL REPRESSION IN MACEDONIA

PLACING BETS FOR A QUANT RING AT THE HONG KONG JOCKEY CLUB

BUT BY 1993, WE KNOW SHE WAS WORKING AT THE FX AND INTEREST RATE OPTIONS TRADING DESK OF A LARGE WALL STREET FIRM, ALONGSIDE HOT AND UN.

BLUE'S CAREER IS BETTER DOCUMENTED...

WELL-REVIEWED BOOKS AND PUBLICATIONS

DISTINGUISHED DEGREES

CHAIRMANSHIP OF AN IMPORTANT INVESTIGATING COMMISSION

WHEN SCANDAL HIT RED'S FIRM...

...BLUE WAS ASKED TO TAKE OVER.

BLUE'S FIRST HIRE WAS A TOP RISK MANAGER.

NOTHING YOU HEAR ABOUT BLOOD SUCKER IS TRUE.

SHE WAS BORN IN SUBURBAN CLEVELAND, NOT SOME MYSTERIOUS PLACE WITH A PAST OF UNSPEAKABLE HORRORS.

HER FIRST JOB WAS AN ASSISTANT BANK LOAN OFFICER, NOT ENFORCING POLITICAL ORTHODOXY IN HUNGARY.

DOGS DID NOT RUN WHIMPERING WHEN SHE APPEARED. IN FACT, SHE OWNED CHAMPION SHOW DOGS.

SHE HAD A GREAT SENSE OF HUMOR AND AN INFECTIOUS LAUGH.

SHE ONLY COLLECTED COFFINS. SHE DIDN'T SLEEP IN THEM.

373

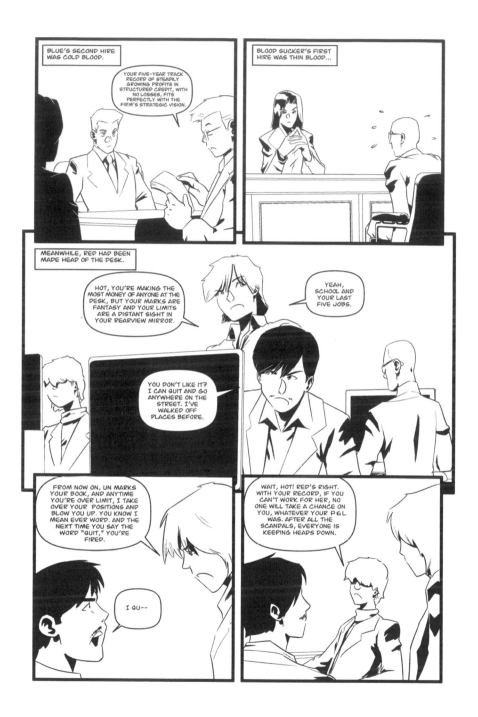

BLUE'S SECOND HIRE WAS COLD BLOOD.

YOUR FIVE-YEAR TRACK RECORD OF STEADILY GROWING PROFITS IN STRUCTURED CREDIT, WITH NO LOSSES, FITS PERFECTLY WITH THE FIRM'S STRATEGIC VISION.

BLOOD SUCKER'S FIRST HIRE WAS THIN BLOOD...

MEANWHILE, RED HAD BEEN MADE HEAD OF THE DESK.

HOT, YOU'RE MAKING THE MOST MONEY OF ANYONE AT THE DESK, BUT YOUR MARKS ARE FANTASY AND YOUR LIMITS ARE A DISTANT SIGHT IN YOUR REARVIEW MIRROR.

YEAH, SCHOOL AND YOUR LAST FIVE JOBS.

YOU DON'T LIKE IT? I CAN QUIT AND GO ANYWHERE ON THE STREET. I'VE WALKED OFF PLACES BEFORE.

FROM NOW ON, UN MARKS YOUR BOOK, AND ANYTIME YOU'RE OVER LIMIT, I TAKE OVER YOUR POSITIONS AND BLOW YOU UP. YOU KNOW I MEAN EVER WORD. AND THE NEXT TIME YOU SAY THE WORD "QUIT," YOU'RE FIRED.

I QU--

WAIT, HOT! RED'S RIGHT. WITH YOUR RECORD, IF YOU CAN'T WORK FOR HER, NO ONE WILL TAKE A CHANCE ON YOU, WHATEVER YOUR P&L WAS. AFTER ALL THE SCANDALS, EVERYONE IS KEEPING HEADS DOWN.

WE NEED TO FIND AN EXTRA FIVE HUNDRED MILLION IN EARNINGS TO MAKE OUR QUARTERLY TARGET.

YOU MIGHT AS WELL FACE IT. WE DIDN'T MAKE IT. THIS QUARTER LAST YEAR, EVERYTHING WENT OUR WAY. WE CAN'T GROW 10% FROM THAT.

I CAN GET YOU THE EARNINGS.

HOW? THE QUARTER'S OVER.

BUT THE BOOKS AREN'T CLOSED. I'LL CHANGE SOME PARAMETERS IN THE MODEL.

BLUE, YOU CAN'T KEEP LYING FOREVER. IF YOU DO THIS, YOU'LL HAVE TO LIE EVEN MORE NEXT TIME. SOONER OR LATER, YOU HAVE TO TELL THE SHAREHOLDERS THAT THIS IS A RISK BUSINESS. IT CAN'T GROW STEADILY EVERY QUARTER.

NO YOU DON'T.

BUT WON'T ANALYSTS QUESTION COLD'S MARKS?

NOT WITH MY COMBINATION OF TECHNICAL JARGON AND PSYCHOTIC OVERCONFIDENCE.

THIS HAS ALREADY GONE TOO FAR. COLD HAS NEARLY A TRILLION DOLLARS ON THE BALANCE SHEET THAT RENFIELD LISTS AT ZERO RISK. I HAVE NO IDEA WHAT THE REAL VALUE OF THOSE POSITIONS ARE. WE MIGHT BE INSOLVENT.

THAT'S NOT MY NAME.

377

CEO BLUE BLOOD DID EVERYTHING ACCORDING TO THE BEST EXPERT ADVICE. ANY CRITICISM IS MONDAY MORNING QUARTERBACKING.

BLUE IS NOW A DEAN OF A MAJOR BUSINESS SCHOOL, CONSIDERED CERTAIN TO GET A HIGH FINANCIAL POST IN THE NEXT ADMINISTRATION.

RISK MANAGER BLOOD SUCKER IMPOSED THE HIGHEST PROFESSIONAL STANDARD.

SHE IS NOW HEAD OF RISK AT ANOTHER MAJOR FIRM.

THIN BLOOD HAS IMPECCABLE CREDENTIALS.

I SAW IT ALL COMING. NOBODY LISTENED TO ME.

HE IS CURRENTLY LOOKING FOR AN APPROPRIATE POSITION.

COLD BLOOD POSSESSED AN EXTRAORDINARY AND BRILLIANT VISION THAT WOULD HAVE WORKED BUT FOR IRRATIONAL MARKET EVENTS.

NEXT TIME, FOR SURE.

HE IS CURRENTLY A SYSTEMIC RISK REGULATOR.

HOT BLOOD WAS THE MOST SUCCESSFUL TRADER ON WALL STREET, BROUGHT DOWN BY IRRATIONAL MARKET EVENTS.

HE IS CURRENTLY RAISING MONEY TO LAUNCH A HEDGE FUND.

DESK HEAD UN BLOODED FOLLOWED ALL THE RULES.

HE WILL BE THE RISK MANAGER AT HOT BLOOD'S NEW FUND.

THE BLAME RESTS ON RED BLOOD.

SHE HAS A LONG HISTORY OF SERIAL FAILURES AND IGNORING ESTABLISHED WISDOM. WHILE SHE HAD A FEW SUCCESSES AS WELL, SHE FAILED TO START SLOWLY AND GROW EXPONENTIALLY. SHE PLANNED FOR SUCCESS WHEN SHE LAUNCHED AND FAILED FAST WHEN SHE FAILED, DESPITE COMMON KNOWLEDGE THAT YOU PLAN CAREFULLY FOR FAILURE AND ONCE YOU DO LAUNCH YOU NEVER GIVE UP. SHE CUT BACK ON LONG-ESTABLISHED, SUCCESSFUL STRATEGIES THAT EVERYONE AGREED WERE SOUND, JUST AT THE POINT THEY COULD MAKE SOME REAL MONEY.

CURRENT WHEREABOUTS UNKNOWN.

Postmortem

We've come a long way together, unless you are one of the people who go right to the last chapter. You know how I feel about probability theory and money, about human evolution and financial markets, about risk and people. We have even covered history, religion, politics, current events, and a lot of other stuff. I hope you had some fun and learned some things.

As you can see from the chapter heading, I am going to close out with a postmortem. In my years as a risk manager, I have had many of these. I learned a few things about how to do them right. You have a bunch of unhappy people gathered in a room to discuss a large loss of money or other disaster. For the purposes of this chapter, we are going to discuss the financial crisis that began in 2007 and is still playing out as I write this.

I always begin by asking people to think like a Bayesian. How shall we update our prior beliefs? In other words, what did we just learn? As long as you both survive and learn, no crisis is a complete loss. Often you discover that most of your loss was actually a gain—you learned that something you thought was valuable was not. That's an addition to knowledge, not a subtraction from wealth, however much it feels like a loss. The same is true if you learned that something you thought was safe was dangerous or that someone you thought could be trusted could not or that something smart was dumb. You never had something to lose; you just thought you did. And now you are wiser and no poorer.

What did we learn from the financial crisis? The most obvious lesson is that large, diversified, regulated financial institutions should become extinct. Since they all either failed or would have failed absent massive government intervention, and since governments cannot afford a second round of bailouts, the wise course is to break them up or shut them down. It's pointless to discuss which features of which institutions were good or bad; they all failed. There is something basically wrong with the design. I think it is conflicts of interests, but whatever it is, it is 100 percent fatal.

I claim authority on this point. Unless you have worked in the middle office of some of these institutions for over a decade and have enough outside experiences to make useful comparisons, I don't think you can understand the deep design deficiencies inherent in their structure. I feel like a doctor who has been treating patients for many years, whose advice is ignored in a debate between policy wonks arguing from aggregate national health statistics and faith healers of various stripes; or a combat commander whose experience is deemed irrelevant as Pentagon game theorists argue with politicians. If big diversified regulated financial institutions are to survive and do well, they will have to strengthen their middle offices, hire back risk takers, embrace all forms of good risk, and focus obsessively on the good of their customers. And some of them have to fail. If anything, the reforms I see to date work in the opposite directions.

The other major lesson is a new aspect of the danger of leverage. We always knew leverage was dangerous, of course, but we did not appreciate the full reason. If you have $100 and buy $100 of stock, you have risk. If you have $100, borrow $100, and buy $200 of stock, you have twice the risk. This is not the danger of leverage. It just means you multiply your gains and losses by a factor. If you want to do this, it's not a danger. Levering up a safe stock 2 to 1 can be safer than holding a more volatile stock without leverage.

Some naive people imagine this kind of leverage when they hear banks were levered up 40 or 50 to 1. No bank borrowed $49 to add to its $1 and bought $50 of stock. Any such institution would go bankrupt very quickly. What banks did for the most part was to use leverage to offset risk. If the bank found itself holding a billion dollars' worth of U.S. Treasuries, for example, it might enter into a futures contract to offset the risk. That means it now has 2 to 1 gross notional leverage, since it has a billion dollars' worth of Treasuries plus a billion-dollar notional short futures position. But it clearly has far less risk than when it was unlevered, before it entered into the futures contract. Its only risks now are that there might be some problem with the futures clearinghouse or some mismatch between the Treasuries it holds and the Treasuries deliverable under the futures contracts. Otherwise, it does not care if Treasury prices go up or down, or even if the U.S. government defaults.

We always knew there were some risks to this kind of leverage, but they seemed much smaller than the risks you eliminated by hedging. We learned that was not necessarily true. In a severe credit crunch and liquidity crisis, even good leverage, the kind that offsets your risks, could kill.

The next step is to think like a frequentist. What things did other people learn that were really just fluctuations in a random walk? U.S. Treasury bonds did great during the crisis, but that might not happen next time. A lot of people decided that illiquid investments were bad, without distinguishing carefully between the disaster of investments that were supposed to be liquid but weren't versus investments everyone knew were illiquid all along. In general, you get overpaid for taking on illiquidity. Most investors pay too much for more liquidity than they need.

Another example of overreaction is the idea that all subprime mortgages are bad. In fact, subprime mortgages have a long history of doing good for both borrower and lender. People who make fun of the weakened underwriting standards used for subprime loans generally don't know how little good strong underwriting standards do. They call no-doc loans "liar loans," when those are the only loans that don't encourage lying. Lots of people with prime mortgages lied on their applications. They may have borrowed a down payment from a relative, or moved money between a bank and brokerage account to double-count assets, or claimed an anticipated bonus that was fantasy.

Careful quantitative analysis of the data shows that conventional subprime loans actually did better than expected given the decline in housing prices and the recession. Different loans served different populations. No-income-verification loans worked for undocumented immigrants and tax evaders who had cash income that could not be backed up by legal documents. These people had assets and income, but could not provide verification. Young people with lots of education debt had no assets to make a down payment, but plenty of income to service the loan. One hundred percent loan to value loans made sense for them. People with poor credit histories due to divorce, illness, or business failure often had enough assets and income to be decent credit risks anyway.

The problem was mainly in loans that had multiple underwriting flaws. The worst were known as NINJA loans (no income, no job, no assets; and yes, it should be NINJNA). This is a basic theoretical point. Overlooking one flaw in an application that has excess strength in another area makes sense. Refusing to do that, whether you're talking about a home mortgage or a job applicant or a new idea or a spouse, shows a rigid thinking that will miss many opportunities. But when an application consists entirely of flaws, there is no reason to overlook anything. These are not opportunities, they are wishful thinking.

In some cases, fraudulent prime loans were more of an issue than subprime loans. Losing 100 percent on a pool expected to have 0.1 percent losses is a bigger shock than losing 30 percent on a pool expected to have 10 percent losses. And even a small amount of fraud spooks the market because it means every pool is at risk.

It actually is a good idea to get lots of people in homes, and it's worth experiencing some failures in the effort. I understand some people have objections to helping tax evaders and illegal immigrants, who were among the beneficiaries of subprime underwriting. Personally I wish the best for everyone, legal or ill, and have a Westerner's (or maybe it's a gambler's) instinctive sympathy for anyone on the run from the government. And some loans were predatory, going to people who could not possibly benefit from them or who were charged unfairly high rates of interest. But most people who earned homes with the help of subprime mortgages were unobjectionable heroes, pulling themselves into the middle class with hard work and shrewd risk-taking. I hope that support for that kind of thing, both in mortgage underwriting and other forms of giving people chances, will not be a casualty of the crisis.

At this point in the postmortem we have learned what we could and identified new opportunities. Now comes thinking like a poker player. Quantitative risk managers do not ask whether the risk was good or bad, but instead, was the risk the right size? And, more important, how do we size the risk in the future?

Suppose, for example, you ran a program for five years and made 10 percent return on capital the first year, then 20 percent, 30 percent, and 40 percent, before losing 50 percent in the fifth year. Everyone tends to focus on the disaster of losing 50 percent. But you do have an overall 20 percent profit over the five-year period. A simple question is: Would you have done better to run the entire program at a higher or lower level of risk? If you hadn't done the program at all, you would have no profit. If you had done it at half the size, you would have made 5 percent, 10 percent, 15 percent, and 20 percent, and then lost 25 percent, for 19.5 percent profit over the period, slightly worse than you actually did. If you had done the program at twice the size, your returns would have been 20 percent, 40 percent, 60 percent, and 80 percent, followed by –100 percent, which would have wiped you out. It turns out that at 77 percent of the level of risk you actually took you would have maximized your return at 23 percent for the period. So you would have been better off sizing the program somewhat smaller.

This, of course, is a toy example. In a real postmortem the decisions that led up to the loss will be far more complicated. It is still worth asking if you could have improved things by systematically taking more or less risk. For example, total U.S. civilian employment rose 9.0 percent from the end of 1999 to its peak in November 2007. It then fell 5.9 percent by December 2009. Since then it has risen 1.4 percent for a total growth over the period of 4.0 percent.

Of course, losing 5.9 percent of civilian jobs during the recession of 2008 and 2009 was a terrible hardship. If there had been less risk in the financial system, the job losses would presumably have been less. We would not expect zero job losses; after all, there have always been periodic credit crunches and recessions. But it seems likely that a lower-risk financial system would have meant smaller job losses.

It seems equally likely, however, that a lower-risk financial system would have produced less growth during the good times. Let's suppose we believe that reduced financial risk taking could have cut the job losses during the recession from 5.9 percent to 3.0 percent. If those same changes had reduced monthly job growth in all the other months by 30 percent, we would have ended up with fewer jobs today. That means if you think cutting risk over the past decade would have been a good idea, you have to think you know how to cut out more than 50 percent of the losses while losing less than 30 percent of the gains. You have to be pretty smart to do that. It's not impossible, but I would have to see a lot of evidence of your skill before trusting your judgment. An awful lot of people think they know how to eliminate 100 percent of the losses with no effect on gains, but I have never seen this done, and the people who claim the ability to do this are not the first ones I would trust with the job.

Now, someone might argue that even with less total job growth, we would be better off with fewer ups and downs and fewer disruptions to people's lives. I think there is an optimum level of ups and downs that leads to the most long-term happiness for individuals and the most long-term productivity for businesses. And I think that level is a lot higher than most people think, possibly higher than what we have experienced recently. Immediately after losing a job, people almost always feel bad. But looking back on a life, a lot of job losses turn out to be blessings in disguise. A bad job is lost and a good career is found as a result. Sometimes you have to shake things up to get them to fall into the right places. But these are all things we can argue over in the postmortem. These are constructive discussions: How much could we have cut losses, and what would have been the effect on gains? Knowing what we know now, how would we have sized the bets? What were the costs and benefits of the variation along the way?

I certainly do not have all the answers about what caused the financial crisis and what we should do in the future. What I do have is a lot of experience in running constructive meetings after disasters. Considering events from the perspective of a Bayesian, then the view of a frequentist, then a poker player's angle usually leads to a pretty good plan for the future.

In the end, there is no magic to risk management. Risk managers cannot prevent bad things from happening. They cannot guarantee that there will be no surprises. They cannot survive every disaster. Moreover, there is no deep wisdom in the field. Risk management takes lots of hard detail work; it is no shortcut to anything. Nevertheless, it is a revolutionary advance in human organization. I have spent half my life exploring it, and in this book I have passed along all that I have learned. I hope you benefit from my experience.

A Risk Management Curriculum

Over the last few years, several universities have created degree programs in risk management and some professional schools now allow it as a specialization. I have interviewed graduates of some of these programs and remain generally unimpressed. In some cases, the programs are repackagings of portfolio management mathematics and regulatory risk reporting detail, cynically sold at exorbitant prices to students who are good at math and desperate to find jobs.

In other cases, the effort seems sincere and includes some valuable material, but suffers from a superficial and narrow focus. As I hope I've convinced you, risk management requires some radical rethinking of probability theory and economics. That can only happen if you go back to the fundamentals and insist on rigor. I have also argued that a risk manager must cast her net of learning wide, beyond probability and economics to accounting, data processing, psychology, law, logic, history, and philosophy among other fields.

The single most valuable skill in a new employee for financial risk management is deep understanding of real financial data in a real firm. Someone who knows nothing about finance or risk but can get reliable numbers is worth gold, and I will be happy to train her in everything else she needs. Someone who can do everything else, but bases conclusions on unreliable data, is worthless.

Unfortunately, getting reliable data requires skills not easily taught by academic instructors. Therefore, I believe a good risk management program should require applicants to have at least two years' experience in financial operations, financial control, or financial information technology. With that base, operations management, accounting, and computer science professors, most of whom either will have practical experience or will keep up with professional practice, can teach meaningful theory to improve the process. I'm not talking about a vocational degree for students who merely want to learn how the job is done now; I'm talking about a professional degree that includes the skills necessary to advance the state of the art.

Once you have data, it's nice if you know what to do with it. The kind of statistics usually taught to nonstatisticians is, in my opinion, worse than useless, at least for a risk manager. This curriculum needs a rigorous foundation in statistics which requires reading original sources in the philosophy, mathematics, and logic of probability along with serious professional intellectual histories of the field. I would cover as wide a ground as possible. Many smart people have written on these subjects and a diverse knowledge of the range of approaches is more valuable to a risk manager than great expertise in any single approach. Until we really understand probability (if we ever do), we need to teach it broadly. Fortunately, this is the kind of teaching good universities excel at.

The third leg of a risk manager's theoretical education concerns people. At the individual level, that encompasses behavioral studies and cognitive psychology, also welfare economics (here you have to be careful: there's a lot of nonsense in welfare economics that would not be tolerated in the first two fields, because they are data-driven). There should be special focus on how people make actual risk decisions. Law is another field that has useful insights into how people deal with risk, both before and after the fact. At the group level, that means studying history of good and bad risk taking in different aspects of human affairs. There should be plenty of good faculty members to teach the courses on individual risk taking. While historians or economists could probably handle the group courses, I think this is an obvious opportunity for visiting lecturers to discuss specifics of risk taking in wars, financial institutions, politics, professional gambling, venture capital, and scientific research; any field in which you can find a speaker able to distill experiences for the students.

That brings us to the practical courses. Clearly we need some on risk reporting. There are three kinds of risk reports: internal, regulatory, and financial. Internal comes in both front office and back office flavors (the other two are exclusively middle office). Each one probably requires a course on how to produce and interpret the numbers. There is an analogy there to the course Financial Statement Analysis, usually shared in a business school between the accounting and finance departments. It is traditional for each professor to begin the course by telling students anything they learned on the subject from the other department is nonsense. Accounting professors tend to teach how knowledge of how the statements are produced can lead to useful inferences. Finance professors are apt to emphasize statistical relations between the reported numbers and objective reality (usually that means market prices). In fact, both perspectives are essential, and the most useful information is a product of combining them. Risk reporting should be taught in that cross-disciplinary spirit.

There are some other practical courses like law and regulation of risk, the risk management industry, using standard commercial risk management products and professional standards and ethics. Somewhere in there you have to teach what a risk manager actually does. I think this is appropriate for a program-long course that meets weekly in a variety of formats, some small group case studies, some program-wide lectures, some individual projects, and some presentations from practicing risk managers.

Naturally, it's not enough to teach in classrooms. Students must actually do things to learn. There are four things I think any risk management degree should require. All of them are required for risk managers, but few of the graduates of these programs will become risk managers. One reason is that there are far more back-office risk reporting jobs than risk management jobs. Another is that the risk management jobs usually go to people with business experience in trading or portfolio management, or whatever other business is being risk managed. These people will not typically be applicants to risk management degree programs. Nevertheless, everyone in any risk job should have some experience or at least simulated experience in managing risk.

The first requirement is extensive practical calculation of VaRs, in as many different applications as possible. Any sort of objective data that is available daily can be used: total receipts by the university parking service, inches of rain reported in New York's Central Park, number of times the letter P appears in the USA Today lead story. Students should have an automated system that posts a VaR before midnight the night before the information becomes available. The system must post all the time, even if input data are missing or the student is away or sick or there is a problem with the university computer system (a box could be available for paper submissions in a power failure). The VaR should pass a standard backtest. For this purpose, an 80 percent VaR is practical compromise between the desire to focus on the tail of the distribution and the need for reliable validation over relatively short periods of time.

The second requirement is experience tracking down numbers. I have in mind here something like the proportion of tractors in the United States that run on gasoline. A good source is statistics cited blithely in news articles. Looking into things like this, students discover definitional issues in the most straightforward-seeming questions. There will be lots of data available, not all directly on point, and much of it wrong. Tracing through to sources and cross-checking in clever ways against objective information teaches both skepticism about all reported data and skills for verifying things.

Third, I believe it's very important to have experience doing real research in models of risk other than coin flips. That means providing statistical assistance to projects in evolutionary biology, quantum physics, behavioral game theory or any other field that works with risk and progressed beyond the seventeenth century. I don't think you can appreciate these ideas from lectures and toy examples. There's a lot of difference between a homework problem and a genuine research issue—one whose answer is both unknown and important. I can see this as either a requirement prior to admission—many students will already have done this—or an integrated part of the program.

Finally, students must have some experience taking risk. Anyone who is not confident that he can walk into a casino and win has no business telling others how to manage risk. And the guy who is confident but wrong is the least qualified. I'm not just talking about beating the games here. That's just a matter of figuring things out. I mean making real bankroll decisions with real meaningful stakes. That takes knowledge and faith in your knowledge, and discipline.

Okay, I know no university is going to make blackjack card counting, poker, and sports betting into graduation requirements. They're not going to send their students to Macau with $10,000 and tell them, "Don't come back until you double it." But the schools have to find some way to make the computations real, to teach students what it means to bet aggressively on the calculations.

How can we do this, without betting real money and without tainting the program with cards, dice, and sports bets? Here's a proposal. Each quarter each student is given $1,000 play money to bet at Iowa Electronic Markets. If you're not familiar with that, it offers real money small bets on various issues like election results, weather, movie grosses, and so on. But I would allow students to bet play money at the mid of the bid and ask prices. This is a huge advantage; if you bet real money you either have to pay the ask or receive the bid, or else work your order, which opens you up to the possibility of adverse selection (that is, no one will hit your bid unless you set it too high). It's not too hard to win playing this way.

Students would have to double the play money by the end of the quarter, or start over the next quarter with a new play $1,000. One successful doubling and you're done. But if you haven't succeeded by graduation, no degree. Okay, no school is going to deny a degree to a student for something as silly as being a bad bettor, even if the whole point of the degree is risk management. But there has to be some meaningful penalty, perhaps an additional paper requirement.

It would take some courage for any school to offer such a program. But that's okay, because only a risk-taking school should offer it. Who wants a risk management degree awarded by an institution afraid to deviate from staid consensus? Even more, who wants to hire someone who wants that degree?

I doubt anyone will implement my idea. I will be surprised if anyone in the risk management degree business even takes it seriously. But I suspect some innovators will move in my general direction. They'll probably do a better job than me. After all, I'm no expert in education. I do know there is vast room for improvement in the existing programs, and that more imagination and courage are needed. I hope one day to meet someone with a risk management degree whom I want to hire.

One Hundred Useful Books

I've been interested in this stuff for many years, and I read a lot. This chapter lists 100 of the more useful books. I did not limit the list to books I agreed with; I wanted to present a range of opinions. I tried to include mostly books of about the same technical level as this one, and I have noted the ones that require more or less math. I do not list more than one book per author. Many of the authors mentioned here are prolific. I have picked the book most directly relevant to mine and leave it to you to select among their other books if you are so inclined. By that logic I had to regretfully omit my other books (but they're great). In addition, I have picked mostly recent books and relatively obscure books. The classics everyone likes are easy to find.

I start with the books that take on the subject of *Red-Blooded Risk* most directly. Nassim Taleb is best known for his *Black Swan*, but his earlier book, *Fooled by Randomness: The Hidden Role of Chance in Life and in the Markets*, tackles many of the same issues as my book, with somewhat different results. We more or less agree on the problem, but go in opposite directions to find solutions. *A Demon of Our Own Design: Markets, Hedge Funds, and the Perils of Financial Innovation* by Richard Bookstaber comes at things from a third direction. Dylan Evans's forthcoming *Risk Intelligence: How to Live with Uncertainty* focuses on similar ideas in settings beyond finance. *Iceberg Risk: An Adventure in Portfolio Theory* is Kent Osband's brilliant and provocative communication of related ideas, and a pretty good novel to boot. The history of the Kelly criterion is told in *Fortune's Formula: The Untold Story of the*

Scientific Betting System That Beat the Casinos and Wall Street by William Poundstone.

If your interest is philosophy of statistics, with emphasis on practical implications, you can do no better than Jimmy Savage's great work, *The Foundations of Statistics*. His son Sam wrote *The Flaw of Averages: Why We Underestimate Risk in the Face of Uncertainty*. Both books are readable without deep quantitative training, but Sam's is the easier one to tackle. Two other classics are Bruno de Finetti's *Philosophical Lectures on Probability* and Abraham Wald's *Statistical Decision Functions*. These are a bit tougher going than the Savage works. For data analysis, *The Jackknife, the Bootstrap, and Other Resampling Plans* by Brad Efron is great. Also consider *Exploratory Data Analysis* by John Tukey.

The magnum opus of statistical history is Steve Stigler's *The History of Statistics: The Measurement of Uncertainty before 1900*. Ian Hacking covers the same material with somewhat more emphasis on ideas than history in *The Emergence of Probability: A Philosophical Study of Early Ideas about Probability, Induction and Statistical Inference*. Two excellent popular histories are *Chances Are: Adventures in Probability* by Michael Kaplan and *Chance, Luck, and Statistics* by Horace Levinson.

Is God a Mathematician? by Mario Livio is about the philosophy of quantification rather than risk, but it has a lot of relevance to *Red-Blooded Risk*.

The anthropology of money and exchange is covered in some worthwhile books. C. A. Gregory wrote *Savage Money*, about the introduction of money to traditional societies. A good summary of research is *Barter, Exchange and Value: An Anthropological Approach*, edited by Caroline Humphrey and Stephen Hugh-Jones. Three books that cover the field chronologically among them are *The Anthropology of Economy: Community, Market, and Culture* by Stephen Gudeman, *Stone Age Economics* by Marshall Sahlins, and *Bronze Age Economics: The Beginnings of Political Economies* by Timothy Earle. The classic of the field remains Karl Polanyi's *The Great Transformation*. Matt Ridley wrote a popular account in *The Rational Optimist: How Prosperity Evolves* and came to similar conclusions as Paul Seabright's *The Company of Strangers: A Natural History of Economic Life*.

The early modern history of money is described in Niall Ferguson's *The Cash Nexus: Money and Power in the Modern World, 1700–2000* and Tim Park's *Medici Money: Banking, Metaphysics, and Art in Fifteenth-Century Florence*. A bit later, early U.S. history is covered by Stephen Mihm in *A Nation of Counterfeiters: Capitalists, Con Men, and the Making of the United States*; Jane Kamensky in *The Exchange Artist: A Tale of High-Flying Speculation and America's First Banking Collapse*; Simon Johnson in *13 Bankers: The Wall Street Takeover and the Next Financial Meltdown*; and Scott Sandage in *Born Losers: A History of Failure in America*.

For the twentieth and twenty-first centuries we have *The New Lombard Street: How the Fed Became the Dealer of Last Resort* by Perry Mehrling, *Exorbitant Privilege: The Rise and Fall of the Dollar and the Future of the International Monetary System* by Barry Eichengreen, *Capital Ideas: The Improbable Origins of Modern Wall Street* by Peter Bernstein, *The Death of the Banker: The Decline and Fall of the Great Financial Dynasties and the Triumph of the Small Investor* by Ron Chernow, *The Greed Merchants: How the Investment Banks Played the Free Market Game* by Philip Augar, and *The Myth of the Rational Market: A History of Risk, Reward, and Delusion on Wall Street* by Justin Fox.

The bible of advantage gamblers is James Grosjean's *Beyond Counting: Exploiting Casino Games from Blackjack to Video Poker*. Peter Griffin was one of the best mathematician/gamblers. He wrote *The Theory of Blackjack: The Compleat Card Counter's Guide to the Casino Game of 21*. For sports betting, *Conquering Risk: Attacking Vegas and Wall Street* by Elihu Feustel is a good choice.

Reuven and Gabrielle Brenner wrote the definitive history on gambling, *Gambling and Speculation: A Theory, a History, and a Future of Some Human Decisions* (disclaimer: I co-authored a book with the Brenners). A popular general history is *Bad Bet: The Inside Story of the Glamour, Glitz, and Danger of America's Gambling Industry* by Tim O'Brien. Richard Hoffer meditated on gambling while visiting places where people gamble in *Jackpot Nation: Rambling and Gambling across Our Landscape of Luck*. For the most important gambling game, poker, James McManus wrote the best history, *Cowboys Full: The Story of Poker*, while Brandon Adams supplied the best novel, *Broke: A Poker Novel* (with honorable mentions to *The Cincinnati Kid*, by Richard Jessup, *King of a Small World* by Rick Bennet, and *The Man with the Golden Arm* by Nelson Algren).

Fischer Black wrote a great finance book that almost nobody read, *Exploring General Equilibrium* (Perry Mehrling wrote the definitive Fischer Black biography, *Fischer Black and the Revolutionary Idea of Finance*, but it didn't make the list because I included another Mehrling book). In one of Fischer's last communications to me he wrote that he did not expect to live to see the book published, and "It will probably be remaindered before the Fall because economists do not take criticism well." I lobbied hard for years to get MIT Press to reissue this book, and I also nagged John Wiley & Sons to reissue his *Business Cycles and Equilibrium*. I was finally successful with Wiley in 2009 and MIT in 2010, so both books are now easily available. In the process of doing this, I appealed for help from one of Fischer's daughters, Alethea Black (whose book of short stories, *I Knew You'd Be Lovely*, is wonderful, but has nothing to do with anything in this book, except perhaps for an autobiographical story featuring a little-known side of Fischer). I told her copies of *Exploring General Equilibrium* were going for over $1,000 on eBay. Her eyes widened as she exclaimed, "I have BOXES of them in my attic."

The standard introduction to quantitative finance is *Paul Wilmott Introduces Quantitative Finance* by, of course, Paul Wilmott. A few years ago Paul told me he had ceased being a person and had transformed into a brand. Antti Ilmanen wrote an excellent guide to the theory and practice of quant strategies, *Expected Returns: An Investor's Guide to Harvesting Market Rewards*. More technical works on the subject are *Algorithmic Trading and DMA: An Introduction to Direct Access Trading Strategies* by Barry Johnson, *Inside the Black Box: The Simple Truth about Quantitative Trading* by Rishi K. Narang, and *Multifractal Volatility: Theory, Forecasting, and Pricing* by Laurent E. Calvet.

The view of quantitative finance described in *Red-Blooded Risk* has a lot of overlap with two pathbreaking but eccentric works: *The Handbook of Portfolio Mathematics: Formulas for Optimal Allocation & Leverage* by Ralph Vince and *Finding Alpha: The Search for Alpha When Risk and Return Break Down* by Eric Falkenstein. A more famous pathbreaking and eccentric work is Benoit Mandelbrot's *The (Mis)behavior of Markets*.

Two of the best books on the future of finance are *The New Financial Order: Risk in the 21st Century* by Robert J. Shiller and *Financing the Future: Market-Based Innovations for Growth* by Franklin Allen and Glenn Yago. Both cover quite a bit of history to ground their predictions in something solid.

If you like to study your quantitative finance through people, Espen Haug's *Derivatives Models on Models* is an excellent choice. Also consider *The Quants: How a New Breed of Math Whizzes Conquered Wall Street and Nearly Destroyed It* by Scott Patterson, *My Life as a Quant: Reflections on Physics and Finance* by Emanuel Derman, *Inside the House of Money: Top Hedge Fund Traders on Profiting in the Global Markets* by Steven Drobny, and *More Money Than God: Hedge Funds and the Making of a New Elite* by Sebastian Mallaby.

The Economic Function of Futures Markets by Jeffrey Williams remains after 20 years the only really good account of this subject.

If you want to know about trading, Michael W. Covel's account of the famous so-called turtle experiment, in which more or less randomly chosen novices were trained to trade, is illuminating. The title is *The Complete TurtleTrader: How 23 Novice Investors Became Overnight Millionaires.* Curtis Faith was one for the original turtles, and he describes his methods in *Trading from Your Gut: How to Use Right Brain Instinct & Left Brain Smarts to Become a Master Trader.* But the classic account of trading is *The Education of a Speculator* by Victor Niederhoffer.

For practical finance, a great book is *John Bogle on Investing: The First 50 Years* by John Bogle. John has not become a brand, but he does have a large and raucous base of fans. They call themselves Bogleheads. David Einhorn is one of the great qualitative investors in the world. He wrote *Fooling Some of the People All of the Time: A Long Short (and Now Complete) Story.* David got a lot of attention in early 2007 by predicting that Lehman Brothers would collapse. I did a point-counterpoint debate with him at the time. Fortunately, I conceded at the outset that his opinion about Lehman's leverage and probable fate was far better than mine. My disagreement was with his view on capital and risk management in general.

A good book for the mathematics of financial risk analysis is *Portfolio Risk Analysis* by Gregory Connor, Lisa R. Goldberg, and Robert A. Korajczyk. This is a technical work. Riccardo Rebonato is one of the original risk managers. His best-known book is *Plight of the Fortunetellers,* but his *Coherent Stress Testing: A Bayesian Approach to the Analysis of Financial Stress* has more technical material about risk management. Christian Gollier wrote a technical account of the mathematics of risk from an economics rather than a finance perspective, *The Economics of Risk and Time.*

There are many great works on the unreliability of numbers and quantitative analysis, and why unvalidated straightforward theories of how the world works are always wrong. Some of the best are *Trust in Numbers* by Theodore M. Porter, *The Politics of Large Numbers: A History of Statistical Reasoning* by Alain Desrosières, *The Logic of Failure: Recognizing and Avoiding Error in Complex Situations* by

Dietrich Dorner, and *Useless Arithmetic: Why Environmental Scientists Can't Predict the Future* by Orrin H. Pilkey. Peter Rutland shows how quantitative planning worked in practice, in *The Myth of the Plan: Lessons of Soviet Planning Experience*.

The same ideas are treated in more optimistic ways by authors who emphasize the positive roles of uncertainty and failure. Good examples are *To Engineer Is Human: The Role of Failure in Successful Design* by Henry Petroski, *Inviting Disaster: Lessons from the Edge of Technology* by James R. Chiles, *Normal Accidents: Living with High-Risk Technologies* by Charles Perrow, *The Limits of Safety* by Scott Douglas Sagan, *The Upside of Turbulence: Seizing Opportunity in an Uncertain World* by Donald N. Sull, and *The Checklist Manifesto: How to Get Things Right* by Atul Gawande.

I have four recommendations if your interest is game theory. All are technical but readable. I went to Harvard with Drew Fudenberg, who wrote (with David Levine) *A Long-Run Collaboration on Games with Long-Run Patient Players*. A few years later, Colin Camerer was in the University of Chicago PhD program with me. He wrote *Behavioral Game Theory: Experiments in Strategic Interaction*. Many years later I argued over some of the ideas in both our books with Colin at the Milken Institute Global Conference. Michael Bacharach died before finishing his pathbreaking work *Beyond Individual Choice: Teams and Frames in Game Theory*. The editors did not do a good job of completing the work and putting it in book form, but the ideas are clear nonetheless. The best survey work on game theory is *The Bounds of Reason: Game Theory and the Unification of the Behavioral Sciences* by Herbert Gintis. A fifth book, *Predictably Irrational: The Hidden Forces That Shape Our Decisions* by Dan Ariely, describes behavioral experiments in lively terms.

Important psychological dimensions of risk are covered by Robert Alan Burton in *On Being Certain: Believing You Are Right Even When You're Not* and Gregory Berns in *Satisfaction: Sensation Seeking, Novelty, and the Science of Finding True Fulfillment*. While not directly concerned with risk, Darrin M. McMahon's *Happiness: A History* covers a lot of related history and psychology. Kenneth R. French gathered some of the world's top financial economists in Squam Lake, New Hampshire, to discuss the 2007–2009 financial crisis. Martin N. Baily, John Y. Campbell, John H. Cochrane, Douglas W. Diamond, Darrell Duffie, Anil K. Kashyap, Frederic S. Mishkin, Raghuram G. Rajan, David S. Scharfstein, Robert J. Shiller, Hyun

Song Shin, Matthew J. Slaughter, Jeremy C. Stein, and Rene M. Stulz collaborated to write *The Squam Lake Report: Fixing the Financial System*. The result has the strengths and weaknesses of a consensus report, but it remains one of the best places to start understanding recent financial events. *How Big Banks Fail and What to Do about It* by Darrell Duffie is more direct and narrower in focus.

For popular accounts of the crisis, I recommend starting with *All the Devils Are Here: The Hidden History of the Financial Crisis* by Bethany McLean and Joe Nocera. However, the most fun one to read (it is also accurate) is *The Big Short: Inside the Doomsday Machine* by Michael Lewis. You can extend your understanding with *Capital Offense: How Washington's Wise Men Turned America's Future Over to Wall Street* by Michael Hirsh, *Fool's Gold: How the Bold Dream of a Small Tribe at J.P. Morgan Was Corrupted by Wall Street Greed and Unleashed a Catastrophe* by Gillian Tett, and *House of Cards: A Tale of Hubris and Wretched Excess on Wall Street* by William Cohan. Roger Lowenstein wrote an account of the previous disaster, the Nasdive of 2000, in *Origins of the Crash: The Great Bubble and Its Undoing*.

I round out the list with some miscellaneous recommendations. *Free: The Future of a Radical Price* by Chris Anderson gives some ideas about how money is going to be replaced in the future. If you cannot understand how I felt in the 1970s, you might gain some insight from *Strange Days Indeed: The 1970s: The Golden Days of Paranoia* by Francis Wheen. Adam Leitzes wrote the story of eRaider.com in *Bulls, Bears, and Brains: Investing with the Best and Brightest of the Financial Internet*. *Still Life with a Bridle* is a wonderful collection by Zbigniew Herbert, from which I took that excerpt about the black tulip.

Finally, *Hong Kong on Air* is an exciting, racy, and financially interesting book by Muhammad Cohen, who helped edit this book. And if you like the illustrations in *Red-Blooded Risk*, check out *The Complete Plays of William Shakespeare* by Eric Kim. You get every one of the Bard's plays, reduced to essentials in two-panel comic strips.

About the Author

Aaron Brown is risk manager at AQR Capital Management in Greenwich, Connecticut. His previous books are *The Poker Face of Wall Street* (John Wiley & Sons, 2006, selected one of the 10 best books of 2006 by *BusinessWeek*) and *A World of Chance* (with Reuven and Gabrielle Brenner, Cambridge University Press, 2008). In his 30-year Wall Street career, he has been a trader, portfolio manager, head of mortgage securities, and risk manager for institutions including Citigroup and Morgan Stanley. He also served a stint as a finance professor, and was among the top poker players in the world during the 1970s and 1980s. He is a regular columnist for two financial journals: *Wilmott* and *Quantum* and contributes frequently to the professional literature in journals, periodicals, and book chapters. He holds degrees in Applied Mathematics from Harvard and Finance and Statistics from the University of Chicago Booth School of Business. He lives on the Upper West Side of Manhattan with his wife, Deborah Pastor, and has two children, Aviva who goes to high school and Jacob who is an undergraduate at the University of Chicago.

About the Illustrator

Eric Kim began his career in comics with the series *Love as a Foreign Language,* published by Oni Press. He has also illustrated *Degrassi: The Next Generation Vol. 3,* created the comic strip series *Battle Academy, The Sidesteppers* (which appeared in *Owl* magazine), *Streta,* and *The Complete Plays of William Shakespeare.* His next comics project will be coming out through Oni Press.

"It's been a real privilege to work with Aaron Brown on this project. Comics has always been my passion, and utilizing the medium to help explain economic concepts is a contribution that I'm happy to make. I hope readers enjoy the works presented here, and hope we get a chance to collaborate again!"

Index